EGON RONAY'S
Champagne Mumm
Guide 1995

4

Paris

Restaurants, brasseries, bistros and hotels

CHAMPAGNE
FONDEE EN 1827
G.H. MUMM & Cⁱᵉ
REIMS · FRANCE

Egon Ronay's Guides
35 Tadema Road
London SW10 0PZ

Consultant **Egon Ronay**
Editorial Director **Bernard Branco**
Managing Editor **Andrew Eliel**
Listings Editor **Peter Long**
Publishing Director **Angela Nicholson**
Sales and Marketing Director **Stephen Prendergast**

Chairman **Roy Ackerman**
Leading Guides Ltd part of the Richbell Group of Companies

Cover Design © **Elizabeth Ayer**
Cover Concept © **Chris Ackerman-Eveleigh**
Cover Illustration © **Ian Drury**

First Published 1995 by Macmillan
Publishers Ltd, Cavaye Place,
London SW10 9PG

9 8 7 6 5 4 3 2 1

ISBN 0 333 6264-43

Typeset in Great Britain by Spottiswoode Ballantyne,
Colchester, Essex.
Printed and bound in Great Britain by BPC Hazell Books Ltd
All inspections of establishments are
anonymous and carried out by Egon Ronay's
Guides' team of professional inspectors.
Inspectors may reveal their identities in order
to check all the rooms and other facilities.
The Guide is independent in its editorial selection
and does not accept advertising, payment or
hospitality from listed establishments.

Contents

How to use this Guide

Hotels (H) and Restaurants (R) are listed in alphabetical order within their arrondissements. Room prices are quoted per night for a double room with private facilities; prices will often vary considerably according to the season and the length of stay. Breakfast is not usually included in the price. Meal prices are for two people – three courses à la carte, a modest bottle of wine, and coffee. We do not quote a meal price for a few, generally fairly informal establishments such as wine bars. Prices on French menus are always inclusive of all taxes and service. Opening times and closures are liable to alteration, and it's always best to book. The nearest Metro station (M°) is shown for each hotel/restaurant. Bear in mind that many restaurants are closed during August, when most Parisians take their holidays. A list of restaurants open during August will be found from page 287, along with restaurants with weekend opening and late opening.

A map of all Paris appears on pages 28 and 29, and general information plus major tourist attractions on the two pages before the map. Each arrondissement is preceded by a map of that arrondissement, with

hotel and restaurant entries plotted by number. The map reference and number will be found by each entry. Opposite each map are listed major local places of interest with phone numbers and nearest Metros.

We award one, two or three stars for excellence of cooking. One star represents cooking much above average, two outstanding cooking, and three the best in Paris. A list of starred restaurants is on page 8. The ☞ symbol denotes our particular favourite restaurants. These do not necessarily serve the best food, but they are certainly places we can thoroughly recommend as providing a real atmosphere and taste of Paris, whether a humble bistro or one of the Grand tables (see list on page 10).

All establishments (240 hotels, 390 restaurants) are listed alphabetically in the index at the back of the book. A glossary of French menu words starts on page 293.

To call Paris from the UK dial 010-33 1 then the 8-digit number (from 16 April 1995 010 changes to 00). To call Paris from elsewhere in France start with 1 16, then dial the 8-digit number.

CHAMPAGNE

FONDÉE EN 1827

G.H. **MUMM** & C.ᴵᴱ

REIMS~FRANCE

Welcome to the 1995 edition of *Egon Ronay's Champagne Mumm Guide to Paris*. Now in its second edition, the Guide remains true to its original design, giving detail of the very best Paris has to offer - whatever your pocket. And so, for the second year, this distinctive guide contains a unique collection of around 600 of the best Parisian restaurants, brasseries, bistros and hotels - to give you a real flavour of the excellence available. For those who relish indulging in the luxury of good food and fine wine, served in the right environment, this is an essential travelling companion.

At Mumm we have been making fine Champagne since 1827 and just as the guide offers quality and choice, Mumm Cordon Rouge offers a quality wine suitable for all occasions. Ideal for festivities and joyous occasions, Champagne Mumm is enjoyed in top restaurants and hotels throughout Paris and indeed, the world over. It is widely recognised by the bold red stripe that adorns every bottle - an image which was inspired by France's highest award, the Légion d'Honneur.

Since its founding, the House of Mumm has been committed to excellence, maintaining quality and style which is still the measure of a fine and prestigious Champagne. Champagne Mumm can be enjoyed at any time of the day - as a light, elegant and refreshing drink on its own or as the perfect accompaniment to a menu degustation.

We are delighted to be associated with *Egon Ronay's Champagne Mumm Guide to Paris,* for the second consecutive year. The guide continues our links with gastronomic excellence throughout the world and is particularly relevant this year with the new "Chunnel" link between London and Paris. In short, we hope this guide will enrich your visit to Paris and help make it both an enjoyable and unforgettable experience.

Finally, if you have the time to visit the Champagne region, we would very much like to welcome you to the home of Champagne Mumm in Reims - which is within easy travelling distance of Paris. For specific details please telephone (33) 26 49 59 70.

On behalf of Champagne Mumm, I very much hope that you enjoy your 'séjour' in France.

Hubert Millet

Hubert Millet
President, Champagne G.H. Mumm

Introduction by Peter Long

Much of Paris is currently looking like a vast building site. Whole areas, especially on the Eastern side, are being redeveloped, and down-at-heel charm is being replaced all too often by unappealing modernity. Moreover, construction of the new Météor metro line is turning major roads into open-cast mines, making the notorious traffic problems even more of a headache and filling the newspapers with column-metres of complaints (the street scene is in some ways quite similar to London's – cyclists hurtle through red lights, Pizza delivery boys risk their own and others' lives on their mopeds, and the policemen and beggars both seem to be getting younger). The occasional avant-garde edifice is, in its way, as remarkable as what it replaced. Nothing in its day could have been more extraordinary than the Eiffel Tower, and a century later it's the Pompidou Centre, the Louvre Pyramid, the Grande Arche at La Défense and the Palais Omnisports de Paris at Bercy.

Plenty of Paris mercifully remains unmined and unmodernised, so it is still one of the most 'walkable' of capital cities, with something to take the eye (and often the breath) at every turn. That something might be the Eiffel Tower, Notre Dame, Sacré Coeur or the Seine, but equally it might be a half-hidden garden, one of the city's dozen or more major cemeteries, a beguiling street café, or a bustling, colourful open market. Food markets are a feature of all parts of Paris, from the patrician suburbs of Neuilly to the cosmopitan crush of the 20th arrondissement. They're all worth a visit, but those of special appeal include the small, charming Rue Mouffetard in the 5th, Rue de Seine/Rue de Buci in the Latin Quarter, the Rue des Belles-Feuilles at Avenue Victor Hugo in the 16th, Rue de Levis in the 17th and the covered Marché St Quentin just down from Gare de l'Est in the 10th.

A price level (or more) up from the markets are the shops – boulangeries, patisseries, fromageries and charcuteries by the thousand, many of whose window displays would cause a pedestrian traffic jam if transferred to a London street. On two sides of Place de la Madeleine, Fauchon really does bring walkers to a halt; the displays of cakes, pastries and prepared foods are succulent works of art, and this world-renowned shop is a must for all foodies. On another side of the same Place, Hédiard is a smaller version of Fauchon and among its delectable offerings are perhaps the best fruit jellies (pâtes de fruits) in the world. Actually, it's not all that much smaller, having recently expanded upwards to include, among other things, a restaurant. Next door in this locality of luxury food shops is La Maison de la Truffe, an Aladdin's cave of truffles, foie gras, caviar and smoked fish. Just around the corner in Rue Vignon is La Ferme St Hubert, a speciality cheese shop with a restaurant attached.

Food is never far away from the thoughts of most Parisians, and for them and visitors to the city the choice of restaurants is astonishing. Snacking is not what the natives are used to, and many outlets are appealing to man's greedier nature with some remarkable offers. The name of the game is 'à volonté', a game played most enthusiastically by the Bistro Romain chain. In the Opéra branch at least, you can keep ordering refills of beef or salmon carpaccio (a better bet in any case than some of the *plats cuisinés*), or stoke up on seconds of chips and pasta. If you order the excellent gorgonzola and goat's cheese you might have to ask them to remove the board if you don't want to make yourself ill. Still more appealing is the grappa, which you can sip to your heart's content before reeling off into the night. At Chez Clément (see index) they have a similar deal with oysters, grilled meats and profiteroles with hot chocolate. Here too you can have your way with the cheese, in this case a first-rate Camembert.

The popular Batifol chain of traditional bistros gets by in fine style without such offers (though I once slurped my way throught most of a largish bowl of apple compote left on the table). Batifols have built their name on value for money, a warm welcome and reliability. Two of the very best in my view are Batifol Bercy (42 Boulevard Bercy 75012), and the Batifol at 6 Place Maréchal Juin 75017, especially if you sit outside on a summer's evening; larger and less 'personal' is the recently opened late-nighter in the touristy Boulevard des Italiens.

The Paris restaurant scene is one of continuous evolution, and even though the fast food invasion has taken its toll, there remains an amazingly wide choice to suit all pockets and tastes. The cuisines of the world are represented, some more successfully than others. We have found, for example, that even the 'best' of the Indian restaurants are really recommendable only for their shellfish – more elaborate cooked dishes can often disappoint. Figs and salmon seem to be the year's most fashionable ingredients, the former baked, poached, sliced in tarts, soused in wine, the latter most trendily appearing raw as *saumon tartare*. Oriental produce is also flavour of the month, particularly ginger, lemon grass and soya.

Enjoy your stay in Paris.

Star List

1st Arr
★★   Carré des Feuillants
       Gérard Besson
       Le Grand Véfour
★   Goumard-Prunier
       Mercure Galant
       Le Meurice
       Ritz, L'Espadon

2nd Arr
★★   Drouant
★   Pile ou Face

4th Arr
★★   L'Ambroisie
★   Benoit
       Bistrot du Dome
       Miravile

5th Arr
★★★   La Tour d'Argent
★   La Timonerie

6th Arr
★   Les Bookinistes
       Le Chat Grippé
       Hotel Lutétia, Le Paris
       Relais Louis XIII

7th Arr
★★   Le Divellec
       Duquesnoy
★   L'Arpège
       Le Bellecour
       La Bourdonnais, La Cantine
          des Gourmets
       La Ferme Saint-Simon
       Jules Verne
       Le Récamier

8th Arr
★★★   Taillevent
★★   Hotel de Crillon, Les
          Ambassadeurs
       Lasserre
       Laurent
       Ledoyen
★   Le Bristol
       Chiberta
       George V, Les Princes
          Restaurant
       Lucas Carton
       La Marée
       Vancouver
       Hotel Vernet, Les Elysées du
          Vernet

9th Arr
★   La Table d'Anvers

11th Arr
★   A Sousceyrac

12th Arr
★   Fouquet's Bastille
       L'Oulette
       Au Pressoir
       La Sologne
       Au Trou Gascon

14th Arr
★   La Cagouille

15th Arr
★   Morot-Gaudry
       Le Relais de Sèvres

16th Arr
★★★   Faugeron
       Le Parc Victor Hugo, Joël
          Robuchon
★★   Le Pré Catelan
★   La Butte Chaillot
       Conti
       Le Parc Victor Hugo, Le
          Relais du Parc
       La Petite Tour
       Relais d'Auteuil
       Le Toit de Passy
       Vivarois

17th Arr
★★★   Guy Savoy
★★   Apicius
       Michel Rostang
★   Amphyclès
       Faucher
       Le Manoir de Paris
       Le Méridien Paris Etoile,
          Le Clos Longchamp
       Le Petit Colombier
       Sormani

20th Arr
★   Les Allobroges

Around Paris
★   Trianon Palace, Les Trois
          Marches

Champagne List – our personal favourites

1st Arr

L'Ami Léon
Carré des Feuillants
Gaya Rive Droite
Juveniles
Paolo Petrini
Pharamond

2nd Arr

Chez Georges
Les Noces de Jeanette

3rd Arr

Bar à Huitres

4th Arr

Bistrot du Dome
A L'Impasse (Chez Robert)
Jo Goldenberg

5th Arr

Bar à Huitres

6th Arr

Les Bookinistes
Brasserie Lipp
Le Chat Grippé
Mariage Frères

7th Arr

Chez Françoise
Duquesnoy
Le Récamier

8th Arr

Ledoyen
Taillevent

9th Arr

Chartier

10th Arr

Aux Deux Canards
Terminus Nord

11th Arr

Astier
Cormillot Bistro Lyonnais
Nioullaville
Le Villaret

12th Arr

L'Oulette
La Sologne

13th Arr

Le Petit Marguery

14th Arr

Bar à Huitres
Le Bistrot du Dome
La Coupole

15th Arr

La Farigoule
Le Gastroquet

16th Arr

Brasserie de la Poste
Brasserie Stella
La Butte Chaillot
Faugeron
Le Parc Victor Hugo, Le Relais
    du Parc
Paul Chene
La Petite Tour
Relais d'Auteuil

17th Arr

Le Bistrot d'à Coté
Bistrot de l'Etoile
Chez Georges
Goldenberg
Le Petit Colombier
Pétrus
Le Relais de Venise (L'Entrecote)

18th Arr

La Galerie

20th Arr

Les Allobroges

Hotel of the Year

Ritz
15 place Vendome 75001

Since being opened by César Ritz in 1898, this hotel, and his name, have become a synonym for opulence, luxury and service. Owner Mohammed Al Fayed (of Harrods fame) and his brothers have spent $150 million in recent years, adding the Ritz Health Club with its vast Romanesque swimming pool and the Ritz Club, where members and guests can dance till dawn; they have also refurbished the splendid Louis XIV interiors and brought modern-day comforts to elegant bedrooms – all ensuring that the Ritz continues to live up to its own legend.

Restaurant of the Year

Faugeron
52 rue de Longchamp 75116

In a city not short of a good restaurant or two, Henri Faugeron's immaculate cooking never fails to please, whether it is his comforting *oeufs coque Faugeron* (soft-boiled hen's eggs with puréed truffles and brioche 'soldiers'), a moreish tournedos of lobster with cep ravioli or game, a speciality in season. Add luxurious surroundings that do not intimidate, service that is correct but never overbearing (supervised with quiet charm by Gerlindé Faugeron), and an outstanding wine list overseen by sommelier Jean-Claude Jambon and you have a Restaurant of the Year, where all aspects combine to create a memorable dining experience.

A great Champagne is born

Reims, March 1, 1827 saw the birth of a new house of champagne, "P.A. Mumm et Co.". The founding fathers, Gottlieb Mumm and his two brothers, Jules and Edouard, recognised masters of the art, came from a long line of wealthy German wine-makers and owned vineyards in the Rhine Valley.

From the very first year, Mumm met with resounding success that was even further inspired, in 1875, with the creation of the incomparable "Cordon Rouge", now hailed as the model and symbol of champagne. In 1838, with Gottlieb's son, Georges Hermann de Mumm, the position and prestige of the house of Mumm were established and it took on the name "G.H.Mumm & Cie".

Ever since, the perfection and style of Mumm have been acclaimed the world over.

Fine soils and noble wines

Since the turn of the century Mumm has been recognised as one of the most famous "vineyard houses" in the Champagne region. The estate contains some of the finest crus – Côte des Blancs, Montagne de Reims, Vallée de la Marne and now covers more than three hundred hectares of superlative soil. With such quality grapes, Mumm produces champagnes from a palette of the finest crus, each with an individual flavour, every cuvée endowed with finesse, elegance and freshness.

Harmony

Each Mumm champagne is unique. Tradition, precision and true affection go into each and every bottle of Mumm champagne. To achieve perfection for such harmony, from twenty-five to as many as forty crus are blended to produce one single cuvée. A great champagne can only enjoy grace, elegance and longevity through the blending of the finest grape varieties.

A subtle art

Every year, the art of producing a cuvée is a truly creative endeavour. By increasing the number of sources and maintaining strict control of the quality of the wines, Mumm has expanded the subtle range of its incomparable style. After tasting more than a hundred wines in the cellars, a selection is made of those to be blended. Subtle marriages of taste depend on the skill and art of the cellar-master and on the entire team.

For perfect balance, the best wines, best crus and best grapes are selected: Chardonnays from the Côte des Blancs offer elegance and finesse, Pinots Noirs from the Montagne de Reims adds a rich wine flavour, while Pinots Meunier from the Vallée de la Marne are lively and fruity. Subtlety, nobility and grace, together with strength and longevity combine in precious alchemy, yielding the perfection of Mumm champagnes. And so the unparalleled quality of Mumm wines continues from year to year.

The prestige of Mumm

First produced in 1875, the celebrated cuvée Cordon Rouge, bearing the emblem of the French Légion d'Honneur is now a symbol of refinement and respect for tradition. Ever since the Roaring Twenties, no celebration nor gala has been complete without the magic bottles bearing the name of Mumm. Seven other cuvées now make up the full range: vintage and non-vintage Cordon Rouge brut, vintage Cordon Rosé, Cordon Vert, Mumm de Cramant, René Lalou and, the height of perfection, Grand Cordon de Mumm.

Inspiration, transcending style

As ambassadors of excellence and a unique lifestyle, Mumm champagnes have long been partners in artistic ventures and noble endeavours. The famous Cordon Rouge has inspired such creative geniuses as Utrillo, Brayer, Chapelain-Midy, Carzou and Foujita who decorated the chapel of "Notre Dame de la Paix" in Reims. Mumm has also been a source of inspiration for great sailors. Since 1977 it has organised the famous "Champagne Mumm Admiral's Cup" and, more recently, the prestigious "Champagne Mumm World Cup".

VINTAGE CORDON ROSÉ

Colour
Twirling, pink salmon. Subtle hints of gold and crimson. Springtime sprightliness and freshness.

Nose
Convincing and teasing. Aromas of cunningly-scented red fruit.

Palate
Generously firm, yet full of courteousness. Soothingly round, velvety and fresh. A fleetingly... lingering dream.

Tasting
Its youthful finesse is its hope and pride. The table's pleasures it sees as white meats and cheeses. It is at any time to be desired a symbol of love and happiness.

GRAND CORDON

Colour
Laced with jade and gold. Roguishly gracious bubbles.

Nose
Floral and convincingly persuasive. Aromas of delicate earthy flavours. Ample, balanced and fruity.

Palate
Grace and charm, finesse and elegance, showing a smilingly personable presence. A discreet personality and a fine character.

Tasting
A fine, enchanting cuvée, caressingly and poetically evocative of pleasure. A champagne full of freshness and jollity, sweet at any time of the day, a byword for pleasure and love. An excellent apéritif, it is better still before meat, with starters and fish if the meal is to be champagne only.

RENÉ LALOU

Colour
Noble, eager bubbles. Stylish and proud in its bearing. Gold and jade form its colour.

Nose
Unctuous and enthralling. Aromas of blossoming hawthorn. Proud and fiery all along.

Palate
Strikes as frank and heady. Fruity, pressing, sweet and long. Generous, powerful, smiling and strong.

Tasting
A harmonious, pulpy, yet gracious wine. A desirable cuvée for the inquiring and informed palate. A champagne for all seasons, a noble wine to preside over a grand dinner.

MUMM DE CRAMANT

Colour
A blend of jade and light. A light froth is to this champagne what delicate features are to a woman's face.

Nose
Full of freshness and youth. Noble wood seasoned with great spirits. Perky aromas of new-born vine-shoots.

Palate
Gentle, remarkably delicate impression. Lingering and caressingly voluptuous. Graceful, poetical finish.

Tasting
Fond of smiling lips, it will give joy and cheerfulness as an apéritif. Early in the meal, it will get on fine with fish, pastry and shellfish.

TASTING NOTES
BY THE CELLAR-MASTER AT MUMM!

CORDON ROUGE

Colour

Eager, exciting bubbles. Brilliant, full and laced with dreams. Golden on wheat straw background.

Nose

Ample, colourful and fruity. Redolent of smoking greengage jam.

Palate

A strong personality and decisive character... with velvet roundness. Chivalrous courtship of tastebuds. Transient touch of almond and peach. Lingering powerfully, charming and virile.

Tasting

A loyal, steady cuvée, the blend showing powerful body yet delicate form. Acts magnetically, for apéritif, and is a sprightly companion throughout a meal. A gem of a champagne, harmoniously combining many crus.

VINTAGE CORDON ROUGE

Colour

Delicate and harmonious bright tints. Light straw with a touch of mellow gold. Attractively eager yet gentle bubbles.

Nose

Earthy caress on a fresh spring morning. Aromas of healthy, fleshy yellow apples. Decisive, frank and full of go.

Palate

Reassuringly soft-angled robustness. Gallant and vivacious. A gentle touch on the tastebuds.

Tasting

A robust, lively wine eager to live long. It will enhance meat and poultry in the midst of a meal. A happy marriage of power and elegance and a smiling cuvée.

CORDON VERT

Colour

Mellow gold with amber tints. Bold confident bubbles.

Nose

Pulpy and fleshy. Penetratingly soothing. Velvet aromas of melting pear.

Palate

Heralding untold pleasures. Tastebuds under sugary spell. Top-bred glucose languorous and long.

Tasting

A symphony of many crus brought together in sweet alliance. A wine made from fully ripe selected grapes. An indispensable companion of refined desserts.

Paris in Focus

Sacré-Coeur

Moulin Rouge

Bofinger – 4th arr

Classic metro sign

Public gardens – 17th arr

Place des Vosges

Relais de Venise (l'Entrecôte) – 17th arr

Place des Vosges

Hotel Saint James Paris – 16th arr

Bistrot du Dome – 4th arr

...Metro for short

Citroën traction avant

At the foot of Sacré-Coeur

Jardin des Plantes

Eurostar – a Capital Way To Travel

The London Waterloo-Paris Gare du Nord Channel Tunnel connection experienced many initial teething problems – almost too many to enumerate. In years to come, however, perhaps even bathysiderodromophobes (those with a fear of underground rail travel) will have succumbed to the benefits of whizzing from London to Paris at up to 300km per hour (approx 186 miles per hour) – though for a few years travel on the British side of the Chunnel will be somewhat slower. Travelling time as a result is currently three hours, though when the new track is finally laid journey times will be reduced to just over two hours. This will further emphasise the benefits of the new service, which will make travelling to Paris as easy and effortless as travelling to Birmingham or Bristol. Checking-in time is a minimum of 20 minutes before departure with a few easy procedures to observe. Great attention is paid to the security aspect, which is airline-style. There are plenty of trolleys – a must for those with baggage as the trains are some 400 metres in length; and staff are plentiful, highly visible in their smart Pierre Balmain sunshine yellow and navy blue uniforms. On board, apart from storage space near the doors, there is precious little room for large baggage, though there are overhead racks. There is slightly more leg room in first class, and the seats are wider. Otherwise, apart from the availability of food, there's not much to choose between the two classes of service. The journey itself is remarkably quiet and the only evidence that you're in the 20-minute tunnel section is a slight whooshing noise which you're not too aware of at the start of the tunnel, but which becomes noticeable by its absence when you emerge at Calais.

Food in first class – airline-style but of better quality – is included in the ticket price; breakfast is served on morning journeys and dinner during evening travel. Menus are planned by Lenotre, the renowned patisserie, and breakfast could begin with a dish of delicious fresh red berries in a raspberry sauce accompanied by fromage frais, followed by either a Continental cold plate of Emmental and good quality sliced ham – a generous portion, plus rye bread; or a cooked breakfast which can be a little disappointing – and indeed was on a press journey (whose start was delayed by an hour): the scrambled eggs were rather rubbery, the bacon lacking in flavour and the mushrooms overcooked. The accompanying Porkinsons chipolata sausage was enjoyable, with a good meaty flavour and texture. Bread rolls were well baked, hard rather than lightly crusty. To finish came cold croissants, *pains au chocolat* and ample pots of quite decent filter coffee. For dinner, the set menu could begin with a plate of cold chargrilled vegetables, with a little tub of good mustardy vinaigrette served separately. Bread rolls appear to have been part of the morning delivery; they had softened a little and lost their fresh baked quality. The choice of main course could be grilled fillet of beef with vegetables or grilled cod with lardons and buttered mixed vegetables. The steak turned out rather overdone and grey-looking and the fish was served skin side up; the fish itself was fine but the skin was rather charred. Vegetables were overcooked and mushy. To finish there was a choice of fresh fruit or a slice of excellent strawberry tart, also fine French cheeses as well as coffee and two complimentary alcoholic drinks.

A super service is presented by young, cheerful and very helpful staff. A pity the caterers are too ambitious food-wise. In the conditions that obtain here it is not appropriate to offer the likes of scrambled eggs or grilled dishes, both needing more careful cooking to be enjoyable. Instead, the caterers should concentrate on simpler preparations more suited to the on-board facilities. Main meals should be casserole-type dishes – why not a good *coq au vin* or navarin of lamb, for instance, and for breakfast perhaps a kedgeree (hard-boiled eggs being the only way of cooking eggs that lends itself to advance preparation).

To Paris and back –
24 hours with Andrew Eliel

Now that the Eurostar Channel Tunnel trains are in operation, comparisons can be made between ways of travelling from city centre to city centre. For Londoners it is certainly both quicker by Eurostar, not to mention less stressful and remarkably hassle-free. In fact, it can take even less than half the time of the quickest sea crossing including the trains on either side.

At present, of course, there are many more flights and choices of airport available than trains to and from Paris. A flight from Heathrow to Charles de Gaulle, for instance, takes an hour, but you must add on the time and cost of getting to and from the airports, the minimum check-in time and the wait for baggage reclaim (unless you travel with hand luggage only).

Without a prior reservation, I took the last Paris flight on a Monday night and flew British Midland from Heathrow, due to leave at 9.10pm, though actually leaving twenty minutes late. Allowing myself time to get to the airport, to purchase a ticket and to check in, I left central London by underground at 7pm, arriving at the ticket desk in Terminal 1 Heathrow at 8.20pm. The over-the-counter cost of a standard one-way ticket was £95, including airport tax. Refreshments available included a small baguette filled with paté, a Jaffa cake bar and choice of drink. The luxury of a hot towel was offered. Passengers (the plane was perhaps half full) disembarked at the futuristic Terminal 2, Charles de Gaulle, at 11.20pm, too late for buses into the city centre: these stop at 11pm! There was a 15-minute wait for a shuttle bus to the RER station, where all the ticket offices were closed and none of the automatic ticket machines were working. A train left at 11.42pm, arriving at the Gare du Nord at 00.15am, over four hours after I left central London (with the hour's time difference).

Returning from Paris the following day, I got to the Gare du Nord at 4.30pm, in time to purchase a standard one-way over-the-counter Eurostar ticket (£77.50) and check in, a minimum of 20 minutes before departure. The train left a few minutes later than the advertised 5.09pm and arrived 6 minutes late at Waterloo at 7.15pm, 24 hours after I left the day before. The journey is quiet and relaxing; security and passport control are similar to an airport's, seating is comparable both in comfort and space to that of airlines; there are two buffet cars per train plus a trolley service. A BLT sandwich and small bottle of mineral water cost £3.50. Hot snacks available in the buffet car include an egg & bacon muffin at £2.50, pizza at £3.25, and a toasted cheese & ham sandwich at £2.75. Afternoon tea costs £2.50, and there is the usual array of sandwiches, crisps, biscuits, cakes and drinks, hot or cold.

In between my travels, I stayed at the **Hotel Lancaster** (belonging, as we went to press, to the Savoy Group of Hotels), a lovely Parisian town house, hidden away just off the Champs Elysées – see entry in 8th Arrondissement. It is supremely comfortable and old-fashioned in the best sense, with handsome furniture, tasteful paintings and works of art, lots of marble, rugs and especially beautiful floral arrangements in both bedrooms and public areas. Impeccable staff glide around effortlessly, and an added bonus here is the delightful inner courtyard patio, the perfect spot, even on a balmy November morning. Typical of the standard of rooms found here is a rooftop terrace suite with views of the top of the Eiffel Tower and the Sacré Coeur in the distance, though admittedly it is twice the price of a double room. Breakfast the following morning included fresh orange juice, assorted brioches, croissants, breads and good coffee.

For lunch I tried the Restaurant **Morot-Gaudry** (see 15th Arrondissement), sited on the eighth floor of a 30s apartment block overlooking the Eiffel Tower. The 220F *Carte d'Affaires* is a real bargain, including as it does four courses and a choice of eleven decent bottles of wine, perhaps a Domaine Commanderie de St Jean, Chardonnay 1993. A little appetiser, tiny cubes of lobster mousse in its own sauce, preceded a starter of *charlotte de St Jacques, sauce homardine*, a colourfully studded scallop mousse/terrine structure, followed by braised guinea fowl (*pintade braisée aux choux verts*) served with shredded cabbage and bacon strips. The dish would have been further enhanced by the appearance of some sort of potato, sadly lacking. Next the cheese trolley is wheeled in front of you, mostly soft and goat's cheeses in fine condition served with walnut bread. I finished with a *charlotte au chocolat et manadarine*, beautifully and artistically made, the top glazed, the sauce containing segments of the fruit. All in all, a fine meal.

There was just time for a brief look and tea at **Hédiard**, a wonderful, enticing and expensive food and wine shop at 21 Place de la Madeleine (see 8th arrondissement).

Le Shuttle

An 'Overture Service' journey has been the only opportunity to sample the Folkestone to Calais Channel Tunnel shuttle train before we go to press. Due to go into full operation before Christmas, with prices still to be determined, the system will begin with at least one train per hour. A junction off the M20 6 miles from Folkestone and 11 miles from Dover ferry terminals leads to 14 vehicle check-ins and a very smart high-tech passenger terminal with banking, snacks (not fully operational on the Overture Service), a bookshop and a chemist as well as a Duty Free shop (while it still exists). The general intention is for cars to proceed from check-in straight to the loading lines via security and border controls and from there to either of the two ramps leading down to the long queen bee-like shuttle. Cars enter on the lower or upper deck at one end and continue down the length of the train. There are approximately six cars per compartment (each of which is shuttered) and information is available both on overhead displays and via the PA system. There's also a special radio channel with light music and even lighter chatter. The compartments only allow limited movement though hydraulic doors allow access to other compartments and to the stairs which connect with the lower decks, where the toilets are located. The average journey time of 35 minutes is very smooth, very quiet and very uneventful. With all border formalities taken care of at the point of departure, when you arrive at the outward destination (Coquelles just outside Calais), it's out of the other end of the train and from there straight through on to the motorway networks and away. Likewise on the inward journey to Folkestone there are no hold-ups between the train and the M20.

The Hovercraft still offers the fastest road-to-road service through the frequency of crossings and Channel sea conditions can cause problems. Of all the comparable short-trip crossings Le Shuttle causes the least hassle, though sitting in your car for 35 or so minutes is somewhat akin to sitting on the car deck of a ferry, albeit for a much shorter period and in lighter, brighter and cleaner surroundings. You also have limited views of the outside through the small, square, porthole-like windows, though the major part of the journey is of course in the tunnel.

Paris – General Information

Useful Telephone Numbers
To call Paris from the UK dial 010-33 1 then the 8 digit number (from 16 April 1995 010 will change to 00).
Central Tourist Information, 127 ave des Champs Elysées 75008, Tel 49 52 53 54, M° Etoile

British Consulate, 9 ave Hoche 75008, Tel 42 66 38 10
British Embassy, Commercial Section, 35 rue du Faubourg St Honoré 75009, Tel 42 66 91 42

Flight Information
Charles de Gaulle/Roissy 48 62 22 80
Orly 49 75 15 15

City Air Terminals
Etoile 42 99 20 18
Invalides 43 23 97 10
Porte Maillot 42 99 20 18

Rail Travel
Eurostar booking in UK 01233 617 575
French Railways Ltd
179 Piccadilly London W1 0171-493 9731
RATP information 43 46 14 14
SNCF information 45 82 50 50 – main lines
                 45 65 60 00 – suburbs

Public Holidays: New Year's Day, Easter Mon, 1, 8 & 25 May, 4 & 5 Jun, 14 Jul, 15 Aug, 1 & 11 Nov, Christmas Day.

School Holidays: 20 Dec-8 Jan, 17 Feb-18 Mar, 6 Apr-2 May, 6 Jul-5 Sep, 21 Oct-6 Nov

Popular Annual Events 1994
SMT (Tourism & Travel Show) Paris – Porte de Versailles – 22-27 Mar
Paris Marathon 2 Apr
Foire de Paris 27 Apr-4 May
Tennis – French Open 29 May-11 Jun
Air show 11, 17, 18 Jun
Tour de France 2-23 Jul
Paris "Halle that Jazz" festival at La Villette 30 Jun-8 Jul
Bastille Day celebrated throughout France 14 Jul
Paris caravanning and open-air show (Le Bourget) 23 Sep-1 Oct
Paris Jazz Festival May-Oct
Prix de l'Arc de Triomphe 1 Oct
Fair of Contemporary Art 7-15 Oct
International Boat Show 1-11 Dec

Major Places of Interest by arrondissement

1 Tuileries, Louvre, Chatelet, Halles
2 Théatre des Variétés, Bibliothèque Nationale, Bourse, Sentier, Reaumur-Sébastopol
3 Temple, Arts et Métiers, Le Marais
4 Hotel de Ville, Centre Georges Pompidou, St Paul, Place des Vosges, Bastille
5 Panthéon, Bd St Germain, Bd St Michel, Jardin des Plantes
6 St Germain des Prés, Odéon, Luxembourg, St Michel
7 Invalides, Ecole Militaire, Sèvres-Babylone, Tour Eiffel, Champ de Mars
8 Etoile, Parc Monceau, Champs Elysées, Concorde, Madeleine, Gare St Lazare
9 Pigalle, Opéra, Bd Haussmann
10 Gare du Nord, Gare de l'Est, Bd de Magenta
11 République, Bd Voltaire
12 Reuilly, Daumesnil, Gare de Lyon
13 Gare d'Austerlitz, Gobelins, Place d'Italie, Porte d'Ivry
14 Montparnasse, Raspail, Denfert Rochereau, Porte d'Orléans, Porte de Vanves
15 Gare Montparnasse, Bienvenue, Pasteur, Grenelle, Porte de Versailles, Convention, La Motte Picquet
16 Passy, Victor Hugo, Trocadéro, Auteuil, Porte de St Cloud
17 Wagram, Ternes, Péreire, Ave de Villiers, Palais des Congrès, Porte de Clichy
18 Montmartre, Sacré Coeur, Porte de Clignancourt
19 Belleville, La Villette, Buttes-Chaumont
20 Père Lachaise Cemetery, Gambetta, Ménilmontant

See the title page of each arrondissement for local places of interest. The best way to visit museums is with a Carte Musée, valid for 1, 3 or 5 days. Buy them at a museum or major metro station and jump the queue at 65 museums in and around Paris.

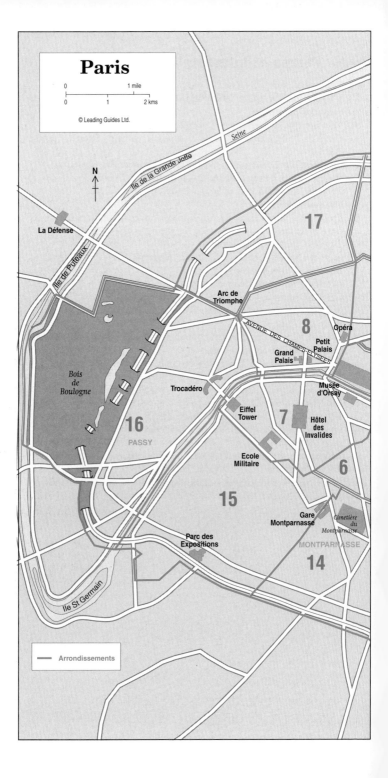

Paris

0 _____ 1 mile
0 _____ 1 _____ 2 kms

© Leading Guides Ltd.

Seine

Île de la Grande Jatte

N

La Défense

Île de Puteaux

17

Arc de Triomphe

AVENUE DES CHAMPS-ELYSEES

8

Opéra

Petit Palais

Grand Palais

Bois de Boulogne

Trocadéro

Musée d'Orsay

Eiffel Tower

7

Hôtel des Invalides

16

PASSY

6

Ecole Militaire

15

Gare Montparnasse

Cimetière du Montparnasse

Parc des Expositions

MONTPARNASSE

Île St Germain

14

Arrondissements

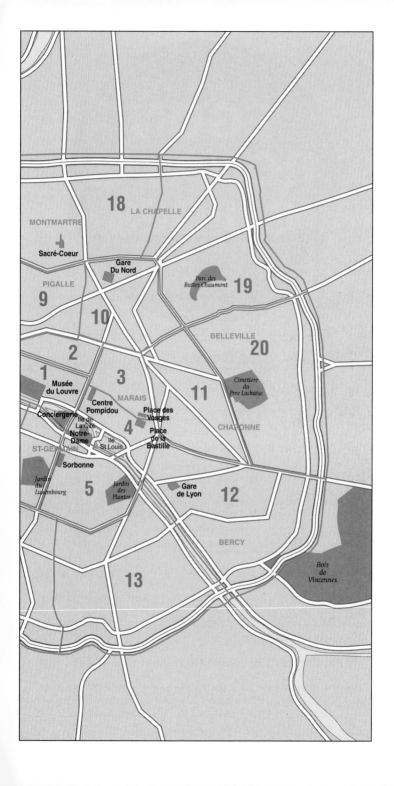

MONTMARTRE

18   LA CHAPELLE

Sacré-Coeur

Gare
Du Nord

Parc des
Buttes Chaumont

PIGALLE

9

19

10

BELLEVILLE

2

20

1

3

Musée
du Louvre

MARAIS

Centre
Pompidou

Cimetière
du
Père Lachaise

Conciergerie

Île de
La Cité

Place des
Vosges

11

4

Notre-
Dame

Île
St Louis

Place
de la
Bastille

CHARONNE

ST-GERMAIN

Sorbonne

Jardin
du
Luxembourg

5

Jardin
des
Plantes

Gare
de Lyon

12

BERCY

13

Bois
de
Vincennes

Recommended by
EGON RONAY'S GUIDES
1995

YOUR GUARANTEE
OF
QUALITY AND INDEPENDENCE

- Establishment inspections are anonymous
- Inspections are undertaken by qualified Egon Ronay's Guides inspectors
- The Guides are completely independent in their editorial selection
- The Guides do not accept advertising, hospitality or payment from listed establishments

Hotels & Restaurants	Pubs & Inns
Europe	Just a Bite
Family Hotels & Restaurants	Paris
Oriental Restaurants	Ireland
New Zealand & South Pacific	Australia

Egon Ronay's Guides are available from all good bookshops or can be ordered from Leading Guides, 35 Tadema Road, London SW10 0PZ
Tel: 071-352 2485 / 352 0019 Fax: 071-376 5071

1st Arrondissement
Places of Interest

Louvre 40 20 50 50
   Pyramide 40 20 51 51
   Musée des Arts Decoratifs 42 60 32 14, M° Palais-Royal/Musée
   du Louvre
Jardin des Tuileries
Musée de l'Orangerie, 40 39 38 74, M° Concorde
Forum des Halles, 40 39 38 74, M° Chatelet/Les Halles
St Eustache, 42 36 31 05, M° Chatelet/Les Halles
Ste Chapelle, 43 54 30 09, M° Cité
Conciergerie, 43 54 30 06, M° Cité/Chatelet
Comédie Française, 40 15 00 15, M° Palais-Royal
Théatre Musical de Paris, 40 28 28 40, M° Chatelet
Palais de Justice, 44 32 50 00, M° Cité

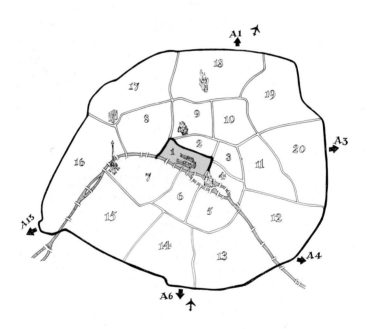

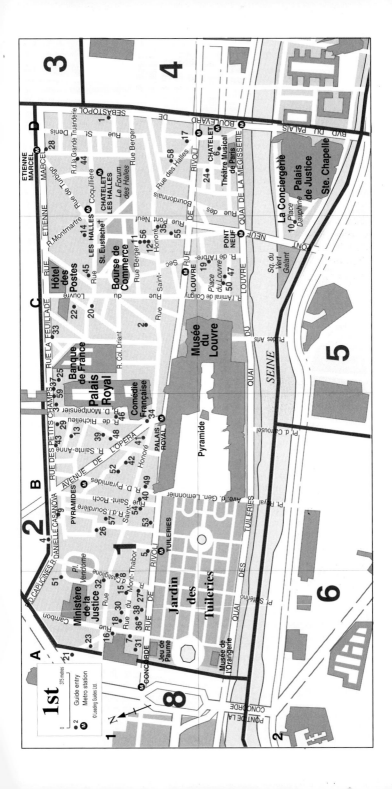

Agora
Map D1.1

Tel 42 33 46 02   Fax 42 33 80 99   **H**

7 rue de la Cossonnerie 75001   **M° Les Halles**
Rooms 29   Double from 370F

From the 1900 facade steps lead up to reception, where a welcome
awaits from smiling staff and a pair of budgies in a period cage.
Bedrooms, all with modern bath or shower/wc facilities, extend
over five floors (there's a lift), with rooms on the top floor having
the charm of sloping ceilings. Reception and room service operate
24 hours. *Amex, Mastercard, Visa.*

L'Ami Léon
Map C1.2

Tel 42 33 06 20   **R**

11 rue Jean-Jacques Rousseau 75001   **M° Louvre**
Seats 20   Meal for 2 approx 350F

Tiny, old-fashioned restaurant with just half a dozen tables hidden
away behind its heavy lace curtains. The eponymous Léon works
single-handed in the kitchen while Madame does everything front
of house. A short carte that changes with the seasons might include
hot pheasant paté, tourain perigourdine (soup), fillet of lamb with
cumin, veal kidneys with sorrel and wild boar with cranberries.
For afters there's *fondant au chocolat*, seasonal fruit tart and *crème
brulée*. The *prix-fixe*, with about three choices at each stage,
is excellent value for money. Short selection of French bottles
plus a Cote de Ventoux by the 25cl *pichet. L 12-2 D 7.30-10.
Closed L Sat, all Sun, 1 week May, 14 Jul-15 Aug & Public
Holidays. Mastercard, Visa.*

Armand au Palais-Royal
Map B1.3

Tel 42 60 05 11   Fax 42 96 16 24   **R**

6 rue de Beaujolais 75001   **M° Palais-Royal**
Seats 40   Meal for 2 approx 700F

Named after Armand's Jean du Plessis, Duc de Richelieu, the
restaurant is located in an old stone-faced building looking at the
back of the Palais-Royal. The setting is romantic, with candle-
light, beamed ceilings and rich upholstery, and Bruno Roupie's
intelligent, innovative cooking combines classic and modern
in happy harmony. He admits to no specialities, and the menu
changes with the seasons, but typical dishes might include *crepe
de maïs au foie gras chaud, effeuillé de raie au chou vert* or *gratin
de langoustines et sole, sauce champagne* plus some delicious chocolate
desserts. French wines span the regions and the price range. Set
menus: L 170-260F D 240-350F. No à la carte. *L 12-2 D 8-10.30.
Closed L Sat, all Sun. Amex, Mastercard, Visa.*

Brasserie Munichoise
Map B1.4

Tel 42 61 47 16   **R**

5 rue Danielle Casanova 75001   **M° Pyramides/Opéra**
Seats 60   Meal for 2 approx 300F

First-floor restaurant with Alpine chalet decor, a friendly welcome
and a menu of German/French inspiration. Specialities include
salami and Baltic herrings to start, then an assortment of sausages;
beef goulash; knuckle of pork roasted, moistened with beer and

served with choucroute; *cochon de lait* (suckling pig) and, to round
off a hearty, convivial meal, apple strudel. Alsace is the most
favoured region on the wine list but most people drink beer,
of which there is a wide variety on tap. Try Bitburger, a German
pils which takes five minutes to serve properly. If all you want is a
nibble they serve grilled sausages along with the beer at a small
bar on the ground floor. *Meals noon-1am (Sat from 5.30).*
Closed L Sat & all Sun. Mastercard, Visa.

Brighton
Map B1.5

H

Tel 42 60 30 03   Fax 42 60 41 78

218 rue de Rivoli 75001   **M° Tuileries**
Rooms 70   Double from 640F

Japanese-owned hotel in a 19th-century building with a prestigious
position facing the Tuileries. Bedrooms are on five floors and both
size and decor vary considerably. Largest rooms overlooking the
Rivoli Gardens are on a grand scale, with lofty moulded ceilings,
brass beds and handsome period furnishings. A couple
of bathrooms boast spectacular mosaics – much in demand for
magazine 'shoots'. At the top of the building, under the eaves,
rooms are small but very charming. The **Salon de Thé** is a relaxing
spot for a light snack. Room service till 8pm. Friendly,
professional staff. *Amex, Diners, Mastercard, Visa.*

Britannique
Map D2.6

H

Tel 42 33 74 59   Fax 42 33 82 65

20 ave Victoria 75001   **M° Chatelet/Les Halles**
Rooms 40   Double from 732F

In a side street between Rue de Rivoli and the Seine, the
Britannique is handily placed for tourists, being just a short walk
from both the Ile de la Cité and the Louvre. Bedrooms are all of a
similar standard, with direct-dial phones, mini-bars, safes,
soundproofing and 10-channel TV. All have private bathrooms
(a few shower/wc only). Reading room and TV lounge but
no restaurant. *Amex, Diners, Mastercard, Visa.*

Cambon
Map A1.7

H

Tel 42 60 38 09   Fax 42 60 30 59

3 rue Cambon 75001   **M° Concorde**
Rooms 43   Double from 1280F

Concorde, the Tuileries garden, Madeleine and the Champs
Elysées are all moments away from the Cambon, a privately
owned hotel where bedrooms all have double beds and a range
of modern comforts from air-conditioning and mini-bar to room
safe and cable TV. No restaurant but breakfast is included in the
room price. *Amex, Diners, Mastercard, Visa.*

Carré des Feuillants   ★★
Map A1.8

R

Tel 42 86 82 82   Fax 42 86 07 71

14 rue de Castiglione 75001   **M° Tuileries**
Seats 70   Meal for 2 approx 1100F

Charming restaurant in an arcade off the Rue de Rivoli with three
elegant bourgeois-style dining rooms and a glass-covered
courtyard. Alain Dutournier's accomplished cooking is firmly

See over

based in his native Gascony with a strong awareness of the seasons, as in the six-course no-choice "Ideas of the Season" menu which, for an extra 180F, comes with glasses of four different wines chosen to complement the various courses; this menu is only available if taken by the whole table. Typical dishes from an autumn *carte* included a terrine of venison with poached fruits, deep-fried eel with spicy herb salad, sole with grilled fennel, *garbure béarnaise à l'ancienne*, roast Pauillac lamb, wild partridge roasted *à la ventreche craquante* and chicken pan-fried 'Rossini' with duck foie gras, clear truffle-flavoured jus and fricassee of artichokes. Most of the desserts – like croustade of figs with nougat ice cream, *peche de vigne au romarin* and dark chocolate gateau – are prepared to order and need to be specified at the beginning of the meal. Huge wine list, over 1300 bins, is mostly French but other European and some New World producers are also represented. Set L 280F Set L & D (*dégustation*) 560F. *L 12-2.30 D 7.30-10.30.* **Closed** *L Sat, all Sun & Aug. Amex, Diners, Mastercard, Visa.*

Les Cartes Postales   Map B1.9

| Tel 42 61 02 93 | R |

7 rue Gomboust 75001   M° **Pyramides**
Seats 30   Meal for 2 approx 750F

A changing collection of framed art-postcards down one wall explains the name of this little restaurant where the cooking is rather more ambitious than the decor. Yoshimasa Watanabe's menu includes dishes with an Oriental influence – marinated mackerel with Chinese herbs, brill half-cooked and half-raw in the Japanese fashion – along with the likes of croustade of pheasant and foie gras, red mullet fried in Provençal herbs with green peppercorn vinaigrette, and veal sweetbreads braised with wild mushrooms. Look out for a classic chocolate gateau among the desserts. Wines are exclusively French. Set L 135F Set L& D 285F & 350F. *L 12-2 D 6.30-10.30.* **Closed** *L Sat, all Sun. Mastercard, Visa.*

Le Caveau du Palais   Map C2.10

| Tel 43 26 04 28   Fax 43 26 81 84 | R |

17-19 place Dauphine 75001   M° **Pont-Neuf**
Seats 60 (+ 30 outdoor)   Meal for 2 approx 500F

On one of the prettiest squares in Paris, the house was built in 1604, and much of the original fabric remains. Cooking is traditional and competent: *moelle de boeuf, salade de cervelle, blanquette de veau, coquilles St Jacques aux pates fraiches* – individual dishes vary according to the season. The owner has been here since 1972, and her son owns the next-door wine bar, where wines by the glass accompany sandwiches and snacks. Set L & D 160F. *L 12.15-2.30 D 7.15-10.30.* **Closed** *Sat (Oct-May), Sun & 24 Dec-2 Jan. Amex, Mastercard, Visa.*

Chez Clovis   Map C1.11

| Tel & Fax 42 33 97 07 | R |

33 rue Berger 75001   M° **Les Halles**
Seats 100 (+ 50 outdoor)   Meal for 2 approx 450F

Famous, traditional bistro by Les Halles, personally run by the same family for over 50 years. The unspoilt interior is full

of black and white photographs of Les Halles in the old days when
it was the main food market for Paris. The menu, which they
describe as 'cuisine à l'ancienne', is full of specialities such as stuffed
neck of duck, *blanquette de veau à l'ancienne*, foie gras of duck
in aspic, *tete de veau sauce gribiche*, hot Lyonnaise sausage with
lentils, and breadcrumbed pig's trotters with sauce béarnaise.
Unusually for a Parisian restaurant there are some 20 wines
available by the glass (small or large). Set L & D 89F and 98F.
L 12-3 D 7-12 (Fri & Sat till 1am). **Closed** *Sun. Amex,
Mastercard, Visa.*

Chez Elle   Map C1.12

| Tel 45 08 04 10 | **R** |

7 rue des Prouvaires 75001   Mᵒ Chatelet/Les Halles
Seats 50 (+ 18 outdoor)   Meal for 2 approx 450F

Turn-of-the-century, black and white photographs of female nudes
bedeck the walls of this unpretentious restaurant near Les Halles.
The traditional menu does not change much, with mussels
marinière or *à la crème, escargots de Bourgogne, oeufs en meurette*
amongst the starters, salmon *en papillote*, sole meunière, grilled
fillet of beef, *magret* of duck and veal kidneys *grandmère* typifying
the main dishes and familiar desserts such as crème brulée,
chocolate mousse, floating islands and the tart of the day. Amongst
the tables there is one that can accommodate up to 12 diners.
Set D 95F. *L 12-2.30 D 8-11 (occasionally till midnight Thu & Fri)*.
Closed *Sat, Sun & Public Holidays. Amex, Visa.*

Chez Pauline   Map B1.13

| Tel 42 96 20 70   Fax 49 27 99 89 | **R** |

5 rue Villedo 75001   Mᵒ Pyramides
Seats 80   Meal for 2 approx 840F

Zinc bar, red banquettes, mirrored walls and moulded ceiling all
add up to an archetypal Parisian bistro. Although he is not from
Burgundy, that is where chef-patron M Gervain's heart lies and
it is the inspiration for his menu. Particular specialities include
a warm salad of *tete de veau* with *sauce gribiche, jambon persillé*,
rabbit terrine *en gelée de vin blanc*, roast Bresse chicken (for two
persons) the wings served with *gratin dauphinoise* potatoes and the
legs with salad, *boeuf bourguignon* served with tagliatelle and,
among the desserts, a dark chocolate gateau with *crème anglaise* and
vanilla ice cream. Burgundy and Beaujolais are, unsurprisingly, the
best represented regions on the wine list. Set L & D 220F. *L 12.15-
2.30 D 7.15-10.30*. **Closed** *Sat (except D Oct-Feb) & Sun. Amex,
Mastercard, Visa.*

Au Cochon d'Or des Halles   Map C1.14

| Tel 42 36 38 31 | **R** |

31 rue du Jour 75001   Mᵒ Les Halles
Seats 25   Meal for 2 approx 500F

A classic bistro menu that's strong on meat, with grilled veal
kidneys, pork with garlic and rib of beef for two among the
specialities. *Carré d'agneau* is another favourite, and there's always
a daily special such as *tête de veau*. *L 12-2.30 D 7.30-10.30*.
Closed *Sun. Amex, Mastercard, Visa.*

Hotel du Continent
Tel 42 60 75 32   Fax 42 61 52 22

Map A1.15
H

30 rue du Mont-Thabor 75001
Rooms 28

M° Concorde
Double from 580F

In the same group and offering basically the same facilities as the
Louvre St-Honoré and the *Saint-Romain*. This one is equally well
situated, moments from the Tuileries and round the corner from
Place Vendome. No restaurant. *Amex, Diners, Mastercard, Visa.*

Demeure Hotel Castille
Tel 42 61 55 20   Fax 40 15 94 64

Map A1.16
H

37 rue Cambon 75001
Rooms 87

M° Madeleine
Double from 2200F

Rubbing shoulders with Chanel and the Ritz, the Castille is itself
certainly not lacking in either style or luxury. Italian Renaissance-
style decor features 18th-century paintings, old engravings, rich
damask fabrics and imported marble. A central courtyard,
complete with fountain and murals, is overlooked by many of the
bedrooms. These are decorated in one of four colour schemes and
come with air-conditioning, three telephones per room, multi-
channel TV and marble bathrooms that boast towelling robes,
high-quality toiletries and separate WCs. 24 new bedrooms (they
have taken over the building next door) are due to open early
in 1995. 24hr room service. Parking for five cars. *Amex, Diners,
Mastercard, Visa.*

Hotel des Ducs d'Anjou
Tel 42 36 92 24   Fax 42 36 16 63

Map D1.17
H

1 rue Ste-Opportune 75001
Rooms 38

M° Chatelet
Double from 600F

Comfortable accommodation in a central location. Rooms are
generally not all that large, the best pair being two on the top
floor with mansard ceilings. Three cheaper rooms have shower
only, with a shared WC along the corridor. No restaurant. *Amex,
Diners, Mastercard, Visa.*

> Note: from April 16 1995 the
> international dialling code 010 changes to 00

Duminy-Vendome
Tel 42 60 32 80   Fax 42 96 07 83

Map A1.18
H

3 rue du Mont-Thabor 75001
Rooms 79

M° Tuileries
Double from 800F

Built on the site of a convent, this is a hotel of charm just
5 minutes from the Louvre. Bedrooms are furnished variously
with old pieces and modern, but all have marble bathrooms and
the usual amenities. Next door to the hotel is the house where the
poet Alfred de Musset lived. Breakfast is included in the room
price. No restaurant. *Amex, Diners, Mastercard, Visa.*

Fellini
Map C2.19

Tel 42 60 90 66   **R**

47 rue de l'Arbre-Sec 75001   **M° Louvre**
Seats 40   Meal for 2 approx 550F

With exposed stone walls this is the more attractive of the two
Fellinis (the other is in the 15th) and has an atmospheric stone
vaulted cellar for private parties of up to 25. Described as 'creative
Italian cuisine' the menu nevertheless offers plenty of familiar
sounding dishes – *spaghetti alle vongole*, bruschetta with Parma ham
and mozzarella, breast of chicken glazed with Marsala, *scampi
al forno*, tiramisu, zabaglione – along with the likes of carpaccio
of tuna with olive oil and fennel, smoked bresaola on a bed
of rocket, sea bass with herbs and giant prawns sautéed with
artichokes. Classy, but pricey, Italian wine list but there are plans
to introduce some more affordable bottles and perhaps also some
French wines. Set L 110F. *L 12-3 D 7-11.30. Mastercard, Visa.*

La Fermette du Sud-Ouest
Map C1.20

Tel 42 36 73 55   **R**

31 rue Coquillière 75001   **M° Palais-Royal/Louvre**
Seats 35   Meal for 2 approx 440F

Dating back to the 16th century, this unpretentious, welcoming
restaurant features rough stone walls, old beams and the cooking
of South-West France. Home-made *boudins* and terrines,
cochonnailles, confit de canard with ceps, cassoulet, *feuilleté à l'orange*
and *tarte tatin* are all big on flavour and satisfaction level. A choice
of just six wines – one each from Cahors, Buzet and Madiran plus
three from Bordeaux – all served on a pay-for-what-you drink
basis. Set L 145F. *L 12-2.30 D 7.30-10.30.* **Closed** *Sun & 1 week
mid Aug. Mastercard, Visa.*

> The best way to get around Paris is by bus or metro – buy a
> book of tickets (carnet) at any metro station and save money

Gaya Rive Droite
Map A1.21

Tel 42 60 43 03   Fax 42 60 04 54   **R**

17 rue Duphot 75001   **M° Madeleine**
Seats 85   Meal for 2 approx 600F

A new name: it was formerly just Gaya, but a sister restaurant
has now opened on the Left Bank (see *Gaya Rive Gauche*). Both
are scions of *Goumard-Prunier* (*qv*) just down the street from this
address. Describing itself as a 'Bistrot de la Mer', it has a menu
which changes daily according to the market, offering
wonderfully fresh, simply prepared fish dishes like fried monkfish
with tartare sauce, grilled John Dory with tarragon and a peppery
fish soup, all swiftly served by waiters in blue-bibbed aprons.
On two bustling floors the decor features some fine ornamental
blue and white tiling that dates from the turn of the century when
this was a Portuguese bar – apparently serving only port wine.
L 12-2.30 D 7-10.30. **Closed** *Sun & 2 weeks Aug. Amex,
Mastercard, Visa.*

Gérard Besson   ★★   Map C1.22
Tel 42 33 14 74   Fax 42 33 85 71   R

5 rue Coq-Héron 75001   Mᵒ Les Halles/Palais-Royal
Seats 45   Meal for 2 approx 1100F

Well-spaced tables with immaculate settings, old paintings and
silver carafes in display cases are all part of the elegant scenery, but
it's Gérard Besson's superb cooking which takes centre stage at this
outstanding restaurant in the old Les Halles area. The marriage
of traditional cuisine with innovative flair delights in dishes like
escalope of foie gras on puréed Puy lentils with wild duck essence;
a *petite marmite* of scallops in a chicken bouillon with fresh herbs
and vegetables; Bresse chicken cooked with a gratin of macaroni
and foie gras and a classical *sauce albuféra*; sole braised
in champagne which is then reduced and thickened with orange
butter to make the sauce and served with a gratin of spinach; and
amongst the desserts a hot praline soufflé with almond milk ice
cream and a bitter chocolate mousse on a base of rice soufflé with
a pistachio-flavoured *sauce anglaise*. Classy French wine list with
just a handful of foreign interlopers. Set L 260F Set L & D 480F
(*dégustation*) & 750F (game menu, in season only). *L 12-2.30
D 7.30-10.30.* **Closed** *L Sat & all Sun.* Amex, Diners,
Mastercard, Visa.

Goumard-Prunier   ★   Map A1.23
Tel 42 60 36 07   Fax 42 60 04 54   R

9 rue Duphot 75001   Mᵒ Madeleine
Seats 100   Meal for 2 approx 1350F

For well over 100 years the name of this most famous of seafood
restaurants was simply 'Prunier'. The prefix arrived in 1992 along
with Jean-Claude Goumard, who effectively saved the restaurant
and who, along with chef Georges Landriot, continues to enhance
its reputation. Jean-Claude's early morning trips to Rungis market
ensure that only the best and freshest of seafood arrives in the
kitchen, where George's light, modern touch makes the very best
of it. Current specialities inlcude fish soufflé with saffron, *craquants
de langoustines et salade d'herbes*, fricassee of mussels with girolle
mushrooms, *rougets de roche en bécasse* and line-caught bass grilled
with artichokes and Indian peppers. They also have a stylishly
fitted out motor-yacht on the Seine for private parties of up to 36
people. *L 12-2.30 D 7-10.30.* **Closed** *Sun (except Sep-Mar) & Mon.*
Amex, Diners, Mastercard, Visa.

Grand Hotel de Champagne   Map D2.24
Tel 42 36 60 00   Fax 45 08 43 33   H

17 rue Jean-Lantier 75001   Mᵒ Chatelet/Les Halles
Rooms 43   Double from 640F

The facade is simple enough, but inside, the hotel has been kept
in 'Old Paris' style, with beams and exposed stonework in most
bedrooms. Each room is different in detail, and some have terraces
where guests can enjoy one of the hotel's selling points – a
gourmet breakfast buffet (55F) including charcuterie, cheese,
patisserie, cereals, fruit tarts, fruit salad, etc. No restaurant. *Amex,
Diners, Mastercard, Visa.*

Le Grand Véfour ★★ Map C1.25

| Tel 42 96 56 27   Fax 42 86 80 71 | **R** |

17 rue de Beaujolais 75001 **Mº Bourse**
Seats 55 Meal for 2 approx 1350F

A historic restaurant that can trace its origins back to a café opened in 1784 in one wing of the then new Palais Royal. It has numbered Bonaparte's Josephine and the writers Colette and Jean Cocteau among regular customers in the past. Now owned by the Taittinger group, and with its richly ornate original interior restored, Le Grand Véfour has regained its former glory and with Guy Martin in the kitchen it's firmly back on the culinary map too. Current specialities on the carte include *ravioles de foie gras, crème truffée;* scallops with polenta and sweet garlic; *saumon mi-cuit en terrine, lait fumé aux graines de pavot;* red mullet with a light sauce made from its liver; *parmentier de queue de boeuf aux truffes;* and amongst the desserts a *gourmandise au chocolat.* Unsurprisingly Taittinger champagne heads the wine list. One red and one white wine are available by the glass. Air-conditioned. Valet parking. Set L 305F Set L & D 750F ('Menu Plaisir', *dégustation*). *L 12.30-2.15 D 7.30-10.15.* **Closed** *Sat, Sun & Aug. Amex, Diners, Mastercard, Visa.*

A la Grille Saint-Honoré Map B1.26

| Tel 42 61 00 93   Fax 47 03 31 64 | **R** |

15 place du Marché St-Honoré 75001 **Mº Tuileries**
Seats 60 (+25 outside) Meal for 2 approx 650F

Chef-patron Jean Speyer is down at the markets each morning choosing only the best and freshest of produce for what is essentially a *cuisine d'auteur* at his intimate restaurant on the corner of the Place du Marché. There are both English and Japanese versions of a *carte* that might include a warm lobster and raw spinach salad, hot cake of ceps with tarragon, sautéed scampi with truffle juice and young lamb in a light curry sauce with baby vegetables. Game is the speciality in season. Wine list majors on Bordeaux. Set L & D 180F. *L 12-2.30 D 7-10.30.* **Closed** *Sun, also Mon (except Oct-Dec), 10 days Christmas & 1st 3 wks Aug. Amex, Diners, Mastercard, Visa.*

Hotel Inter-Continental Map A1.27

| Tel 44 77 11 11   Fax 44 77 14 60 | **HR** |

3 rue Castiglione 75001 **Mº Concorde/Tuileries**
Rooms 450 Double from 2100F

Built in 1878 around an elegant courtyard, this highly luxurious hotel has an ideal location between the Place Vendome and the Place de la Concorde with some rooms overlooking the Tuileries gardens. Air-conditioned bedrooms offer every possible comfort and include some 70 suites. The service lives up to the surroundings and includes 24hr room service, valet parking and a well-connected concierge. Breakfast options include perhaps the best Japanese breakfast in town. Of various function rooms the stunning Salon Imperial with its marble columns, glittering chandeliers and ornate gilt mouldings is among the most beautiful in the city and is a listed national monument. *Amex, Diners, Mastercard, Visa.*

See over

Terrasse Fleurie
Tel 44 77 10 44 ›
Seats 32 (**+**140 outdoor)

Passing through the lobby of the hotel, this appealing restaurant
comes into view through the columns that surround the central
courtyard. In summer, the tables and chairs spread out on to the
courtyard itself. The interior has a 'winter garden' decor with
a marble floor, large windows and fixed conservatory blinds
across the glass ceiling. Chef Raoul Gaiga's *carte*, which comes
with English translations, changes with the seasons, the fixed-price
lunch weekly. Lobster rigatoni *au gratin*, eggs *en cocotte* with
truffles, sole with celery confit, pigeon and foie gras in puff pastry,
young rabbit sautéed with artichokes and sweet garlic, chicken
casserole with a butter and herb sauce and beef fillet with spices
are typical of the 'nouvelle' inspired dishes. At night one can
choose the gourmet *dégustation* menu and enjoy seven of Raoul's
creations served in appropriately small portions. This menu
is served only to an entire table. Extensive wine list with two
or three available by the glass. Set L 270F Set D450F. *L 12-3 D 7-
10.* **Closed** *last week Dec.*

Joe Allen
Map D1.28

| Tel 42 36 70 13   Fax 40 28 06 94 | **R** |

30 rue Pierre Lescot 75001   M° Etienne Marcel
Seats 115 (+ 32 outside)   Meal for 2 approx 450F

Modelled on the New York original, (there's another in London),
the decor of exposed brick walls, bare-board floor and check
tablecloths goes along with a brash, informal atmosphere. The
menu, written in American with French sub-titles, ranges from
Buffalo chicken wings with blue cheese dip and roasted red
pepper with feta cheese and basil to T-bone steak, 'Sloppy Joe'
BBQ ribs and grilled swordfish with wild rice salad. Puds are
as American as brownies and pecan pie. Some 10 or so wines
by the glass plus a selection of beers. A special brunch menu is the
only choice weekends and Public Holidays. *Meals noon-1am (till
4pm Sat, Sun & Public Holidays). Amex, Mastercard, Visa.*

Juveniles

| Tel 42 97 46 49   Fax 47 03 36 93 | **R** |

47 rue de Richelieu 75001   M° Palais Royal/Bourse

Englishman Tim Johnston is a wine merchant, and sometime
vigneron, rather than a restaurateur, but his cheerfully informal
tapas bar gives customers an excellent excuse to sample his wines
whilst enjoying a flavoursome nibble. The tapas range from
tapénade of aubergine with toast and a fricassee of chanterelle and
pied du mouton mushrooms to succulent roast quail with chicory
salad and rabbit with chutney. There are also *plats* such as steamed
salmon with saffron, tuna steak with fresh coriander and
ratatouille, lamb curry and liver with bacon. Cheeses include
Cheddar and Stilton or go for one of the puds: chocolate cake,
apple crumble with vanilla ice cream, tiramisu. Wines, of which
some 14 or so are available by the glass, major on the Cote
du Rhone; sherry is also a speciality. Set meal (tapas for two) 138F
(220F with wine). *Meals noon-11pm (12-3 & 7-11 Mon & Sat).*
Closed *Sun. Mastercard, Visa.*

Kinugawa
Map A1.30

R

Tel 42 60 65 07   Fax 42 60 45 21

9 rue Mont-Thabor 75001
Seats 80

Mᵒ Tuileries
Meal for 2 approx 800F

Bright Japanese restaurant with a menu that's strong on seafood:
salmon eggs and salted fish guts among the starters, steamed
seafood flavoured with saké, 15 varieties of sashimi including sea
bream, tuna, octopus and oysters as well as grilled shrimps and the
day's choice grilled with a teriyaki sauce or prawn fritters. Meat-
eaters weigh in with sliced beef and ginger, roast beef with
ponzou sauce, cold roast duck, quail teriyaki and a sustaining pot-
au-feu (shabu shabu). For special occasions try the Kaiseki (chef's
recommendation) menu (545F). There's a sister restaurant of the
same name in the 8th (4 rue Saint Philippe Tel 45 63 08 07) with
the same hours and closures. Set L 240F. *L 12-2.30 D 7-10.*
Closed *Sun, 24 Dec-5 Jan. Amex, Diners, Mastercard, Visa.*

Lescure
Map A1.31

R

Tel 42 60 18 91   Fax 40 15 91 27

7 rue de Mondovi 75001
Seats 38 (+ 20 outdoor)

Mᵒ Concorde
Meal for 2 approx 280F

Traditional home cooking at very kind prices in a rustic, convivial
restaurant that's been in the same family since 1919. *Paté en croute
chaud, confit de canard, cassoulet,* poached haddock, *boeuf
bourguignon,* seasonal game and boiled stuffed chicken show that
this is not a centre of culinary revolution. The *carte* changes every
two weeks, the *prix-fixe* never. Speciality Cahors and Macon
wines – you only pay for what you drink. No bookings. Set L &
D 100F. *L 12-2.15 D 7-10.15.* ***Closed*** *D Sat, all Sun & Aug.*
Mastercard, Visa.

Lotti
Map A1.32

H

Tel 42 60 37 34   Fax 40 15 93 56

7 rue Castiglione 75001
Rooms 133

Mᵒ Opéra/Tuileries/Concorde
Double from 1900F

Built in 1900 and opened as a hotel ten years later, the Lotti
is now run by the Italian chain Jolly Hotels. Peace and comfort are
keynotes, from the elegant reception area to bedrooms decorated
in various Louis and Empire styles. Top-floor rooms, with sloping
ceilings, are reserved for non-smokers. All rooms feature multi-
channel TV, radio, direct-dial phones, mini-bar, air-conditioning
and soundproofing. Room service till midnight. Valet parking.
Amex, Diners, Mastercard, Visa.

Louis XIV
Map C1.33

R

Tel 40 26 20 81

1bis place des Victoires 75001
Seats 80 (+ 24 outdoor)

Mᵒ Bourse
Meal for 2 approx 560F

Archetypical bistro near the Banque de France where chef Dugat's
Lyonnaise cooking has been keeping his customers happy for
a quarter of a century: *tete roulée au Beaujolais, oeuf en gelée, foie
de veau lyonnaise, andouillette mitonnée, boeuf bourguignon.* Less often
encountered dishes include *tablier de sapeur* – pieces of beef
seasoned with mustard, breadcrumbed and fried, sprinkled

See over

(optionally) with sherry vinegar, and *cervelle des canuts* – fromage frais beaten with shallots, vinegar, white wine and herbs. Set L & D 165F (210F with wine). *L 12-2.30 D 7.30-10.30.* **Closed** *Sat, Sun & Aug. Mastercard, Visa.*

Hotel du Louvre
Map B1.34

Tel 44 58 38 38   Fax 44 58 38 01   H

place André Malraux 75001   M⁰ Palais-Royal
Rooms 200   Double from 1300F

Between the Louvre and the Palais-Royal stands this handsome hotel whose accommodation, extending over 5 floors, includes 16 junior suites and 4 full suites. Bedroom size and decor vary – some art deco, some in quiet pastels – but all are well appointed, with up-to-date telephone systems and multi-channel TV, while individual air-conditioning keeps things comfortable. High levels of service extend to valet parking, porterage, 24hr room service and an efficient concierge. **Le Defender** bar features an evening pianist. *Amex, Diners, Mastercard, Visa.*

Louvre Saint-Honoré
Map C1.35

Tel 42 96 23 23   Fax 42 96 21 61   H

141 rue St-Honoré 75001   M⁰ Louvre
Rooms 40   Double from 840F

Two period buildings, one of eight storeys, the other of seven, are divided by a glass pyramid covering a courtyard – the setting for a relaxed breakfast. Some of the modern bedrooms overlook this courtyard, others the road. The hotel, just a few steps from the Louvre, is part of Hotels les Beaux Logis de Paris, also responsible for *l'Hotel du Continent* and *Hotel St-Romain* (see entries). No restaurant. *Amex, Diners, Mastercard, Visa.*

Mayfair
Map A1.36

Tel 42 60 38 14   Fax 40 15 04 78   H

3 rue Rouget-de-L'Isle 75001   M⁰ Concorde
Rooms 53   Double from 1650F

Just off Rue de Rivoli (and, like that renowned thoroughfare, dating from 1880), there's an elegant feel to public areas that comprise a lobby-cum-lounge with ornate gilt light fittings, and a cosy wood-panelled bar with tapestry panels where breakfast is also served; there is no restaurant. Recently refurbished bedrooms, though mostly not large, are stylishly decorated and offer all sorts of comforts from mini-bar and room safe to multi-channel TV and good bathrooms, all with showers over tubs. Most rooms are air-conditioned. Room service till 9pm. No parking of their own but the hotel can reserve spaces in a nearby garage. *Amex, Diners, Mastercard, Visa.*

Mercure Galant   ★
Map C1.37

Tel 42 96 98 89   Fax 42 96 08 89   R

15 rue des Petits Champs 75001   M⁰ Pyramides
Seats 80   Meal for 2 approx 1100F

Classic cooking in tranquil comfort is the order of the day at Pierre Ferranti's recently redecorated 19th-century restaurant near the Palais Royal. Lobster salad with citrus fruits; *turbot roti, legumes à l'huile de curry*; fillet of Charolais beef with bone marrow *en papillotte*, and *mille et une feuilles du Mercure* are specialities from a menu that might also include such dishes as a feuilleté of fresh snails with mushrooms, fricassee of chicken with morel mushrooms and a tempting dessert involving chocolate and orange combined in three different ways. On the wine list are 120 Bordeaux and 20 burgundies. Set L 210F Set D 400F. *L 12.15-2.30 D 7.15-10.30.* **Closed** *L Sat, all Sun & Public Holidays. Amex, Mastercard, Visa.*

Meurice   Map A1.38

| Tel 44 58 10 10   Fax 44 58 10 17 | **HR** |

228 rue de Rivoli 75001   **Mᴼ Tuileries**
Rooms 180   Double room from 2550F

Dating from the time when Prefect Haussman was replanning Paris, the Meurice, with its location overlooking the Tuileries Gardens, quickly established itself as a favourite of the Imperial Court. More recently it has become a haunt of the literati with the jury of a new literary prize 'Le Jury du Prix Novembre' making their home here. Following the hotel's acquistion by the Ciga group in 1988 considerable refurbishment has returned the sparkle to the stunning Salon Pompadour, with its elaborate gilt decoration, and other public rooms, and restored the hotel's position amongst the best in Paris. Antique furniture, fresh flowers, original paintings and the occasional marble fireplace are among the elements that bring individuality and luxury to both the bedrooms and the 37 suites. Bathrooms are marble and standards of service are high. Valet parking. *Amex, Diners, Mastercard, Visa.*

Le Meurice   ★
Seats 50   Meal for 2 approx 1000F

Marc Marchand's menu changes with the seasons in this exquisitely appointed restaurant, but on Wednesdays you might get all four seasons at once, as Vivaldi is often included in the musical 'saveurs lyriques' evenings. Ballotine of duck foie gras with grape purée, marinated salmon and scallops with a mustard and beetroot sauce, perch with ceps and a compote of red cabbage, supreme of pheasant with foie gras and a pineapple soufflé with passion fruit sorbet were amongst the dishes indicated as specialities on a recent lunchtime menu. Extensive French wine list, full of famous names, and with a good sprinkling of half bottles. Set L 300F Set D 380F (inclusive of wine) & 420F (Wed only). *L 12-2.30 D 7.30-10.30.*

Molière   Map B1.39

| Tel 42 96 22 01   Fax 42 60 48 68 | **H** |

21 rue Molière 75001   **Mᴼ Palais Royal/Pyramides**
Rooms 32   Double from 560F

Handily situated for many of the major Parisian sights, this is a small hotel of charm and character, with particularly pleasant staff and a reservation book that's generally filled with regulars. It's typically 19th century in appearance, and the bedrooms, spread over seven floors and ranging in style from Louis XV to 1930s, look out on to either a little flowery courtyard or the small street.   *See over*

Top-floor rooms have sloping ceilings, some rooms have balconies and all are sound-proofed. Cable TV includes English channels. 11 of the rooms have shower/WC only. No restaurant. *Amex, Diners, Mastercard, Visa.*

Montana-Tuileries   Map B1.40

Tel 42 60 35 10   Fax 42 61 12 28   **H**

12 rue St-Roch 75001   **M⁰ Tuileries**
Rooms 25   Double from 580F

The building dates from 1800 and became a hotel in 1945. Bedrooms are individual in their detail, with generally simple modern furnishings and the expected modern comforts (just three rooms have shower/wc only). Rooms on the fifth floor have little balconies. The hotel is just across the road from the Louvre and the Tuileries. Room service in the daytime only. No restaurant. *Amex, Diners, Mastercard, Visa.*

Normandy   Map B1.41

Tel 42 60 30 21   Fax 42 60 45 81   **H**

7 rue de l'Echelle 75001   **M⁰ Musée du Louvre/Palais-Royal**
Rooms 123   Double from 1375F

Built in 1877 to a Haussmann design, the hotel is three stone-faced buildings which have kept their original style. In the hall are marble columns and three enormous chandeliers; the reception desks are all in wood, as is the English bar with its velvet curtains and leather seats. In the bedrooms, which include eight suites, the same sense of tradition prevails, and many of the bathrooms retain their splendid old fittings. Room service from 6.30am to 9.45pm. *Amex, Diners, Mastercard, Visa.*

Paolo Petrini   Map B1.42

Tel 42 60 56 22   Fax 42 36 55 50   **R**

9 rue d'Argenteuil 75001   **M⁰ Pyramides**
Seats 30   Meal for 2 approx 650F

Paolo Petrini is doing wonders for the reputation of Italian cooking at his tiny restaurant in a side street close to Palais Royal. The decor is modern Italian, of the sort that looks simple but does not come cheap, and reflects Paolo's own contemporary approach to mainly north Italian dishes, particularly those of his native Tuscany. Cep soup with bread and pumpkin; bresaola with olive oil, goat's cheese and lemon; pappardelle with ragout of hare; gnocchi with tomato, basil, mint and ricotta cheese; stuffed baby pigeon with a Barbaresco sauce; rabbit casseroled with celery, bacon and green olives, and *semifreddo sole di Sicilia* (semi-frozen lemon and orange cake) typify a menu that comes with both French and English translations. Home-baked Tuscan schiacciata bread topped with olive oil, rosemary and rock salt arrives with the menu and unless you're keen to visit the dentist don't forget to dunk the rock-hard little biscuit that comes with the coffee. Paolo's passion for food is matched only by his passion for wine. "There is no good kitchen without a good cellar", a philosophy reflected in the well-chosen, if shortish, list of Italian wines of which five are available by the glass. *L 12-2.30 D 7.30-11. **Closed** L Sat, all Sun & Aug. Amex, Mastercard, Visa.*

La Passion

Map B1.43

Tel 42 97 53 41   **R**

41 rue Petits-Champs 75001   M° Pyramides/4 Septembre
Seats 45   Meal for 2 approx 600F

One wall of this little restaurant is covered with a trompe l'oeil mural of windows opening onto the Place des Victoires, another is largely mirrored. Add fresh flowers on the tables and some foodie watercolours and the whole effect is quite charming. Chef-patron Gilles Zellenwarger puts his own signature, and slight Alsace accent, on traditonally-based dishes: *foie gras de canard* (something of a speciality), mussel soup, fricassée of sole *fines herbes, daube de boeuf, croustade de pigeon à la bordelaise,* mille feuille of skate wing with tarragon. Set L & D 170F/200F/360F (*dégustation). L 12-2.30 D 7.30-10.* **Closed** *L Sat, all Sun & Aug. Amex, Mastercard, Visa.*

Pharamond

Map D1.44

Tel 42 33 06 72   Fax 40 28 01 81   **R**

24 rue de la Grande Truanderie 75001   M° Les Halles
Seats 95   Meal for 2 approx 750F

Listed as a historic monument for its extravagant Belle Epoque interior, this restaurant near Les Halles features traditional Normandy cuisine: *tripes à la mode de Caen,* galette of rabbit, cod stew with sweet garlic. *Canette au citron* and *coquilles St Jacques au cidre* are particular specialities. The menu changes with the seasons. Set L 180F Set D 250F. *L 12-2.30 D 7.30-10.30.* **Closed** *L Mon, all Sun. Amex, Diners, Visa.*

Au Pied de Cochon

Map C1.45

Tel 42 36 11 75   Fax 45 08 48 90   **R**

6 rue Coquillière 75001   M° Halles
Seats 280 (+ 60 outdoor)   Meal for 2 approx 520F

Open day and night (*every* day and *every* night), this brasserie has a warm place in the hearts of Parisians, out-of-town French and visitors from overseas. In bright convivial surroundings helped along by young, relaxed staff, they tuck into what they've always tucked into: onion soup, fish soup, oysters and clams, snails, foie gras, the renowned pig's trotters, grilled salmon and grilled steaks, fruit tarts and profiteroles. The wine list majors on Beaujolais (with all the Crus Beaujolais coming from Duboeuf) but all the main French regions are covered. House wine is a Costières de Nimes from the owner's own vineyard. *Meals 24 hours a day. Amex, Diners, Mastercard, Visa.*

Pierre au Palais-Royal

Map B1.46

Tel 42 96 09 17   Fax 42 96 09 62   **R**

10 rue Richelieu 75001   M° Palais-Royal
Seats 50   Meal for 2 approx 700F

Charming restaurant *du quartier* where the handwritten menu changes twice a week, and some dishes even more often according to the vagaries of the market. Popular dishes include *jambon persillé,* chicken liver terrine, brill with sorrel, wild duck with

See over

blackberries and *boeuf ficelle à la ménagère*. Duck foie gras, served either hot with sherry vinegar or cold in a terrine, is a more or less permanent feature of the menu. Exclusively French wine list is strongest in Bordeaux where it ranges all the way up to Pétrus. Set L & D 210F. *L 12-2.30 D 7-10.30.* **Closed** *Sat, Sun, Aug & Public Holidays. Amex, Diners, Mastercard, Visa.*

Hotel de la Place du Louvre   Map C2.47

Tel 42 33 78 68   Fax 42 33 09 95   **H**

21 rue des Pretres-St-Germain-l'Auxerrois 75001   **M⁰ Louvre/Pont Neuf**
Rooms 20   Double from 670F

An ancient building opposite the church which gives the street its name. Bedrooms, all named after different artists and boasting a print of their work, come with mini-bars, safes, numerous TV channels and all the usual modern conveniences. There's no restaurant, but breakfast is served either in bedrooms or in the 14th-century Cellar of the Musketeers. Room service during the day. Laundry service. *Amex, Diners, Mastercard, Visa.*

For a glossary of menu terms see page 293

Le Poquelin   Map B1.48

Tel 42 96 22 19   Fax 42 96 05 72   **R**

17 rue Molière 75001   **M⁰ Palais-Royal**
Seats 45   Meal for 2 approx 600F

Michel and Maggy Guillaumin have been running their little restaurant next to the Comédie Française for more than 20 years, he in the kitchen, she the charming and outgoing hostess. The decorative theme is the Comédie and Molière (Jean Baptiste Poquelin). Market-fresh produce contributes to the success of dishes like steamed lobster with creamy lemon sauce, stewed turbot with smoked bacon, shoulder of lamb roasted with two kinds of cabbage and veal kidney with mustard sauce. Amongst the desserts the freshly-baked individual apple tart (order at the beginning of the meal) has been a firm favourite ever since the restaurant opened. The fixed-price menu changes monthly, the *carte* seasonally. In addition to the regular wine list there is always a good value Bordeaux of the month at 120F and, also changing monthly, a selection of four wines from some of the more obscure French regions. Set L & D 185F. *L 12-2 D 7.30-10.30.* **Closed** *L Sat, all Sun & 1st 3 wks Aug. Amex, Diners, Mastercard, Visa.*

Regina Paris   Map B1.49

Tel 42 60 31 10   Fax 40 15 95 16   **H**

2 place des Pyramides 75001   **M⁰ Palais-Royal/Tuileries**
Rooms 130   Double from 1500F

Elegant public areas at this traditional hotel opposite the Louvre include a chandeliered lobby with carved mahogany desk and a wood panelled bar with red leather upholstery. Antique-furnished bedrooms come with all the usual amenities and some have air-conditioning. *Amex, Diners, Mastercard, Visa.*

Le Relais du Louvre
Map C2.50

| Tel 40 41 96 42 | Fax 40 41 96 44 | **H** |

19 rue des Pretres St-Germain-l'Auxerrois 75001   **Mᵒ Louvre/Pont-Neuf**
Rooms 20   Double from 780F

Just 18 bedrooms and 2 suites in a charming hotel with a long and
interesting history. From 1800 to 1941 it was the seat of the
'Journal des Débats' – the French Hansard – and its ground floor
was the famous Café Momus, a rendezvous of intellectuals and
Bohemians. Individually appointed bedrooms have antique
furniture and rich co-ordinating fabrics, plus modern amenities
like points for fax and computers. Four singles have shower/wc
only. Breakfast is served only in the bedrooms. *Amex, Diners,
Mastercard, Visa.*

Ritz
Map A1.51

| Tel 43 16 33 33 | Fax 43 16 36 68 | **H R** |

15 place Vendome 75001   **Mᵒ Opéra**
Rooms 187   Double from 3200F

One of the world's *special* hotels, the very name a by-word for
opulence and luxury. Opened by César Ritz in 1898, the hotel
is still in private hands and is unconnected with other hotels
bearing the same name. Marble columns, deep carpets, rich drapes,
glittering chandeliers and lashings of gilt distinguish the classic
Louis XIV decor of the main public areas of a hotel that offers just
about everything a guest might need, from the Ritz Health Club
(stunning Romanesque swimming pool with underwater music
and trompe l'oeil sky, Turkish baths, squash courts, hairdressers
and every conceivable beauty treatment), and afternoon tea served
to the sound of a harp in the peaceful statuary-filled Vendome
garden, to the exclusive Ritz Club for dining and dancing till
dawn and a shopping gallery that is almost 100 yards long and
lined with some 90 showcases of luxury goods, all of which can
be bought from the Ritz boutique, making it unnecessary for even
the most ardent shopper ever to leave the hotel. In August 1994
the famous Hemingway Bar was reopened 50 years to the day
after he 'liberated' the Ritz from the German occupation – small
and cosy with warm, wood-panelled walls and leather upholstery
it now features a bust of 'Papa' Hemingway along with
memorabilia and photos of some of the other famous literati
(Proust, Jean-Paul Sartre, Oscar Wilde, J D Salinger) who have
patronised the bar over the years. To this day writers and
jounalists can use the Hemingway Bar as a mailing address. The
bar is closed on Sunday and Monday. Upstairs, bedrooms come
with marble fireplaces, chandeliers, gilt-framed mirrors, watered-
silk panelled walls, tapestry hangings at the bedhead and light
switches in the form of golden keys – and these are just the
'standard' rooms. Even bedroom corridors boast chandeliers and
damask-covered walls. There are 45 luxurious suites, some named
after famous former guests such as Coco Chanel, Scott Fitzgerald
and the Duke of Windsor. All mod cons are here, of course, from
air-conditioning to bedside controls to operate the exterior
window awnings. Only the mini-bars look a bit out of place.
Marble bathrooms feature huge bath tubs, taps in the form
of silver swans, enveloping robes and toiletries of the highest
quality along with bidets, twin wash basins and two telephones.   *See over*

Service is exemplary, with a ratio of nearly three staff members
to every guest bedroom. Just a touch of one of the three differently
coloured, jewel-like buttons at the side of the bed will summon
waiter, chambermaid or valet and you can even arrange to have
your own personal butler. A truly exceptional hotel of which
Hemingway wrote "When I dream of the afterlife in heaven, the
action always takes place at the Paris Ritz". A worthy winner
of our first Paris Hotel of the Year Award. *Amex, Diners,
Mastercard, Visa.*

L'Espadon   ★
Seats 60   Meal for 2 approx 1500F

A Second Empire room of delicate elegance, where the exact
shade of turquoise in a trompe l'oeil sky is picked up in the
trimmings for elaborate drapes that adorn high windows (which
open on to the Vendome gardens for summer dining) and
matching mirrored 'windows' that surround the room, giving it a
satisfying symmetry. Add Venetian glass 'flower vase' lights set on
sconces around the walls and you have a setting into which the
wing-collared, be-tailed waiters fit perfectly. A typically
thoughtful Ritz touch is the little gilt hook discreetly tucked away
on the side of each chair to accommodate handbags. The first chef
at the Ritz was the great Auguste Escoffier, who also designed the
original kitchens, and it is from his classic tradition that long-
serving chef Guy Legay has developed his own style taking into
account modern trends. *Menus dégustation* are where a chef
generally likes to 'show off' but here it is perhaps the 'safe' choice
while such dishes as a sashimi of lightly smoked salmon with a
tartare of sea bass and caviar cream sauce, fillets of red mullet with
its sautéed liver and Provençal vegetables, half a saddle of lamb
wrapped in its 'epigram' with tarragon and served with aubergine
'caviar' and a confit of sweet peppers, and a 'bombe' of fresh
cream-cheese and champagne sorbet with a coulis of redcurrants
appear on the *carte* along with classics like lobster bisque, sole
meunière and hot soufflés. A respectable cheese trolley comes with
their own excellent bread. Impressive wine list full of classic
names from Bordeaux and Burgundy. *L 12-3 D 7.30-11.*

Le Ruban Bleu   Map B1.52
Tel 42 61 47 53   R
29 rue d'Argenteuil 75001   M° Pyramides
Seats 40   Meal for 2 approx 530F

A former maitre d' on the liner *Normandie* decorated this 1940s
restaurant, so the blue riband that runs along the cream-painted
walls is explained. Regulars in this banking district return day
after day for lunch, and neither the chef nor the charming and
conscientious patronne lets them down. The cuisine is traditional
(with an emphasis on fish), lightened and freshened for health-
conscious executives: smoked Loire eel in aspic; noisettes
of monkfish with peppercorns; bass with spices and sorrel;
mignons of veal with summer vegetables; gratin of red fruits;
croustade of apples and Calvados. The Loire predominates on an
all-French wine list. *L only 12-2.15.* **Closed** *Sat, Sun, Aug &
1 wk Christmas. Diners, Mastercard, Visa.*

Saint-James et Albany
Map B1.53

| Tel 44 58 43 21   Fax 44 58 43 11 | **H** |

202 rue de Rivoli 75001   M⁰ Tuileries
Rooms 211   Double from 950F

Built as a rather grand private house during the reign of Louis
XIV, the Saint-James et Albany now offers good modern
bedrooms to complement period public areas which include
a courtyard garden. Ideally located between the posh shops of the
Rue St Honoré and the Tuileries gardens. Room service till 10pm.
Private parking. *Amex, Diners, Mastercard, Visa.*

Saint-Romain
Map B1.54

| Tel 42 60 31 70   Fax 42 60 10 69 | **H** |

5 rue St-Roch 75001   M⁰ Tuileries
Rooms 34   Double from 650F

One of the three hotels in the Beaux Logis de Paris group, along
with *Hotel du Continent* and the *Louvre St-Honoré* (see entries).
This one has a certain country air. No restaurant but a stone-
vaulted breakfast room in the basement. *Amex, Diners,
Mastercard, Visa.*

Tonic Hotel les Halles
Map C1.55

| Tel 42 33 00 71   Fax 40 26 06 86 | **H** |

12-13 rue du Roule 75001   M⁰ Louvre
Rooms 34   Double from 590F

Part of a small chain (others in Paris are at Bd St Germain and
Odéon), this one, in an old building, was totally renovated in the
summer of 1993. Bedrooms, which come with all the usual extras plus
bathrooms with either whirlpool tubs or multi-jet showers – both incorporating a steam
bath. Breakfast is included in the room price. No restaurant. *Amex,
Diners, Mastercard, Visa.*

> Note: from April 16 1995 the
> international dialling code 010 changes to 00

La Tour de Montlhéry
Map C1.56

| Tel 42 36 21 82 | **R** |

5 rue des Prouvaires 75001   M⁰ Chatelet/Les Halles
Seats 60   Meal for 2 approx 450F

Lovely old restaurant near Les Halles with timbered exterior and
tiled floor, old beams, exposed stone walls and red check table
cloths inside. With some famous faces amongst its clientèle it's
worth booking for dishes such as *haricot de mouton* (served out
of huge porcelain dishes), *terrine de poisson*, braised salmon with
mustard sauce, *cote de boeuf*, gateau of chicken livers, blanquette
of veal and *cote d'agneau grillée*. Blackboard menu. Drink the house
Brouilly. Open 24hrs (although sometimes with a break between
7-11 in the morning and 6-8 in the evening). ***Closed** Sat, Sun &
14 Jul-15 Aug. Mastercard, Visa.*

Hotel des Tuileries
Map B1.57

| Tel 42 61 04 17   Fax 49 27 91 56 | **H** |

10 rue Saint-Hyacinthe 75001   M⁰ **Tuileries/Pyramides**
Rooms 26   Double from 790F

Double-glazing ensures peace and quiet at this small family-run
hotel set in an 18th-century mansion near the Louvre. Bedrooms
combine a period feel – antique-style furniture, chandeliers – with
modern conveniences such as direct-dial phones, TVs and mini-
bars. No restaurant. *Amex, Diners, Mastercard, Visa.*

Velloni
Map D1.58

| Tel 42 21 12 50 | **R** |

22 rue des Halles 75001   M⁰ **Chatelet/Les Halles**
Seats 65   Meal for 2 approx 500F

Classic Italian cooking, with specialities from chef-patron Stefano
Cuccini's native Tuscany, continues to please at this smart modern
restaurant by Les Halles. Pasta dishes might include spaghetti
or rigatoni with a devilled sauce or taglierini with a ragout
of fresh crab and meat dishes a Tuscan-style fillet of beef or veal
kidneys 'Trifola'. Fish dishes vary daily according to the market.
Finish with some Italian cheeses or a pud such as bitter chocolate
terrine with coffee sauce. An excellent all-Italian wine list includes
a Chianti from the vineyard of Stefano's father. Set L&D 130F.
L 12-2.30 D 7.30-11. **Closed** *Sun 2 wks mid-Aug. Amex, Diners,*
Mastercard, Visa.

Willi's Wine Bar
Map B1.59

| Tel 42 61 05 09   Fax 47 03 36 93 | **R** |

13 rue des Petits-Champs 75001   M⁰ **Bourse/Palais-Royal**
Seats 40   Meal for 2 approx 450F

Posters by local artists adorn the white walls of a wine bar whose
speciality is wines from the Rhone Valley but where New World
wines also get a look in. Shortish menu which changes daily
to reflect the markets and the season: crab salad with herbs, confit
of quail with spiced peaches, sauté of lamb with rosemary, calf's
liver sautéed with sage and peppercorns, steamed cod with
an olive tapénade and *marmelade* of aubergine, caramelised apricot
tart and terrine of bitter chocolate 'Willi's' show the style.
A dozen wines, changing weekly, are available by the glass
or carafe. In the same ownership is 'Juveniles' (*qv*) at 47 rue
de Richelieu. Set L & D 155F. ***Open*** *11-11 (L 12-2.30 D 7-11, light*
snacks served at the bar at other times). Mastercard, Visa.

56

2nd Arrondissement
Places of Interest

Bourse, 42 33 99 83, M° Bourse
Bibliothèque Nationale, 47 03 81 26, M° Bourse
Théatre des Variétés, 42 33 09 92, M° Bourse, Rue Montmartre
Opéra Comique, 42 60 04 99, M° Richelieu-Drouot
Boulevard des Italiens

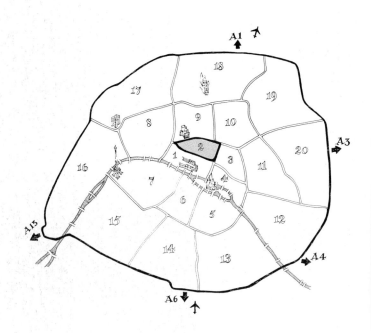

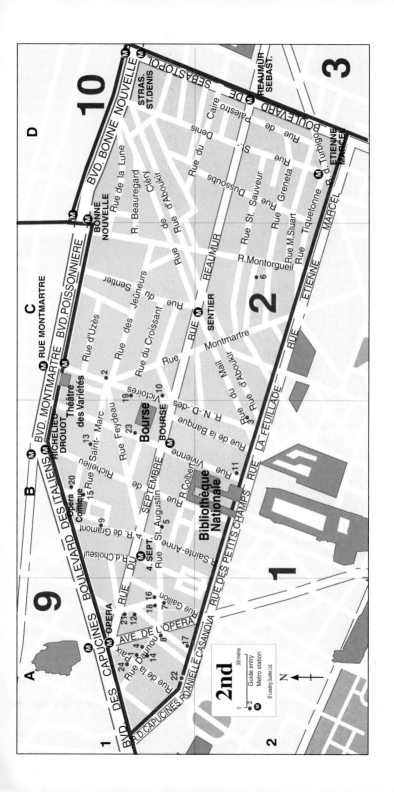

2nd

A B C D

9 10 3

1 2

1 BVD. DES CAPUCINES
BVD. DES ITALIENS
BVD. MONTMARTRE
BVD. POISSONNIERE
BVD. BONNE NOUVELLE

RUE MONTMARTRE
BONNE NOUVELLE

STRAS. ST.DENIS

BOULEVARD DE SEBASTOPOL

REAUMUR SEBAST.

RICHELIEU DROUOT

Théâtre des Variétés

OPERA

Opéra Comique

Rue de la Paix
Rue Daunou
Rue Danielle Casanova
Rue de Gramont
Rue St. Augustin
Rue Sainte-Anne
Rue d.Choiseul
Rue de Gaillon

AVE. DE L'OPERA

4. SEPT.
RUE DU 4 SEPTEMBRE

Rue de la Bourse
Rue Vivienne
Rue de Richelieu
Rue Saint-Marc
Rue Feydeau
Rue d'Uzès
Rue des Jeûneurs
Rue du Sentier
Rue du Croissant
Rue Montmartre

BOURSE
Bourse

R. N.-D.-des-Victoires
R.Colbert
Rue Vivienne

RUE DE LA FEUILLADE
RUE DES PETITS CHAMPS

Bibliothèque Nationale

SENTIER

RUE REAUMUR

R.Montorgueil
Rue St. Sauveur
Rue Greneta
Rue Tiquetonne
Rue M.Stuart

Rue Dussoubs
Rue St. Denis
Rue d'Aboukir
Rue de Cléry
R. Beauregard
Rue de la Lune

Carré de Palestro

RUE ETIENNE MARCEL
R. d. Turbigo
ETIENNE MARCEL

Rue du Mail
Rue d'Aboukir
Rue de la Banque
Rue Montmartre

2nd

0 300 metres

• 2 Guide entry
Ⓜ Metro station

© Leading Guides Ltd

N

• 1 • 4 • 24
• 14 • 22
• 8 • 17
• 12 • 21
• 18 • 16
• 7
• 9 • 20 • 15
• 13 • 2
• 5
• 11
• 19 • 10 • 23
• 3
• 6

Arco Tapas y Vinos

Map A1.1

Tel 42 60 07 20   Fax 42 60 45 13   **R**

12 rue Daunou 75002   **M⁰ Opéra**
Seats 60   Meal for 2 approx 500F

A former English club, with high vaulted ceiling, carved wood
panelling and a stone fireplace. The tapas are among the best
in town, spanning fried squid, moules piquantes, chorizo in white
wine, prawn croquettes, fried eggs with pimentos, Serrano ham
and, of course, Spanish omelette. To accompany this tempting
assortment is a distinguished cellar of Spanish wines majoring
on Catalonia. *Open 9am-midnight (hot food 12-3 & 7-11 only).*
Closed Sun. Mastercard, Visa.

Auberge Perraudin

Map C1.2

Tel 42 36 71 09   **R**

164 rue Montmartre 75002   **M⁰ Rue Montmartre**
Seats 37   Meal for 2 approx 400F

Unpretentious restaurant with a hospitable atmosphere where
regular customers are treated more like friends. There is no longer
a set menu as such but a list of the days dishes is written up on
a blackboard: *salade tiède de lentilles paysanne*, a selection of terrines
'Père Claude', *trio de la Sainte-Cochon* (three different ways with
pork). Also known as La Cave du Père Claude – Père Claude
being a sister establishment in the 15th. Note that they now open
for dinner. *L 12-2.30 D 7.30-10. Closed Sat, Sun & 3 weeks Aug.*
Mastercard, Visa.

For a glossary of menu terms see page 293

Chez Georges

Map B2.3

Tel 42 60 07 11   **R**

1 rue du Mail 75002   **M⁰ Bourse**
Seats 60   Meal for 2 approx 520F

Serving simple food with fine wine has been a family tradition for
five generations, currently upheld by Bernard Brouillet (along
with M Devouges who has been in the kitchen here for 25 years)
at this archetypal brasserie – crisply-clothed tables squeezed
together against banquettes down each side of a long room with
mirrored walls – near the Place des Victoires. On one side of the
menu (handwritten but nostalgically reproduced in pink and
mauve on an ancient Roneo machine) are listed the likes
of jambon persillé, celery rémoulade, rillettes of goose (which
come in an earthenware pot from which you help yourself, along
with a large jar of gherkins), grilled turbot with béarnaise sauce,
and grilled lamb cutlets with haricots verts. On the other side
is printed a wine list that is full of famous names including all the
first-growth clarets, and burgundies such as Richebourg, La Tache
(both from Romanée-Conti) and Echezeaux. Some dozen wines
are available by the glass – if you're strong-willed that is, as the
bottles are left on the table and you pay for what you drink.
L 12-2 D 7-9.30. Closed Sun, 1st 2 wks Aug, Public Holidays.
Amex, Mastercard, Visa.

Country Life

Map A1.4

Tel 42 97 48 51 ·

R

6 rue Daunou 75002
Seats 120

M° Opéra
Meal for 2 approx 124F (food only)

Modest vegetarian buffet to the rear of a health food shop near the
Opéra. For a fixed price of 62F (pay on entry) choose from half
a dozen hot items – bean casserole, couscous, leeks in white sauce –
and a simple salad bar. Air-conditioned. Unlicensed. *Open*
L 11.30-2.30 D 6.30-10. *Closed D Fri, all Sat, Sun & Public*
Holidays. No credit cards.

Coup de Coeur

Map B1.5

Tel 47 03 45 70

R

19 rue St Augustin 75002
Seats 60

M° 4 Septembre
Meal for 2 approx 500F

A restaurant on two floors with a subtle English look to the decor.
The kitchen, however, in the charge of Thierry Lebland whose
background includes the *Cote St Jacques* at Joigny and the *Grand
Véfour* in Paris, is strictly French with such dishes as *gelée
de volailles aux champignons* and *loup de mer aux épices douces*
demonstrating Thierry's classically based modern style. Short wine
list but full of familiar names, mostly from Bordeaux. Set L 98F
Set L & D 135F & 270F. *L 12-2.30 D 7-10.30.* *Closed L Sat, all*
Sun. Amex, Mastercard, Visa.

Aux Crus de Bourgogne

Map C2.6

Tel 42 33 48 24   Fax 40 26 66 41

R

3 rue Bachaumont 75002
Seats 80 (+ 25 outdoor)

M° Les Halles
Meal for 2 approx 450F

Turn of the century bistro with mirrored walls, red and white
check tablecloths, plenty of parlour plants and a classic bistro
menu holding no surprises. *Filet de boeuf aux morilles, confit
de canard, pied de porc* and *cotes d'agneau grillées* typify the choice.
Grilled lobster is a regular fixture on Thursdays. Modest, handwritten list of some 20 exclusively French wines. *L 12-2.30 D 8-
10.30.* *Closed Sat, Sun & 1st 3 weeks Aug. Mastercard, Visa.*

Drouant   ★★

Map A1.7

Tel 42 65 15 16   Fax 49 24 02 15

R

18 place Gaillon 75002
Seats 70

M° 4 Septembre
Meal for 2 approx 1400F

A short stroll from the Place de l'Opéra with a restaurant as well
as a café, Drouant is distinguished by its elegant art deco styling.
Under the same ownership as the Jules Verne, on the second
storey of the Eiffel Tower, it lies close to the Paris Bourse, so
lunchtimes are invariably busy with diners from the business
community. Louis Grondard's cooking is of extremely well
thought-out dishes prepared in a style that's decidedly modern but
retaining a clear classical pedigree. Some dishes are indeed Drouant
all-time favourites, notably salmon smoked over beechwood, 'blue'
lobster grilled with its coral and rib of Charolais beef with bone
marrow. Specialities with a more contemporary ring include
charlotte of langoustines with confit aubergines, pig's trotter in a   *See over*

salad with a terrine of Roseval potatoes, fillet of John Dory and
baby squid with a saffron-infused jus and noisettes of veal *à la
brunoise, cannelloni au parmesan*. Simpler dishes (and considerably
cheaper) are offered on the Café menu, which operates for diner
and supper right up to midnight. Delightful desserts should not be
missed – try honey ice cream with gentian or *biscuits croquants*
with chocolate and a ginger cream. Set L 290F Set D 600F
(*dégustation*). *L 12-2.30 D 7-10.30.* **Closed** *D 25 Dec & 1 Jan.*
Amex, Diners, Mastercard, Visa.

Edouard VII   Map A1.8

Tel 42 61 56 90   Fax 42 61 47 73   **HR**

39 ave de l'Opéra 75002   **Mᵒ Opéra**
Rooms 70   Double from 1200F

Occupying seven floors of a 17th-century building between the
Opéra and the Seine and not far from Place Vendome, the hotel
enjoys a prime city-centre location. Generally spacious bedrooms
(there are just four singles with shower and wc only) are
traditionally furnished and come complete with double-glazing
and air-conditioning as well as all the usual comforts. *Amex,
Diners, Mastercard, Visa.*

Restaurant Delmonico
Tel 42 61 44 26
Seats 60   Meal for 2 approx 450F

Comfortable hotel restaurant with good service and traditional
French cooking. In addition to the à la carte there is a fixed-price
menu de saison offering four choices at each stage: crayfish salad,
Bayonne ham with melon, beef terrine with carrots and salmon
with fresh herbs to start, perhaps, followed by pan-fried steak with
Roquefort butter, a light chicken curry, smoked haddock with
sorrel, or saffron *fruits de mer*. Fruit charlotte, iced passion fruit
mousse and apple tart to finish. Set L & D 158F. *L 12.30-2.30
D 7.30-10.* **Closed** *Sat, Sun & Aug.*

Favart   Map B1.9

Tel 42 97 59 83   Fax 40 15 95 58   **H**

5 rue Marivaux 75002   **Mᵒ Richelieu-Drouot**
Rooms 37   Double from 620F

An 18th-century building opposite the Opéra Comique, classed
a historic monument and for a spell the home in exile of the
painter Goya. Individually decorated bedrooms, one in period
style, all come with mini-bar, safe and multi-channel TV. Room
prices are inclusive of breakfast. No restaurant. *Amex, Diners,
Mastercard, Visa.*

Gallopin   Map C1.10

Tel 42 36 45 38   Fax 42 36 10 32   **R**

40 rue Notre Dame des Victoires 75002   **Mᵒ Bourse**
Seats 120 (+ 30 outdoor)   Meal for 2 approx 460F

Reminiscent of the Paris of Zola, Baudelaire and Rimbaud, the
decor here has changed little since 1876 when the restaurant first
opened: moulded ceilings, brass and lots of mahogany, including
a huge solid block that provides the counter for a small bar at the
entrance. Lots of traditional favourites are to be found on the

carte, from fish soup and *rosette de Lyon* to *coq au Brouilly* and
grilled pig's trotters. Particular specialities include entrecote
Gallopin, *pièce de boeuf à la moelle*, steak tartare and calf's liver with
green peppercorns. A small section of the menu depends upon
what enthusiastic chef-patron M Wagrez has found in the market
that day. Good value set dinner at 150F. The wine list tries
to offer good wines at affordable prices. About half the list
is devoted to Bordeaux. Set D 150F. *L 11.30-3 D 7.30-11.30.*
Closed *Sat & Sun. Amex, Diners, Mastercard, Visa.*

Le Grand Colbert

Map B2.11

| Tel 42 86 87 88   Fax 42 86 82 65 | **R** |

2 rue Vivienne 75002   **M⁰ Bourse**
Seats 100   Meal for 2 approx 500F

A historic brasserie within an arcade dating from the 1830s.
Decor features a fine frescoed frieze in classical style above
mirrored walls stuck with current play bills. A popular haunt
of the theatrical crowd (it's in the heart of the theatre district) the
atmosphere really begins to buzz after the evening performances
making this a good choice for late dining. The varied menu
changes daily: endive and Roquefort salad, chicken liver terrine,
turbotin braised in mustard, salmon *unilatéral* (sautéed skin side
down only), calf's liver with sherry and baby onions, saddle
of lamb Provençal. Champagne comes by the 50cl carafe (125F).
Air-conditioned. Set L & D: 155, 200, 245 & 300F. *L 12-3 D 7-*
1am. **Closed** *Aug. Amex, Mastercard, Visa.*

L'Horset Opéra

Map A1.12

| Tel 44 71 87 00   Fax 42 66 55 54 | **H** |

18 rue d'Antin 75002   **M⁰ Opéra**
Rooms 54   Double from 1300F

In the heart of the city just by the Opéra, l'Horset offers modern
amenities and air-conditioned comfort behind its period facade.
Day rooms include the bar **Le Diapason**, a favourite place for
cocktails. Room service throughout the day and evening. *Amex,*
Diners, Mastercard, Visa.

Aux Lyonnais

Map B1.13

| Tel 42 96 65 04   Fax 42 97 42 95 | **R** |

32 rue Saint-Marc 75002   **M⁰ Bourse/ Richelieu-Drouot**
Seats 120   Meal for 2 approx 300F

The *plat du jour* changes daily but, apart from a few seasonal
variations, the *carte* at this traditional 1900s bistro is fairly static.
M Jandot's cooking has a Lyonnais slant: sausages with *salade frisée*
or *pommes à l'huile, la grosse quenelle comme à Lyon, brochet au beurre*
blanc, confit of duck with sauté potatoes, chicken with tarragon
and mushroom cream sauce, grilled pig's trotters. Finish with the
likes of poire Belle Hélène, café or chocolate Liégeois, *oeuf à la*
neige or crème caramel. Shortish wine list, mostly from Beaujolais
and the Cote du Rhone, with most also in half bottles. Separate list
of mineral waters – they were up to 20 at the last count. Busiest
at lunchtimes. Set L & D 87F. *L 11.30-3 D 6.30-12.* **Closed** *L Sat,*
all Sun. Amex, Diners, Mastercard, Visa.

Le Moï

Map A1.14

| Tel 47 03 92 05 | **R** |

5 rue Daunou 75002   **M° Opera**
Seats 36   Meal for 2 approx 400F

Established by Mme Oggéri in 1965, this Vietnamese restaurant
has recently moved to its new address from one in the 16th. The
short all-day menu is simply arranged with all starters – Chinese
soup with pork and egg noodles, salade Moï, raviolis Vietnamiens
– at 45F, meat main dishes – pork with ginger, grilled chicken
brochettes with saté and coconut milk, grilled beef with lemon
grass – at 65F, a couple of fish dishes at 95F and desserts – fruit
beignets; soya, caramel and ginger flan – all at 35F. Just a handful
of French wines and some Chinese beer to drink. Set L 79F. *Meals
noon-10pm.* **Closed** *L Sat, all Sun. Amex, Diners, Mastercard.*

Les Noces de Jeannette

Map B1.15

| Tel 42 96 36 89 Fax 47 03 97 31 | **R** |

14 rue Favart 75002   **M° Richelieu Drouot**
Seats 60   Meal for 2 approx 320F

In the throbbing heart of the city, near the Opéra, the restaurant
takes its name from a one-act comic opera by Massé. One of the
street-level upstairs rooms is decorated with operetta posters, while
the other is a tribute to French films of the 30s, 40s and 50s.
Several upstairs rooms are used for private parties. The 159F menu
is all-inclusive: aperitif, three courses, wine and coffee – and there's
even a plate of butter with the basket of bread. Les Noces has
earned its reputation with reliable, traditional bistro cooking, and
a daily special always supplements the nine or ten main-course
options. Monday brings navarin of lamb, Wednesday a sustaining
pot au feu, Friday bouillabaisse, Saturday and Sunday brochettes
of lamb with rosemary. Salad of Roquefort and walnuts, salmon
rillettes and *parfait de foie de volaille aux pistaches* are typical
starters; cod with salmon roe, grilled andouillette and pork hock
with lentils are popular central dishes; and Brie de Meaux is an
alternative to desserts such as *truffe glacée au chocolat, pruneaux
d'Agen au Cahors* or crème caramel. Owner Patrick Fracheboud
takes excellent personal care of his customers. Set L & D 159F.
L 12-2 D 7-10.30. Amex, Diners, Mastercard, Visa.

Note: from April 16 1995 the
international dialling code 010 changes to 00

Hotel de Noailles

Map A1.16

| Tel 47 42 92 90 Fax 49 24 92 71 | **H** |

9 rue de la Michodière 75002   **M° Opéra/4 Septembre**
Rooms 58   Double from 750F

A period facade conceals a hotel of striking modern design, with
metal, wood and glass combining in style. Bedrooms, most
of which enjoy a quiet location overlooking the courtyards, have
a Japanese theme. *Amex, Mastercard, Visa.*

Passy Mandarin

Map A1.17

Tel 42 61 25 50

R

6 rue d'Antin 75002   M° Opéra
Seats 100   Meal for 2 approx 500F

A sumptuously appointed Chinese restaurant with dim sum and lacquered duck among the specialities. *Closed* Sunday, otherwise details as for entry in 16th arrondissement.

Pierre "A la Fontaine Gaillon"

Map A1.18

Tel 42 65 87 04   Fax 47 42 82 84

R

place Gaillon 75002   M° Opéra
Seats 120   Meal for 2 approx 650F

A 17th-century town house with a string of royal owners before becoming a restaurant in the 1880s, although it was only in 1984 that it gained its present grand interior with several rooms done out in different period styles. The menu is a mixture of traditional dishes – *rosette de Lyon, tete de veau sauce gribiche,* grilled tournedos steak with béarnaise sauce – with more modish offerings such as salmon *unilatéral* (grilled on the skin side only) and baby turbot with rhubarb and cider. The daily-changing section of the menu concentrates on seafood – a speciality here. Set D 165F. *L 12-3 D 7-12.30am.* **Closed** *L Sat, all Sun & Aug. Amex, Diners, Mastercard, Visa.*

Pile ou Face   ★

Map C1.19

Tel 42 33 64 33   Fax 42 36 61 09

R

52bis rue Notre-Dame-des-Victoires 75002   M° Bourse
Seats 40   Meal for 2 approx 850F

Heads you win, tails you can't lose at this warm, cosy restaurant on two floors with burgundy red walls and a small bar/greeting area near the entrance. Much of the produce used – ducks, foie gras, eggs, rabbits, pigeons, chicken – comes from their own farm in Normandy and appears in many of their specialities: escalope of foie gras with ginger bread, scrambled eggs with morel purée, *marmalade de lapin parfumée au romarin,* pigeon roasted with truffle oil and served with pan-fried foie gras; other dishes include *mousse de brochet aux pistaches, pintade au cerfeuil poelée de chataignes* and a *crème brulée* with honey. Lunch is a fixed-price affair of four courses (including cheese) of dishes taken from the evening menus with about half a dozen choices at each stage. An all-French wine list favours Bordeaux. Set L 235F Set D 280 & 320F. *L 12-2 D 8-10.* **Closed** *Sat, Sun, Aug & 25 Dec-1 Jan. Mastercard, Visa.*

Café Runtz

Map B1.20

Tel 42 96 69 86

R

16 rue Favart 75002   M° Richelieu-Drouot
Seats 95   Meal for 2 approx 400F

With a corner site near the Opéra Comique, Odette Leport's restaurant/*salon de thé* sports engraved glass panels and mirrors topped with pictures of some of her theatrical customers. Mealtimes bring a menu of Alsatian specialities; the main courses majoring on choucroute which is served with black pudding, ham, sausages and fish while the hors d'oeuvre include the likes of *salade*   *See over*

strasbourgeoise, smoked Alsace ham and a warm onion tart. The
menu formule includes a half bottle of wine along with a main dish
and dessert. From 9am-midnight (except while lunch is being
served) one can drop in just for one of their own home-baked
pastries. The wines of Alsace are well represented on a short list.
Open *9am-midnight. (L 11.45-2.30 D 6.30-11.30).* **Closed** *Sat,
Sun & Aug. Amex, Mastercard, Visa.*

Le Saint Amour   Map A1.21

Tel 47 42 63 82   **R**

8 rue Port Mahon 75002   **Mᴼ Opéra**
Seats 70   Meal for 2 approx 750F

By the Bourse and the major banks, a restaurant of refinement,
busy at lunchtime but still intimate. Cooking is classic and careful,
typified by *foie gras de canard, oeufs meurette* and lobster salad
to start; turbot hollandaise, monkfish with lentils, veal kidneys
with shallots and thyme-infused rack of lamb for mains; and
crème brulée, millefeuille and *nougat glacé* to finish. The
restaurant has a history going back 60 years. Set L & D 155F.
L 12-2.30 D 7-10.15. **Closed** *L Sat, all Sun & mid Jul-mid Aug.
Amex, Diners, Mastercard, Visa.*

Le Stendhal   Map A1.22

Tel 44 58 52 52   Fax 44 58 52 00   **H**

22 rue Danielle-Casanova 75002   **Mᴼ Pyramides**
Rooms 21   Double from 1510F

In a building once occupied by the author after whom it is named,
Le Stendhal is an intimate hotel of considerable luxury and
comfort. Bedrooms, which include several suites, boast designer
fabrics and all sorts of modern comforts from air-conditioning and
double-glazing to mini-bar, room safe, and a second phone line for
your fax. There's a clubby day room with dado panelling, green-
shaded lights and shelves of books and the stone-vaulted basement
houses the breakfast room. Room service from 11am to 11pm.
Amex, Diners, Mastercard, Visa.

Vaudeville   Map B1.23

Tel 40 20 04 62   **R**

29 rue Vivienne 75002   **Mᴼ Bourse**
Seats 145 (+100 outside)   Meal for 2 approx 550F

Classic turn-of-the-century brasserie opposite the Paris Bourse.
Marble walls, mirrors, art deco light fittings, closely packed tables
and friendly, efficient service from waiters who carry trays
shoulder-high laden with the oysters and other shellfish that are
a speciality here and which can also be bought from a pavement
stall to take away. The *carte* caters for meat-eaters with such
offerings as parsleyed lamb provençale, fillet of beef with
Périgourdine sauce and various grills. Good range of puds from
floating islands, gratin of fresh figs with wine sabayon, and *tarte
aux pommes* to the popular *café liégeois*. From 6 to 11am breakfast
(39F) is served either in the bar or the main restaurant. Set D (and
L Sun & Public Holidays) 185F and a late-night menu at 109F,
served from 10pm onwards. *L 12-3.30 D 7-2am.* **Closed** *D 24 Dec.
Amex, Diners, Mastercard, Visa.*

Westminster
Map A1.24

Tel 42 61 57 46   Fax 42 60 30 66

HR

13 rue de la Paix 75002
M° Opéra

Rooms 102
Double from 1800F

Handily placed between the Opéra and Place Vendome, the
Westminster boasts a lobby in traditionally grand style – marbled
columns, coffered ceiling, large floral display – that sets the tone
for elegant, individually decorated bedrooms and suites with
antique-style furniture and coloured marble bathrooms. 24hr
room service. Private parking for 10 cars. *Amex, Diners,
Mastercard, Visa.*

Restaurant Le Celadon
Tel 47 03 40 42

Seats 55
Meal for 2 approx 1000F

Formerly sous chef here, Emmanuel Hodencq has now settled into
the top job with cooking to match the stylish dining room of Le
Celadon with its glittering chandeliers and polished service.
Terrine of foie gras, *escabèche*, red mullet with rosemary and garlic
oil, saddle of rabbit with mangetout and gratin of fruits with .
an almond milk sorbet show the range. Set L & D 220F & 290F.
L 12-2 D 7.30-10.30. **Closed** *Sat, Sun, Public Holidays & Aug.*

3rd Arrondissement
Places of Interest

Archives Nationales, 40 27 62 18, M° Rambuteau
Musée Picasso, 42 71 25 21, M° St Paul/Chemin Vert
Musée Carnavalet (History of Paris), 42 72 21 13, M° St Paul/Chemin
Vert
Place des Vosges, M° Bastille/Chemin Vert/St Paul
Place de la République
Musée Cognacq-Jay (18th-century collection), 40 27 07 21,
    M° St Paul
Musée de la Chasse et la Nature, 42 72 86 43,
    M° Hotel de Ville/Rambuteau

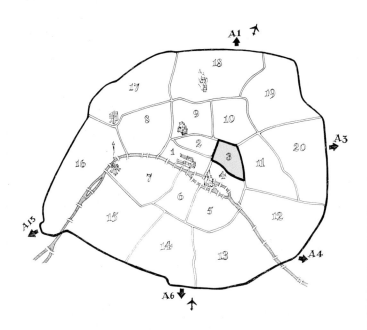

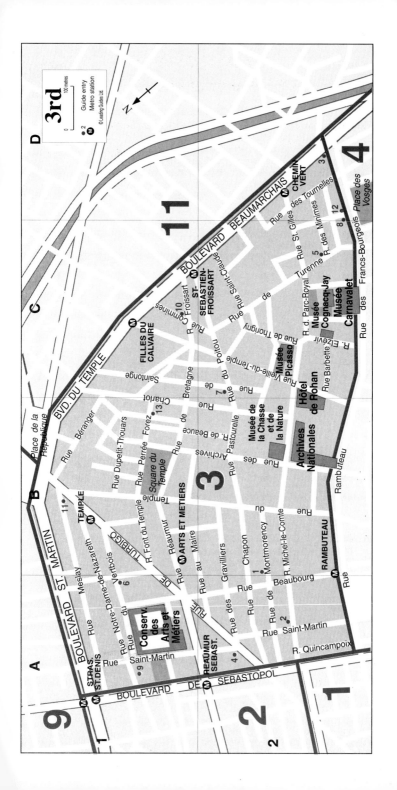

L'Alisier   Map B2.1

Tel 42 72 31 04   Fax 42 72 74 83   **R**

26 rue Montmorency 75003   **M° Rambuteau**
Seats 45   Meal for 2 approx 400F

Twin brothers run L'Alisier, Jean-Luc Dodeman in the kitchen,
Jean-François in the dining room, which is done out in traditional
Paris bistro style (there is also a private room in Louis XVI style).
The menu (159F in the evening including an aperitif and coffee)
mixes modern and traditional: *pipérade en vinaigrette au thon fumé,
salade tiède de ris de veau à l'huile de noix, filet de lotte au beurre
de basilic, supreme de volaille au porto, cote de boeuf grillé, tarte fine à la
cassonade et sorbet yaourt, tomate farcie en pot pourri de fruits secs.*
*L 12-2 D 7.30-10. **Closed** Sat, Sun & Aug. Amex, Mastercard, Visa.*

Ambassade d'Auvergne   Map A2.2

Tel 42 72 31 22   Fax 42 78 85 47   **R**

22 rue de Grenier St Lazare 75003   **M° Rambuteau**
Seats 100   Meal for 2 approx 500F

Appropriately named, the rustic decor is as authentic as the food
here representing the Auvergne region of France. Six separate
dining rooms, each holding up to 20 people, are individually
decorated – one with cooking utensils, another with pictures,
a third with tapestries, and so on. Specialities include ham from
the Auvergne, cabbage and Roquefort soup, a warm salad of Puy
lentils, *saucisse d'Auvergne aligot* ("elle file, file notre purée"), *confit
de canard* and *filet de boeuf de salers.* Choose à la carte or from the
summer *menu fraicheur* (160F). Also at 160F is the *menu gourmet
pressé.* *L 12-2 D 7.30-10.30. **Closed** 2 wks in summer. Amex,
Mastercard, Visa.*

Bar à Huitres   Map D2.3

Tel 48 87 98 92   •   **R**

33 bd Beaumarchais 75003   **M° Bastille**

Restaurant de poissons. See entry in 14th arrondissement.

The best way to get around Paris is by bus or metro – buy a
book of tickets (carnet) at any metro station and save money

Bellevue et du Chariot d'Or   Map A1.4

Tel 48 87 45 60   Fax 48 87 95 04   **H**

39 rue de Turbigo 75003   **M° Réaumur-Sebastopol**
Rooms 59   Double from 470F

An old building, now renovated, near the Centre Pompidou.
Lofty reception and breakfast room. Modern bar. Functional
bedrooms, all with bath/WC, comprise 30 twins, 24 doubles and
5 triples. The Chariot d'Or recalls an alley behind the hotel down
which a bride-to-be rode in a chariot with her dowry (usually
flowers and gold). Her betrothed would meet her at the other
end. The hotel has no restaurant. Room rate quoted includes
breakfast. *Amex, Diners, Mastercard, Visa.*

Hotel des Chevaliers

Map C2.5

Tel 42 72 73 47   Fax 42 72 54 10   **H**

30 rue de Turenne 75003   **M⁰ St Paul/Bastille**
Rooms 24   Double from 560F

The Place des Vosges and the Picasso Museum are both a few steps
away from this friendly little Marais hotel, whose comfortable
modern bedrooms (done out in pink, blue or yellow) are spread
over five floors; rooms at the top have sloping roofs. Breakfast
is served in the vaulted 17th-century cellar (no restaurant). This
hotel is a popular choice with fashion and cinema people. Plans
were afoot as we went to press for expanding the reception area
and installing air-conditioning. *Amex, Mastercard, Visa.*

Chez l'Ami Louis

Map A1.6

Tel 48 87 77 48   **R**

32 rue du Vertbois 75003   **M⁰ Arts et Métiers**
Seats 50   Meal for 2 approx 1400F

A restaurant since 1930, and for many years using an old wood-
fired oven for preparing most of the main courses, which mainly
take their inspiration from the South West. Portions are
enormous, preparation simple, prices on the à la carte-only menu
very high. Foie gras, snails, *coquilles St Jacques à la provençale*, roast
lamb, and game in season are the specialities and the chips are
impressively large and perfectly cooked. Most renowned of all the
dishes is perhaps the marvellous roast Challans chickens. Long
wine list (over 200 bins – all French). *L 12-2.15 D 8-11.*
Closed *Mon & Tues. Amex, Mastercard, Visa.*

Chez Nénesse

Map C2.7

Tel 42 78 46 49   **R**

17 rue Saintonge 75003   **M⁰ Filles-du-Calvaire**
Seats 42   Meal for 2 approx 450F

A fine old neighbourhood bistro, very typical of the *quartier*,
with menus that change with market availability; chef Le Meur
is particularly happy preparing fish and game. Salmon tartare with
ginger, terrine of St Jacques served warm with a chive sauce,
mullet with marrow, lamb fillet with fresh mint and venison
steak with redcurrants typify his menu. *L 12-2 D 7.45-10.*
Closed *Sat, Sun, 1 week Feb & all Aug. Mastercard, Visa.*

La Guirlande de Julie

Map D2.8

Tel 48 87 94 07   **R**

25 place des Vosges 75003   **M⁰ Bastille**
Seats 50   Meal for 2 approx 400F

Part of the Tour d'Argent group (as is *Coconnas* also in Place des
Vosges but in the 4th arrondissement), Julie is open long hours
every day for teas, snacks and full meals. *Pot au feu* is the house
speciality – a classic cold-weather dish, but this restaurant's best
feature is its 40-seater terrace, a boon in warm weather. The à la
carte choice is quite varied, and there are set menus at 65F (plat
du jour L Mon-Fri), 85F (L Mon-Fri) & 165F (L & D daily). *Meals
noon-midnight.* ***Closed*** *Jan. Mastercard, Visa.*

Little Palace Hotel   Map A1.9

Tel 42 72 08 15   Fax 42 72 45 81   **H**

4 rue Salomon-de-Caus 75003   M⁰ Strasbourg-St-Denis
Rooms 57   Double from 620F

Opposite the Square Chautemps in the old Arts et Métiers quarter.
The building is old, but inside is modern. Nearly half the
bedrooms have bath/wc, and these overlook the courtyard. The
rest, with shower/wc, face the front. Offerings in the restaurant
include a 400-ish calorie *menu minceur*. *Amex, Mastercard, Visa.*

Hotel du Marais   Map C1.10

Tel 48 87 78 27   Fax 48 87 09 01   **H**

2bis rue Commines 75003   M⁰ St Seb-Froissart/Filles-du-Calvaire
Rooms 39   Double from 390F

Simple modern accommodation in old Paris, between Bastille and
République. 12 rooms have bath/wc, the rest shower/wc. *Amex,
Mastercard, Visa.*

Meslay République   Map B1.11

Tel 42 72 79 79   Fax 42 72 76 94   **H**

3 rue Meslay 75003   M⁰ République
Rooms 39   Double from 660F

A listed building in one of the oldest parts of Paris, just a few steps
from Place de la République. All the bedrooms are en-suite and
accessories include automatic alarms, direct-dial phones and mini-
bars. No restaurant. *Amex, Diners, Mastercard, Visa.*

Pavillon de la Reine   Map D2.12

Tel 42 77 96 40   Fax 42 77 63 06   **H**

28 place des Vosges 75003   M⁰ Chemin-Vert
Rooms 50   Double from 1500F

Set back from one of the finest and most beautiful squares in Paris
(built in the 17th century and exquisitely renovated over the last
few years), the entrance to this hotel is an attractive hall with
massive exposed beams and stone-tiled floor. Comfortable
furnishings and handsome antiques complete the attractive picture.
Tastefully decorated bedrooms, all air-conditioned, vary in size
and colour, and overlook either the garden or the flowered
courtyard. 24hr reception and room service. Porter, concierge,
laundry service. Breakfast 90F Continental 130F English. No
restaurant. Private parking (free for 20 cars). *Amex, Diners,
Mastercard, Visa.*

Hotel du Vieux Saule   Map B1.13

Tel 42 72 01 14   Fax 40 27 88 21   **H**

6 rue Picardie 75003   M⁰ République
Rooms 31   Double from 460F

The facade dates from 1830, but the vaulted cellars are three
centuries older. Rooms differ in detail floor by floor; simple
in their decor, they are quite well equipped: cable TV, hairdryer,
safe, trouser press and iron. Eight have baths, the rest showers.
Garage 60F for a day or a night. Buffet breakfast 45F. Sauna.
A decent address in the Marais, and part of the vast Inter-Hotel
network. *Amex, Diners, Mastercard.*

CHAMPAGNE
FONDÉE EN 1827

G.H. MUMM & Cᴵᴱ
REIMS~FRANCE

4th Arrondissement
Places of Interest

Centre Georges Pompidou, Musée d'Art Moderne 44 78 12 33,
  Mº Hotel de Ville/Rambuteau
Notre Dame, 43 26 07 39; Crypt, 43 29 83 51, Mº Cité
Hotel de Ville, 42 76 59 28, Mº Hotel de Ville
Pavillon de l'Arsenal (town planning, architecture), 42 76 33 97
(42 76 63 46), Mº Sully Morland
Place des Vosges
Maison de Victor Hugo, 42 72 10 16, Mº Bastille/St Paul/Chemin
Vert, Le Marais
Théatre de la Ville, 42 74 22 77, Mº Chatelet

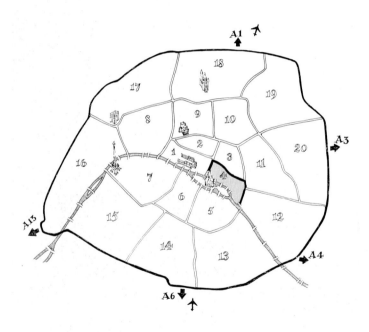

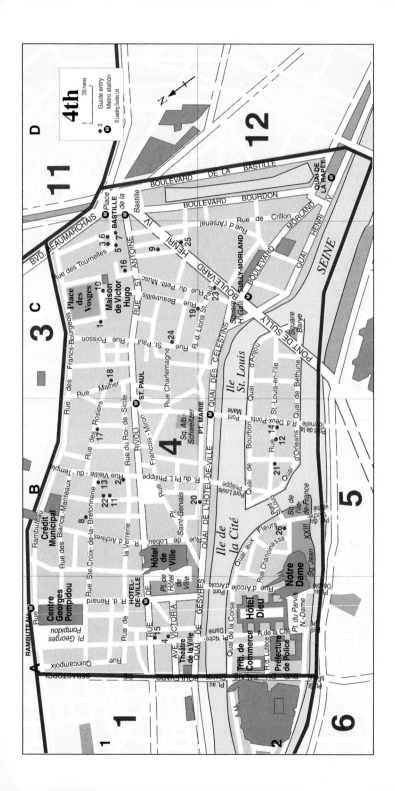

L'Ambroisie ★★   Map C1.1

Tel 42 78 51 45   **R**

9 place des Vosges 75004   **M° Bastille/St-Paul**
Seats 35   Meal for 2 approx 1800F

The restored 17th-century Place des Vosges is one of the major
architectural glories of Paris, and no less glorious in culinary terms
is Bernard Pacaud's refined and exclusive restaurant set back under
the arcaded buildings surrounding the square. The restaurant's
interior reflects the 17th-century atmosphere with a hanging
tapestry, Thonet chairs, stone floors and rich wood. In these
elegant surroundings, excellent and beautifully-crafted dishes are
served. Bernard is admired for the fact that he never leaves his
kitchen to visit the dining-room in order to acknowledge his
clients' praise for some of the best cooking in Paris. Instead
he leaves that up to his charming wife. The menu is changed
according to the season, the weather and the chef's mood: in the
autumn, for example, he might suggest duck foie gras terrine
served with a compote of fresh figs as a starter, followed by grilled
Bresse chicken with *sauce diable* and *pommes Darphin*, or pastry
cases of langoustine tails with a lightly curried sauce, and a dark
chocolate tart with vanilla ice cream or raspberry millefeuille
to finish. Snails in lettuce leaves with coriander seeds, lobster
minestrone with a shellfish jus and *croustillant* of saddle of lamb
with rosemary butter are other signature dishes. On wines,
sommelier Pierre Le Mouillac is on hand to offer his expert
advice. Reservations well in advance essential. *L 12-2.30
D 8-10.15.* **Closed** *Sun, Mon, 2 wks Feb & 3 wks Aug. Amex,
Mastercard, Visa.*

Axial Beaubourg   Map B1.2

Tel 42 72 72 22   Fax 42 72 03 53   **H**

11 rue du Temple 75004   **M° Hotel de Ville**
Rooms 39   Double from 730F

A six-storey hotel in the Marais, close to the Hotel de Ville and
the Centre Pompidou. Simple modern comforts in a renovated
period building. Breakfast is included in the room price quoted.
No restaurant. *Amex, Diners, Mastercard, Visa.*

For a glossary of menu terms see page 293

Bastille Speria   Map C1.3

Tel 42 72 04 01   Fax 42 72 56 38   **H**

1 rue de la Bastille 75004   **M° Bastille**
Rooms 42   Double from 600F

A warm welcome awaits visitors to the Bastille Speria, a peaceful
but well-located hotel in an old corner building which was
completely modernised internally a few years back and
is refurbished on a regular basis. Bedrooms have all the basic
modern comforts, and on the first floor there are two quiet sitting
areas. No restaurant. *Amex, Diners, Mastercard, Visa.*

Benoit ★
Map A1.4

| Tel 42 72 25 76   Fax 42 72 45 68 | R |

20 rue Saint-Martin 75004
Seats 70

Mᵒ Chatelet/Hotel de Ville
Meal for 2 approx 900F

There are two dining rooms in this elegant Parisian bistro with its old parquet floors, red velvet banquettes, white table linen, pretty glass and silver cutlery. The classic bourgeois dishes of France that are not so easy to find nowadays can nevertheless be found here, most of which need a lengthy cooking time: *cassoulet maison*, knuckle of veal *provençale*, casseroled duck (for 2) or the very traditional *boeuf mode*. The wine list is uniquely French and nothing is available by the glass. *L 12-2 D 8-10.* **Closed** *Sat, Sun & 1st 3 wks Aug. No credit cards.*

Bistrot du Dome ★
Map C1.5

| Tel 48 04 88 44   Fax 48 04 00 59 | R |

2 rue de la Bastille 75004
Seats 80

Mᵒ Bastille
Meal for 2 approx 500F

An offshoot of the renowned Brasserie Dome and a sister restaurant to the Montparnasse Bistrot (14th arr), with the same effective decor mix of rag-painted walls, fish tiles and plastic grapes as table lights and on the vine overhead, and the same à la carte ideas on the blackboard menu. The menu is all fish, the cooking skilful and relatively unembellished: an excellent dish of peppers stuffed with brandade lapped by a thick tomato sauce, clams sautéed with thyme, *poelée de crevettes grises vivantes, friture d'éperlans, encornets à la plancha*, skate salad, *St Jacques provençale*, rascasse with olive oil potato purée, *bourride, solettes meunière*, whole bream buttery-braised with new potatoes and cloves of garlic in their skins. St Nectaire farmhouse cheese, or simple sweets like chocolate cake, lemon tart, pineapple or gratin of pears round off a very good meal. All the wines are 98F per bottle, 20F by the glass. See photo page 22. *L 12.15-2.30 D 7.30-11. Amex, Mastercard, Visa.*

Bofinger
Map C1.6

| Tel 42 72 87 82   Fax 42 72 97 68 | R |

7 rue de la Bastille 75004
Seats 300

Mᵒ Bastille
Meal for 2 approx 550F

Five magnificent rooms with stunning Belle Epoque decor make up one of the capital's best known classic brasseries. Opened in 1864, it has seen a few ups and downs, but with the current owners its status as one of the 'musts' for visitors has been restored. If you're eating classic Bofinger you're eating oysters and other shellfish, foie gras, choucroute, steak tartare, grills and home-produced patisserie and ices. But there's plenty more besides on the menus, where the best value is provided by the 166F all-in *prix-fixe* of three courses and a half-bottle of wine. Recent successes on this menu have included a terrine of St Jacques with lobster sauce and *jambonette de canard* stuffed with foie gras. See photo page 19. *L 12-3 D 6.30-1am (Sat/Sun noon-1am). Amex, Diners, Mastercard, Visa.*

Le Bistrot de Bofinger
Map C1.7

Tel 42 72 05 23
R

6 rue de la Bastille 75004
Mᵒ Bastille
Seats 100
Meal for 2 approx 400F

The Brasserie has spawned a bistro, directly opposite and quite
grand in its own right, with 40s frescoes, light wood, brass, huge
mirrors and potted plants. Oysters, foie gras, raw marinated
salmon, venison terrine and fish soup are typical starters, while
main courses include cassoulet, andouillette, and fillet of plaice.
Steak tartare is a speciality cold dish, salad of citrus fruits
a trademark dessert. A la carte, or set menus at 98F (lunch except
Sunday) and 163F including an aperitif, three courses, half-a-bottle
of wine and coffee. All the wines are available by the glass (20F).
L 12-3 D 7-12. Amex, Diners, Mastercard, Visa.

Hotel de la Bretonnerie
Map B1.8

Tel 48 87 77 63   Fax 42 77 26 78
H

22 rue Ste-Croix de la Bretonnerie 75004
Mᵒ Hotel de Ville
Rooms 30
Double from 620F

A four-storey 17th-century building renovated with style and
taste. A continuing programme keeps things spick and span in the
bedrooms (no two the same), whose furnishings are generally
18th-century or Louis Philippe, and whose bathrooms are modern
and roomy. Accommodation is flexible (rates are 620F-800F) and
extra guests can be put up for 50-100F. Day rooms (lots of beams
in evidence) are quiet and relaxing, and the vaulted cellar is used
as a breakfast room. No restaurant. ***Closed** Aug. Mastercard, Visa.*

Hotel Castex
Map C1.9

Tel 42 72 31 52   Fax 42 72 57 91
H

5 rue Castex 75004
Mᵒ Bastille/Sully-Morland
Rooms 27
Double from 330F

Family-run, friendly, neatly kept, simple and quiet – a budget
hotel near Place de la Bastille. It was founded in 1919, and the
owners really know about traditional hospitality. Bedrooms (21
doubles, 5 singles, 1 triple) are fairly basic (though direct-dial
phones are installed) and some rooms at lower rates have a toilet
along the corridor. Breakfast/TV room and patio. ***Closed** Aug.
Mastercard, Visa.*

Coconnas
Map C1.10

Tel 42 78 58 16
R

2bis place des Vosges 75004
Mᵒ Chemin Vert/Bastille
Seats 60 (+ 70 outdoor)
Meal for 2 approx 500F

When the weather's fair, the terrace is the place to be, set in the
cloisters of one of the most stunning squares in Paris. The menu
at this offshoot of *La Tour d'Argent* is old-fashioned and more
or less invariable: classic preparations of foie gras, duck, *merlan*,
marquise, and specialities *poule au pot du Bon Roy Henry, petit salé*
and hot soufflés. Set menu 160F. Plenty of wines by the glass. See
also *La Guirlande de Julie* in the same Place but in the 3rd
arrondissement. *L 12-2 D 7.30-10 (must book). **Closed** Mon, also
Tues Oct 1-April 1. Amex, Diners, Mastercard, Visa.*

Le Coude Fou
Map B1.11

| Tel 42 77 15 16 | R |

12 rue du Bourg-Tibourg 75004   **M° Hotel de Ville**
Seats 70   Meal for 2 approx 450F

Traditional bistro with a modern touch. Simple wooden tables
and chairs, and original "naive" frescoes depicting country scenes
provide a slightly unusual setting for some excellent cooking.
Some dishes are well established in the bistro repertoire – *terrines,
foie gras de canard, crottin de chèvre chaud, foie de veau vinaigre
de framboise*, saddle of lamb with tarragon sauce – while others
may be on the way – *couscous d'anchois frais au citron vert,
langoustines roties au beurre de réglisse*. Current specialities are *poulet
au citron* and *entrecote au Bleu d'Auvergne*. Wine is taken seriously
here too, and a solid list of mostly recent vintages is supplemented
by a monthly-changing selection of wines by the glass. Choose à la
carte, or take the 110F menu (three courses and two glasses
of wine). *L 12-2.30 D 8-12 (book).* **Closed** *L Sun. Amex,
Mastercard, Visa.*

Hotel des Deux-Iles
Map B2.12

| Tel 43 26 13 35   Fax 43 29 60 25 | H |

59 rue St-Louis-en-l'Ile 75004   **M° Pont-Marie**
Rooms 17   Double from 810F

17th-century building with the feeling of a family home. Pretty
bedrooms (4 singles, 13 doubles), have Provençal-style fabrics,
cane furniture and blue Portuguese bathroom tiles, multi-channel
TV, radio, hairdryers. Virtually next door (65) and offering
similar facilities is the **Hotel Lutèce** (Tel 43 26 23 52/Fax 43 29
60 25). (The **Galiléo**, in the 8th arrondissement (Tel 47 20 66 06)
is in the same ownership.) No restaurant. *No credit cards.*

Le Fond de Cour
Map B1.13

| Tel 42 74 71 52   Fax 48 04 91 12 | R |

3 rue St-Croix de la Bretonnerie 75004   **M° Hotel de Ville**
Seats 40 (+ 45 outdoor)   Meal for 2 approx 520F

Changing artwork adorns the walls of a softly lit, pretty room
at the far end of a courtyard, where tables are set in the summer.
Menu is a mixture of traditional and contemporary, exemplified
by langoustine ravioli with ginger, fricassee of snails with garlic
and polenta, *croustillant* of duck with a sweet-sour sauce and fillet
of beef Rossini. A particularly interesting December special was
ostrich fillet with poached pears. Set menu: L from 108F. *L 12-2
D 7-11. (Sat from 7.30)* **Closed** *L Sat, all Sun, Public Holidays.
Mastercard, Visa.*

Au Gourmet de l'Isle
Map B2.14

| Tel 43 26 79 27 | R |

42 rue St Louis-en-l'Ile 75004   **M° Pont-Marie**
Seats 60   Meal for 2 approx 400F

The secret corners of the charming Ile St Louis are secrets
no longer. The whole place is awash with tourists, most of whom
at some time or other seem to be queuing at the excellent   *See over*

Berthillon ice cream shops. There's a big choice of restaurants, many of them blatantly touristy, some more obviously traditional Parisian. One of the best of the latter, especially in terms of value for money, is this interesting little place with two rooms of tables under old beams, and a vaulted stone basement. The 130F menu (there's also an à la carte) includes classics such as *oeuf en meurette, boudin, terrine de foie de volaille, ris d'agneau with a port sauce, andouillette AAAAA* (*Association Amicale des Amateurs d'Andouillettes Authentiques*), guinea fowl with cabbage or lentils, *crème caramel*, compote of apples and pears in red wine. House specialities are *fond d'artichaut* topped with a poached egg and sauce gribiche, and a pork equivalent of coq au vin. *L 12-2 D 7-10.* **Closed** *Mon & Tues. Amex, Diners, Mastercard, Visa.*

Le Grizzli   Map A1.15

Tel 48 87 77 56   **R**

7 rue St-Martin 75004   Mᴼ **Chatelet/Rambuteau**
Seats 50 (+ 35 outdoor)   Meal for 2 approx 400F

The road is St Martin but the newest inhabitant is St Michael – the latest Marks & Spencer store is just a few steps away from this classic bistro established in 1902. Cooking is a mix of bistro standards and dishes from the South-West of France (produce is regularly delivered direct from the Auvergne). Among the specialities are *haricots tarbais, calamares à l'encre, cassoulet, fricot de veau aux cèpes séchés, foie gras, jambon au couteau, confit de canard* and salmon, sole, lamb cutlets or *faux-filet* of beef grilled and served on a slate. Set menus: L 110F, L & D 145F. *L 12-2.30 D 7.30-11.* **Closed** *Sun. Amex, Mastercard, Visa.*

A l'Impasse (Chez Robert)   Map C1.16

Tel 42 72 08 45   **R**

4 impasse Guémenée 75004   Mᴼ **Bastille**
Seats 60 (+ 20 outdoor)   Meal for 2 approx 400F

Run by the fourth generation of the family Collard, this splendid little bistro is located in a cul-de-sac moments away from Place des Vosges and Place de la Bastille. The atmosphere is intimate, with carefully restored ceiling beams and exposed sandstone walls, red-tiled floors, and candles are lit in the evenings on tables bedecked with white linen cloths and serviettes. Cooking by chef M Vulcain is traditional, and many visitors (including us!) cite the *blanquette de veau à l'ancienne* as among the best in Paris. Other choices could include minted skate terrine, *gateau de foie de volaille à la bressanne,* Madeira-sauced kidneys, *boeuf bourguignon*, their special way with sweetbreads and *tripes à la quercysoise* (tomatoes, herbs, spices, white wine, garlic). A short wine list (by bottle, pichet and glass), and a couple of dozen beers. *L 12-1.45 D 7.30-11.* **Closed** *L Sat and Mon, all Sun & Aug. Mastercard, Visa (no cheques).*

Jo Goldenberg   Map B1.17

Tel 48 87 20 16   Fax 42 78 15 29   **R**

7 rue des Rosiers 75004   Mᴼ **St-Paul**
Seats 100 (+ 60 outdoor)   Meal for 2 approx 250F

In a street of similar establishments, this is the best known Jewish caterer in town, open all day, 364 days a year, as both deli and restaurant. The deli/take-away is at the front, the restaurant behind it, and in summer a large terrace comes into its own. Zakouskis (15 different fillings), blinis, home-cooked pastrami, gefilte fish and smoked salmon are among the snack favourites, while daily dishes run from stuffed cabbage leaves to escalope Vienna-style, moussaka, goulash and chicken with paprika. *Meals 9am to 1am.* **Closed** *Jewish day of atonement. Amex, Diners, Mastercard, Visa.*

Hotel Malher   Map C1.18

Tel 42 72 60 92 Fax 42 72 25 37	H

5 rue Malher 75004   **M° St-Paul**
Rooms 31   Double from 570F

Spick-and-span accommodation in a prime location for visiting the Marais. Family-run for three generations and recently redecorated throughout, the Hotel Malher has 31 rooms, 24 with bath/wc, 2 with shower/wc, all with direct-dial phone, cable TV, mini-bar and hairdryer. Conference room (up to 18 people). Breakfast room in the vaulted cellars. No restaurant. *Amex, Mastercard, Visa.*

Le Maraicher   Map C1.19

Tel 42 71 42 49	R

5 rue Beautreillis 75004   **M° Sully-Morland**
Seats 28   Meal for 2 approx 500F

A relative newcomer in the Marais, with exposed stone walls, wooden beams, antique floor tiles, neat white tablecloths and a sophisticated style of cooking. The new chef continues a style that is almost always just a little bit different: *raviolis de pétoncles aux copeaux de courgettes à la graine de sésame, salade de magret de canard confit au paprika, supreme de bar à l'essence de Brouilly, foie de veau au vinaigre de framboise.* One of the speciality desserts is *l'assiette de tout citron.* Set menus: L 120F D 175F/295F *(dégustation). L 12-2.30 D 8-11.15.* **Closed** *L Mon, all Sun, Aug. Amex, Mastercard, Visa.*

Miravile   ★   Map B2.20

Tel 42 74 72 22 Fax 42 74 67 55	R

72 quai de l'Hotel de Ville 75004   **M° Pont-Marie/Hotel de Ville**
Seats 75   Meal for 2 approx 650F

Gilles Epié's fashionable and elegant restaurant enjoys a prime location by the Seine, just beyond the Hotel de Ville. His cooking is innovative and invariably interesting, and the flavours of the Mediterranean are often to the fore. Signature dishes include rémoulade of duck liver with celeriac, caramelised beignets of foie gras with port, baked tuna with bacon and mature Parmesan, rabbit with pistou-flavoured ratatouille and saddle of lamb with aubergine caviar. Cherries Jubilee is a superb sweet, so too the warm chocolate mousse (chaudcolat) with coconut ice cream. See also *Campagne et Provence* in the 5th arrondissement. Set menu 220F. *L 12-2 D 7.30-10.30.* **Closed** *L Sat, all Sun, Aug, 25 Dec, 1 Jan. Amex, Mastercard, Visa.*

Au Monde des Chimères

Map B2.21

Tel 43 54 45 27

R

69 rue St Louis-en-l'Ile 75004
Seats 40

M° Pont-Marie
Meal for 2 approx 500F

This charming bistro in a 17th-century building with exposed
stone walls and beams on the Ile St Louis serves the traditional,
bourgeois French family cooking (chef Cécile Ibane) which
is rapidly disappearing along with the way of life it represents. The
menu could suggest mussel soup (served as main course), *brandade
de morue*, chicken with 40 garlic cloves or Pauillac lamb preceded
by the house speciality *L'Oeuf de Jean* – a pan-fried escalope of foie
gras, deglazed with vinegar and honey and served with a poached
egg. Puddings are all the classics – floating islands, chocolate
mousse, *nougat glacé* or a hot apple tart (20 minutes wait). Set
menus: L 85F, L & D 155F. *L 12.30-2.30 D 7.30-10.30.*
***Closed** Sun, Mon & Mar school holidays. Amex, Mastercard, Visa.*

Rivoli Notre Dame

Map B1.22

Tel 42 78 47 39   Fax 40 29 07 00

H

19 rue du Bourg-Tibourg 75004
Rooms 31

M° Hotel de Ville
Double from 610F

17th-century stone-faced building in the historic Marais quarter.
Bedrooms, refurbished a couple of years ago, are equipped with
TV, mini-bar, and hairdryer. Breakfast can be served in either the
bedrooms or the vaulted cellars. No restaurant. *Amex, Diners,
Mastercard, Visa.*

Hotel Saint-Louis-Marais

Map C2.23

Tel 48 87 87 04   Fax 48 87 33 26

H

1 rue Charles V 75004
Rooms 15

M° Bastille/St-Paul/Sully-Morland
Double from 590F

An old building (once a convent) in the ancient Marais district.
Bedrooms are traditional in style, with few accessories but modern
bath/shower rooms. No restaurant. *Mastercard, Visa.*

Hotel du 7e Art

Map C1.24

Tel 42 77 04 03   Fax 42 77 69 10

H

20 rue St-Paul 75004
Rooms 23

M° St-Paul
Double from 620F

17th-century building in the classic mould, in the historic Marais
quarter. The hotel was renovated quite recently, and takes the
American cinema (especially 40s to 60s) as its decorative theme.
Reception resembles a cinema cash desk, every inch of space being
covered with posters, photos and bills. Bedrooms, including two
small suites, have sound-proofing, direct-dial phones, safes and en-
suite bath or shower. Four floors, no lift. No room service, but
sandwiches and snacks can be provided in the bar. All rooms can
be singles or doubles (310F per person per night). *Amex, Diners,
Mastercard, Visa.*

Le Vieux Bistro

Map B2.26

Tel 43 54 18 95   Fax 44 07 35 63

R

14 rue du Cloitre-Notre-Dame 75004

M° Cité

Seats 40 (+ 10 outdoor)

Meal for 2 approx 650F

Real bistro food in a real bistro in the tourist hubbub north
of Notre Dame. The bar and furniture are all authentic pieces
from the beginning of the century, offset by an original tiled
floor, old mirrors and claret-coloured tablecloths. Lunch and
candle-lit dinners share the same menu of classics, prepared
by long-serving chef M Verlataine: *paté de tete à l'ancienne,
poireaux vinaigrette, saucisson chaud pommes à l'huile, quenelles
de brochet sauce Nantua, sole meunière, civet de canard, andouillette
au Sancerre, rognon de veau sauce moutarde, coeur de filet à la moelle
en papillote, tarte tatin flambée au Calvados avec crème fraiche.* Meats
are served very rare. 60 or so wines on the list – none by the glass
but they'll open a bottle and you pay for what you drink. Quick,
young, friendly service. *L 12-2 D 7.30-10.30 (book).*
Closed 25 Dec. Mastercard, Visa.

Woolloomooloo

Map C1.25

Tel 42 72 32 11   Fax 42 72 32 21

R

36 bd Henri IV 75004

M° Bastille

Seats 60 (+25 outside)

Meal for 2 approx 650F

Everything about this airy, clean-cut restaurant from head chef
Bernard Plaisted and all the front of house staff to the background
(it's not at all intrusive) tape of natural 'outback' sounds,
is determindly Australian. Opened in the autumn of '94, it has
already found a following for its bold, modern antipodean
cooking that combines the flavours of the Asia Pacific rim with
those of the Mediterranean. Marinated quail with baked polenta
and houmus; chicken laksa with noodles, tofu and *bok choy* (a hot
spicy soup); Thai green chicken curry with jasmin rice; braised
duck leg with black mushroom dumpling and mustard greens;
veal and roasted pumpkin pie with spicy tomato sauce and lime
tart with grilled figs demonstrate Bernard's unrestrained style. The
lunch menu (written in French, the evening carte is in English
with French translations) is shorter and cheaper than the dinner
menu and when we were last here, just before Christmas, there
were plans to introduce a 'tapas' menu at the bar. The fixed-price
menus offer two choices at each stage and are priced for either
two or three courses. The majority of the wines are Australian,
with several available by the glass. Set L 95F/115F Set
D 130F/150F. *L 12-2.30 D 7.30-11 (till 11.30 Fri & Sat).*
Closed *L Sat, all Sun,* 25 & 26 Dec. Mastercard, Visa.

5th Arrondissement
Places of Interest

Sorbonne, M° Cluny-La Sorbonne

Panthéon (tombs of Voltaire, Rousseau, Hugo, Zola), 43 54 34 51,
   M° Cardinal Lemoine/ Place Monge

Musée d'Histoire Naturelle

Jardin des Plantes, 40 79 30 00, M° Gare d'Austerlitz

Institut du Monde Arabe, 40 51 38 38, M° Jussieu/Cardinal
Lemoine/Sully Morland

Musée National du Moyen-Age-Thermes de Cluny, 43 25 62 00,
   M° Saint-Michel/Cluny La Sorbonne

Institut Océanographique, 46 33 08 61, M° Luxembourg (RER)

Rue Mouffetard (market)

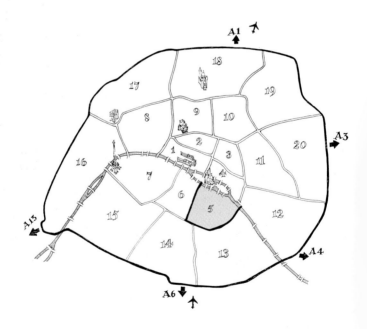

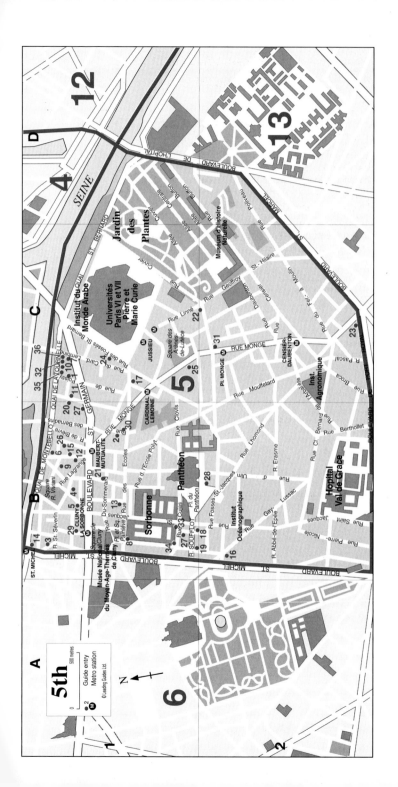

Restaurant A

Map C1.1

Tel 46 33 85 54   **R**

5 rue de Poissy 75005   Mᵒ Maubert-Mutualité
Seats 50   Meal for 2 approx 500F

In order to deter the casual tourist Kien Huynh, the chef
proprietor has deliberately kept the exterior fairly low-key. The
largely local crowd who frequent the restaurant can relax in a
stylish interior and enjoy classical Chinese dishes, many of which
are from the Imperial Court. Imperial prawns (prepared with
sugar, salt, pepper and honey), a Hunan speciality of ham cooked
with honey and a *marmite de canard maison* – a duck dish with
lotus nuts and mushrooms which requires 48 hours notice. Diners
are often entertained by the chef's artistry with rice paste, carving
a selection from up to 250 different animals before them. *L 12-3
D 7-11.* **Closed** *L Mon. Amex, Mastercard, Visa.*

Agora St-Germain

Map B1.2

Tel 46 34 13 00   Fax 46 34 75 05   **H**

42 rue des Bernardins 75005   Mᵒ Maubert-Mutualité
Rooms 39   Double from 660F

Just to the south of Boulevard St-Germain the hotel has a small,
warmly decorated marble-floored reception and cosily decorated
bedrooms which have the advantage of being quite well
soundproofed. Half look out over the street while the rest, and
quietest, have views over a small garden. All have a good range
of amenities and there's a characterful brick-lined, stone-floored
basement breakfast room. *Amex, Diners, Mastercard, Visa.*

Hotel d'Albe

Map B2.3

Tel 46 34 09 70   Fax 40 46 85 70   **H**

1 rue de la Harpe 75005   Mᵒ St-Michel
Rooms 45   Double from 580F

Located in a busy pedestrianised street in the very heart of the
Latin Quarter, the hotel has a smart modern decor throughout.
The reception is compact, as are the bedrooms, but this
is compensated by the use of bright colours and good lighting.
There's a lift to the first five of the six floors. All rooms have
en suite facilities with half having shower and wc facilities. All
benefit from satellite TVs, direct-dial phones and room safes.
Breakfast is taken in a modern café-like basement dining room.
Amex, Diners, Mastercard, Visa.

Auberge des Deux Signes

Map B1.4

Tel 43 25 46 56   Fax 46 31 20 49   **R**

46 rue Galande 75005   Mᵒ Maubert-Mutualité
Seats 170   Meal for 2 approx 1000F

George Dhulster's is one of the most characterful of all Parisian
restaurants thanks to a splendid location and very appealing decor.
A Gothic window, all that remains of the 15th-century Chapelle
Sainte Blaise which was destroyed in 1770, now forms part of one
of the thick stone walls. Heavy beams, vaulted ceilings and
an early 17th-century Louis XIII-style decor on the inside and
exterior views over a charming square and the church of St Julien-
Le-Pauvre create a suitably impressive setting for what is largely

traditional country-style cooking. Beef ravioli with cabbage
enlivened with ginger and roast rack of lamb with thyme and
an aubergine charlotte typify the choice and delicious desserts such
as champagne sabayon with fresh fruit round off a well-balanced
meal. *L 12-2.30 D 7.30-10.30.* **Closed** *L Sat, all Sun & Aug. Amex,
Diners, Mastercard, Visa.*

Bar à Huitres   Map B1.5

| Tel 44 07 27 37 | **R** |

33 rue Saint-Jacques 75005   M^o **Maubert-Mutualité**

Restaurant de poissons. See entry in 14th arrondissement.

Le Bistro du Port   Map B1.6

| Tel 40 51 73 19 | **R** |

13 quai Montebello 75005   M^o **Maubert-Mutualité**
Seats 30 (+15 outside)   Meal for 2 approx 500F

Overlooking Ile de la Cité the quayside terrace of this attractive
bistro offers a splendid view of Notre Dame. The menu changes
with the seasons and though traditionally based, creative flourishes
abound and there's excellent use of spices and herbs. Specialities
include roast Scottish salmon with an aromatic glaze and fillet
of duck with olives. There are excellent desserts too, including
a mango *tarte tatin. L 12.30-2.30 D 8-10.30.* **Closed** *Mon, Tue,
10 days Aug. Mastercard, Visa.*

Le Bistrot d'à Coté   Map C1.7

| Tel 43 54 59 10 | **R** |

16 bd St-Germain 75005   M^o **Maubert-Mutualité**
Seats 65 (+10 outside)   Meal for 2 approx 450F

Formerly Chez Raffatin et Honorine, Michel Rostang's bistro
is one of four scattered throughout the city. This one's the furthest
from the original, which is in Ave de Villiers (17th
arrondissement), properly *d'à coté.* Here, as in the others, the menu
changes every few months though the specialities remain fairly
constant. These include a brochette of mussels with a mushroom
salad, veal kidneys with pig's trotters and a macaroni gratin and
to finish a hot Valrhona chocolate soufflé. Set menu: 178F. *L 12-
2.30 D 7-11.* **Closed** *L Sat, all Sun. Amex, Mastercard, Visa.*

For a glossary of menu terms see page 293

Brasserie Balzar   Map B1.8

| Tel 43 54 13 67   Fax 44 07 14 91 | **R** |

49 rue des Ecoles 75005   M^o **Cluny la Sorbonne**
Seats 85   Meal for 2 approx 550F

Traditional brasserie with restrained 30s decor, serving classic
brasserie cuisine from noon till past midnight. Specialities include
choucroute garnie, pied de porc pané, raie au beurre fondu and *foie gras
de canard.* Of the wines about a dozen are available by the generous
glassful (15cl). *Meals noon-12.30am.* **Closed** *August and 1 week
Christmas. Amex, Mastercard, Visa.*

La Bucherie
Map B1.9

| Tel 43 54 78 06   Fax 46 34 54 02 | R |

41 rue de la Bucherie 75005 M° St-Michel
Seats 100 (+ 30 outdoor) Meal for 2 approx 920F

Dishes such as oysters in champagne sauce, langoustines with
lentils, fillets of red mullet with basil, jugged hare and desserts
such as *quenelles de pomme à la vanille* have been keeping Bernard
Bosque's customers here happy for over 30 years. With classical
background music the decor features much attractive woodwork
and contemporary art around the walls. In the afternoon (3-7pm)
one can also take tea and pastries – rhubarb tart, chocolate cake –
at armchairs around the fireplace with magazines and the day's
newspapers provided. Set menu: 230F. *L 12-2.30 D 7-12.30.*
Amex, Diners, Mastercard, Visa.

Campagne et Provence
Map C1.10

| Tel 43 54 05 17 | R |

25 quai de la Tournelle 75005 M° Maubert-Mutualité
Seats 40 Meal for 2 approx 450F

The interior has a simple rusticity. There are Mediterranean-blue
straw-seated chairs and numerous dried grass and flower
arrangements with a particularly huge display just inside the
entrance of what is a small, cosy restaurant with a mellow, creamy
decor. The menu, conceived by Gilles Epié of *Miravile* (*qv*),
is Provence-based and is light and flavourful. Starters include pan-
fried scallops served on a bed of tomato, onion and olives, a gratin
of skate with lentils and tarragon, a salad of olives, with
or without garlic, followed by a red mullet bouillabaisse with
fennel, sea bass under a crust of mozzarella and tomato flavoured
with fennel, or rabbit stuffed with hazelnuts and almonds.
To finish, a lavender crème brulée, warm fig tart with vanilla ice
or tiramisu. Excellent choice of Provençal rosé wines from a list
that stays mainly below 100F. *L 12.30-2 D 7.30-11 (Fri, Sat till
1am).* **Closed** *L Sat & Mon, all Sun, 25 Dec. Mastercard, Visa.*

Chez Toutoune
Map C1.11

| Tel 43 26 56 81   Fax 43 25 35 93 | R |

5 rue Pontoise 75005 M° Maubert-Mutualité
Seats 60 Meal for 2 approx 450F

A comfortable bistro just off the Boulevard St-Germain where
Colette (Toutoune) Dejean's fixed-price menu offers good-value
Provençal-inspired cooking. A soup course precedes the starters –
country terrine with aspic and olives, *escabèche, céleri rémoulade,*
snail gougère with garlic butter – and a cheese of the day between
main dish – guinea fowl with rosemary and ratatouille, roast cod
with a fennel and extra virgin olive oil purée – and dessert. The
latter might include *tarte tatin* with quince, *gateau au chocolat très
noir* or fresh roast figs with a passion fruit coulis. Wines from
Colette's native Midi. Set menu: 160F. *L 12-2 D 7.45-11.*
Closed *L Mon, all Sun. Amex, Mastercard, Visa.*

Chieng-Mai
Map B1.12

Tel 43 25 45 45
R

12 rue Frédéric Sauton 75005
M⁰ Maubert-Mutualité
Seats 100
Meal for 2 approx 400F

One of the best Thai restaurants in town – popular too, so worth
booking – with seating on two air-conditioned floors. Order
prawn soup with lemon grass; beef salad with galangal (an
aromatic root); spiced fish steamed in a banana leaf; pork satay;
sautéed beef with peppers; duck and chicken fried with ginger;
and to finish a cooling and unusual Thai red bean and coconut
milk ice cream or coconut milk jelly with fruits and ice cream.
A novelty on the otherwise French wine list is an offering from
China 'Nuit de Chine', both red and white. Several set menus
from 120-173F per person plus à la carte. *L 12-2.30 D 7-11.*
Closed *Sun, 1st 2 wks Aug, 2 wks Christmas. Amex,
Mastercard, Visa.*

Hotel du Collège de France
Map B1.13

Tel 43 26 78 36   Fax 46 34 58 29
H

7 rue Thénard 75005
M⁰ Maubert-Mutualité
Rooms 29
Double from 500F

In a quiet back street near the Sorbonne in the heart of the Latin
Quarter. Rooms on the sixth floor are the largest and most
characterful with beams and balconies but need to be reserved five
or six months in advance. No room service, no restaurant. *Amex,
Mastercard, Visa.*

Le Départ de Saint-Michel
Map B1.14

Tel 43 54 24 55
R

1 pl Saint-Michel 75005
M⁰ St-Michel

Tables and chairs are arranged in outward-facing rows in order
to watch the 'theatre of life' from this long-hours brasserie at a
very busy crossroads by the Seine. The menu is quite extensive
and varied, ranging from light snacks and pastries to a few more
substantial dishes such as a speciality of *pavé au poivre*, a thick
peppered steak served with French fries, French beans or spaghetti.
Pride of place, however, must go to the *croque campagnard* –
a *croque monsieur* that ranks among the best in Paris. It is prepared
on a long slice of excellent country bread, the gruyère cheese
topping nicely browned. *Amex, Mastercard, Visa.*

Dodin-Bouffant
Map B1.15

Tel 43 25 25 14   Fax 43 29 52 61
R

25 rue Frédéric Sauton 75005
M⁰ Maubert-Mutualité
Seats 60 (+40 outside)
Meal for 2 approx 800F

Somewhere in character between a bistro and a *grande brasserie
de luxe*, Dodin-Bouffant's combination of outstanding classical
French cooking and realistic (by top Parisian standards) pricing
make it a very popular, bustling sort of place. A non-smoking
room on the first floor is a little more peaceful and cosy. Philippe
Valin's menu is strong on seafood – *daube d'huitres et pied de porc*,
monkfish provençale and lobster with garlic – along with hearty
bistro fare and market 'specials' such as *blanquette d'agneau*. Good

See over

wine list. Set menu: 195F. *L 12-2.15 D 7.30-11.* **Closed** *L Sat, all Sun, 10 days Christmas and 15 days mid-Aug. Amex, Diners, Mastercard, Visa.*

E Marty

Map C2.23

Tel 43 31 39 51

R

20 ave des Gobelins 75005
Seats 60

M° **Les Gobelins**
Meal for 2 approx 450F

At the junction of Avenue des Gobelins, Boulevard de Port Royal and Boulevard St Marcel, the first-floor brasserie with decorative hints of its 30s origins offers a selection of very fresh and delicious shellfish including plump, juicy Normandy oysters, queen scallops sautéed in butter and very tender grilled lobster from the tank. One or two items, like the feuilleté speciality, may disappoint. In the ground-floor restaurant the *plateau de fruits de mer* is a popular and excellent choice. *L 12-2.30 D 7-10.30. Amex, Diners, Mastercard, Visa.*

Elysa Luxembourg

Map B2.16

Tel 43 25 31 74   Fax 46 34 53 27

H

6 rue Gay-Lussac 75005
Rooms 30

M° **Luxembourg (RER)**
Double from 620F

Near the Luxembourg Gardens close to the heart of the Latin Quarter. Neat bedrooms, with TV, radio alarms and mini-bars, are decorated in pastel shades and feature en-suite marble bathrooms. The basement breakfast room has a cellar-like ambience with exposed stone walls. *Amex, Diners, Mastercard, Visa.*

Familia

Map C1.17

Tel 43 54 55 27   Fax 43 29 61 77

H

11 rue des Ecoles 75005
Rooms 30

M° **Cardinal Lemoine**
Double from 395F

Now with triple glazing in all bedrooms and walls hung with artwork by fine-arts students this is a family-run hotel in the Latin Quarter. Well-equipped bedrooms have multi-channel TV (including BBC), mini-bar and hairdryer. A number of rooms have private balconies. No room service. *Amex, Diners, Mastercard, Visa.*

Les Fontaines

Map B1.18

Tel 43 26 42 80

R

9 rue Soufflot 75005
Seats 70

M° **Luxembourg (RER)**
Meal for 2 approx 500F

This café/brasserie between the Luxembourg gardens and the Pantheon corner has kept everything very traditional – the decor as much as the cuisine. Little known by the tourists, it's extremely popular with its regular clientele of university staff, editors and other locals. Everyone sits elbow-to-elbow to enjoy such specialities as smoked salmon crêpes with vegetables or a fish terrine with a fresh tomato coulis, followed by roast pigeon with wild mushrooms, *rognons de veau dijonnaise, homard grillé* or poached brill with thyme. There's always a home-made fruit

tart to finish. Like many Parisian cafés, business starts at 7.45am
and finishes at 1am. No set menu. *L 12-3 D 7.15-10.30.*
Closed Sun & Aug. Mastercard, Visa.

La Gueuze
Map B1.19

| Tel 43 54 63 00   Fax 43 54 12 59 | **R** |

19 rue Soufflot 75005
Seats 200

M^o Luxembourg (RER)
Meal for 2 approx 300F

A few paces from the Luxembourg Gardens, the speciality here
is the vast selection of some 150 beers from around the world.
There are 61 bottled Belgian beers with 12 more on draught. The
menu is familiar, headed by *moules marinière* and the almost
obligatory *frites*. Portions are hearty and Belgian favourites
include *carbonnade flamande*. There's a short daily list of blackboard
specials such as grilled sea bass with a mousseline sauce and,
to finish, enjoyable minty profiteroles. *Meals noon-2am (Fri & Sat
till 4.30am). Closed Sun. Mastercard, Visa.*

Inajiku
Map C1.20

| Tel 43 54 70 07   Fax 40 51 74 44 | **R** |

14 rue Pontoise 75005
Seats 55

M^o Maubert-Mutualité
Meal for 2 approx 450F

Relatively inexpensive Japanese teppan-yaki bar with each table
(for 7-8 people – it's normal to share) having its own hot plate
at which the prawns, scallops, beef and salmon are cooked before
your very eyes. Teppan-yaki menus include tofu, rice and
vegetables and begin at 95F (for chicken, leek and sesame). Also
sushi and sashimi menus at 168F and 188F (both 138F
at lunchtime). Finish with jasmine tea-flavoured sorbet. Drink
Japanese beer. *L 12-2.30 D 7-11. Closed Sun and Aug.
Mastercard, Visa.*

Le Jardin de Cluny
Map B1.21

| Tel 43 54 22 66   Fax 40 51 03 36 | **H** |

9 rue du Sommerard 75005
Rooms 40

M^o Maubert-Mutualité
Double from 735F

The stone-vaulted basement breakfast room here may be of
ancient origin but bedrooms above are rather more up-to-date
with air-conditioning, remote-control TVs (including English
language channels), direct-dial phones and mini-bars.
No restaurant. *Amex, Diners, Mastercard, Visa.*

Le Jardin des Plantes
Map C1.22

| Tel 47 07 06 20   Fax 47 07 62 74 | **H** |

5 rue Linné 75005
Rooms 33

M^o Jussieu
Double from 500F

Start the day with breakfast on the top-floor terrace of this
appealing hotel in a quiet street behind the Botanical Gardens.
Bedrooms, all with TV, mini-bar and hairdryer, have floral wall
coverings, a different flower for each floor, and matching
bedcovers and curtains. A brasserie/tea room on the ground floor
closes at 9pm. *Amex, Diners, Mastercard, Visa.*

Moissonnier

Map C1.24

Tel 43 29 87 65

R

28 rue des Fossés St Bernard 75005
Seats 70

M° Jussieu
Meal for 2 approx 500F

Authentic old-fashioned family-run bistro with simple decor and
homely atmosphere. Lyonnaise and Franche-Comté specialities (in
huge portions) include about a dozen assorted hors d'oeuvre from
giant *saladiers lyonnaises* (*salades de pied de veau, de gras double,
de cervelas, de boeuf*); *petit salé, couennes et lentilles; civet de lapereau
aux pates fraiches; tablier de sapeur* ('fireman's apron' –
breadcrumbed tripe with sauce gribiche); *meringues glacées, sauce
chocolat chaud; entremets citron, coulis de framboises.* Wines, many
from Beaujolais, include some recherché items like *vin jaune* from
the Jura. No set menu. *L 12-2.30 D 7-10.* **Closed** *D Sun, all
Mon & Aug. Mastercard, Visa*

Hotel des Nations

Map C1.25

Tel 43 26 45 24   Fax 46 34 00 13

H

54 rue Monge 75005
Rooms 38

M° Cardinal Lemoine
Double from 600F

On the main Rue Monge, but double glazing throughout keeps
the traffic noise away from the bedrooms, which are simple and
modern, all decorated in soft pastel shades. A few look out on to
a plant-filled courtyard while others can accommodate up to four
people. All have TV and radio. Public rooms include a bar and
lounge area. No restaurant. *Amex, Diners, Mastercard, Visa.*

Hotel de Notre Dame

Map B1.26

Tel 43 26 79 00   Fax 46 33 50 11

H

19 rue Maitre Albert 75005
Rooms 34

M° Maubert-Mutualité
Double from 690F

In a quiet side street between the Boulevard St-Germain and the
Seine and opposite Notre Dame. The reception/bar area is given
a slightly rustic feel by timber ceiling beams that also feature
in many of the bedrooms which are mostly furnished in a classical
style. All have TV, mini-bar and hairdryer as well as a wall safe.
No restaurant. *Amex, Mastercard, Visa.*

Au Pactole

Map B1.27

Tel 46 33 31 31   Fax 46 33 07 60

R

44 bd St-Germain 75005
Seats 45 (+ 8 outside)

M° Maubert-Mutualité
Meal for 2 approx 700F

Resembling a rather smart private dining room – pictures, shelves
of books, crystal chandeliers – Roland Magne's increasingly
appreciated restaurant has enormous charm, thanks to Noëlle, his
wife, as well as the fine food served here. The cuisine is classically-
based but interpreted with Roland's own inventiveness: *raviolis
d'escargots à la crème d'ail, escalope de saumon au pistou*, fricassee
of lobster with ginger, stuffed pig's trotter, *tarte au chocolat*, and
iced Grand Marnier soufflé with an orange coulis. In addition
to the à la carte there's a five-course menu gourmand (279F) and
a limited choice business lunch (149F). *L 12-2.30 D 7-10.45.*
Closed *L Sat, all Sun. Amex, Mastercard, Visa.*

Hotel du Panthéon
Map B2.28

Tel 43 54 32 95   Fax 43 26 64 65   **H**

19 place du Panthéon 75005
Rooms 34

M° St-Michel
Double from 765F

Near the Luxembourg Gardens, an 18th-century mansion facing
the Panthéon. Spacious, individually decorated bedrooms, some
with fabric-covered walls, feature exposed beams and country-
style furniture. All have air-conditioning, mini-bars and cable
television. The *Hotel des Grand Hommes* (Tel 46 34 19 60), next
door, and in the same ownership, is similar in style and pricing.
Amex, Diners, Mastercard, Visa.

Parc St-Séverin
Map B1.29

Tel 43 54 32 17   Fax 43 54 70 71   **H**

22 rue de la Parcheminerie 75005
Rooms 27

M° St-Michel/Cluny la Sorbonne
Double from 550F

A 1930s hotel renovated in the late 1980s. Bright bedrooms, very
recently refurbished, have a mix of antique and modern furniture
and boast cable TV, hairdryers, mini-bars, private safes and well-
lit bathrooms. Four rooms have balconies, the best (at 1500F)
a large terrace overlooking the church of St-Severin and the
rooftops of the Latin Quarter. *Amex, Mastercard, Visa.*

Hotel Résidence Henri IV
Map B1.30

Tel 44 41 31 81   Fax 46 33 93 22   **H**

50 rue des Bernardins 75005
Rooms 14

M° Maubert-Mutualité
Double from 900F

By Square Paul-Langevin and Rue des Ecoles, this intimate hotel
boasts some nice moulded ceilings and other period features. The
nine bedrooms and five apartments vary considerably in size but
all have kitchenette, mini-bar and cable TV. *Amex,
Mastercard, Visa.*

Hotel Résidence Saint Christophe
Map C2.31

Tel 43 31 81 54   Fax 43 31 12 54   **H**

17 rue Lacépède 75005
Rooms 31

M° Place Monge
Double from 650F

Both the refurbished bedrooms and public areas are furnished
in Louis XV style at an elegant little hotel near the Botanical
Gardens. TVs, mini-bars and hairdryers are standard features.
No restaurant. *Amex, Diners, Mastercard, Visa.*

La Rotisserie du Beaujolais
Map C1.32

Tel 43 54 17 47   **R**

19 quai de la Tournelle 75005
Seats 50

M° Maubert-Mutualité
Meal for 2 approx 440F

Quayside bistro with view of Notre Dame from a covered terrace,
in the same ownership as, and across the road from, the renowned
Tour d'Argent. Many of the ingredients come direct from Lyons
(as does the antique bar counter) for a menu that might include
the likes of fresh foie gras, *poulet roti, confit de canard* and *tete
de veau sauce ravigote.* Spit-roasted meats are a speciality of the   *See over*

kitchen, which is open to the dining room. Short wine list
concentrates on Beaujolais. No set menu. *L 12-2.30 D 7.30-11.30.*
Closed *Mon. Mastercard, Visa.*

Select   Map B1.33

Tel 46 34 14 80   Fax 46 34 51 79   **H**

1 place Sorbonne 75005   **Mᵒ Luxembourg/Odéon**
Rooms 68   Double from 780F

A 15th-century facade conceals a very modern interior centering
on a plant-filled atrium. Double-glazed bedrooms, some recently
refurbished, others completely renovated, mix contemporary
furnishings and style with exposed ceiling beams and some natural
stone walls. All are air-conditioned and have TVs and hairdryers.
Breakfast is served in a stone-vaulted basement. *Amex, Diners,
Mastercard, Visa.*

Hotel de la Sorbonne   Map B1.34

Tel 43 54 58 08   Fax 40 51 05 18   **H**

6 rue Victor-Cousin 75005   **Mᵒ Cluny la Sorbonne**
Rooms 37   Double from 410F

Small family-run hotel by the Sorbonne, just around the corner
from the Luxembourg Gardens. A little rattan-furnished
conservatory sitting area looks on to a plant-filled courtyard. En-
suite bedrooms – 11 with bath-tub the rest with shower/wc only
– have country-style decor in a variety of colour schemes and such
conveniences as cable TV, hairdryer and safe. *Mastercard, Visa.*

La Timonerie   ★   Map C1.35

Tel 43 25 44 42   **R**

35 quai de la Tournelle 75005   **Mᵒ Maubert-Mutualité**
Seats 20   Meal for 2 approx 800F

The walls of Philippe de Givenchy's charming little restaurant are
lined with natural wood and decorated with old etchings. Having
worked with Chibois and Senderens, his cuisine is very refined
and personalised. At lunchtime, his four-course *carte menu* (220F)
offers six choices at each course and is a slightly abbreviated
version of the evening *carte*. Typical of his highly individual style
is an old country recipe from the Poitou area, *petatou Poitevin,*
a goat's cheese and potato tart served with a chive sauce, as well
as boudin ravioli with a subtle vinegar sauce, an aubergine-topped
pizza with thyme and mussels in chicken bouillon with vermicelli.
Main courses might be roast sea bream with tarragon and pimento
and suckling pig-stuffed cabbage. He uses mainly inexpensive cuts
of fish and meat creating with them dishes of great sophistication,
for instance mackerel with cumin, warm potatoes, lemon confit
and mint, and pig's cheeks with crackling and vegetables.
To finish, a *tarte fine au chocolat* or a cherry *clafoutis* – desserts have
to be ordered at the beginning of the meal. Pedestrian wine list,
quite highly priced – cheapest champagne 350F! Parking
is permitted on the quai after 7.30pm. *L 12-2.30 D 7.30-10.30.*
Closed *L Mon, all Sun. Mastercard, Visa.*

La Tour d'Argent ★★★

Tel 43 54 23 31 | Fax 44 07 12 04

R

Map C1.36

15 quai de la Tournelle 75005
Seats 110

Mᵒ St-Paul
Meal for 2 approx 2000F

Spectacular views of the Seine and Notre Dame from the coveted
window tables are but one of the many special features of the
restaurant. This is a sumptuous, truly luxurious and very
expensive establishment that has been a major landmark on the
Parisian restaurant scene for a great many years. The duck *à la
presse* is another of its hallmarks and is so well known that
it doesn't even appear on the menu. Numbered certificates are
issued with each and numbers are fast approaching the million
mark. Though a few lighter dishes have been incorporated in line
with current trends the *carte* remains very traditional and classical,
complementing the sophisticated setting and polished, professional
service. The autumn/winter menu includes *foie gras d'oie des Trois
Empereurs*, apparently named after three Far Eastern emperors who
have successively enjoyed this dish of delicate goose liver quenelles
with truffles. *Quenelles de brochet* are buttery, creamy pike
quenelles with a rich mushroom mousseline and *huitres chaudes à la
Pompadour* are fat belon oysters poached on a bed of spinach and
glazed with a champagne sabayon. Main dishes feature specialities
like *filet de boeuf Tour d'Argent*, the fillet topped with a slice
of pan-fried foie gras alongside a bordelaise sauce and *pommes
soufflées*, *poussin Revenga* – a boned baby chicken stuffed with
a foie gras and truffle mousse with a Perigueux sauce on the side –
while to finish there are luxurious desserts such as warm chocolate
millefeuille, a flambé of peaches with raspberry eau de vie or a
gratin of apples with raisins and walnuts. Wines come from
a fabulous cellar which also houses a museum of wine. The set
lunch menu at 375F represents a more manageable option if the
carte is deemed prohibitive and the **Comptoires de la Tour
d'Argent** opposite is available for the purchase of luxury
souvenirs and food items all bearing the restaurant's coat of arms.
L 12-2 D 8-10. **Closed** *Mon. Amex, Diners, Mastercard, Visa.*

Hotel des Trois Collèges

Tel 43 54 67 30 | Fax 46 34 02 99

H

Map B1.37

16 rue Cujas 75005
Rooms 44

Mᵒ Cluny la Sorbonne
Double from 450F

Between the Panthéon and the Luxembourg Gardens, a period
building conceals a simple modern interior. Bedrooms have deep
red carpets, white furniture and beige walls. Many have recently
been renovated. All have TVs and hairdryers. A *salon de thé* was
due to open as we went to press. *Amex, Diners, Mastercard, Visa.*

Note: from April 16 1995 the
international dialling code 010 changes to 00

6th Arrondissement
Places of Interest

Jardin du Luxembourg
St Sulpice
St Germain-des-Prés
Musée Delacroix, 43 54 04 87, M° Saint Germain-des-Prés
Latin Quarter, Boulevard St Germain, Boulevard St Michel
Hotel des Monnaies, 40 46 55 35, M° Pont Neuf
Latin Quarter

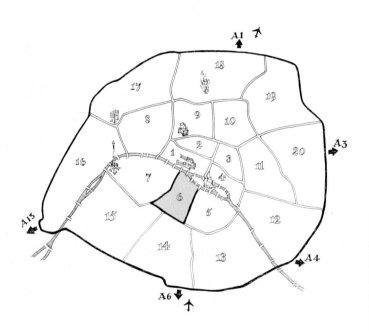

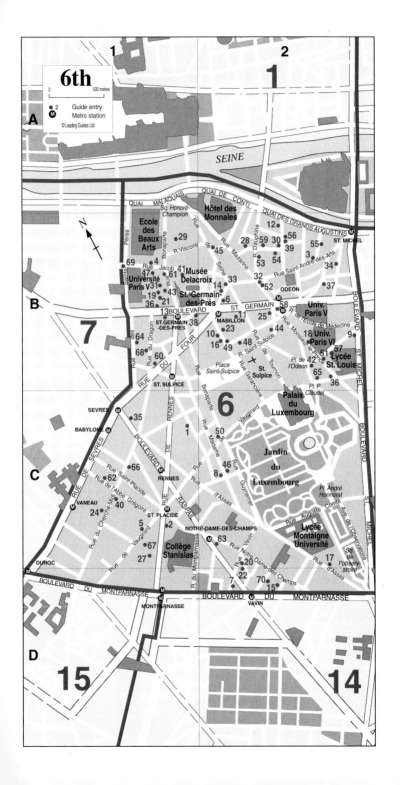

Hotel de l'Abbaye Saint-Germain   Map C1.1

Tel 45 44 38 11   Fax 45 48 07 86   **H**

10 rue Cassette 75006   **Mᵒ St-Sulpice**
Rooms 46   Double from 960F

Its sacred role is far in the past, but this old convent remains
a place of peace and calm. None of the bedrooms give on to the
road, and there's a great garden on the inside where alfresco
breakfasts are served. Bedrooms are comfortable, though not
particularly roomy, and there are tubs in all the bathrooms. One
room has a terrace. The rate quoted above is for a standard room;
larger rooms are priced much higher, and at the top of the range
are duplex suites with their own terraces. Room service till
midnight. Three lounges, modern bar. No restaurant. *Amex,
Mastercard, Visa.*

Acacias Saint-Germain   Map C1.2

Tel 45 48 97 38   Fax 45 44 63 57   **H**

151bis rue de Rennes 75006   **Mᵒ St-Placide**
Rooms 41   Double from 750F

In the Left Bank triangle of the Latin Quarter, Saint-Germain-des-
Prés and Montparnasse, this hotel (built in 1856 and a private
house till 1930, now a listed building) offers space and comfort,
plus a delightful little summer garden (overlooked by five family
rooms). Top-floor rooms are spacious, with sloping ceilings and
views over the Paris rooftops. 20 bedrooms have been totally
refurbished in a classic English style. All have satellite
TV (including Japanese broadcasts), a mini-bar, hairdryer and safe.
Among the offerings are 24hr room service and 24hr availability
of breakfast (Continental as well as cooked), laundry, baby-sitting
and fluent English. Special low rates in winter, July and August,
and interesting package deals. *Amex, Diners, Mastercard, Visa.*

Allard   Map B2.3

Tel 43 26 48 23   **R**

41 rue Saint André-des-Arts 75006   **Mᵒ Odéon/St-Michel**
Seats 65   Meal for 2 approx 650F

A lively, authentic bistro, its decor splendidly unchanged since
it opened at the turn of the century, its appeal as strong as ever.
The handwritten menu offers time-honoured specialities that
include *jambon persillé, saucisson chaud lyonnais,* sole meunière,
poached turbot with beurre blanc, Bresse chicken with girolles
and – perhaps most famous of all – duck with olives, lamb stew
and partridge with cabbage. Set menus: 150F (L only) and 200F.
L 12-2 D 7.30-10. **Closed** *Sun, Aug, 23 Dec-3 Jan. Amex, Diners,
Mastercard, Visa.*

Hotel d'Angleterre   Map B1.4

Tel 42 60 34 72   Fax 42 60 16 93   **H**

44 rue Jacob 75006   **Mᵒ St-Germain-des-Prés**
Rooms 27   Double from 750F

Once the British Embassy, and later home to Ernest Hemingway,
this charming hotel has its own delightful patio garden, the perfect
spot to enjoy a leisurely breakfast or a quiet drink in fine weather.

Character abounds in the elegant reception rooms that feature
period furniture, objets d'art and fine paintings, and the bedrooms
(some with four-posters, all with satellite TV, direct-dial
telephone, hairdryer and small safe) are especially attractive, with
original beams, exposed stone walls, comfortably large beds and
generous seating. Bathrooms, with basins set in freestanding
antique vanity units, have painted tiles and give the impression
of being old-fashioned, but are in fact up-to-date, with decent
plumbing. Daytime room service, no restaurant. *Amex, Diners,
Mastercard, Visa.*

Aramis Saint-Germain
Map C1.5

Tel 45 48 03 75   Fax 45 44 99 29   **H**

124 rue de Rennes 75006   **Mᵒ St-Placide**
Rooms 42   Double from 600F

An appealing hotel offering high standards of comfort and
traditional hospitality to a largely non-French clientèle. Bedrooms
vary in detail, 20 having recently been redecorated, but all are
attractive and relaxing with TV, video, mini-bar and hairdryer;
some are air-conditioned, some have whirlpool baths. A pianist
sometimes plays in the bar. The vaulted cellar makes
an atmospheric function/meeting room for up to 30.
No restaurant. 24-hour public parking 100 metres away. *Amex,
Diners, Mastercard, Visa.*

L'Arbuci
Map B2.6

Tel 44 41 14 14   Fax 44 41 14 10   **R**

25 rue de Buci 75006   **Mᵒ Mabillon**
Seats 220   Meal for 2 approx 480F

One of a family of brasseries in Paris, this one specialises in oysters,
shellfish and various meat and fish dishes cooked on the rotisserie.
A special menu of 121F offers nine oysters no. 5, and a pork, beef
and chicken brochette with potato purée while a 128F menu
offers oysters *à volonté* – you can eat as many as you want! Among
the alternative hot and cold starters are small brochettes of mussels
en pipérade or a chicken salad with hazelnut oil. The rotisserie
is also useful for desserts such as a banana roasted in its skin and
flambéed with Grand Marnier or fresh fruit on a brochette with
a chocolate sauce. Jazz club in the basement. *Meals 11am-1.30am.
Amex, Mastercard, Visa.*

Atelier Montparnasse
Map D2.7

Tel 46 33 60 00   Fax 40 51 04 21   **H**

49 rue Vavin 75006   **Mᵒ Vavin**
Rooms 17   Double from 700F

Owner Marie-José Tible has completed the redecoration of her
modern hotel near, but not quite amid the bustle of Montparnasse.
Each bedroom is named after a famous artist, and each floor has
a different colour scheme. All rooms are double-glazed and feature
TV, mini-bar and hairdryer. There are tubs in all the bathrooms,
where mosaic representations of the works of Montparnasse artists
are an attractive feature. *Amex, Diners, Mastercard, Visa.*

Hotel de l'Avenir
Map C2.8

| Tel 45 48 84 54   Fax 45 49 26 80 | **H** |

65 rue Madame 75006
Rooms 35

M⁰ St-Placide/Notre-Dame-des-Champs
Double from 520F

In a quiet street a few paces from the Luxembourg Gardens
between Montparnasse and the Latin Quarter, l'Avenir offers the
usual facilities in bedrooms, half of which have bath/wc en suite,
the rest shower/wc. There is sound-proofing as well as direct-dial
phones, hairdryers and safes. No room service, no restaurant.
Amex, Mastercard, Visa.

Belloy St-Germain
Map B2.9

| Tel 46 34 26 50   Fax 46 34 66 18 | **H** |

2 rue Racine 75006
Rooms 50

M⁰ Odéon/Cluny la Sorbonne
Double from 910F

The building is turn-of-the-century, reception is after Louis XIII
and renovation carried out 3 years ago has brought
a contemporary look to the bedrooms, which include suites and
triples. 15 rooms have shower/wc only but all have cable TV,
hairdryer and mini-bar. Public parking 200 metres away. *Amex,
Mastercard, Visa.*

Bistro de la Grille
Map B2.10

| Tel 43 54 16 87 | **R** |

14 rue Mabillon 75006
Seats 60 (+ 50 outdoor)

M⁰ Mabillon
Meal for 2 approx 500F

A real old-fashioned Parisian bistro popular with both locals and
tourists. Its reputation is based firmly on traditional French cuisine,
typified by *terrine de lapin, saucisses, sauté de veau aux olives, magret
de canard, daube provençale, fondant au chocolat* and gratin of fruits.
The bistro is decorated with black and white photographs of the
stars of early French cinema. Set menus: L 80F & 120F D 150F.
Meals noon-12.30am. **Closed** *L Sun. Mastercard, Visa.*

> The best way to get around Paris is by bus or metro – buy a
> book of tickets (carnet) at any metro station and save money

Le Bistrot d'Alex
Map B2.11

| Tel 43 54 09 53 | **R** |

2 rue Clément 75006
Seats 40

M⁰ Odéon/Mabillon
Meal for 2 approx 550F

The decor is red and gold, and numerous paintings by Moretti
adorn the walls. The cooking is a lightened mix of Lyonnais and
Provençal: *rosette de Lyon, saucisson pistaché, gras double,* salad
of lamb's trotters, Bresse chicken cooked *en vessie* with
mushrooms, and on Wednesdays a *pot au feu.* Desserts include
a good *flan à l'orange* and *mousse au chocolat.* There is no house
wine though a traditional Lyonnais *pot de vin* is available
(46cl – 30F) Set menus: L & D 140F, 190F. *L 12-2 D 7.30-10.*
Closed *Sun, 1 wk Christmas. Amex, Mastercard, Visa.*

Les Bookinistes ★

Map B2.12

Tel 43 25 54 94   Fax 43 25 23 07

R

53 quai des Grands Augustins 75006
Seats 70

M° St-Michel
Meal for 2 approx 500F

Decor is a stylish 'designer-distressed' blend of soft creamy hues
with small colourful highlights gouged out of the plaster on the
walls. Napery is a summery pale yellow and with minimalist
black chairs and cleverly diffused lighting the ambience
complements the short, modish menu. A blackboard lists a further
brief but enticing selection of the day's specials. Both this and the
menu proper feature innovative and well-prepared dishes that are
composed with attention to detail. A carpaccio of paper-thin slices
of raw tuna comes with raw baby vegetables dribbled with
anchovy essence topped with a crisp round of fine parmesan-
flavoured pastry, chicken liver terrine is accompanied by an apple
chutney and pumpkin soup has a garnish of potato rissoles, ham
and tapénade. Main dishes could be milk-fed veal braised with
mushrooms served with a gratin of marrows, or breast of young
chicken marinated in spices and roasted with cabbage and a confit
of lemons. Set L 160F. *L 12-2.30 D 7-12.* **Closed** *Sat & Sun. Amex,
Mastercard, Visa.*

Brasserie Lipp

Map B1.13

Tel 45 48 53 91   Fax 45 44 33 20

R

151 bd Saint Germain 75006
Seats 150

M° St-Germain-des-Prés
Meal for 2 approx 560F

Perhaps the capital's most famous brasserie, founded in 1880
by Léonard Lipp. It now has a 20s decor of ceramics, mirrors and
painted ceiling (and is classed as a historic monument). It was, and
is, the haunt of the famous, from Malraux to Madonna, from
Hemingway to Harrison Ford. Throughout its long opening hours
it serves a classic brasserie menu of bourgeois cuisine, and listed
as specialities are *cervelas rémoulade*, Bismarck herrings, grilled
stuffed pig's trotters, and choucroute with pork knuckle. The
choice is extensive and each day there are additional dishes such
as fricassee of chicken with sorrel sauce and rice or fillets of brill
with courgettes. On Thursday there's cassoulet, on Saturday roast
leg of lamb with puréed potatoes or white haricot beans. To finish,
a selection of traditional desserts that includes *baba au rhum*,
millefeuille and profiteroles with hot chocolate sauce.
Meals 10am-1am. Amex, Diners, Mastercard, Visa.

Hotel Buci-Latin

Map B2.14

Tel 43 29 07 20   Fax 43 29 67 44

H

34 rue de Buci 75006
Rooms 27

M° Mabillon
Double from 970F

A few yards from Boulevard St-Germain, the hotel was created
just three years ago. A great deal of thought went into the decor,
which is stylish and impressively modern. The foyer, with its
collection of old toys, is spacious and welcoming. There's a small
bar just inside the entrance and the breakfast room with its water
garden and Mediterranean decor is on the lower ground floor.
Breakfast is included in the room price. Bedrooms are arranged
on both sides of the street and each is identically furnished. They   *See over*

are warm and appealing, with terracotta-coloured walls and
curved lightwood furniture with good-size beds. Each has 21-
channel TV, a mini-bar and ample storage space in Oriental
wardrobes. Bathrooms are splendidly up to date (but note the
old-fashioned taps) and boast a host of extras. *Amex, Diners,
Mastercard, Visa.*

Café des Deux Magots
Map B1.21

Tel 45 48 55 25
R

6 pl Saint-Germain-des-Prés 75006
Mᵒ St-Germain-des-Prés

Opened in 1885, this, one of the typical Parisian boulevard cafés,
stands on a corner opposite the church of St-Germain-des-Prés.
Rows of tables and chairs spill out on to the pavement. Hugely
popular as a meeting place, it is the haunt of writers, artists,
politicians and tourists. Former patrons have included Simone
de Beauvoir, Hemingway and Truman Capote. If you're hungry
for conversation, this is the place to be. *Meals 7.30am-1.30am.
Mastercard, Visa.*

Café de Flore
Map B1.26

Tel 45 48 55 26
R

172 bd St Germain 75006
Mᵒ St-Germain-des-Prés

Along with *Les Deux Magots* one of the most renowned *cafés
littéraires* and the birthplace of existentialism, the café
is a good place for people-watching, less so for its savouries.
Meals 7am-1.30am. Amex.

Le Caméléon
Map D2.15

Tel 43 20 63 43   Fax 43 27 97 91
R

6 rue de Chevreuse 75006
Mᵒ Raspail/Vavin
Seats 45
Meal for 2 approx 480F

Montparnasse bistro strongly evocative of 20s Paris, with its
original decor of black banquettes, marble-topped tables, and
painted flowery wallpaper. But the food's the thing here:
straightforward bistro fare with some modern touches spans salad
of oxtail, salt cod provençale, entrecote sauce bordelaise, *confit
de canard*, pear *clafoutis* and chocolate and orange mousse. The
Loire figures prominently on the wine list. Le Caméléon is run
in splendid style by Raymond Faucher and his wife. *L 12-2
D 8-10.30.* **Closed** *Sat & Sun. Diners, Mastercard, Visa.*

Aux Charpentiers
Map B2.16

Tel 43 26 30 05   Fax 46 33 07 98
R

10 rue Mabillon 75006
Mᵒ Mabillon
Seats 100 (+ 20 outdoor)
Meal for 2 approx 500F

Once the eating place of the guild of carpenters, the restaurant has
the timeless quality of a typical French bistro. The menu offers
a long list of starters including fresh duck foie gras – best with
a chilled glass of Sauternes, *fromage de tete aux échalotes* and *soupe
de poissons.* For a main course there's a daily special such as veal
Marengo on Mondays, *boeuf à la mode* on Tuesdays and pot
au feu on Thursdays. Otherwise the selection includes roast duck
with an olive and port sauce, roast Bresse chicken or a delicious
piece of beef fillet cooked in a paper bag with carrots and pieces

of bone marrow. Simple sweets to finish such as tarte tatin, crème caramel or a *clafoutis* of mirabelles. *L 12-3 D 7-11.30.* **Closed** *Sun. Amex, Diners, Mastercard, Visa.*

Le Chat Grippé   ★   Map C2.17

Tel 43 54 70 00   **R**

87 rue d'Assas 75006   **M⁰ Port-Royal**
Seats 44   Meal for 2 approx 800F

A small, quiet, elegantly appointed restaurant with a restrained decor of deep burgundy and grey with smoked mirror panelling, pink napery and tall, black, rattan chairs. The menu is a studied example of carefully thought-out modern combinations, the use of subtle spicing put to good effect. The *menu dégustation* is a perfect and well-balanced option, allowing the diner to sample delicious and very varied courses from the *carte*, which changes with the seasons. To begin, a superb appetiser of jellied mussels with a chive cream might be followed by a duck foie gras terrine with Sauternes jelly and sea salt. Next a consommé-like soup of sliced scallops, baby clams and oyster with wild mushrooms and the merest hint of ginger followed by a small fillet of salmon cooked crisp and accompanied by a soya and garlic sauce with deep-fried parsley, tomato and a roasted garlic clove. For a main course a simple pigeon breast and leg are served roasted with delicate spicing and garnished with fondant potatoes and apple slices in honey. A delicious Cabécou de Rocamadour follows, dribbled with olive oil, a side salad and nut and raisin bread served alongside. The dessert could be a hot caramel soufflé with a caramel ice cream served separately in a tuile basket. Coffee and petits fours round off a classy meal in welcoming surroundings. Set L 160F Set L & D 235F. *L 12-2.30 D 7.30-10.30.* **Closed** *L Sat, all Mon & Aug. Mastercard, Visa.*

Chez Maitre Paul   Map B2.18

Tel 43 54 74 59   Fax 46 34 58 33   **R**

12 rue Monsieur-le-Prince 75006   **M⁰ Odéon**
Seats 55   Meal for 2 approx 450F

The Jura/Franche-Comté region of eastern France provides the inspiration for the menu at this grand little restaurant which has been in the same family since opening nearly 30 years ago. The specialities are basically unchanged down the years – splendid smoked sausages (*brésil*) and other charcuterie, sole fillets cooked with Chateau-Chalon, veal sweetbreads with morels, chicken cooked in Arbois (the yellow wine of the Jura), chocolate gateau, the day's fruit tart. Set menu 180F. *L 12.15-2.30 D 7.15-10.30.* **Closed** *L Sat, all Sun. Amex, Diners, Mastercard, Visa.*

Crystal Hotel   Map B1.19

Tel 45 48 85 14   Fax 45 49 16 45   **H**

24 rue St-Benoit 75006   **M⁰ St-Germain-des-Prés**
Rooms 26   Double from 718F

Just seconds from Boulevard St-Germain, the Crystal provides charm and comfort in traditional surroundings, with affable service provided by the *directrice* and her staff. Bedrooms are fairly simple, but bright and cheerful, some also being air-conditioned, and there's one suite. Nine of the rooms have   *See over*

shower/wc only but all have TV, mini-bar, safe and hairdryer.
Room price includes breakfast. There is no room service. The
owners are also responsible for a nearby *salon de thé*, *l'Arlequin*,
at 25 rue St André des Arts. *Amex, Diners, Mastercard, Visa.*

Danemark   Map C2.20

Tel 43 26 93 78   Fax 46 34 66 06   **H**

21 rue Vavin 75006   M° Vavin/Notre-Dame-des-Champs
Rooms 15   Double from 620F

A neat little hotel, in business for 100 years and now with
completely renovated bedrooms. Outside is painted a cheerful
blue, while in the public area there's something of the look of the
30s, with blues and greys in evidence. Bedrooms have a smart
contemporary decor, with furniture in mahogany, oak or ash
(depending on the storey). Satellite TV, mini-bar and hairdryer
are common to all. All bathrooms have tubs, no. 10 a whirlpool
bath. *Amex, Diners, Mastercard, Visa.*

Dominique   Map C2.22

Tel 43 27 08 80   **R**

19 rue Bréa 75006   M° Vavin
Seats 100   Meal for 2 approx 500F

Russian restaurant/take-away/bar/shop that's been established
in Montparnasse for many years. Decor is old Russian – 'Kremlin-
style' – and the cooking is reliable, wholesome and full of flavour:
zakouskis (hors d'oeuvre), borsch, blinis, sturgeon à la russe, beef
stroganoff, vatrouchka (tart with fromage blanc and fruit
preserve). Accompanying this gutsy food are classic wines and
a variety of vodkas. Set menu: 153F. *L 12.15-2.15 D 7.15-10.30.*
***Closed** 1 wk Feb/Mar, 15 Jul-15 Aug. Amex, Diners,
Mastercard, Visa.*

L'Ecaille de PCB   Map B2.23

Tel 43 26 73 70   Fax 46 33 07 98   **R**

5 rue Mabillon 75006   M° Odéon/Mabillon/St-Germain-des-Prés
Seats 40 (+ 10 outdoor)   Meal for 2 approx 650F

Mahogany and brass give this splendid place the look of a ship,
which is quite appropriate for a restaurant specialising totally
in seafood. Simple preparation, mainly grilling with sauces served
separately, emphasises the quality of the produce in dishes such
as *escabèche* of fresh sardines, Scottish salmon *à l'unilatéral*, roast
John Dory with grain mustard, osso buco of monkfish 'orientale',
Brittany lobsters grilled, poached or served in a salad. Options
include a three-course *menu minceur* (600 calories) at 210F and a set
menu at 125F. *L 12-3 D 7.30-11.* ***Closed** L Sat, all Sun. Amex,
Mastercard, Visa.*

Ferrandi   Map C1.24

Tel 42 22 97 40   Fax 45 44 89 97   **H**

92 rue du Cherche-Midi 75006   M° Vaneau
Rooms 42   Double from 560F

A discreet and charming bed and breakfast hotel peacefully
situated in an early 19th-century building opposite the *Musée
Hébert* (paintings by Ernest Hébert), just north of the

Montparnasse area. The cluttered entrance hall has an open fireplace with an elaborate gilt mirror above and chandelier, and individually decorated bedrooms (on four floors, there is a lift) have period freestanding furniture, heavy drapes and pink marble bathrooms; some of the larger ones boast four-posters or half-testers. Double-glazed to avoid street noise, all the bedrooms have mod cons such as satellite TV, hairdryer and telephone. Bar. Patio. *Amex, Diners, Mastercard, Visa.*

Hotel de Fleurie
Map B2.25

Tel 43 29 59 81   Fax 43 29 68 44   **H**

32 rue Grégoire-de-Tours 75006   M° Odéon/St-Germain-des-Prés
Rooms 29   Double from 810F

The family owners of this exceptionally pleasant little hotel on the corner of Boulevard St-Germain completely renovated it when they took over a few years ago. They continue to make improvements, the latest being the installation of air-conditioning. Bedrooms are bright and spacious, traditional in style, and their bathrooms are clad in marble, with hairdryers and heated towel rails. Children under 12 stay free in parents' room. No restaurant but breakfast is served in a bright stone-lined cellar. *Amex, Diners, Mastercard, Visa.*

For a glossary of menu terms see page 293

Grand Hotel Littré
Map C1.27

Tel 45 44 38 68   Fax 45 44 88 13   **H**

9 rue Littré 75006   M° Montparnasse
Rooms 97   Double from 895F

Bedrooms in this 19th-century building come in various sizes but all are traditional in style, with amply sized beds, solid furnishings and large bath or shower rooms. All have satellite TV, hairdryer and safe. The English bar is contrastingly more modern with plain wood panelling. There's a limited amount of reservable parking in a private garage (120F for 24 hours). *Amex, Diners, Mastercard, Visa.*

L'Heure Gourmande
Map B2.28

Tel 46 34 00 40   **R**

22 passage Dauphine 75006   M° Odéon
Seats 54 (+8 outside)   Meal for 2 approx 220F

Passage Dauphine is a charming alleyway which connects Rue Mazarine to Rue Dauphine. Step down to enter a cosy dining room with extra table space on a mezzanine level. The feel is charming and feminine with antique furniture, Liberty fabrics and mismatched crockery. From a simple slice of one of the delicious home-made pastries (*tarte au chocolat amer, clafoutis,* or crumble *aux fruits rouges*), hot chocolate *à l'ancienne,* fresh fruit juices or Berthillon ice cream, to more elaborate *assiettes gourmandes* (*petit salé aux lentilles, brandade de morue*), the quality menu caters for all needs. *Open 11-7.* **Closed** *Sun, Aug & Public Holidays. Diners, Mastercard, Visa.*

L'Hotel
Map B1.29

| Tel 43 25 27 22   Fax 43 25 64 81 | **HR** |

13 rue des Beaux-Arts 75006   **M° Mabillon**
Rooms 27   Double from 1700F

In the late 19th century, when it was known as the Hotel d'Alsace,
Oscar Wilde first took refuge, then died here ("I am dying beyond
my means") in 1900. Restored by owner Guy-Louis Duboucheron
and re-opened in 1968, the hotel retains many original features,
with Wilde's room reconstructed and Mistinguett's furniture
restored. Spacious and air-conditioned bedrooms, all en-suite and
some with balconies, are a mixture of styles (even Baroque) and
offer satellite TV and direct-dial telephone. Breakfast and other
meals are served in vaulted cellars. *Amex, Diners, Mastercard, Visa.*

Le Belier
Seats 100   Meal for 2 approx 500F

Red walls, green carpet, paintings and sculpted steel animals; the
busy decor is crowned by a noisy stone fountain with gigantic
flower arrangement. Christian Schuliar is now well established
and offers a very recherché classic cuisine of well-presented,
precisely cooked dishes. From the menu carte: *poelée de langoustines
sur pousses d'épinard, raie au chou vert et thym, queue de boeuf braisée
carottes persillées, poires au vin rouge et à la cannelle.* Set L & D 180F.
L 12-2 D 7.30-midnight.

Jacques Cagna
Map B2.30

| Tel 43 26 49 39   Fax 43 54 54 48 | **R** |

14 rue des Grands-Augustins 75006   **M° St-Michel**
Seats 55   Meal for 2 approx 1200F

A small, discreet doorway in an ancient, narrow street leads into
a tiny, cosy reception. The dining room is up on the first floor and
its 16th-century decor is both well preserved and very appealing.
The ceiling is heavily beamed, the walls, part oak-panelled, are
hung with fine old oil paintings and the salmon-pink upholstery
lends itself perfectly to the setting. The menu is of classic dishes
with a few nods to modernity. The selection is lengthy and varied
and changes with the seasons. After an *amuse gueule* of a tiny duck
beignet with red pepper sauce and a quail's egg in aspic the choice
could include two small lidded puff pastry cases, one filled with
lightly sautéed baby scallops, the other with pieces of lobster on a
bed of spinach. A very delicate sea-urchin butter accompanies,
together with a lobster claw. Other options might be langoustine
beignets on a salad with artichoke crisps and a gazpacho sauce
or carpaccio of bream with celery rémoulade and caviar. Main
courses range from baked John Dory accompanied by a selection
of tiny stuffed vegetables to duck from Challans roasted with
orange and lemon zests and served with a red burgundy sauce and
fillet of Scottish beef with Perigord truffles and Anna potatoes.
In the winter season there's a good selection of game running from
crisply roasted partridge served off the bone with chopped
Brussels sprouts and bacon to Scottish grouse, venison, hare and
wild boar. To finish the speciality is the dinky, bagel-sized Paris-
Brest (a memory of Jacques Cagna's childhood). Filled with piped
hazelnut cream, it is delicious. Equally impressive is the Black

Forest gateau garnished with cherries from Burgundy and paper-thin, crisp tuile biscuits. *L 12-2 D 7.30-10.30.* **Closed** *Sat, Sun, Aug & Christmas. Amex, Diners, Mastercard, Visa.*

Latitudes Saint Germain   Map B1.31

Tel 42 61 53 53   Fax 49 27 09 33   **H**

7-11 rue St Benoit 75006   **Mᵒ St-Germain-des-Prés**
Rooms 117   Double from 670F

Practical modern hotel (opened in 1988) which retains its turn-of-the-century facade. Air-conditioning, satellite TV, mini-bar, and hairdryer come as standard in the spacious, pastel-hued bedrooms. Continental breakfasts can be taken in the rooms or from the bright, cheerful buffet in the breakfast room. The hotel is just a few steps away from the bustle of the Boulevard St-Germain, but those few steps are enough to provide a fair measure of peace and quiet (unless you're in the cellar listening to jazz). *Amex, Diners, Mastercard, Visa.*

Left Bank   Map B2.32

Tel 43 54 01 70   Fax 43 26 17 14   **H**

9 rue de l'Ancienne Comédie 75006   **Mᵒ Odéon**
Rooms 31   Double from 990F

The building dates from 1750, but it has been a hotel only since 1989. It offers high standards of comfort and service. It's a handsome place, too, with antique furniture, tapestries, stone walls and fine wood panelling, oak beams and a little interior garden. Bedrooms are very well appointed – air-conditioning, double-glazing, safes, direct-dial phones, mini-bars, multi-channel TV, marble bathrooms with hairdryers. One room is equipped for disabled guests. *Amex, Diners, Mastercard, Visa.*

Hotel de la Louisiane   Map B2.23

Tel 43 29 59 30   Fax 46 34 23 87   **H**

60 rue de Seine 75006   **Mᵒ St-Germain-des-Prés/Odéon**
Rooms 80   Double from 600F

The location is a splendid one, directly across from an excellent supermarket in a street that bustles with all manner of food stalls. The accommodation is very basic, though the beds are quite comfortable. Rooms have direct-dial phones but little else, and bath tubs are on the small side. The breakfast room offers sliced breads and help-yourself filter coffee; far better to visit the shops and stalls, where you'll find some outstanding pastries and filled baguettes. **Closed** *6-26 Dec.*

La Lozère   Map B2.34

Tel 43 54 26 64   Fax 44 07 00 43   **R**

4 rue Hautefeuille 75006   **Mᵒ St-Michel**
Seats 38   Meal for 2 approx 300F

This beamed, stone-walled restaurant is owned by the tourist office of the Lozère region of central France, and the tables and chairs were made by craftsmen from that area. The menu has a similar provenance, and among the hearty *spécialités lozériennes* are warming winter soups, omelettes and *tripoux* as well as cold pork   *See over* confit salad and *andouillette*. Thursday evening brings *l'aligot d'Aubrac*, a potato purée with melted Tomme cheese, garlic and crème fraiche served with Lozère sausage. Wines are mostly from the Languedoc/Roussillon. Set menus: L 91F, L & D 121F, 145F. *L 12-2 D 7.30-10.15. **Closed** Sun, Mon, Aug, Christmas-New Year. Mastercard, Visa.*

Hotel Lutétia   Map C1.35

Tel 49 54 46 46   Fax 49 54 46 00   **HR**

45 bd Raspail 75006   **M°** Sèvres-Babylone
Rooms 283   Double from 990F

One of the grandest and most famous of the Left Bank hotels, opened in 1910 and renovated in magnificent art deco style in 1983, under the direction of Sonia Rykiel. Day rooms are splendid in their size and appointments – marble, gilt, velvet, Lalique, Takis sculptures, glass screens from the 30s – and the **Bar Lutèce**, looking down on the vast reception area has long been a favourite meeting place of the smart set. A pianist plays in the evening, jazz trios make frequent appearances and the barman and his assistant are stars in the world of mixing and inventing cocktails. There are no less than 12 conference rooms, the largest seating 450 theatre-style. The bedrooms, elegantly done out in grey, purple and gold, have the style of the 30s (ornate period furnishings, octagonal bedheads, mahogany wardrobes, bathrooms in light marble and black faïence), and the amenities of today, including 17-channel TVs, air-conditioning, sound-proofing and, for rooms overlooking the street, double-glazing. *Amex, Diners, Mastercard, Visa.*

Le Paris   ★
Tel 49 54 46 90
Seats 35   Meal for 2 approx 1000F

Designed to recreate the splendid dining room of the liner *Normandie*, destroyed by fire in New York Harbour, this is the hotel's small yet refined main restaurant. Here Philippe Renard deploys his considerable talents which combine classical skills (he's a disciple of the school of Escoffier) and a real sense of creativity. Other influences are culinary leading lights like Troisgros at Roanne and Lameloise at Chagny. The major menu (495F with wine) offers alternatives at each stage: after *amuse gueule* a choice of perhaps smoked salmon with a rémoulade of radish and parsley or wild duck terrine with foie gras and wild mushroom compote, then a remarkable dish of lobster and pig's head with green lentils or beef tournedos with herbs and mustard accompanied by boulangère potatoes and for dessert a splendid confection of chocolate and liquorice with Agen prune ice cream. Set menus 250F (L only) 350F and 495F (wine included). *L 12-2 D 7.30-11. **Closed** Sat, Sun & Aug.*

Brasserie Lutétia, the hotel's second restaurant (with separate entrance round the corner in Rue de Sèvres) is open from 7 to 10 for breakfast, then from noon to midnight for a menu of grand brasserie classics including *fruits de mer*, salmon with sorrel, *andouillette de Troyes* and *crème brulée à la vanille*. A la carte or a variety of prix-fixe menus.

Luxembourg
Map C2.36

Tel 43 25 35 90   Fax 43 26 60 84   H

4 rue de Vaugirard 75006
M° **Odéon**
Rooms 33
Double from 680F

Peace, comfort and a charming welcome a few steps from the
Luxembourg Gardens and Palace. Bedrooms are of reasonable size
and furnished with reproduction Louis XVI pieces; they all offer
modern amenities such as TV, mini-bar, hairdryer and safe.
A buffet breakfast is served in the vaulted cellars. Small courtyard
garden. No restaurant. *Amex, Diners, Mastercard, Visa.*

Hotel Du Lys
Map B2.37

Tel 43 26 97 57   Fax 43 26 97 57   H

23 rue Serpente 75006
M° **St-Michel**
Rooms 22
Double from 460F

In a narrow street right in the very heart of the Latin Quarter, the
hotel occupies a well-preserved 17th-century building. The
location is excellent as it is so central, Boulevard St-Germain being
just round the corner, and yet it is surprisingly quiet. Run by the
second generation of the same family, it has an atmosphere that
is both welcoming and homely. Bedrooms are furnished with care
and taste, individually decorated and full of charm. All have TV,
hairdryer and neat, simple bathrooms. Breakfast is included in the
room rate. There is no room service and no restaurant.
No credit cards.

Madison
Map B1.38

Tel 40 51 60 00   Fax 40 51 60 01   H

143 bd St-Germain 75006
M° **St-Germain-des-Prés**
Rooms 55
Double from 960F

Set slightly back from the Boulevard, a handsome hotel with
balconied bedrooms overlooking either street or courtyard.
Accessories include double glazing, air-conditioning, 10-channel
TV, direct-dial phone and mini-bar. Continental breakfast served
in the rooms or a buffet breakfast is offered in the dining room.
24-hour bar/*salon de thé*. A child under 12 may be accommodated
free in its parents' room. *Amex, Diners, Mastercard, Visa.*

Mariage Frères
Map B2.39

Tel 40 51 82 50   Fax 44 07 07 52   R

13 rue des Grands-Augustins 75006
M° **Odéon**

Both an experience in *savoir vivre* and a trip back in time, the
menu of this exceptional tea shop located in a 17th-century
building offers an almost never-ending list (actually 450) of teas.
The colonial atmosphere of the first-floor dining room with its
high ceiling and green plants contrasts with the vaulted basement
so typical of St-Germain-des-Prés. The menu is almost entirely
focused on tea with *escalope de saumon au thé vert Mat Uji* (salmon
scented with green tea) *charlotte d'un jardin de thé* (scented with
Casablanca tea) and *madeleines au thé*, scones and muffins served
with tea jelly. A place highly recommended for afternoon teas and
pastries, but unfortunately not to the budget traveller. The

See over

original shop is in the centre of Le Marais at 30 rue du Bourg-Tibourg 75004, Tel 42 72 28 11. *Open 12-6.* **Closed** *15 Aug-21 Aug. Amex, Diners, Mastercard, Visa.*

La Marlotte   Map C1.40

Tel 45 48 86 79   Fax 45 44 34 80   **R**

55 rue Cherche-Midi 75006   M⁰ Sèvres-Babylone
Seats 80 (+ 30 outdoor)   Meal for 2 approx 460F

A very civilised spot, with smart customers and staff. The room is rustic-elegant with old paintings on papered walls, attractive flower displays and candle-light in the evening. Cooking is careful and classically based, with a Savoyard slant. Typical dishes run from *terrine de canard* and seasonal salads to chicken fricassee, veal kidneys with mustard sauce, boudin with apples and daily fish specials – bass bordelaise, brochette of monkfish with fennel. *Grande terrine de crème caramel* is an unmissable dessert. *L 12-3 D 8-11.* **Closed** *Sat, Sun, Aug. Amex, Diners, Mastercard, Visa.*

Hotel des Marronniers   Map B1.41

Tel 43 25 30 60   Fax 40 46 83 56   **H**

21 rue Jacob 75006   M⁰ St-Germain-des-Prés
Rooms 37   Double from 640F

Peace is a commodity in plentiful supply at this really delightful little hotel, whose ancient origins may still be traced (one wall of the sous-sol dates from Henry IV). Bedrooms (all with bath/wc or shower/wc ensuite) have a romantic, rustic appeal. One of the most attractive features is a little informal garden. Ask for a room overlooking this garden – one at the top will also get you a view of the belfry of St-Germain-des-Prés. *No credit cards.*

La Méditerranée   Map B2.42

Tel 43 26 46 75   Fax 44 07 00 57   **R**

place de l'Odéon 75006   M⁰ Odéon
Seats 120   Meal for 2 approx 600F

"Spécialités de la mer", prepared carefully and mostly grilled are the stock in trade of this elegant restaurant, whose main room is the work of the renowned theatre decorator Bréard. There are three private rooms on the first floor, and a terrace (covered in white) facing the Odéon Theatre. The menu includes *brandade de morue, bouillabaisse,* grilled bass with fennel, fillets of John Dory with garlic and fresh tomatoes, éventail of salmon with parsley sauce, sea bream in red wine as well as crawfish, lobster, red mullet, turbot and sole. There's the odd meat dish too, such as duck aiguillettes with peaches. Set menus: 185F/215F. *L 12-3 D 7-11. Amex, Diners, Mastercard, Visa.*

Le Muniche   Map B1.43

Tel 46 33 62 09   Fax 45 66 47 64   **R**

22 rue Guillaume Apollinaire 75006   M⁰ St-Germain-des-Prés
Seats 140 (+ 80 outdoor)   Meal for 2 approx 360F

Like its neighbour *Le Petit Zinc,* Le Muniche throbs with life throughout most of its opening hours. In the two handsome rooms designed by Slavik, the crowds tuck into *plateaux de fruits*

de mer, andouillettes, calf's liver, roast lamb (carved at the table),
duck confit and choucroute. Set menu: L & D 148F. *Meals noon-
2am. Amex, Diners, Mastercard, Visa.*

Hotel de l'Odéon   Map B2.44

Tel 43 25 70 11   Fax 43 29 97 34   **H**

13 rue St-Sulpice 75006   **M⁰ Odéon**
Rooms 29   Double from 740F

16th-century building in the Latin Quarter, with no bedroom the
same as its neighbour. Tasteful period furnishings and a generally
cosy feel make up for a lack of size in some rooms; all have
private bathrooms, with tubs in all but two. The majority are
now air-conditioned and have cable TV, safe and hairdryer. Most
rooms overlook the little interior garden. *Amex, Diners,
Mastercard, Visa.*

La Palette   Map B2.45

Tel 43 26 68 15   **R**

43 rue de Seine 75006   **M⁰ Odéon/Mabillon/St-Germain-des-Prés**
Seats 100 (plus terrace 100)   Meal for 2 approx 200F

In amongst the tiny streets of the Left Bank is a corner café
appropriately named given the number of galleries in the vicinity.
Relatively unchanged since the early 1900s, the walls are wood-
panelled and have colourful faïence tiling as well; it is best
experienced in the summer when seating is placed under the trees
or on the pavement. This is a family business where good homely
cooking by members of the said family is only on offer
at lunchtime when the *plat du jour* (55F) could be tenderloin pork
with lentils, roast beef with potato purée or breadcrumbed
escalope with petits pois. The patronne's fruit tarts are well worth
saving space for – raspberry, tatin or lemon. *Open 8am-2am (meals
12-3).* **Closed** *Sun, Aug, 8 days Feb/Mar (school holidays).
No credit cards.*

Perreyve   Map C2.46

Tel 45 48 35 01   Fax 42 84 03 30   **H**

63 rue Madame 75006   **M⁰ Notre-Dame-des-Champs/St-Placide**
Rooms 30   Double from 430F

Comfort and style on a small scale in a modernised hotel near the
Luxembourg Gardens. There's a pleasant sitting room on the
ground floor. No restaurant but room service is available. *Amex,
Diners, Mastercard, Visa.*

Le Petit St Benoit   Map B1.47

Tel 42 60 27 92   **R**

4 rue St Benoit 75006   **M⁰ St-Germain-des-Prés**
Seats 50 (+ 50 outdoor)   Meal for 2 approx 260F

Very homely cooking in friendly surroundings – the terrace is a
favourite spot for a lively discussion on any topic under the sun.
Outside or in, regulars tuck into familiar dishes like *hachis
parmentier, boeuf bourguignon, gigot d'agneau* or *blanquette de veau,*
with *museau vinaigrette* or herring fillets to start and a fruit tart
to round things off. The place has a very traditional look, with old   *See over*

mirrors and clocks, railway-style luggage racks for coats, plain wooden tables and red tablecloths. *L 12-2.30 D 7-10.30.* **Closed** *Sat, Sun. No credit cards.*

Le Petit Vatel   Map B2.48

| Tel 43 54 28 49 | R |

5 rue Lobineau 75006   **Mᵒ Odéon/Mabillon**
Seats 22 (+ 10 outdoor)   Meal for 2 approx 200F

A restaurant in the tradition of the Latin Quarter, long popular with students and artists. French home-cooking covers such dishes as vegetable soup, *hachis parmentier*, roast pork with thyme, Toulouse sausages, *boeuf bourguignon* and a daily fish special. To finish, a couple of cheeses, crème caramel, Mont-Blanc, chocolate gateau. Set menus: L 59F D 87F. *L 12-3 D 7-midnight (Sat all day noon-1am).* **Closed** *L Sun. Amex, Diners, Mastercard, Visa.*

La Petite Cour   Map B2.49

| Tel 43 26 52 26   Fax 44 07 11 53 | R |

8 rue Mabillon 75006   **Mᵒ Mabillon**
Seats 48   Meal for 2 approx 500F

The ancient level of Rue Mabillon was several feet below the present one and the restaurant, located on this old street, now more of a courtyard, is approached across a narrow stone bridge and down a series of steps. In summer, tables and parasols provide a delightful spot for alfresco dining. Likewise the interior is utterly charming. Rich burgundy velour seating, which could have come from the boudoirs of courtesans, and soft-apricot silky fabric-covered walls hung with framed oil paintings provide a suitably romantic ambience. The food is up to date with offerings such as thinly sliced raw scallops topped with finely grated raw radish and a truffle oil dressing or langoustine ravioli with tarragon. *Canard sauvage 'col vert' roti, sauce aux épices* – roast wild duck with a fragrant spicy sauce, and *mignons de biche Grand Veneur aux airelles* (venison fillet with cranberries and a rich game sauce) are typical main dishes. Quite enjoyable sweets include a vanilla *crème brulée*, figs and pears poached in Saumur wine or a small tart of apples, clementines and prunes. Set menus: L 150F and 165F D 185F. *L 12-3 D 7-11.30. Mastercard, Visa.*

Au Plaisir des Pains   Map C2.50

| Tel 45 48 40 45 | R |

62 rue de Vaugirard 75006   **Mᵒ Saint Sulpice**

Appetising pastries, jars of honey and traditional jams decorate the window. The shop has a tiny, light-green dining room with darkwood tables and chairs on the first floor. M Arella is in charge wielding his mighty whisk to create deliciously light savouries: *tarte à la tomate, feuilleté au Roquefort, sandwich aux poivrons grillés* (grilled peppers served in warm Greek bread), and mouth-watering desserts such as *fondant au chocolat* and Berthillon ice cream making it an unusual and high-quality sandwich shop. *Open 10am-8pm.* **Closed** *Sun, Bank Holidays, 2 wks Aug. No credit cards.*

Polidor

Map B2.51

`Tel 43 26 95 34`   **R**

41 rue Monsieur-le-Prince 75006   **Mᵒ Odéon**
Seats 120   Meal for 2 approx 240F

One of the real survivors, not greatly changed in the past 100+ years. The art deco lighting is quite a feature, the uneven ceiling may look as though it's about to fall down and the floor is not quite even but it's all part of the charm, and it would be a shame to change it. Long-serving waitresses distribute homely, traditional dishes like pumpkin soup, *blanquette de veau*, beef bourguignon, chicken *basquaise* and duck with petits pois. The home-made patisserie is particularly good, the chocolate tart, a speciality, being always in great demand. Set menus: L 55F L & D 100F. *L 12-2.30 D 7-12.30 (Sun to 11). No credit cards.*

Le Procope

Map B2.52

`Tel 43 26 99 20   Fax 43 54 16 86`   **R**

13 rue de l'Ancienne Comédie 75006   **Mᵒ Odéon**
Seats 220   Meal for 2 approx 500F

The oldest café in Paris, now restored to its 17th-century splendour. The menu calls it "Le Rendezvous des Arts et des Lettres" and indeed in its 300-year history Le Procope has entertained many leading lights of French literature, from Balzac to Voltaire. The menu sticks mainly to reasonably prepared brasserie food, with oysters, whiting Colbert, duck à l'orange, fillet of beef béarnaise and guinea fowl with Calvados among the popular choices. Sorbets and ice creams are the speciality desserts, all made on the premises. Rhone bottles head the wine list. Set menus: 99F, 290F. *Meals 11am-1am. Amex, Diners, Mastercard, Visa.*

Le Régent

Map B2.53

`Tel 46 34 59 80   Fax 40 51 05 07`   **H**

61 rue Dauphine 75006   **Mᵒ Odéon**
Rooms 25   Double from 750F

Traditional and modern features blend happily at the Régent, an 18th-century mansion in the heart of St-Germain-des-Prés. Old stonework and painted beams take the eye in reception, and the breakfast room is a vaulted cellar. Bedrooms are decorated in a variety of pleasing, well co-ordinated styles and shades, all are air-conditioned and sound-proofed, with direct-dial phones, satellite TV, digitally-coded safes and mini-bars. Bathrooms feature marble or hand-painted Italian tiles. Children under 12 are accommodated free with parents in the larger rooms. There's no restaurant, but the renowned **Café des Deux Magots** (*qv*) in the same ownership is not far away. *Amex, Diners, Mastercard, Visa.*

Relais Christine

Map B2.54

`Tel 43 26 71 80   Fax 43 26 89 38`   **H**

3 rue Christine 75006   **Mᵒ St-Michel**
Rooms 51   Double from 1580F

You enter through wrought-iron gates and a bricked courtyard, resplendent with small trees and shrubs. The hotel, quite close   *See over*

to Notre-Dame and situated just south of the river in a quiet street
near St-Germain-des-Prés, was once a 16th-century abbey (note the
stone-vaulted medieval breakfast room and discreet panelled
lounge with leather sofas), and still has lots of character in the
recently refurbished bedrooms, which overlook either the small,
pretty garden or courtyard, and provide all the expected comforts
alongside period furniture and fine paintings. The *Pavillon de la
Reine* (*qv*) in the 3rd arrondissement is under the same ownership.
Garden. *Amex, Diners, Mastercard, Visa.*

Relais Hotel du Vieux Paris   Map B2.55

| Tel 43 54 41 66   Fax 43 26 00 15 | **H** |

9 rue Git-le-Coeur 75006   **M⁰ St-Michel**
Rooms 20   Double from 990F

A hotel with a history going back to 1480. It once belonged to the
Duc de Luynes and more recently was a favourite with the Beat
generation including Kerouac, Burroughs and Ginsberg as well
as the artists Picasso, Matisse and Giacometti. Completely
renovated in 1991, it is a comfortable, roomy and well-appointed
place. Accommodation comprises 13 rooms and 7 suites, and three
of the latter have mezzanines and magnificent views over the
rooftops. Beams, handsome furnishings, 19-channel TV, mini-bar,
safe and marble-finished bathrooms (whirlpool baths in suites) all
make for a pleasant stay. Fax and laundry service; airport pick-up
can be arranged. *Amex, Mastercard, Visa.*

Relais Louis XIII   ★   Map B2.56

| Tel 43 26 75 96 | **R** |

8 rue des Grands-Augustins 75006   **M⁰ St-Michel**
Seats 55   Meal for 2 approx 1000F

Built on the remains of the Grands-Augustins monastery (dating
back to early 17th century), the restaurant retains many relics
of the past. Magnificent beams and timbered walls have been
perfectly preserved and are the back-drop to tapestries and objets
d'art of the period. The classical French cuisine offers Landes duck
foie gras or langoustine ravioli with tarragon followed perhaps
by John Dory with a prawn sauce, fricassee of Breton lobster with
Sauternes or fillet of beef with Périgord truffles. Finish with
a chocolate mousse. Set menus: L 190F, 240F D 250F, 350F.
L 12.15-2.15 D 7.30-10.15. **Closed** *L Mon, all Sun & early Aug.*
Amex, Diners, Mastercard, Visa.

Relais Médicis   Map B2.57

| Tel 43 26 00 60   Fax 40 46 83 39 | **H** |

23 rue Racine 75006   **M⁰ Odéon**
Rooms 16   Double from 980F

Two 18th-century buildings of three storeys are separated by a
pretty little patio garden with a fountain. The whole place has
been designed to give a country feel, and the well-appointed
bedrooms feature flowery Impressionist-style fabrics and warm,
pastel-coloured walls. Painted woodwork, antiques and old
photographs add to the period appeal, while air-conditioning and
sound-proofing keep things peaceful and comfortable. The
handsome marble bathrooms have separate wcs. Room price
includes breakfast. *Amex, Diners, Mastercard, Visa.*

Relais St Germain   Map B2.58

Tel 43 29 12 05   Fax 46 33 45 30   **H**

9 carrefour de l'Odéon 75006   **Mᵒ Odéon**
Rooms 20   Double from 1450F

The building is 17th-century, and the inside of this delightful little
place is done out in colourful country style, with flowery fabrics,
antique furniture and beams. A small building next door, also
from the same period, has been purchased and converted to nine
smart, new bedrooms. Modern comforts such as cable TV, mini-
bar, safe and hairdryer are not lacking in any and bathrooms,
finished in marble, have tubs, shower and separate wcs. The top-
floor suite, which has a terrace, is reached by a little staircase from
the 5th (other floors are served by a lift). A generous Continental
breakfast (included in room price) is served in the rooms
or downstairs. The hotel stands at the bustling Odéon crossroads.
Amex, Diners, Mastercard, Visa.

Note: from April 16 1995 the
international dialling code 010 changes to 00

La Rotisserie d'en Face   Map B2.59

Tel 43 26 40 98   Fax 43 54 54 48   **R**

2 rue Christine 75006   **Mᵒ Odéon/St Michel**
Seats 85   Meal for 2 approx 520F

This is Jacques Cagna's informal modern, buzzy and inexpensive
dining option. It stands across the road from his main restaurant
and features an imaginative three-course fixed-price multiple-
choice menu beginning with *terrine de lièvre à la sauge salade
de cresson* – terrine of hare with sage and watercress; *paté en croute
de canard au foie gras maison* – duck and foie gras paté baked
in pastry, *assiette de coquillages et tagliatelles au pistou* – noodles with
shellfish in a thin cream and basil sauce. Main dishes include fish
such as grilled Scottish salmon with endives and lime, and hake
with salsa verde, baby clams and peas as well as meat options like
grilled entrecote with a béarnaise sauce, moussaka, and pig cheek
with carrots and fondant potatoes. The rotisserie produces rack
of lamb with thyme and Challans chicken with a purée of potatoes
among a short selection. Desserts are generally good, including
a super warm apple tart. It's a fun place but the service can
be brusque and the food doesn't always live up to expectations.
Menu-carte: L 145F (2 courses), D 185F (3 courses). *L 12-2.30
D 7-11 (Fri & Sat to 11.30).* **Closed** *L Sat, all Sun. Mastercard, Visa.*

Hotel de Saint-Germain   Map B1.60

Tel 45 48 91 64   Fax 45 48 46 22   **H**

50 rue du Four 75006   **Mᵒ St-Sulpice/Sèvres-Babylone**
Rooms 30   Double from 695F

"Cute and cosy" bedrooms, half of which have just been
renovated, the rest due to be completed when this guide
is published, have lightwood furnishings and Laura Ashley looks.
Direct-dial phone, TV; mini-bar, and safe help make this a quiet,
civilised little retreat. *Amex, Diners, Mastercard, Visa.*

Hotel Saint-Germain-des-Prés   Map B1.61

Tel 43 26 00 19   Fax 40 46 83 63   **H**

36 rue Bonaparte 75006   **M° St-Germain-des-Prés**
Rooms 30   Double from 950F

A traditionally-run hotel decorated in a quaintly old-fashioned
style and located in an old street at the heart of St-Germain-des-
Prés. Bedrooms, though not large, are comfortably appointed –
air-conditioning, double-glazing, TV (some with cable), safe,
direct-dial phone, mini-bar – and many have beamed ceilings.
There are five suites. *Mastercard, Visa.*

Saint Grégoire   Map C1.62

Tel 45 48 23 23   Fax 45 48 33 95   **H**

43 rue de l'Abbé-Grégoire 75006   **M° St-Placide**
Rooms 20   Double from 760F

An 18th-century mansion modernised into a charming hotel with
a snug, brightly decorated lounge, a little garden and a cellar
breakfast room. Bedrooms (a few with balconies) feature pastel
colour schemes, a largely traditional decor and some handsome
antiques. Two rooms on the 6th floor are air-conditioned. The
hotel is between the Boulevards Raspail and Montparnasse. *Amex,
Diners, Mastercard, Visa.*

Sainte-Beuve   Map C2.63

Tel 45 48 20 07   Fax 45 48 67 52   **H**

9 rue Ste-Beuve 75006   **M° Notre-Dame-des-Champs**
Rooms 23   Double from 680F

Accommodation at this 19th-century building just off Boulevard
Raspail comprises double rooms, doubles de luxe, junior suites and
apartments. Price varies according to size, with the apartments
at the top of the range at 1600F. Furnishings are a careful blend
of old and new, David Hicks being responsible for the interior
design. Attractive tiled bathrooms. Garden bar. *Amex,
Mastercard, Visa.*

Hotel des Saints-Pères   Map B1.64

Tel 45 44 50 00   Fax 45 44 90 83   **H**

65 rue des Saints-Pères 75006   **M° St-Germain-des-Prés/Sèvres-Babylone**
Rooms 39   Double from 700F

Built in the 17th century by Louis XVI's architect Gittard and
though now much modernised, the hotel has kept a certain
traditional style and charm. Most of the bedrooms have a quiet
setting overlooking the courtyard garden where, when the
weather's kind, breakfast and tea can be taken. There are lounges
and a bar but no restaurant. *Amex, Mastercard, Visa.*

Hotel Sénateur   Map B2.65

Tel 43 26 08 83   Fax 46 34 04 66   **H**

10 rue Vaugirard 75006   **M° Odéon**
Rooms 44   Double from 680F

Completely renovated in 1992, the Sénateur has a contemporary,
functional designer look, with a little greenery to brighten the
public areas; bedrooms use carefully co-ordinated colour schemes.

Bedrooms and duplexes are equipped with private facilities (some shower/wc only), satellite TV and mini-bars. Top-floor rooms enjoy splendid views. Supervised car park next to the hotel, which is in the heart of St-Germain-des-Prés. *Amex, Diners, Mastercard, Visa.*

Taverne Basque   Map C1.66

Tel 42 22 51 07   **R**

45 rue du Cherche-Midi 75006   **M⁰ St-Placide/Sèvres-Babylone**
Seats 50   Meal for 2 approx 450F

Run by Pierre Alcorta and his family, this is very much a homely, local restaurant. The decor has warmth and character too, with dark wood-strip panelled walls hung with colourful pictures and Basque artefacts suspended from the beamed ceiling. The food is simple, flavoursome and well prepared. Specialities from the South-West region of France include a hot starter of pipérade – a sort of scrambled egg mixture with tomato and onion. This comes topped with slices of raw cured ham. *Ttoro* (fish soup), cold goose confit, roast duck breast with honey from the Pyrenees and Toulouse cassoulet are typical offerings. There are daily specials too such as venison medallions *Grand Veneur*, tuna steak *basquaise* and poached haddock. Good desserts round things off well. Service is charming. Set menus: L & D 150F/190F (incl. drink). *L 12-2 D 7.30-10.30. **Closed** L Sat, all Sun, 1st 2 wks Aug. Amex, Diners, Mastercard, Visa.*

Victoria Palace Hotel   Map C1.67

Tel 45 44 38 16   Fax 45 49 23 75   **H**

6 rue Blaise-Desgoffe 75006   **M⁰ St-Placide/Montparnasse**
Rooms 111   Double from 936F

A choice of accommodation (some rooms recently renovated) in a large, old-fashioned hotel between Montparnasse and St-Germain-des-Prés. Tariff ranges from 870F for a single to 1400F for a de luxe double. Bar. Private parking for 12 cars (130F of per night). Meeting rooms for up to 15 people. *Amex, Diners, Mastercard, Visa.*

The best way to get around Paris is by bus or metro – buy a book of tickets (carnet) at any metro station and save money

---

La Vigneraie   Map B1.68

Tel 45 48 57 04   **R**

16 rue Dragon 75006   **M⁰ St-Germain-des-Prés/Sèvres-Babylone**
Seats 60   Meal for 2 approx 500F

An old-fashioned *bistro à vins*, where you can drop in for a glass of wine (Bordeaux a speciality) or settle down for a full meal. The menu sticks to classics old and new: salad of spinach and chicken livers, goat's cheese on toast, salmon *à l'unilatéral, pot au feu, gigot d'agneau à la fleur de thym, délice au chocolat*. Set menus: L 75F, L & D 168F. *L 12-2.30 D 7-11.30. **Closed** L Sun, Aug. Amex, Diners, Mastercard, Visa.*

La Villa   Map B1.69

Tel 43 26 60 00   Fax 46 34 63 63   **H**

29 rue Jacob 75006   **M° St-Germain-des-Prés**
Rooms 32   Double from 800F

Originality is stamped all over La Villa, whose ultra-modern
design has been a talking point since its opening a couple of years
ago. Accommodation ranges from '3rd category with shower
or bath' to a senior suite with two bedrooms and a sitting room.
All rooms are sound-proofed and air-conditioned, with mini-bar,
satellite TV and even a telephone extension in the bathroom.
Among the hotel's many unique attractions is its cocktail bar, open
from 6, with the top names in jazz performing live after 10.30
Monday to Saturday. *Amex, Diners, Mastercard, Visa.*

Villa des Artistes   Map D2.70

Tel 43 26 60 86   Fax 43 54 73 70   **H**

9 rue de la Grande-Chaumière 75006   **M° Vavin**
Rooms 59   Double from 650F

Just steps away from Boulevard du Montparnasse, a welcoming
hotel with public rooms done out in art deco style and built
around a neat little courtyard garden with a central fountain.
Standard rooms (price quoted above) have shower/wc, while
de luxe accommodation offers many extras including bathtubs,
air-conditioning, mini-bar and safe. Room rate includes breakfast.
Amex, Diners, Mastercard, Visa.

7th Arrondissement
Places of Interest

Musée d'Orsay, 40 49 48 14, Mº Solferino
Assemblée Nationale, Mº Assemblée Nationale
Hotel des Invalides, Mº Latour-Maubourg/Invalides
Musée de l'Armée (tomb of Napoleon 1st) 45 55 37 70
Tour Eiffel, 45 50 34 56, Mº Bir Hakeim/Trocadéro
Champ de Mars, Mº Ecole Militaire
Ecole Militaire, Mº Ecole Militaire
Les Egouts de Paris (sewers), 47 05 10 29, Mº Alma-Marceau
Musée Auguste Rodin, 47 05 01 34, Mº Varenne

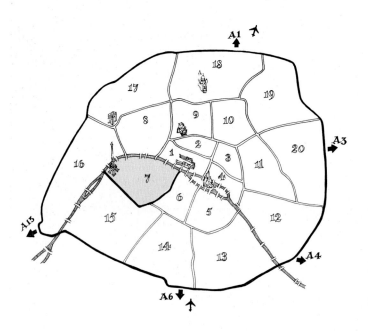

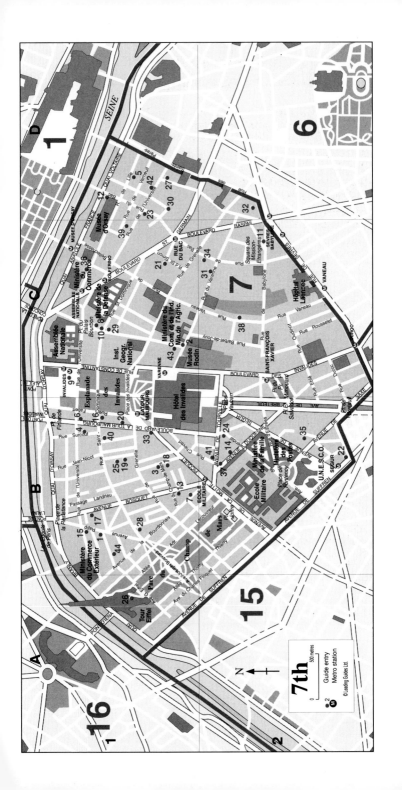

Antoine et Antoinette   Map B1.1

Tel 45 51 75 61   **R**

16 ave Rapp 75007   **M⁰ Alma Marceau**
Seats 45 (+ 22 outdoor)   Meal for 2 approx 500F

Now in his 10th year here, chef-patron Jean-Claude Pernot
presents a seasonal selection of soundly cooked classical French
dishes in his pretty little restaurant. The menus (English translation
available) deal in very straightforward dishes like *cassolette
d'escargots à l'ail doux, ratatouille glacé à l'oeuf, aiguillettes de canard
aux poire épicées*, and *pavé de morue fraiche à l'huile d'olive*.
Millefeuille with red berries is a speciality dessert to order at the
beginning of the meal. Set menu: L & D 130F. *L 12.15-2 D 7.30-
10*. **Closed** *Sat, Sun, 2 wks Aug. Amex, Diners, Mastercard, Visa*.

L'Arpège   ★   Map C1.2

Tel 45 51 47 33   Fax 44 18 98 39   **R**

44 rue de Varenne 75007   **M⁰ Varenne**
Seats 45   Meal for 2 approx 1700F

If it were possible for a cello to cast off its casing and be reborn,
then the splendid bronze and wood sculpture in the entrance
would be the perfect embodiment of such an act. This and
a portrait of the chef's mother, who provided early culinary
inspiration, are the only decoration in a dining room whose
backlit walls are panelled with softly undulating pearwood.
Behind is bare pink stuccoed plaster. The rest, apart from the
white napery, is charcoal grey. All this simple modernity is in
contrast to the sobriety of the setting – a street of grey
government offices (though the Rodin museum is almost directly
across the way). The food is quite extraordinary and there's ample
choice, though a good proportion of the main dishes including the
whole of the *'menu gastronomique'* is for a minimum of two people.
Dishes are assembled in a medley of intricate and complex
flavours, some of which almost defy the senses. To begin, perhaps
a simple dish of clams steamed in a paper bag, a sweet and sour
lobster salad or a cream of wild mushroom soup with Parmesan.
Main dishes include a good choice of fine fish such as John Dory
baked with bay leaves, scallops with a cauliflower purée and skate
with capers and sultanas. Calf's sweetbreads with liquorice,
suckling pig with North African seasonings and rack of Alpine
lamb with walnuts are just a few of the imaginative meat dishes.
Good country cheeses follow and last but not least desserts such
as a chocolate millefeuille, a hot chocolate soufflé or a rather
strange baked tomato filled with a very fine, mainly citrus, dice
topped with a hot syrup. Set menus: L 320F, L & D 820F.
L 12.30-1.30 D 7.30-10.30. **Closed** *L Sun, all Sat. Amex, Diners,
Mastercard, Visa*.

Beaugency   Map B1.3

Tel 47 05 01 63   Fax 45 51 04 96   **H**

21 rue Duvivier 75007   **M⁰ Ecole Militaire**
Rooms 30   Double from 550F

A modern building close to Hotel des Invalides and not too far
from the Eiffel Tower. Brightly decorated, double-glazed
bedrooms, some quite compact, have satellite TV, mini-bar and

hairdryer. There is room service for breakfast or it can be taken
in the cheerful breakfast room with its white rattan furniture and
wall-length mural. *Amex, Diners, Mastercard,Visa.*

Le Bellecour ★   Map B1.4

| Tel 45 55 68 38 | R |

22 rue Surcouf 75007   M° Invalides
Seats 80   Meal for 2 approx 860F

South of the Quai d'Orsay and close to the Esplanade des Invalides,
Bellecour is a restaurant renowned for its Lyonnais specialities such
as *salade de clapotons* (lamb's trotters), *quenelles de brochet*, and Bresse
chicken in vinegar with a gratin of macaroni. These feature on a
carte of well-thought-out modern dishes such as lobster with
turmeric, roast duck with lime and cardamom and lamb loin
chops roasted with sage and served with garlic beignets. Gerald
Goutagny's desserts are a particular forte with an amazing selection
from hot *charlotte soufflé* to caramelised apple tart, a trio of *crèmes
brulées* and a cherry blancmange with sweet almond milk sorbet.
Set menus from 160F. *L 12.30-2.30 D 7.30-10.30.* **Closed** *Sat,
Sun & Aug. Access, Amex, Diners, Visa.*

Bersoly's Saint-Germain   Map D1.5

| Tel 42 60 73 79   Fax 49 27 05 55 | H |

28 rue de Lille 75007   M° Rue du Bac
Rooms 16   Double from 580F

Highlights at this one-time monastery include a warm, friendly
welcome, antiques from the nearby specialist shops, a pretty little
interior courtyard and an atmospheric vaulted cellar where
breakfast is served. Cosy bedrooms are named after painters. All
have cable TV, hairdryer and safe. **Closed** *Aug. Mastercard, Visa.*

La Boule D'Or   Map B1.6

| Tel 47 05 50 18   Fax 47 05 91 21 | R |

13 bd de Latour-Maubourg 75007   M° Invalides
Seats 55   Meal for 2 approx 500F

Contemporary decor, a civilised band of regulars, a charming
owner and a chef with skill and imagination. Dishes are in the
traditional French mainstream, from *compote de lapin au vin blanc*
and *paté de truite de rivière en croute* through poached skate wing
with sabayon and *petit gigot d'agneau au jus de thym* to a speciality
hot lemon soufflé or warm chocolate fondant with raspberry
coulis; these desserts have to be ordered at the beginning of the
meal. Set menu: 170F. *L 11.30-2.30 D 7.30-10.30.* **Closed** *L Sat.
Amex, Diners, Mastercard, Visa.*

La Bourdonnais   Map B1.7

| Tel 47 05 45 42   Fax 45 55 75 54 | HR |

111 ave de la Bourdonnais 75007   M° Ecole Militaire
Rooms 59   Double from 640F

Turn-of-the-century building offering comfortable
accommodation in very traditional Parisian style. *Diners,
Mastercard, Visa.*   *See over*

La Cantine des Gourmets   ★
Tel 47 05 47 96   Fax 45 51 09 29
Seats 60   Meal for 2 approx 1000F

Next door to the hotel at no 113, the restaurant is among the
most popular in town as well as the most cheerful, thanks
to Micheline Coat, who's in overall charge. Provence is the
provenance of Philippe Bardau's cooking, and his background
with Outhier and Maximin means that fine fresh country flavours
are very much to the fore. Among many marvellous dishes on an
autumn menu were a salad of pigeon, almonds and broad beans,
sole meunière with *pommes charlotte à la moelle*, crayfish with
a baby squid risotto, rabbit with rosemary and black olives, and
a choco-caramel dome with *glace nougatine*. Strong showing
of Bordeaux wines. Set menus: L 220F, 420F D 320F, 420F.
*L 12-2.30 D 8-11. **Closed** 25 Dec.*

Bourgogne et Montana   Map C1.8
Tel 45 51 20 22   Fax 45 56 11 98   **H**

3 rue de Bourgogne 75007   **Mᵒ Invalides/Assemblée Nationale**
Rooms 33   Double from 680F

Opposite the Palais Bourbon and very near the Assemblée
Nationale, this traditionally run hotel is in a late 18th-century
building. All its bedrooms are warm and comfortable, furnished
with antiques and period pieces and many have recently been
stylishly renovated. All have cable TV, mini-bar and hairdryer.
Continental breakfast is served in the rooms, a buffet in the
restaurant (closed for main meals Sat, Sun and 1st 3 wks Aug).
Amex, Diners, Mastercard, Visa.

Chez Françoise   Map C1.9
Tel 47 05 49 03   **R**

Aérogare des Invalides 75007   **Mᵒ Invalides**
Seats 150 (+50 outside)   Meal for 2 approx 600F

Not advertised on the esplanade outside – look for it in the
basement of the Invalides Air France bus terminal. A sort of up-
market brasserie, it has made its reputation as the MPs' canteen,
with a relaxed, enjoyable atmosphere. *Foie gras de canard frais
maison, salade de homard vinaigrette tiède à l'huile de noix* and
entrecote d'Angus poelée fondue d'échalotes – nothing is missing from
the classical repertoire and certainly not quality. Compared with
the somewhat pricy à la carte, the set menu with generous
portions, wine and coffee is one of city's best bargains. Private
parking with access in front of 2 rue Fabert. Live piano music, and
live entertainment on Saturday nights. Set L 168F Set D 200F
(wine & coffee included). *L 12-3 D 7-12. Amex, Diners,
Mastercard, Visa.*

Chez Marius   Map C1.10
Tel 45 51 79 42   Fax 47 53 79 56   **R**

5 rue de Bourgogne 75007   **Mᵒ Invalides/Assemblée Nationale**
Seats 55   Meal for 2 approx 600F

Affable chef-patron Michel Perrodo runs a delightful restaurant
specialising in the cuisine of the Mediterranean and particularly
seafood. *Bouillabaisse, queues de langoustes en salade aux Xérès, cigale*

de mer grillé provençale, panaché aux trois poissons à l'armoricaine,
grilled *filet de bar de ligne* with olive oil and lime . . . . these and
similar simply prepared delights keep the regulars happy, and
there's also plenty of choice for meat-eaters (rack of lamb with
Provence herbs and various ways with Bresse chicken are firm
favourites). Set menus: 180F, 250F. *L 12-3 D 7.30-10.30.*
Closed *L Sat, all Sun & Aug. Amex, Diners, Mastercard, Visa.*

Chomel   Map C2.11

Tel 45 48 55 52   Fax 45 48 89 76   **H**

15 rue Chomel 75007   **M⁰ Sèvres-Babylone**
Rooms 23   Double from 650F

A Left Bank hotel in traditional style, recently refurbished, its six
floors served by a lift. Bedrooms, all with private bath or shower
and wc, offer the expected necessaries of direct-dial phone,
hairdryer and mini-bar, plus cable TV (British channels) and
radio. Breakfast may be taken in the bedrooms or in the little
lounge. Parking available below the nearby *Bon Marché* store.
Amex, Diners, Mastercard, Visa.

Christian Constant   Map D1.12

Tel 47 03 30 00   Fax 42 86 97 97   **R**

26 rue du Bac 75007   **M⁰ Rue du Bac**

An excellent pastry shop open all day for fine baking and a few
light savouries. A must are the chocolate delicacies for which
Christian Constant has won a well-deserved reputation. *Fleurs
de Chine* is a light, bitter chocolate mousse with a cocoa sorbet and
jasmin ice cream. The plate of desserts of the day is a real and
worthwhile indulgence. Another Christian Constant (a cousin) is
chef at the *Hotel de Crillon* (*qv*, 8th arrondissement). *Open 8-8.
Mastercard, Visa.*

Clémentine   Map B1.13

Tel 45 51 41 16   **R**

62 ave Bosquet 75007   **M⁰ Ecole Militaire**
Seats 60 (+ 12 outdoor)   Meal for 2 approx 420F

Chef-patron Bernard Przybyl specialises in the cuisine of the
South-West (Cahors) in his snug little restaurant with up-market
bistro decor offering cassoulet, foie gras and dishes such
as *fricassée de rognons de veau* with mustard, *confit de dinde à la
landaise, filet de poulet grillé aux groseilles et citron* and *médaillons
de rouget à l'ail*. Reliable cooking, kind prices, regional wines. Set
menu: 178F (wine included). *L 12-2.30 D 7.30-10.30.*
Closed *L Sat, all Sun & Aug. Mastercard, Visa.*

Derby Eiffel   Map B2.14

Tel 47 05 12 05   Fax 47 05 43 43   **H**

5 ave Duquesne 75007   **M⁰ Ecole Militaire**
Rooms 43   Double from 590F

Not far from the Eiffel Tower and close to Hotel des Invalides,
the Derby's public areas include a relaxing modern lounge and
a courtyard garden. There are also two meeting rooms, for 10 to
40 people. Bedrooms are neat and practical, with satellite TV,
mini-bars and private safes. Underground car park close by. *Amex,
Diners, Mastercard, Visa.*

Les Deux Abeilles
Map B1.15

| Tel 45 55 64 04 | R |

189 rue de l'Université 75007   **M⁰ Alma Marceau**

A family-style tea room with smart 30s decor and careful
management by the lady owner and her daughter. Three rooms
furnished with period pieces have an old-fashioned charm which
fits right into this residential part of the 7th. Light savoury dishes
are offered throughout the day but the real treats are the home-
made pastries on display: *fondant au chocolat*, a rich chocolate cake,
crumble *aux poires et fruits rouges, gateau au fromage blanc*,
(cheesecake) or *tarte soufflée aux framboises*, (raspberry meringue
pie). Seats outside. *Open 9-7.* **Closed** *Sun, Aug. No credit cards.*

Le Divellec   ★★
Map B1.16

| Tel 45 51 91 96   Fax 45 51 31 75 | R |

107 rue de l'Université 75007   **M⁰ Invalides**
Seats 60   Meal for 2 approx 1400F

Jacques Le Divellec is one of the prime exponents of modern fish
cookery. His restaurant, overlooking the Esplanade des Invalides,
has a suitably nautical theme having an aquarium and numerous
paintings of boats, fish and the sea. The cooking style is excitingly
innovative yet relatively uncomplex, the quality and flavour
of the fish taking precedence over elaborate saucing and
obsequious garnishes. A favourite is the juxtaposing of foie gras
and seafood as in langoustines with foie gras terrine, or tournedos
of tuna with truffled duck foie gras. Exquisite starters such as a
salad of lobster with coral vinaigrette, a tartare of bass, salmon and
mullet with virgin olive oil and clams stuffed with garlic and
thyme could precede John Dory with tapénade and a tomato and
olive coulis or roast turbot with a lobster béarnaise and fried
potatoes. The lobster press is an invention of M Le Divellec and
is based on the famous duck press at *Le Tour d'Argent*; it is used
in the preparation of *homard à la presse*. There are a couple of meat
dishes but these are anathema when so much effort has been
expended in the creation of such piscatorial masterpieces. Set
menus from 270F. *L 12-1.30 D 7.30-9.30.* **Closed** *Sun, Mon,
Aug & Christmas. Amex, Diners, Mastercard, Visa.*

Duquesnoy   ★★
Map B1.17

| Tel 47 05 96 78   Fax 44 18 90 57 | R |

6 ave Bosquet 75007   **M⁰ Ecole Militaire**
Seats 45   Meal for 2 approx 1100F

Jean-Paul Duquesnoy prepares haute cuisine dishes for a smart,
civilised clientele in his handsomely decorated, light wood-
panelled restaurant just south of Pont d'Alma. His skill, finesse and
light touch are evident throughout exceptionally enticing menus:
*soupe crémeuse d'haricots tarbais à la truffe noir et crepettes de volaille
de Bresse; bar au vermouth; rouelles d'oignon meunière et duxelle
de champignons; ripopée de boeuf truffé au vin de Graves, quenelles
de moelle et pommes soufflées* and for dessert a light caramelised pear
millefeuille with walnuts. Choosing is a delightful, but difficult
task, and Jean-Paul will do it for you if you (and all at your table)
order the *menu dégustation* of four specialities served in small
portions. The 250F lunchtime menu provides great value for

money. Classic wines accompany the classic food. Françoise
Duquesnoy is a charming and knowledgable hostess. Set menus:
L 250F, L & D 450F/550F (*dégustation*). *L 12-2 D 8-10.*
Closed *L Sat, all Sun, 1st 2 wks Aug, 25 Dec, 1 Jan. Amex,
Mastercard, Visa.*

Ecaille et Plume   Map B1.18

| Tel 45 55 06 72   Fax 45 51 38 35 | R |

25 rue Duvivier 75007   **Mᵒ Ecole Militaire**
Seats 45   Meal for 2 approx 500F

In a romantic setting of soft lights, candles and hunting scenes,
Marie Naël presents a seductive menu of classical dishes based
on the freshest seasonal produce. That means plenty of fish
in summer (*tournedos de lotte au fumet de Bordeaux, polenta
frite*; roast scallops and watercress; and some unusual shellfish –
razor shells, limpets.). There's game in winter, including wild
duck, wild boar, hare and grouse flambéed in whisky. Among the
menu options is the menu club at 150F: you can join the club
after just one meal. Throughout the year look out for special
tasting menus with various themes and national cuisines. Set
menus: L & D 150F, 220F. *L 12-3 D 7.30-11.* **Closed** *L Sat, all
Sun & Aug. Mastercard, Visa.*

Eiffel Park Hotel   Map B1.19

| Tel 45 55 10 01   Fax 47 05 28 68 | H |

17bis rue Amélie 75007   **Mᵒ Latour-Maubourg**
Rooms 36   Double from 780F

Bright, comfortable hotel opened in 1989, possessing well-
appointed modern bedrooms with satellite TV, safe, mini-bar and
hairdryer. There's a great view from the top-floor sun-terrace.
Meeting rooms for up to 30; bar; reading room. *Amex, Diners,
Mastercard, Visa.*

Elysées Maubourg   Map B1.20

| Tel 45 56 10 78   Fax 47 05 65 08 | H |

35 bd de Latour-Maubourg 75007   **Mᵒ Latour-Maubourg**
Rooms 30   Double from 640F

A hotel with stylish, up-to-date bedrooms featuring quality
furnishings. Intimate bar, indoor garden, a meeting room for 15
people and the unusual (for Paris) feature of a sauna in the
basement. Parking des Invalides is 300 metres away. *Amex, Diners,
Mastercard, Visa.*

La Ferme Saint-Simon   ★   Map C1.21

| Tel 45 48 35 74   Fax 40 49 07 31 | R |

6 rue de Saint-Simon 75007   **Mᵒ Rue du Bac**
Seats 90   Meal for 2 approx 700F

A smart, well-respected restaurant in a quiet residential area,
La Ferme comprises cosy dining rooms with a charming, intimate
atmosphere. The menu is thoroughly up-to-date and demonstrates
the chef's creativity and imagination. Dishes include a cold
bouillabaisse set in aspic with a saffron and garlic cream dressing,
fillets of red mullet with saffron and stuffed courgettes, a nage
of sole with mussels and ginger and grilled sea bass with tomato   *See over*

and a basil cream. There are good meat dishes too, as in roast lamb noisettes with stuffed artichokes, a feuilleté of calf's liver with fruit and spices, and a navarin of lamb with broad beans and summer haricots. A speciality is braised knuckle of veal with chanterelle mushrooms and noodles. For dessert, the assortment of fruit tarts needs to be ordered at the beginning of the meal. Set menu: L 165F. *L 12-2 D 7.30-10.15.* **Closed** *L Sat, all Sun & 5-15 Aug. Amex, Diners, Mastercard, Visa.*

Foc-Ly   Map B2.22

| Tel 47 83 27 12 | R |

71 ave de Suffren 75007   **Mᵒ Ségur**
Seats 60   Meal for 2 approx 600F

Specialising in Chinese and Thai cooking, the restaurant has smart lightwood panelling, a comfortable ambience and staff who provide friendly and efficient service. The menu is short and lends a French influence to the cooking with generally mild spicing and the assumption that diners conform to having a starter, main course and dessert. There's a small selection of mostly deep-fried dim sum. Other dishes from a largely simple and uncomplicated selection include delicious *crevettes aux cent fleurs* – giant prawns stuffed with mashed prawns and just a hint of chili, *noix de Saint Jacques à l'aigre douce* – sliced scallops with a mild garlic sauce, and *emincé de canard aux pousses de gingembre et ananas* – tender, lean slices of duck with Japanese pickled ginger and fresh pineapple served in a half pineapple. Relatively inexpensive wine list. Also at 79 Avenue Charles de Gaulle, Neuilly sur Seine. Set menus: L (Sat & Sun only) from 140F D from 140F. *L 12-2 D 7.30-11.* **Closed** *Mon in August & all July. Amex, Diners, Mastercard, Visa.*

Gaya Rive Gauche   Map D1.23

| Tel 45 44 73 73 | R |

44 rue du Bac 75007   **Mᵒ Rue du Bac**
Seats 50 (+10 outside)   Meal for 2 approx 600F

New, sister restaurant to *Gaya Rive Droite* (*qv*) across the river, with whom it shares the successful formula of serving only the best and freshest of fish each day, in simple, uncomplicated fashion. Decor has a nautical flavour with old photos of boats, fishermen and the like around wood-panelled walls. *L 12-2.30 D 7-11.* **Closed** *Sun & 2 weeks Aug. Amex, Mastercard, Visa.*

For a glossary of menu terms see page 293

Grand Hotel de France   Map B2.24

| Tel 47 05 40 49   Fax 45 56 96 78 | H |

102 bd de Latour-Maubourg 75007   **Mᵒ Ecole Militaire**
Rooms 60   Double from 480F

Practical, reasonably priced accommodation with cable TV and mini-bars in a modern (1980s) hotel opposite Invalides and five minutes from the Eiffel Tower. Hotel bar. *Amex, Diners, Mastercard, Visa.*

Les Jardins d'Eiffel

Map B1.25

Tel 47 05 46 21   Fax 45 55 28 08

H

8 rue Amélie 75007   **M° Invalides**
Rooms 80   Double from 860F

A bourgeois building from the beginning of the century has been
turned into a hotel of real comfort and character. There is now
a new wing of 36 bedrooms. Individually decorated, all rooms
have attractive period-style furnishings, neat private bathrooms
and separate wcs, sound-proofing, satellite TV, mini-bars, safes,
direct-dial phones, electric blinds, trouser presses and hairdryers.
New rooms are air-conditioned; rooms with views of the Eiffel
Tower attract a supplement. The hotel also has a sauna. *Amex,
Diners, Mastercard, Visa.*

Jules Verne   ★

Map A1.26

Tel 45 55 61 44   Fax 47 05 29 41

R

2ème Etage Tour Eiffel 75007   **M° Bir Hakeim/Champs de Mars**
Seats 100   Meal for 2 approx 1600F

A private lift transports guests up to the second level of the Eiffel
Tower to this unique setting. The interior decor purposely doesn't
detract from what's outside – everything is black and grey, even
the paintings! Chef Alain Reix specialises in country cooking
(*cuisine du terroir*) with an emphasis on fish and his menus change
in part every two or three days. *Rouget à la provençale*, roast
duck and *entrecote de veau*, *petit pain soufflé de tourteau*, baked
turbot with a foie gras crème, pike-perch with a sauce of smoked
bacon and little calf's trotter pancakes … these and other triumphs
should dispel any inclination towards vertigo. Book several weeks
in advance. Set menus: L 290F (Mon-Fri), D 660F. *L 12.15-2
D 7.15-10. Amex, Diners, Mastercard, Visa.*

Hotel Lenox

Map D1.27

Tel 42 96 10 95   Fax 46 61 52 83

H

9 rue de l'Université 75007   **M° Rue du Bac**
Rooms 34   Double from 680F

The location is a relatively quiet street a short distance from the
heart of St Germain. Sister to the *Lenox* in the 14th (*qv*), it is
virtually identical in its decor and style. There's a spacious and
welcoming entrance hall-cum-lounge and bedrooms have
attractive traditional furnishings complemented by modern
amenities. *Amex, Diners, Mastercard, Visa.*

Londres

Map B1.28

Tel 45 51 63 092   Fax 47 05 28 96

H

1 rue Augereau 75007   **M° Ecole Militaire**
Rooms 30   Double from 580F

A few paces from Champs de Mars and the Eiffel Tower,
a straightforward business and tourist hotel with friendly, helpful
staff. Ten of the cheerful bedrooms have bath/wc, and are at the
back of the hotel, where it's quieter; the rest have shower/wc. All
have satellite TV, mini-bar and hairdryer. *Amex, Diners,
Mastercard, Visa.*

Michel Courtalhac

Map C1.29

Tel 45 55 15 35

R

47 rue de Bourgogne 75007

M° Varenne

Seats 50

Meal for 2 approx 500F

Fresh produce gets simple, careful handling in Michel and Nadine Courtalhac's delightful little beamed, stone-walled restaurant. *Colinot poelé, purée au persil; fricassée de poulet au cresson et au vin jaune; dorade au thym avec pignons et basilic; selle d'agneau roti à l'orientale* and *onglet poelé jus aux herbes* are just a selection of the daily-changing dishes. *Crème brulée avec ses petites madeleines* or a chocolate ganache with coffee sauce are further examples that make this place such an attractive choice. The menu changes every day. Good wines for under 100F. *L 12.30-2.45 D 7.45-10.30. Closed L Sat, all Sun, Aug & 1 wk Christmas. Mastercard, Visa.*

Montalembert

Map D1.30

Tel 45 48 68 11   Fax 42 22 58 19

HR

3 rue Montalembert 75007

M° Rue du Bac

Rooms 56

Double from 1625F

The restored splendour of its 1926 origins incorporates the well-conceived use of many luxurious materials, including marble, leather, wrought iron, cast bronze and a variety of woods. Beyond the entrance the first striking feature is a rug woven to reproduce the handwriting of the Count of Montalembert. Some of the bedrooms have 20's-style furniture, others are in Louis-Philippe style. All are equipped with up-to-the-minute accessories including video recorder (the hotel has a tape library). Bathrooms are particularly luxurious in both look and appointments, with Portuguese marble, chrome and generous towelling and toiletries. There's 24-hour room service. The bar is a popular place for the literary world to meet, and there's an adjoining lounge for quiet relaxation, and a delightful garden patio. Valet parking. *Amex, Diners, Mastercard, Visa.*

Restaurant

Seats 30 (+ 20 outdoor)

Meal for 2 approx 700F

As stylish as the rest of the hotel, with lightwood panelling and black and white photographs. Snacks and more substantial dishes, both traditional and contemporary, are available, but Sunday brunch is what it's best known for. Specialities are *salade d'haricots verts en fond d'artichaut, mini-poireaux et radis; saumon grillé à l'unilatéral, pousses d'épinards en salade; gratin de rhubarbe et fraise.* Set menu: 165F. *Meals noon-10.30pm.*

Le Petit Laurent

Map C2.31

Tel 45 48 79 64   Fax 42 66 68 59

R

38 rue de Varenne 75007

M° Sèvres-Babylone

Seats 35

Meal for 2 approx 600F

In civilised Louis XVI surroundings chef Sylvain Pommier prepares a range of dishes in which classic skills are blended with contemporary touches. Terrine of skate wings with capers and cress, gratin of red mullet with courgettes and tomatoes, a fricassee of calf's sweetbreads and kidneys, and roast rack of lamb with

thyme are typical of his style. Set menus: 175F, 240F. *L 12-2.30
D 7.45-10.15. **Closed** L Sat, all Sun & Aug. Amex, Diners,
Mastercard, Visa.*

Le Récamier   ★

	Map D2.32
Tel 45 48 86 58 Fax 42 22 84 76	**R**

4 rue Récamier 75007   M° Sèvres-Babylone
Seats 80   Meal for 2 approx 800F

A really splendid place for late spring and summer when
Recamier's open-air terrace comes into its own. Extending into
a delightful, pedestrianised cul-de-sac awash with flowers, the
restaurant majors on classics from the Burgundy region such
as beef bourguignon with fresh noodles, and *jambon persillé*.
M Cantegrit, the chef-patron, has been here for 30 years but keeps
abreast of current trends with dishes like skate with mustard
or sole with a champagne sauce and mushroom ravioli. Gratin
dauphinois is a favourite accompaniment, appearing with rack
of lamb, Auvergne-style calf's liver and various steaks. The wine
list is phenomenal – particularly strong in Bordeaux and
champagne. *L 12-2.30 D 7.45-10.30. **Closed** Sun, Public Holidays.
Amex, Diners, Mastercard, Visa.*

Résidence Latour-Maubourg

	Map B1.33
Tel 47 05 16 16 Fax 47 05 16 14	**H**

150 rue de Grenelle 75007   M° Latour-Maubourg
Rooms 10   Double from 650F

Directly across from Hotel des Invalides between Rue Fabert and
Boulevard de Latour Maubourg, the accommodation here
is comfortable and homely. Brand new bathrooms have been
installed on the second floor. Rear rooms offer a greater degree
of tranquillity than those at the front, though the latter are double-
glazed. They are also brighter and more cheerful. Each room has
a TV, two phone lines for the use of lap-tops and fax machines,
and bathrooms have hairdryers. At the rear of the ground floor
is a lounge which in the morning becomes an informal breakfast
room – breakfast is included in the room price. *Mastercard, Visa.*

Saint Germain

	Map C2.34
Tel 45 48 62 92 Fax 45 48 26 89	**H**

88 rue du Bac 75007   M° Rue du Bac
Rooms 29   Double from 630F

An old mansion whose conversion to a hotel has not spoilt its
original character. Beams, moulded ceilings, stone walls and
period furniture all make their contribution, in the individually
and very attractively appointed bedrooms as well as in elegant day
rooms. *Amex, Mastercard, Visa.*

Saxe-Résidence

	Map B2.35
Tel 47 83 98 28 Fax 47 83 85 47	**H**

9 villa Saxe 75007   M° Ségur
Rooms 52   Double from 625F

A particularly peaceful hotel with a neat, functional, 50s look, set
in a residential area by Invalides and the Ecole Militaire. Private   *See over*

facilities, mini-bar, safe, cable TV and direct-dial phones in all
rooms. Resident's bar, meeting room and lounge. Private parking
(free) for five cars. *Amex, Mastercard, Visa.*

Solférino   Map C1.36

| Tel 47 05 85 54   Fax 45 55 51 16 | H |

91 rue de Lille 75007   **M° Solférino**
Rooms 32   Double from 510F

Purpose-built for the Gare d'Orsay (now the Musée d'Orsay) 150
years ago, the Solférino has a quiet, old-fashioned charm,
highlighted by bright bedrooms decorated in creamy pastel shades
and flowery wallpaper, a delightful and very homely little lounge
and a cheerful sky-lit breakfast room. TVs are available on request.
Closed 23 Dec-4 Jan. Mastercard, Visa.

Splendid   Map B2.37

| Tel 45 51 24 77   Fax 44 18 94 60 | H |

29 ave de Tourville/1 ave Duquesne 75007   **M° Ecole Militaire**
Rooms 48   Double from 780F

A fine Haussmann building whose triangular construction affords
views of the Eiffel Tower from all its bedrooms. A few have
balconies and the three small suites have private telephone lines.
Decor is smartly contemporary with a welcoming mirror-lined
reception, very stylish bar and bright, well-decorated bedrooms.
All rooms have satellite TV, mini-bar, safe and hairdryer. *Amex,
Diners, Mastercard, Visa.*

Hotel de Suède   Map C2.38

| Tel 47 05 00 08   Fax 47 05 69 27 | H |

31 rue Vaneau 75007   **M° Varenne**
Rooms 41   Double from 630F

Located south of the Musée d'Orsay with rear rooms overlooking
gardens, the hotel has a very conservative and traditional air.
Panelled public areas are decorated in an elegantly restrained
manner and bedrooms, though not large, have a stylish decor with
pale grey velour-upholstered armchairs and Directoire-style
furniture. TVs and hairdryers are available on request; direct-dial
phones in all rooms. There's a pleasant little interior
courtyard/garden where breakfast or tea may be taken. *Amex,
Mastercard, Visa.*

Tan Dinh   Map C1.39

| Tel 45 44 04 84 | R |

60 rue de Verneuil 75007   **M° Rue du Bac**
Seats 60   Meal for 2 approx 600F

Robert Vifian introduced Paris to the delights of Vietnamese
cooking, and his pastel-toned restaurant continues to produce
traditional Vietnamese dishes with an innovative slant; there's
an exceptional wine list to boot. Mung bean cream with crab won
tons, steamed raviolis with smoked goose, sea bream with ginger,
sautéed lamb with spices and coconut and skewered veal with
cardamom are typical of the MSG-free delights on the menu.
*L 12-2 D 7.30-11. Closed Sun, Aug, some Public Holidays.
No credit cards.*

Thoumieux
Map B1.40
R

| Tel 47 05 49 75   Fax 47 05 36 96 |

79 rue St-Dominique 75007
Seats 120

M⁰ Latour-Maubourg
Meal for 2 approx 400F

The robust dishes of the South-West are among the most popular
orders at this roomy, relaxed restaurant, which has been run
by three generations of the same family since 1922. *Cassoulet,
confit de canard* and foie gras head the list, and other choices
include sole meunière, tuna steak on a bed of leeks and tomato,
and familiar bistro fare (*assiette de crudités, artichaut vinaigrette,
soupe de poissons*, calf's kidneys with a mustard sauce, steaks).
Thoumieux is also a hotel with 10 modern bedrooms (600F
double). Set menu: 57F. *L 12-3.30 D 6.45-12. Sun meals 12-12.
Closed 1 May. Mastercard, Visa.*

Note: from April 16 1995 the
international dialling code 010 changes to 00

Le Tourville
Map B2.41
H

| Tel 47 05 62 62   Fax 47 05 43 90 |

16 ave de Tourville 75007
Rooms 30

M⁰ Ecole Militaire
Double from 760F

A short distance from Les Invalides, the hotel is ideally located for
visiting some of the more important Parisian sights. Behind its
classical facade the lounge and bar have a refined, stylish decor and
bedrooms are warmly and tastefully decorated in soft pastels.
Furnishings are a mix of period and modern. Best of the
accommodation are four rooms with private terraces (1390F) and
three junior suites with whirlpool baths (1990F). *Amex, Diners,
Mastercard, Visa.*

Hotel de l'Université
Map D1.42
H

| Tel 42 61 09 39   Fax 42 60 40 84 |

22 rue de l'Université 75007
Rooms 27

M⁰ Rue du Bac
Double from 800F

17th-century appeal lives on in the shape of beams, antiques and
traditional fabrics retaining much of the charm of the private
residence which it once was. Accommodation, though not
spacious, is comfortable and ranges from singles with shower only
(400F) to top-floor apartments with terraces (triple 1500F).
Mastercard, Visa.

Hotel de Varenne
Map C1.43
H

| Tel 45 51 45 55   Fax 45 51 86 63 |

44 rue de Bourgogne 75007
Rooms 24

M⁰ Varenne
Double from 470F

Recently refurbished in "le style anglais", the Varenne is situated
in an area of government offices just a few paces from Les
Invalides. Some bedrooms face the street (these are double-glazed)
while the rest look over a flowery courtyard where breakfast
is served in the summer. *Amex, Mastercard, Visa.*

Vin Sur Vin

Map B1.44

Tel 47 05 14 20

R

20 rue de Montessuy 75007

M° Alma Marceau

Seats 20

Meal for 2 approx 700F

The menu at this exclusive little restaurant is based round the
wine list, whose 400 wines have been selected by owner Patrice
Vidal. Joachim Grafford, the chef, has been here for 4 years.
Having previously worked at *L'Arpège* (*qv*), his menus are
recherché and imaginative: for instance, a salad of scallops and
sweet peppers, braised endive with foie gras, monkfish with lime
butter, fillet of beef with braised lettuce and cauliflower and calf's
liver with beetroot. *L 12-2 D 8-10.* **Closed** *L Sat & Mon, all Sun,
23 Dec-2 Jan, 2 wks Aug. Mastercard, Visa.*

CHAMPAGNE
FONDÉE EN 1827

G.H. MUMM & C.ᴵᴱ
REIMS~FRANCE

8th Arrondissement
Places of Interest

Champs Elysées
Place de la Concorde – Obélisque, M° Concorde
Place de la Madeleine
Arc de Triomphe, 43 80 31 31, M° Charles de Gaulle-Etoile
Grand Palais, 40 74 80 00, M° Champs-Elysées-Clemenceau
   Palais de la Découverte
Petit Palais, 42 65 12 73, M° Champs-Elysées-Clemenceau
St Augustin, M° St Augustin
Parc Monceau, M° Monceau
Musée Cernuschi, 45 63 50 75, M° Villiers/Monceau
Musée Nissim de Camondo, 45 63 26 32, M° Villiers/Monceau
Galérie Nationale du Jeu de Paume, 42 60 69 69,
   M° Concorde/Tuileries
Pont Alexandre III, M° Invalides/Champs-Elysées-
Clemenceau/Concorde
Palais de La Découverte, 40 74 80 00, M° Franklin D Roosevelt

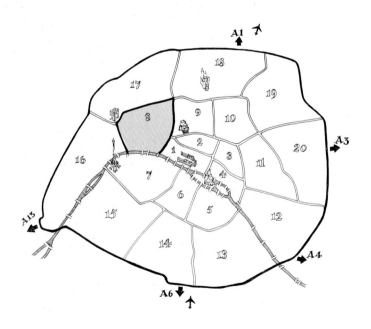

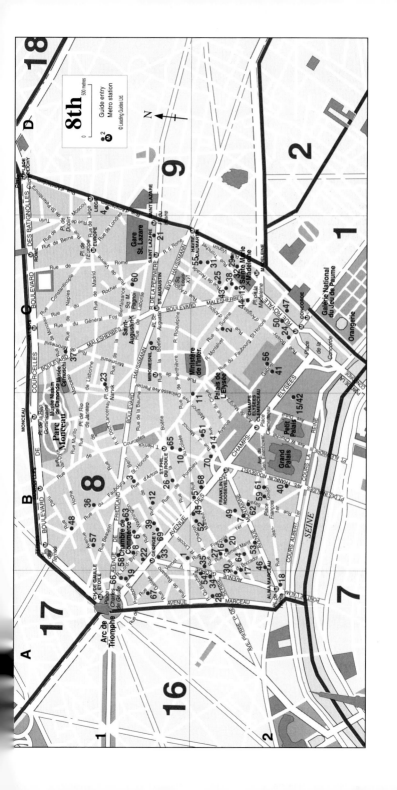

Al Ajami

Map B1.1

Tel 43 59 55 37   Fax 42 56 60 08 **R**

58 rue François 1er 75008 **Mᵒ George V**
Seats 80 (+ 20 outdoor) Meal for 2 approx 550F

Well-established Lebanese restaurant with sister establishments
in Beirut and Riyadh. Refined art deco-style dining room with
oriental touches. Menu of authentic Lebanese dishes plus the
occasional French offering. Set L 105F (weekdays) Set L &
D 125F & 155F. *Meals noon-midnight. Amex, Diners,
Mastercard, Visa.*

Alison

Map C2.2

Tel 42 65 54 00   Fax 42 65 08 17 **H**

21 rue Surène 75008 **Mᵒ Madeleine**
Rooms 35 Double from 550F

Between the Madeleine and the Elysée Palace, near all the smart
shops of the Faubourg Saint Honoré, the Alison provides modest
comfort in the heart of the city. Rooms all have safes.
No restaurant but a stone-vaulted breakfast room-cum-lounge
in the basement. *Amex, Diners, Mastercard, Visa.*

Aux Amis du Beaujolais

Map B1.3

Tel 45 63 92 21   Fax 45 62 70 01 **R**

28 rue d'Artois 75008 **Mᵒ George V/St Philippe-du-Roule**
Seats 95 Meal for 2 approx 400F

In the same family since 1924, this modest bistro, done out in a
cheerful shade of yellow, on the corner of the Rue d'Artois and the
Rue du Berri, can be relied on for some sound, unpretentious
cooking. Bernard Picolet credits his grandmother for the *cuisine
familiale* that features rillettes, earthy terrines and the likes
of celery rémoulade and *rosette du Beaujolais* amongst the starters
and leg of lamb with two kinds of beans, partridge braised with
cabbage and steak *frites* as main dishes on the daily changing
menu. Daily specials are more of a fixture with Monday bringing
a hearty *pot au feu* (complete with large piece of marrowbone),
Tuesday a *boeuf bourguignon* (something of a speciality) and
Wednesday a *noix de veau aux épinards*. Beaujolais, not surprisingly,
dominates the list of wines with the Chénas and Moulin à Vent
arriving by cask to be bottled at the restaurant. Gents have an old-
fashioned hole-in-the-floor loo, ladies are more comfortably
accommodated. *L 12-3 D 6.30-9. **Closed** Sun, 1 week Summer &
1 week Christmas. Mastercard, Visa.*

Androuët

Map D1.4

Tel 48 74 26 93   Fax 49 95 02 54 **R**

41 rue d'Amsterdam 75008 **Mᵒ Gare St-Lazare**
Seats 100 Meal for 2 approx 650F

One of the famous Parisian fromageries, founded in 1909,
Androuët is now owned by Air France. In the restaurant above
the shop, cheese-lovers can indulge to the full in the likes
of *croquette de Camembert*, fillet of beef with Roquefort (both
specialities), *ravioles de chèvre frais* and fillet of lamb with oyster
mushrooms and a *boulette d'Avesnes* cheese sauce. Asterisks on the

menu indicates those few dishes (apart from desserts) that do not involve cheese in one way or another. When it comes to choosing from the splendid cheese tray a good plan is to leave the selection to the knowledgeable waiters who will even advise on the order in which they should be eaten. Set L 165F Set L & D 230F/250F Set D 195F. *L 12-2.30 D 7-10.15.* **Closed** *Sun. Amex, Diners, Mastercard, Visa.*

L'Appart
Map B2.5

Tel 53 75 16 34   **R**

9 rue du Colisée 75008   **M⁰ Franklin D Roosevelt**
Seats 125   Meal for 2 approx 400F

Busy, trendy restaurant on two floors just off the Champs Elysées. Waitresses in smart black suits offer swift service at closely packed tables, or one can eat at the bar downstairs (where there are also tables), from a reasonably priced carte: lentil salad with sherry vinegar, seafood bisque with a little cream and a horseradish quenelle, terrine of rabbit, roast salmon on a bed of cabbage and bacon, entrecote with *pommes Anna*, confit of duck leg. The hot apple flan is large and square and needs to be ordered at the beginning of the meal; other desserts include *baba au rhum*, fruit soup, *poire craquante au chocolat* perfumed with ginger and ice creams and sorbets. Shortish wine list plus lots of cocktails. Sunday lunchtime brings a special 'brunch' menu. Set L 100F & 140F. *L 12-1.30 D 7.30-12.* **Closed** *24 Dec. Amex, Mastercard, Visa.*

Atala
Map B1.6

Tel 45 62 01 62   Fax 42 25 66 38   **H**

10 rue Chateaubriand 75008   **M⁰ George V**
Rooms 50   Double from 950F

The spacious, wood-panelled, marble-floored lobby opens on to a pretty courtyard garden that is the ideal spot for summer breakfasts. Pleasant bedrooms in art deco style all have mini-bars, direct-dial phones and satellite TV and some have balconies. Good central location near the Arc de Triomphe. Private parking for three cars. *Amex, Diners, Mastercard, Visa.*

L'Avenue
Map B2.7

Tel 40 70 14 91   Fax 49 52 08 27   **R**

41 ave Montaigne 75008   **M⁰ Alma-Marceau**
Seats 150   Meal for 2 approx 700F

Haute couture meets haute cuisine at this art deco restaurant much favoured by the fashion world – Dior, Céline and Christian Lacroix are nearby. Actually it's more brasserie style than haute cuisine but in the modish *meridional* style with the likes of tomato, mozzarella and basil salad, snail risotto with pistou, *bouillabaisse de l'Estaque,* calf's liver with parmesan-gratinated polenta, salt pork with green Puy lentils, roast salmon with choucroute and celery, and chicken with tarragon cream sauce. A section of the menu headed *Sur le Pouce* offers quick snacks such as a club sandwich, gravlax and their own salad L'Avenue. Good wines from *Taillevent's* wine shop. *L 12-2.30 D 7-12.30am.* **Closed** *25 Dec. Amex, Mastercard, Visa.*

Balzac
Map B1.8

| Tel 45 61 97 22   Fax 42 25 24 82 | **H** |

6 rue Balzac 75008   **Mº George V**
Rooms 70   Double from 1830F

Although only just off the bustling Champs-Elysées the Balzac
(named, as is the street, after the 19th-century writer) is a haven
of peace and luxury. Built for an aristocrat in 1910, this Belle
Epoque townhouse was completely renovated in 1985. Oil
paintings and antique tapestries grace elegant public areas while
air-conditioning, double-glazing, marble bathrooms and twin
telephone lines add comfort and convenience to the bedrooms,
of which 14 are either 'junior' or 'full' suites. Discreet, attentive
service extends to a 24hr room menu and valet parking. *Amex,
Diners, Mastercard, Visa.*

For a glossary of menu terms see page 293

Le Bistrot du Sommelier
Map C1.9

| Tel 42 65 24 85 | **R** |

97 bd Haussmann 75008   **Mº St Augustin**
Seats 50   Meal for 2 approx 800F

The owner, Philippe Faure-Brac, won awards for best sommelier
in France in 1988 and 'World's Best Sommelier' in 1992. The
wine list is phenomenal, with 900 bottles and no less than 40
wines available by the glass. The decor is themed strongly on wine
and the menu, which comes with English translation, is unfussy,
short and modern. Starters include a terrine of sweetbreads and
morel mushrooms, ham from the Savoie on a green bean and nut
salad, and smoked fish with paprika cream and Russian pancakes.
Among the main dishes are monkfish with aubergines, Bresse
chicken with morels in *vin jaune* from the Jura (with its particular
nutty fragrance) and veal kidneys with pine nuts and smoked
bacon. There's a good selection of cheeses to complement the
wines and sweets include a Sommelier's selection and a Valrhona
chocolate fondant with preserved oranges. *L 12-2.30 D 7.30-11.
Closed Sat, Sun, Aug, 25 Dec-1 Jan. Amex, Mastercard, Visa.*

Le Boeuf sur le Toit
Map B1.10

| Tel 43 59 83 80   Fax 45 63 45 40 | **R** |

34 rue du Colisée 75008   **Mº St Philippe-du-Roule**
Seats 250   Meal for 2 approx 500F

Part of the excellent *Flo* group of traditional Parisian brasseries,
this one in 1920s style is full of mirrors, plants and bustling
waiters. Oysters and other shellfish are a speciality but there
is much else besides: rillettes of fresh and smoked salmon,
andovillettes, melon with smoked ham, blinis with crème fraiche,
salad of duck foie gras, saddle of lamb with tarragon, steak tartare
with matchstick potatoes, rump steak with maitre d'hotel butter,
brill with butter sauce. Set L 109F (inc wine) Set D 185F & 109F
(from 10pm). *Meals noon-2am. **Closed** D 24 Dec. Amex, Diners,
Mastercard, Visa.*

Le Bristol

Map B2.11

Tel 42 66 91 45   Fax 42 66 34 16   **HR**

112 rue du Faubourg St Honoré 75008   **M⁰ Miromesnil**
Rooms 200   Double from 2950F

One of the most expensive but also most luxurious and exclusive
of Paris hotels. Refined day-rooms blend genuine antiques with
fine reproduction pieces and tapestry wall hangings. A peaceful
garden is an unexpected pleasure in a town-centre hotel, as are
views across the rooftops of Paris from the swimming pool. Most
rooms and suites are decorated and furnished in traditional style
but a few, in a wing that was formerly a Carmelite convent, are
more modern in style. Well-drilled staff provide impeccable
service. Good business facilities, a direct link to the Bourse and
several conference rooms. Valet parking. *Amex, Diners,
Mastercard, Visa.*

Restaurant   ★
Seats 60   Meal for 2 approx 1500F

The location of the restaurant changes between summer and
winter, that for the latter being a beautiful circular dining room
with wood-panelling from floor to ceiling, where four paintings
depicting the four seasons look down on small round tables with
Louis XV armchairs and bouquets of flowers; there are several
chandeliers and a large Flemish tapisserie at the end of the room.
Chef Emile Tabourdiau offers plenty of choice with the 330F
menu indicating which dishes can be served swiftly, the chef's
suggested menu of the day priced for either two or three
significant courses (and with some suggested wines) and a short list
of dishes based on the day's market, all in addition to the à la carte.
Whole lobster salad prepared at the table, sea bream caramelised
with honey, truffle omelette, *tete de veau en ravigote à l'huile
de noix*, roast Barbary duck perfumed with ginger, veal kidneys
flambé à la crème de foie gras moutardée and *cote de boeuf grillée* show
the range. Excellent wine list. Set L & D 330F & 450F/620F. *L 12-
2.30 D 7-10.30.*

Hotel California

Map B1.12

Tel 43 59 93 00   Fax 45 61 03 62   **H**

16 rue de Berri 75008   **M⁰ George V**
Rooms 173   Double from 1800F

In a quiet street just off the Champs Elysées, the California is a
hotel with its own distinct personality, part of a small family run
group. Some 3000 original paintings are scattered throughout the
bedrooms and public areas and there's a small art gallery dedicated
to encouraging young artists. Dating from the 1920s, but totally
refurbished a few years ago, the light, airy lobby boasts chandeliers
and rug-strewn marble floors and the leather-upholstered piano
bar, a collection of model boats, another of owner Monsieur
Leroy's interests. Air-conditioned throughout, the individually
decorated bedrooms include a number of full suites, some arranged
for business travellers with a meeting room, others for leisure and
tourists with extra large TVs and one even with a piano. All
rooms come with little extras like sweets from Cambrai (the
family's home town). Bathrooms are marble, a few with shower   *See over*

& wc only. Room service is 24hrs, there is a staffed business
centre, fitness room and valet parking. *Amex, Diners,
Mastercard, Visa.*

Caviar Kaspia   Map C2.13
Tel 42 65 33 52   Fax 42 66 60 11   **R**
17 place de la Madeleine 75008   **Mᵒ Madeleine**

Elegantly informal spot where up-market folk come to nibble
smoked fish and caviar. It's possible to construct a three-course
meal – bortsch before a crab and prawn salad perhaps, with cheese
or pastries to follow – but by no means necessary. Drink iced
vodka or champagne. Above a shop on the ground floor from
where most things that appear on the menu upstairs can be taken
away. *Meals noon-midnight.* **Closed** *Sun. Amex, Diners,
Mastercard, Visa.*

Centre-Ville Matignan   Map B2.14
Tel 42 25 73 01   Fax 42 56 01 39   **H**
3 rue de Ponthieu 75008   **Mᵒ Franklin D Roosevelt**
Rooms 23   Double from 690F

Large scenic murals above the bedheads feature in rooms at this
stylish, centrally located hotel. Up-to-date equipment includes
individually controllable air-conditioning, satellite TV, room safe
and Minitel terminals in each room. A sister hotel near the Arc
de Triomphe (*Centre-Ville Etoile* Tel 43 80 56 18) is very similar
in style with identical prices. *Amex, Diners, Mastercard, Visa.*

Le Cercle Ledoyen   Map B2.15
Tel 47 42 76 02   Fax 47 42 55 01   **R**
carré des Champs Elysées 75008   **Mᵒ Champs-Elysées-Clemenceau**
Seats 80 (+80 outdoor)   Meal for 2 approx 600F

The second restaurant of the two-starred *Ledoyen* (*qv*) and housed
in the same delightful pavilion near the Petit Palais. Here the
decor features a pale, bird's-eye-view map of Paris painted on walls
and ceilings within blond wood-panelling of the same shade. The
cooking and the menu could not be more straightforward with
starters – langoustine consommé, fricassee of wild mushrooms,
oysters – all at 60F, mains – sole meunière, poached haddock with
lemon butter, navarin of lamb, Angus rump steak with shallots –
all 100F and desserts such as *tarte glacée au chocolat*, tiramisu,
caramel mousse with a compote of pears and pancake with
creamed chestnut each priced at 50F, all adding up to excellent
value for money; booking is advisable. *L 12-2 D 7-11.30.*
Closed *Sun. Amex, Diners, Mastercard, Visa.*

Chez André   Map B2.16
Tel 47 20 59 57   Fax 47 20 18 82   **R**
12 rue Marbeuf 75008   **Mᵒ Alma-Marceau**
Seats 100   Meal for 2 approx 500F

Useful eaterie just off the Champs Elysées – about halfway down.
Bistro decor with paper cloths but linen napkins and swift
friendly service. Specialities include rump steak with mustard
sauce, *tete de veau sauce ravigote*, half a crispy roast chicken and
steak tartare plus seafood including various *plateaux de fruits de mer*

(from 119F to 495F). There are also dishes of the day of which some are regulars such as *pot au feu* on Saturdays and *bouillabaisse* on Fridays. Several wines are available by the glass or carafe and about half the shortish list also come in half bottles. *Meals noon-1am. Amex, Diners, Mastercard, Visa.*

Chez Edgard   Map A2.17

| Tel 47 20 51 15   Fax 47 23 94 29 | R |

4 rue Marbeuf 75008   **Mᵒ Alma-Marceau**
Seats 180 (+40 terrace)   Meal for 2 approx 600F

A lively atmosphere pervades this attractive art deco-styled restaurant. The menu is of familiar, classic starters and grills with a quite lengthy specials section which changes daily. The latter includes fish and shellfish dishes typical of South-West France – grilled tuna with tomato and basil, *filets de rougets à l'escabèche*, mackerel with white wine sauce – as well as the likes of veal kidneys with mustard, *tete de veau sauce ravigote* and duck breast with green peppercorn sauce. The day's desserts might include a gratin of raspberries and a caramelised pear tart to supplement such straightforward items as the crème caramel, fruit salad and chocolate mousse to be found on the main menu. *L 12-3 D 7.30-12.30.* **Closed** *Sun & 1st 2 weeks Aug. Amex, Diners, Mastercard, Visa.*

Chez Francis   Map A2.18

| Tel 47 20 86 83   Fax 47 20 43 26 | R |

7 place de l'Alma 75008   **Mᵒ Alma-Marceau**
Seats 160 (+180 outside)   Meal for 2 approx 600F

Immortalised as the setting for a scene in the play 'The Mad Woman of Chaillot' by Jean Giraudoux, this brasserie/restaurant by the Pont d'Alma has been a fashionable meeting place for over a century. From the terrace one can admire the Eiffel Tower, from within, oneself – reflected in the ornately framed amber mirrors, alongside glittering chandeliers. Cooking is uncomplicated with seafood a speciality (the *plateau de fruits de mer* is formidable), which makes for a good *soupe de poissons*. Also simple grills, roast lamb with garlic, steak tartare and the like. Amongst the wines one white (Muscadet) and one red (Bordeaux) are served by the glass. Set meal 180F. *Meals noon-1am. Amex, Diners, Mastercard, Visa.*

Chiberta   ★

| Tel 45 63 77 90   Fax 45 62 85 08 | R |

3 rue Arsène-Houssaye 75008   **Mᵒ Etoile**
Seats 75   Meal for 2 approx 650F

Splendid flower arrangements are a bright spot in the modern, minimalist decor of this restaurant near the Arc de Triomphe. Chef Philippe de Silva's cooking is of a very high order with dishes that are well thought-out, superbly constructed and beautifully presented. There is an underlying complexity to what, on paper, appears relatively simple and straightforward. His art is in successful marriages of ingredients in perfect balance. To begin one can choose from lobster salad with fresh herbs, ravioli filled with truffles and parsley, or fresh duck foie gras. Main dishes will include fish such as bass braised with caviar and   *See over* champagne and John Dory steamed with celery and ginger. Meat dishes could be duck roasted with spices and beef *à la ficelle* with chives and tarragon. Finish with desserts such as *millefeuille à la vanille, vacherin au Grand Marnier* and a chocolate tart with acacia honey ice cream. Good selection of red Bordeaux. Three wines are now available by the glass – whites from Burgundy and Grave and a red from the Médoc. Set L & D 290F. *L 12-2.30 D 7.30-11. Closed Sat, Sun, Public Holidays, Aug & 25 Dec-1 Jan. Amex, Diners, Mastercard, Visa.*

Claridge-Bellman   Map B2.20

| Tel 47 23 54 42   Fax 47 23 08 84 | **H** |

37 rue François 1er 75008   **M⁰ Franklin D Roosevelt**
Rooms 42   Double from 1420F

A small hotel of considerable charm in the quarter of Paris favoured by leading couturiers and perfume houses. Public areas include a panelled reception, cosy bar and sitting room with tapestry covering one wall. Characterful bedrooms – an antique here, chandelier there or old marble fireplace – all come with air-conditioning and mini-bars along with other modern comforts. Room service from 7am-9pm. *Amex, Diners, Mastercard, Visa.*

Concorde Saint-Lazare   Map C1.21

| Tel 40 08 44 44   Fax 42 93 01 20 | **H** |

108 rue Saint-Lazare 75008   **M⁰ Gare St-Lazare**
Rooms 300   Double from 1160F

Splendid old railway hotel built by Gustave Eiffel in the 1880s. The impressive lobby (with plenty of button-backed leather seating) is three storeys high and has been listed as a national monument. Most bedrooms have fairly recently been refurbished in shades of pink or blue. All the usual modern comforts including both cable and satellite TV. About half the rooms are air-conditioned. 24hr room service. Valet parking. *Amex, Diners, Mastercard, Visa.*

Copenhague   Map B1.22

| Tel 44 13 86 26   Fax 42 25 83 10 | **R** |

142 ave des Champs-Elysées 75008   **M⁰ Etoile/George V**
Seats 80   Meal for 2 approx 850F

Scandinavian restaurant on the first floor of the *Maison du Danemark* – look out for the two huge Danish flags – in the Champs Elysées. One section of the menu is described as an *Hommage au Saumon Nordique* with the fish coming smoked, marinated, hot with spinach and mushrooms and *unilatéral.* Set menus include the 'Danish Table' (for 2 people) at 590F and the menu of the day at 240F which includes a glass of aquavit and another of draught Carlsberg. Offerings are by no means exclusively Nordic with other dishes including the likes of fish terrine with watercress, lobster salad with herbs and roast turbot with a devilled sauce. Good selection of Chablis and Bordeaux. On the ground floor, next to a shop selling Danish specialities and filled baguettes to take away, is the simpler **Flora Danica** with unclothed tables and a less expensive menu in similar style to that above. *L 12-2.30 D 7.15-10.30. Closed Sun, Public Holidays, 1 wk Jan & all Aug. Amex, Diners, Mastercard, Visa.*

Le Crétois
Map C1.23

Tel 45 63 34 17   **R**

19 rue Treilhard 75008   M° Miromesnil
Seats 45 (+20 outside)   Meal for 2 approx 370F

Small, very modest bar-bistro with 1950s-style decor and a shabby Greek mural left over, along with the name, from a former proprietor. It's now run by a mother and son team who, in just over a year, have local business folk queueing up for their simple blackboard lunch menu. The likes of warm leeks with raspberry vinaigrette, *saucisse seche d'Auvergne, andouillette*, cassoulet of snails, skirt of beef with shallots, and herring fillets with *pommes à l'huile* are washed down with a choice of some 17 wines, which include most of the *crus Beaujolais*, all available by the glass as well as the bottle. Throughout the day there is a short list of *tartines* (various things on toast – ham, cheese, rillettes etc) and a lunchtime hot dish like a potato galette with confit of duck served at the bar. Cheerful, friendly atmosphere. *Open 7am-6.30pm. (L 12-3.30).* **Closed** *Sat & Sun. Amex, Visa.*

Hotel de Crillon
Map C2.24

Tel 44 71 15 00   Fax 44 71 15 02   **HR**

10 place de la Concorde 75008   M° Concorde
Rooms 163   Double from 3100F

Each capital has its favourite and most reputable *palace*. The Hotel de Crillon, owned by the Taittinger family, maintains the tradition of quality that built the hotel's reputation. The central marble hall has intimate proportions, an open fire and private desks for checking in and out. A history of customers is kept, retaining personal preferences and tastes. From the hall, a few steps lead to the *grand salon d'honneur* looking out on to the patio used as a summer restaurant and *salon de thé* with harp music. Facing the Place de la Concorde, on the southern side of the *salon d'honneur*, is the **Ambassadeurs** restaurant. Different in style and feel, the hotel's second bar and the restaurant **l'Obélisque** have low ceilings and a clubby atmosphere of panelled walls. The hotel's first floor is dedicated to conferences and receptions with a series of linked historic rooms: *salon Marie-Antoinette* with its delightful terrace, *salon des Aigles* and *salon des Batailles* all look out on to the famous obelisk. The salons, carefully decorated, have been solemnly restored to their former glory. Air-conditioned and quiet, the bedrooms are traditional in decor. Many are tastefully decorated by Sonia Rykiel. Bedrooms are particularly roomy, equipped with modern comforts like cable television and mini-bar, plus 24hr room service. Most of the beautiful marble bathrooms have separate shower and bath. Small flats on the top floor have private terraces and breathtaking views of Paris's roofs. Fax machines are available in the bedrooms if needed, there are several conference rooms and secretarial services. *Amex, Diners, Mastercard, Visa.*

Les Ambassadeurs   ★★
Tel 44 71 16 16
Seats 60   Meal for 2 approx 1500F

The decor in this most magnificent of dining rooms radiates refinement – chequered floors, gilded mirrors, trompe l'oeil skies,   *See over*

painted friezes of cherubs, long, majestic night-blue curtains and
tables sparkling with crystal and silver. The grandiose
surroundings have ideal proportions, making the dining room
comfortable and enjoyable rather than intimidating. In this
remarkable setting, Christian Constant can express his talent
without reserve. The menu will change with every season, but the
precision of execution is sure to remain. Instead of the traditional
miniature *amuse-bouche* systematically offered in this category
of restaurant, a refreshing chilled *soupe de cocos* (white beans) with
miniature diced truffle makes a perfect introduction to the meal.
Faithful to tradition, and inspired by it, the chef proposes re-
invented dishes such as foie gras caramelised with acacia honey and
served with a ragout of chestnuts and Jerusalem artichokes; *noisette*
et cotelette de chevreuil 'Grand Veneur', tagliatelle de céleri truffé;
supreme of bass grilled with a coating of sesame seeds and served
with a semolina *du jus de homard,* and scallops pan-fried with
endive hearts and a bitter orange sauce. Talent reaches its zenith
with desserts like the extraordinary *truffe glacée à la fleur de thym*
frais, ganache au chocolat "Manjari" fondue, when a spoonful
of thyme-scented ice cream – like inhaling a bouquet of fresh
thyme – is the perfect answer to the intoxicating richness of the
chocolate sauce. Such accuracy in taste and preparation make
Christian Constant one of the most talented chefs of his
generation. Complementing all this, the service, never stiff, is a joy
in its attention and kindness. Set L & D 330F & 590F (*dégustation*).
L 12-2.30 D 7-10.30.

L'Obélisque
Tel 44 71 15 15
Seats 50   Meal for 2 approx 750F

Separate entrance on Rue Boissy d'Anglas. The elegant wood-
panelled dining room, with touches of red velvet and Lalique
chandeliers, is extremely busy at lunchtime. Supervised
by Christian Constant, the shortish monthly-changing menu
makes life simple by pricing all the starters at 80F, mains at 150F
and desserts at 55F or one can have all three at the reduced price
of 250F. Described as *cuisine du terroir,* typical dishes might include
a terrine of wild mushrooms and herbs, Jerusalem artichoke soup
with foie gras, quenelles of pike gratinated with parmesan, half
a wild duck with roast figs and spices, and rump steak with
shallots and bone marrow. Finish with the likes of a vanilla crème
brulée or chocolate gateau with almond biscuits. Full meals are not
a requirement in this informal restaurant. For wine-lovers the
menu *Les Coordonnées* associates, for 250F, basil-flavoured fresh
pasta with a glass of Chateau Lafite-Rothschild 1983 or the classic
foie gras with Chateau d'Yquem 1987. Set L & D 250F. *L 12-2.30*
D 7-10.30.

Daniel Météry   Map C2.25
Tel 42 65 53 13   Fax 42 66 53 82   **R**
4 rue de l'Arcade 75008   **M° Madeleine**
Seats 45   Meal for 2 approx 650F

Pretty first-floor restaurant with modern decor in pastel shades
and up-to-date cooking from chef-patron Daniel Météry: salmon
cooked *à l'unilatéral*; farmed pigeon roasted with fennel and baby
onions; honey jelly with a coulis of red fruits. Choose from two

fixed-price menus (180F/240F) or a novel 'surprise' menu in which every dish is made with vinegar – from a selection of 25 different sorts. *L 12-2.15 D 7.30-10.15.* **Closed** *L Sat, Sun & Aug. Amex, Mastercard, Visa.*

Hotel de l'Elysées
Map B1.26

Tel 42 65 29 25   Fax 42 65 64 28   **H**

12 rue des Saussaies 75008 — Mᵒ Miromesnil
Rooms 32 — Double from 680F

Theatres, the Elysées Palace, the Madeleine and shopping in the fashionable Rue du Faubourg St-Honoré are all within a short walk of this moderately priced, traditionally-run hotel decorated in Restoration style. Bedrooms vary in size and decor, and some have four-poster or canopied beds. Two suites under the mansard roof boast air-conditioning. *Amex, Diners, Mastercard, Visa.*

L'Etage Baumann
Map B2.27

Tel 47 20 11 11   Fax 47 23 69 65   **R**

15 rue Marbeuf 75008 — Mᵒ Franklin D Roosevelt
Seats 160 — Meal for 2 approx 600F

Formerly called Baumann Marbeuf, but the change of name has not affected the menu, which continues to offer traditional Alsatian cuisine: *crépine de pied de cochon, foie gras de canard maison, choucroute strasbourgeoise.* Smart brasserie-style establishment with a light airy feel, just off the Champs Elysées. A sister restaurant *Baumann Ternes (qv)* is to be found in the 17th at 64 ave des Ternes (a third is in the city of Strasbourg). *L 12-2.30 D 7.30-12.30am.* **Closed** *12-21 Aug. Amex, Diners, Mastercard, Visa.*

Fakhr el Dine
Map A2.28

Tel 47 23 44 42   Fax 47 27 11 39   **R**

1/3 rue Quentin Bauchart 75008 — Mᵒ Georges V
Seats 50 — Meal for 2 approx 500F

Authentic, classical Lebanese cuisine is served in a large dining-room with wall frescoes. The *carte*, which never changes except for the occasional addition, offers a long list of hot and cold hors d'oeuvre followed by grilled meat or fish, or the *plat du jour.* A typical meal might be *rkakat* (feuilleté filled with cheese) or *sambousek* (meat rissoles with pine nuts), followed by *chawarma* (marinated lamb, chopped and roasted on a brochette). Oriental patisseries make for a sweet ending. Or, if you're feeling adventurous, pick one of the mezze (*mezze extra* for 2 people – 10 dishes 330F). Lebanese wines, alcohols and liqueurs are available. Also at 30 rue de Longchamp 75016 (Tel 47 27 90 00) and 2 Rue Fossés St Bernard 75005 (Tel 46 33 47 70). Set L 95F Set L & D 150F & 160F. *L 12-4 D 8-12. Amex, Diners, Mastercard, Visa.*

Fauchon-Le30
Map C2.32

Tel 47 42 56 58   Fax 42 66 38 95   **R**

30 place de la Madeleine 75008 — Mᵒ Madeleine
Seats 80 (+ 20 outside) — Meal for 2 approx 800F

No visit to Paris is complete without a trip to Fauchon, one of the the greatest food shops in the world, with quite wonderful — *See over* window displays. It also houses several eating places, including a caviar bistrot, café/tea room, Italian trattoria and seafood brasserie. The shop occupies a corner of Place de la Madeleine, and the restaurant (at no 30) is on the first floor looking across to the church. Smartly decorated in pastel peach colours, the Roman villa-style restaurant also has a pretty patio terrace garden, as well as tasteful table settings, and some of the dishes reflect what you may see in the shop windows. Chef Bruno Deligne's *carte* might include a steak of turbot with ragout of French beans and herbs, scallops with a leek fondue and star anise, roast sea-bream with shellfish fumet and braised fennel, *navarin d'agneau* with baby vegetables and *penne* with basil, curried veal sweetbreads with coconut milk and some marvellous desserts/pastries/cakes created by *patissier* Pierre Hermé. Excellent coffee, scrumptious petits fours, ordinary wine list. Set D 240F. *L 12.15-2.30 D 7.30-10.30.* **Closed** *Sun. Amex, Diners, Mastercard, Visa.*

La Ferme St Hubert   Map C2.29
Tel 47 42 79 20   R

21 rue Vignon 75008   Mᵒ **Madeleine**
Seats 44 (+16 outside)   Meal for 2 approx 400F

The cheese shop came first, with a stuffed goat in the window and wonderful smells emanating from within. A few years later Henry Voy opened this little restaurant next door. There's nothing fancy – just paper napkins and squares on closely packed tables and a huge black and white photograph of a couple of cows in a field on one wall. Virtually everything on the menu involves cheese in one way or another from starters like *feuilleté au chèvre* and a light, moist Roquefort soufflé to main dishes such as Camembert croquette on a sherry vinegar-dressed salad, gratin dauphinois with smokey bacon, goat's cheese with haddock and vegetables cooked in a paper parcel, fondue Savoyarde and Swiss raclette – the last two for a minimum of two persons. A few simple desserts such as crème brulée and crème caramel. *L 12-3.30 D 7-11.* **Closed** *Sun. Amex, Mastercard, Visa.*

La Fermette Marbeuf   Map A2.30
Tel 47 20 63 53   Fax 40 70 02 11   R

5 rue Marbeuf 75008   Mᵒ **Franklin D Roosevelt**
Seats 150   Meal for 2 approx 600F

In the smart 'Golden Triangle' area, just off the Champs Elysées, the splendid fin-de-siècle decor is almost, but not quite, as big a draw as the cooking: herb salad with *gésiers de canard confit,* feuilletées (leek and onion compote, lamb brains with coriander), wild duck with banana, red mullet with saffron sauce, grilled sole *beurre blanc*, noisettes of venison with a sweet and sour sauce plus grills and desserts such as *nougat glacé* with hot chocolate and fig tart with cinnamon ice cream. Park in the George V or Rue François 1er car parks and present your ticket at the restaurant for 2 hours free parking. Set L & D 160F. *L 12-3 D 7.30-11.30. Amex, Diners, Mastercard, Visa.*

Hotel Folkestone
Map C2.31

| Tel 42 65 73 09   Fax 42 65 64 09 | **H** |

9 rue Castellane 75008   M⁰ Madeleine
Rooms 50   Double from 800F

Smart little hotel just north of the Madeleine. Bedrooms feature
stylish matching fabrics, cable TV and room safes. Rooms on the
fourth floor are air-conditioned. A comfortable sitting area boasts
a stained-glass panel depicting irises and they are particularly
proud of their buffet breakfast. Room service from 7am-5pm.
Amex, Diners, Mastercard, Visa.

Fouquet's
Map B1.33

| Tel 47 23 70 60   Fax 47 20 08 69 | **R** |

99 ave des Champs-Elysées 75008   M⁰ George V
Seats 300 (+ 50 outdoor)   Meal for 2 approx 800F

Brass plaques commemorating each year's winners of the French
cinema's 'César' awards pave the entrance to this institution (listed
as an historic building in 1988) and remind one that it is still very
much a haunt of the famous. Specialities on the main *carte* include
l'assiette de légumes de printemps et son aïoli, calf's liver grilled
or meunière with a potato gateau and *selle d'agneau en croute
d'épices et d'aromes*. Some of these also appear on the *Menu
Tradition* (250F) along with the likes of medallions of foie gras;
fish soup with rouille and croutons; *quenelles de rascasse, coulis
de homard* and *entrecote grillée maitre d'hotel*. Eat on the verandah
to see and be seen, inside or upstairs in the 'Raimu' room (except
weekends) to soak up the atmosphere. All-French wine list with
an emphasis on the Loire and Bordeaux. A snack menu – *croque
monsieur*, omelettes, quiche Lorraine, *rillettes de canard*, sandwiches,
salads – is served in the bar or on the terrace from 11am to 11pm
with breakfast from 8am. Open every day of the year and with
a branch at La Bastille. Pronounce it 'Fooketts'. Set L & D 250F.
L 12-3 D 7-12.30. Amex, Diners, Mastercard, Visa.

George V
Map A2.34

| Tel 47 23 54 00   Fax 47 20 40 00 | **HR** |

31 ave George V 75008   M⁰ George V
Rooms 298   Double from 2560F

Named after an English king, designed by an American (in the
late 1920s) and run by the international Forte group, the George
V is nevertheless very much a Parisian hotel. Grand high-ceilinged
public rooms boast antique furniture, 17th-century tapestries,
objets d'art and even a Renoir, plus lots of fresh flowers all adding
up to an atmosphere of elegance and luxury. Whether staying
in one of the many sumptuous suites or in an individually designed
bedroom one can expect the same high standards of service.
Numerous private function rooms include the wood-panelled
Louis XIII salon with its massive stone fireplace and the Chantilly
room with cool stylised classical murals. Business travellers can
have fax machines installed in their bedrooms; secretarial and
translation services are available on request, and conference
facilities can cater for up to 600. Valet parking. *Amex, Diners,
Mastercard, Visa.*   *See over*

Les Princes Restaurant   ★
Seats 60   Meal for 2 approx 900F

Chandeliers above widely spaced tables with elegant place settings
and a huge floral centrepiece – this is a truly grand hotel dining
room with a suitably expansive menu. The main *carte*
is supplemented by a limited choice fixed-price menu and,
in season, a special game menu. The George V's 'traditional dishes'
are chicken and foie gras in aspic, *gratin de langoustines 'Mère
Filloux'*, spring chicken from Alsace roasted with truffles under its
skin, medallions of beef fillet in claret sauce with shallots and bone
marrow, and apricot soufflé. Other dishes from the *carte* might
be fresh salmon smoked with lapsang souchong tea, *marquise de sole
et mousseline de saumon sauce crevette et coulis de crabe,* breast
of Challans duck roasted in a salt crust, fine honey nougat with
yoghurt, ice cream and raspberries, and rhubarb tart with
blackcurrant cream. If you want to go the whole hog try the no-
choice tasting menu that consists of eight suitably small-sized
courses. A large terrace can seat up to 70 and when it is in use the
dining room itself is not. Wine list is Bordeaux-oriented and
includes plenty of halves plus a couple by the glass. Valet parking.
Set L & D 240F & 450F (*dégustation*). *L 12-2.30 D 7-10.30.*

Les Georgiques   **Map B2.35**
Tel 40 70 10 49   **R**
36 ave George V 75008   **Mᵒ George V**
Seats 60   Meal for 2 approx 1100F

The chef, Katsumaro Ishimaru, is Japanese but the cooking at this
peaceful, panelled restaurant is exclusively French. Foie gras with
truffle sauce, *bisque d'homard*, filet of beef with a shallot confit,
aiguillettes of duck with green peppercorn sauce, *nougat glacé aux
pistaches* and *marquise au chocolat* indicate Katsumaro's classical
leanings. To appreciate his talent to the full the *Menu d'Agrément*
(served only to an entire table) is worth considering. Careful
cooking is matched by correct service. Set L 180F Set L & D 360F.
L 12-2 D 7-10. **Closed** *L Sat & all Sun.* Amex, Diners,
Mastercard, Visa.

Golden Tulip St-Honoré   **Map B1.36**
Tel 49 53 03 03   Fax 40 75 02 00   **HR**
218 rue du Faubourg St-Honoré 75008   **Mᵒ Etoile/Ternes**
Rooms 72   Double from 1700F

A luxurious and particularly well-appointed hotel, built in 1989,
Dutch-owned and boasting function rooms, swimming pool and
its own car park. The rooms and suites are air-conditioned and
sound-proofed, with mini-bars, marble bathrooms, safes, a keycard
security system, satellite TV and points for fax and Minitel. Room
service is available 24 hours a day. *Amex, Diners, Mastercard, Visa.*

Le Relais Vermeer
Seats 70   Meal for 2 approx 700F

Comfortable, cosseting restaurant where chef Frédéric Lecuisinier's
menu of carefully prepared, well-thought-out dishes comes with
English translations. Scallops with crispy beetroot, beef and
vegetable consommé, spiced prawn fricassee with noodles, calf's
liver *lyonnaise*, roast saddle of lamb with forest mushroooms, tart

tatin and crème brulée show the style. In addition to the *menu du jour*, and at the same price, there's a *menu diététique* for the health-conscious. Short but well-balanced list of French wines. Set L & D 195F. *L 12-3 D 7-11. Closed Sun & 1st 3 weeks Aug.*

Le Grenadin
Map C1.37

Tel 45 63 28 92   Fax 45 61 24 76   R

44 rue de Naples 75008   **M⁰ Villiers**
Seats 40   Meal for 2 approx 650F

Pretty pink and green restaurant full of nooks and crannies and especially appealing when candle-lit at night. Chef-patron Patrick Cirotte's cooking is appealingly individualistic with, sometimes, unusual combinations in light, well-balanced dishes. Carpaccio of foie gras with ceps, mussel soup with fresh beans and tarragon, oysters and alfalfa sprouts with lemon cream, fillet of mullet with fennel and capsicum juice, and a tartlet of Saint Chevrin with black radish and Granny Smith apple are typical. Some 450 wines on the list with an emphasis on the Loire – particularly Sancerre. Set L & D 188F, 248F, 298F & 320F. *L 12-2.30 D 7.30-10.30. Closed Sat (except L Nov-Apr), Sun, 14 Jul, 15 Aug, 4 days Christmas & 4 days New Year. Amex, Mastercard, Visa.*

Hédiard
Map C2.38

Tel 43 12 88 99   Fax 43 12 88 98   R

21 place de la Madeleine 75008   **M⁰ Madeleine**
Seats 80   Meal for 2 approx 550F

Established 140 years ago, Hédiard stands in distinguished company among the luxury food shops of Madeleine. At its heart on the first floor is a new restaurant which is open all day from breakfast until late. You can either sit at the bar and perhaps enjoy tapas, a pastry or a speciality tea (the latter is accompanied by a *madeleine* – what else!), or at one of the tables in the spacious restaurant done out in natural wood. Whether you have just one dish, say a *cocotte de légumes d'automne*, or the full gamut – a starter of *paté en croute*, followed by pot-braised beef with its juices and vegetables and ending with a trio of cheeses or a dessert – you are assured of quality and charming service. *Meals 7.30am-11pm. Closed Sun. Amex, Diners, Mastercard, Visa.*

Lancaster
Map B1.39

Tel 40 76 40 76   Fax 40 76 40 00   H

7 rue de Berri 75008   **M⁰ George V**
Rooms 59   Double from 2350F

Successfully achieving its aim of being a Parisian town house *par excellence*, the Lancaster, in the heart of fashionable Paris, is as we go to press, part of London's Savoy group. Style and elegance are its hallmarks. The foyer sets the tone with its mirror-finished cream marble floor. Magnificent flower arrangements and fine antiques grace the public rooms together with tapestries, oil paintings and a collection of eighteenth-century clocks. The bar is softly lit and has pastel-coloured murals. One of the finest features of the hotel is the splendid courtyard, which provides a touch of the countryside so close to the hustle of the Champs-Elysées. The whole place has a comforting, traditional and old-fashioned appeal reflected in the bedrooms with their Persian rugs,   *See over* antique porcelain ornaments and exquisite eighteenth-century artwork. Up-to-date bathrooms feature toiletries from the best *parfumiers* as well as cosseting bathrobes. Modern influences include air-conditioning and mini-bars, though standards of service are very high, making the latter somewhat less than essential. *Amex, Diners, Mastercard, Visa.*

Lasserre   ★★   Map B2.40

Tel 43 59 53 43 Fax 45 63 72 23	R

17 ave Franklin D Roosevelt 75008   **M⁰ Franklin D Roosevelt**
Seats 100   Meal for 2 approx 1500F

Arriving in Paris between the wars at the age of 12, from humble origins in Bayonne, René Lasserre created one of the most notable restaurants in town, one that generates intense loyalty from both customers – regulars have their own Club de la Casserole – and staff, whose former members have their own organisation "Les Anciens de Lasserre" which includes such now famous chefs as Gérard Boyer, Guy Savoy and Marc Haeberlin among its number. Attention to detail is the hallmark of all aspects of both service and decor, the latter including silver table decorations, specially commissioned chandeliers and the famous sliding roof (itself a work of art with stylised figures painted against a blue sky background) that retracts on summer evenings to magical effect. The menu is not so much traditional or old-fashioned as timeless with specialities including a warm salad of sweetbreads and langoustines, clams roasted in their shells with hazelnuts, sole soufflé with a salpicon of shellfish, "Le Ragout '74", escalope of foie gras with grapes, duck with orange "Lasserre" (kept on the menu by popular demand), and, an immovable fixture, the *mesclagne Mère Irma* named after, and based on a dish of, René's mother involving a rich chicken "dumpling" concealing slices of foie gras in a sauce with morel mushrooms and truffle garnish. Chef Bernard Joinville has been here for over 15 years. The vast cellar of over 200,000 bottles is a veritable treasure-house of famous names and rare vintages. Upstairs in the dining room the decanting of old red wines is a serious business too, involving a wonderful collection of antique cut-glass silver-necked pitchers. Valet parking. *L 12.30-2.30 D 7.30-10.30.* **Closed** *L Mon, all Sun & Aug. Amex, Mastercard, Visa.*

Laurent   ★★   Map C2.41

Tel 42 25 00 39 Fax 45 62 45 21	R

41 ave Gabriel 75008   **M⁰ Champs-Elysées-Clemenceau**
Seats 100 (+ 100 outdoor)   Meal for 2 approx 1700F

One of the 'pavilion' restaurants in the gardens at the Place de la Concorde end of the Champs Elysées, Laurent, with its painted neo-classical façade, was built in the 1840s on the site of an older building – probably a hunting lodge of the Louis XIV period. There's a splendid terrace for alfresco dining in the summer. The short menu, devised by Joël Robuchon, with whom chef Philippe Braun trained, is a carefully executed and studied working of modern cooking. Textures and flavours are juxtaposed with great finesse ensuring a level of sophistication and harmony that complements the fine decor. Hors d'oeuvre include *langoustines croustillants au basilic,* aubergine caviar with tomato coulis and *tarte friande aux champignons des sous-bois.* Principal dishes such as *rougets aux saveurs provençales,* roast turbot with puréed potatoes and *cote de veau lait, légumes étuvés au jus* precede desserts like *feuillantine chocolat-noisette,* pineapple fritters with rum ice cream or the pastry trolley. Set menu 380F. *L12.30-2.30 D 7.30-11. **Closed** L Sat, all Sun & Public Holidays. Amex, Diners, Mastercard, Visa.*

Ledoyen ★★	**Map B2.42**
Tel 47 42 35 98 Fax 47 42 55 01	**R**

carré des Champs-Elysées 75008   M⁰ Champs-Elysées-Clemenceau
Seats 50   Meal for 2 approx 1400F

Patronised by Robespierre, painted by Tissot, written about by Maupassant – Ledoyen's claim to be the "most legendary gastronomic address in Paris" is no idle boast. Opened in 1792 (as Chez Doyen) the setting, in a pavilion near the Petit Palais in the Jardin des Champs-Elysées, is incomparable, with the most elegant Napoleonic first-floor dining room looking out over the gardens. Restaurants are all about food, however, and the hotel group which now owns Ledoyen have lured husband and wife team Jean-Paul and Ghislaine Arabian (the former as ebullient manager, the latter to take charge of the kitchen) from their highly acclaimed restaurant in Lille to reinvigorate the cuisine here. Deceptively simple dishes concentrate on taste and flavour rather than spectacular presentation: terrine of hare with warm beetroot salad, scallops in a 'fluffy' liquor perfumed with beer; salmon roasted *en croute de pain noir* with confits of horseradish and radish; risotto of Brittany lobster with wild mushrooms; *pigeonneau mi-roti mi-confit, sauce du sang;* Pyrenean lamb roasted with thyme and leeks, and partridge simply grilled with a seasoned jus. Cheeses come from Roger Alléosse or go for a dessert like crepes Suzette (for two); warm, dark chocolate tart with coconut ice cream or *parfait glacé à la chicorée, pain d'épices* with a beer-flavoured sabayon. Prices are not totally astronomic and one can even find a 50F half bottle of Cotes de Blaye rubbing shoulders with Ch Pétrus on the wine list. Set L 290F Set L & D 520F. *L 12-2 D 7-10.30. **Closed** Sat, Sun & Aug. Amex, Diners, Mastercard, Visa.*

> The best way to get around Paris is by bus or metro – buy a book of tickets (carnet) at any metro station and save money

---

Lido	**Map C2.43**
Tel 42 66 27 37 Fax 42 66 61 23	**H**

4 passage Madeleine 75008   M⁰ Madeleine
Rooms 32   Double from 930F

Reception at this characterful hotel between the Madeleine and the Place de la Concorde boasts an oriental rug, tapestries on the wall and a beamed ceiling. There are more beams in some of the traditionally furnished bedrooms, which offer all sorts of amenities including mini-bar, multi-channel TV, room safe and, in the en-suite marble bathrooms – all of which have tubs – hairdryers. Some rooms are air-conditioned. Buffet breakfast is included in room price. *Amex, Diners, Mastercard, Visa.*

Lucas Carton ★   Map C2.44

Tel 42 65 22 90   Fax 42 65 06 23   **R**

9 place de la Madeleine 75008   **Mᵒ Madeleine**
Seats 100   Meal for 2 approx 1850F

This temple of French gastronomy is actually Japanese-owned now
although Alain Senderens remains in charge of the menu and it is
his genius that came up with such famous creations as *raviolis
de pétoncles* (baby scallops) *aux courgettes* and lobster flavoured
with vanilla. In day-to-day charge of the kitchen though
is Bertrand Gueneron, whose name is now given equal
prominence on the menu. The *carte* is unique in giving the option
of a glass of wine individually chosen to complement each and
every dish, including the puds – a truly wonderful idea. A glass
of '85 Jurançon *moelleux* with the cabbage-wrapped foie gras, for
example, a Chassagne Montrachet 'Morgeot' with a dish of turbot,
risotto and wild mushrooms; Hermitage 'La Sizeranne' '90 with
the *pastilla* of rabbit with foie gras, and with the sweetbreads,
a white Lynch-Bages. Desserts like *mille-feuille à la vanille* (Muscat
de Rivesaltes), pinepple fritters 'pinacolada' (white rum) and
caramelised pears with ginger and red berry ice cream
(Gewurztraminer) are all prepared to order and need to be chosen
at the beginning of the meal. The no-choice 'Menu Lucas Carton'
– served only to the whole table – consists of dishes from the carte
but not always with the same wines. Set L 375F Set L & D 1850F
(with wine). *L 12-2.30 D 8-10.30. **Closed** L Sat, all Sun, 23 Dec-3
Jan & 1st 3 wks Aug. Amex, Mastercard, Visa.*

La Maison d'Alsace   Map B2.45

Tel 43 59 44 24   Fax 42 89 06 62   **R**

39 ave des Champs-Elysées 75008   **Mᵒ Franklin D Roosevelt**
Seats 180 (+ 100 outside)   Meal for 2 approx 550F

Large, lively brasserie, open day and night, with mirrored walls,
banquette seating formed into convivial booths and a terrace
on the Champs Elysées itself. As the name suggests the menu gives
pride of place to the produce and cuisine of Alsace: various
choucroute, escalope of veal with horseradish sauce, foie gras
in Gewurztraminer-flavoured aspic, quiche lorraine, chicken
in Riesling. Shellfish is also a speciality. Short wine list includes all
the grape varieties grown in Alsace plus a few wines from other
areas, or drink the *grande bière d'Alsace à la pression*. From 11pm
till dawn there is a special 119F 'night menu'. *Meals 24 hours a day.
Amex, Diners, Mastercard, Visa.*

Maison Blanche   Map B2.46

Tel 47 23 55 99   Fax 47 20 09 56   **R**

15 ave Montaigne 75008   **Mᵒ Franklin D Roosevelt**
Seats 200   Meal for 2 approx 1100F

On the roof of the Théatre des Champs-Elysées the decor
is modern and the panoramic view of the Paris skyline stunning –
especially at night with the illuminated Eiffel Tower in the middle
distance. Jose Martinez' menu is as up-to-date as the surroundings:
fried duck liver with polenta, asparagus meunière with coriander,
roast tuna with pepper and bone marrow (a speciality), vegetarian

pot au feu, pastilla de homard, coffee blancmange with chocolate
caramel. *L 12-2 D 8-11.* **Closed** *L Sat, all Sun, last week July & 1st
3 weeks Aug. Amex, Mastercard, Visa.*

La Maison du Valais   Map C2.47
Tel 42 60 22 72	R

20 rue Royale 75008   **Mᵒ Madeleine**
Seats 80 (+ 18 outdoor)   Meal for 2 approx 550F

Rustic chalet-style setting with timber walls and cow-hide seats
where Parisians come to eat Swiss fondues and raclettes (slices
of gently melted raclette cheese served with hot potatoes in their
skins). Start with plates of country ham or wafer-thin slices of air-
dried beef. Among the fish dishes, fillets of perch meunière and
wild char, either grilled or meunière, are specialities as is the
emincé de veau 'Valaisan' aux morilles from the meat section.
Desserts are mostly ice cream or sorbet based. Wine list covers all
the French regions plus the Valais area of Switzerland. The house
red (Dole), white (Fendant) and rosé (Valaison) are sold by the
pichet or the glass. Set L & D 210F (inc wine). *L 12.15-2.30
D 7.15-11.30.* **Closed** *Sun. Amex, Diners, Mastercard, Visa.*

La Marée   ★   Map B1.48
Tel 43 80 20 00 Fax 48 88 04 04	R

1 rue Daru 75008   **Mᵒ Ternes**
Seats 70   Meal for 2 approx 1200F

On the corner of Rue du Faubourg St-Honoré. There are a couple
of meat dishes on the menu here but this is overwhelmingly
a seafood restaurant; the name means tide. Particular specialities
include oysters in champagne, lobster roasted with ginger, ravioli
of langoustines, baby turbot with mustard and a *panaché*
of steamed red mullet with line-caught bass. Flemish paintings
decorate the walls. The clever wine list is printed on the inside
of the menu and presented by vintage – youngest first. Three
Spanish, three US and a handful of rural wines apart, it is
magnificently all-French and includes choice wines by the glass.
A 1937 Richebourg is a snip at 6800F. *L 12-2.30 D 8-10.30.*
Closed *Sat, Sun & Aug. Amex, Diners, Mastercard, Visa.*

Le Marignan   Map B2.49
Tel 40 76 34 56 Fax 40 76 34 34	H

12 rue de Marignan 75008   **Mᵒ Franklin D Roosevelt**
Rooms 73   Double from 1600F

South of the Champs Elysées in an elegant neo-Gothic building
with an art deco facade, Le Marignan combines traditional
comforts with modern amenities. Public rooms are a stylish blend
of marble-pillared classicism and the ultra-modern. Scattered
throughout is a collection of sculptures while walls are hung with
an exciting assortment of modern art. Bedrooms, sixteen of which
are suites, include many which are duplexes or have terraces.
Otherwise they are more intimate than spacious but all are air-
conditioned and decorated to a good standard. Bathrooms are
a blend of modern tiling and coloured marble. A notable feature
is the **Salon de Thé** where numerous teas are offered with home-
made pastries. *Amex, Diners, Mastercard, Visa.*

Maxim's
Map C2.50

Tel 42 65 27 94   Fax 40 17 02 91
R

3 rue Royale 75008
M° Concorde
Seats 200
Meal for 2 approx 2000F

For over 100 years Maxim's has been both an institution and
a legend. In the early 1900s the restaurant was in fact bought by a
group of English businessmen – a good excuse for travelling
regularly to Paris on 'inpsection visits'! It is now owned by Pierre
Cardin. Magnificently and grandly decorated in art nouveau style
(it was registered as a national historical monument in 1979), it
has an original facade hidden by the glass terrace; note also the
murals, mirrors, copper decorations, art deco lighting and the glass
roof over the main dining room, once the interior courtyard.
Eating the traditional *cuisine* here does not come cheap, but
as long-serving maitre d' Jean-Pierre Guevel says "for about eleven
hundred francs each, you can enjoy a complete night out, starting
at around 8.30pm for aperitifs, sitting down at, say, 9.15pm and
dancing to the five-piece orchestra from 11pm-2am with a bottle
of champagne on the table". Add too the violinist who serenades
the tables, taking care not to obstruct the tail-coated waiters who
glide effortlessly through the dining rooms. Chef Michel Ménant,
himself in situ for 30 years, oversees the classical cooking – dishes
are first presented to customers before being served over flame
warmers, not often seen these days – typical offerings being duck
terrine, *cotriade* (a Breton fish soup), paupiettes of sole with girolle
mushrooms, chateaubriand sauce béarnaise. Particular specialities
include quail's eggs with caviar, *charlotte* de langoustines, *Billy
by* (cream of mussel soup) and *sole Albert*. Tarts aplenty for dessert,
or maybe a classic soufflé Grand Marnier as well as the usual ice
creams and sorbets. Exalted wines at exalted prices. *L 12.30-2
D 7.30-10.30* **Closed** *Sun. Amex, Diners, Mastercard, Visa.*

For a glossary of menu terms see page 293

Au Petit Montmorency
Map B2.51

Tel 42 25 11 19
R

26 rue Jean-Mermoz 75008
M° Franklin D Roosevelt
Seats 45
Meal for 2 approx 900F

Having extended into the next door corner premises, Au Petit
Montmorency has gained a new front door (and address) around
the corner and can now offer a *salon particulier* for up to 12
people. Daniel Bouche's cooking – a blend of modern and classic
influences – remains the same however, with dishes such as a soup
of morel mushrooms with foie gras toast; tomato, aubergine and
parmesan tart; warm terrine of lobster and broad beans; calf's
liver *bigarade* with balsamic vinegar and fricassee of veal kidneys
and sweetbreads with wild mushrooms. Desserts, many of which
need to be ordered at the beginning of the meal, include
millefeuille of red fruits, hot apple tart with a cider sorbet and
a *grand dessert au chocolat amer*. In addition to the carte there is a
market-based *menu surprise* at 250F. *L 12-2.30 D 7.30-10.30.*
Closed *Sat (except L Easter-Sep), Sun & Aug. Mastercard, Visa.*

Le Pichet
Map B2.52

| Tel 43 59 50 34   Fax 45 63 07 82 | R |

68 rue Pierre Charron 75008   M° Franklin D Roosevelt
Seats 96   Meal for 2 approx 900F

A smart bistro with mirrored walls and plentiful photographs
of celebrity clients – including President Mitterrand. The menu
specialises in fish, with an excellent choice of shellfish, particular
dishes include *panaché de St Jacques et saumon crus*, steak of red tuna
with fresh spinach, *brandade de morue*, oysters poached in sherry,
a duo of sole and langoustines with a fondue of leeks and a warm
vinaigrette. Meat-eaters are not forgotten with the likes of *confit
de canard*, steak bordelaise and best end of lamb roasted with
thyme. Shortish wine list also includes some famous names. *L 12-
2.30 D 7-midnight.* **Closed** *Sat, Sun, 2 wks Christmas & 3 wks Aug.
Amex, Diners, Mastercard, Visa.*

Plaza Athénée
Map B2.53

| Tel 47 23 78 33   Fax 47 20 20 70 | H R |

25 ave Montaigne 75008   M° Alma-Marceau
Rooms 211   Double from 3010F

Surrounded by the great haute-couture houses, the Plaza has its
own inimitable sense of style and has long been a haunt of the
famous – and sometimes infamous; Mata Hari was arrested in the
hotel's darkwood and leather English bar. Other public areas
include a large circular lobby, vaulted Galerie des Gobelins with
pairs of columns down each side, and a verdant courtyard garden
with fountains and red umbrellas that match the awnings of the
balustraded bedroom windows that overlook it. Bedrooms
in either Louis XV, Louis XVI or Regency style are elegant and
comfortable with air-conditioning and ultra-modern bathrooms.
Services include 24-hour room service, hairdressing salon, perfume
boutique, theatre desk and free entry to a gym around the corner.
Forte. Valet parking. *Amex, Diners, Mastercard, Visa.*

Le Régence
80 (+ 80 outdoor)   Meal for 2 approx 1050F

An elegant dining room with fluted pilasters supporting
an elaborate gilded frieze, and widely spaced tables displaying
silver place settings. Very much the Grand Hotel menu in both
style – separate sections for grills, fish etc – and content; the
starters include oysters, caviar, smoked salmon and foie gras.
Amongst the more interesting dishes are ravioli of langoustines
with a tarragon bisque; cabbage-wrapped salmon with fresh herb
vinaigrette; soufflé of lobster 'Plaza Athénée (a speciality); *rognon
de veau rissolé, gratin de macaronis* and roast fillet of lamb with
a wild marjoram jus and celery purée. From a good varied choice
of desserts this would be just the place to enjoy the spectacle that
is crepe Suzette flambée. 500 wines include some from both Italy
and California. *L 12.30-2.15 D 7.30-10.15.*

Relais Plaza
Seats 120   Meal for 2 approx 650F

Informal, all-day eaterie with 1930s decor and entrance direct
from the street as well as from within the hotel. It's breakfast till
11am after which the full menu runs through until the early   *See over*

hours. With something to suit all appetites the choice ranges from
club sandwiches and croque monsieur, via pasta, salads and egg
dishes to lamb curry, sole meunière and grills. Wines available
by the glass. Set menu 285F. *Open 8am-1.30am.*

Prince de Galles   Map A2.54

| Tel 47 23 55 11   Fax 47 20 96 92 | H |

| 33 ave George V 75008 | M⁰ George V |
| Rooms 171 | Double from 3000F |

Now owned by Sheraton Hotels, the Prince de Galles has just
benefited from top-to-toe refurbishment. The tone is set by an
elegant lobby with baronial-style stone walls and central carpeted
island sporting a huge floral display that almost reaches up to
touch the glittering chandelier above; the bar boasts red leather
upholstery and carved wood-panelled walls. A unique feature
of the hotel is its central patio/courtyard, overlooked by many
of the bedrooms, with the enclosing walls completely covered
with original 1927 mosaic tiling – right up to roof level. Air-
conditioned bedrooms are all identically furnished with traditional
freestanding pieces, including leather-topped desk, and with
bedhead walls covered in the same fabric as the quilted bedcovers.
Choose between blue or yellow colour schemes. Peace and quiet
are ensured by almost all the rooms having their own lobby and
service extends to a 24hr room menu and the turning down
of beds in the evening. There is a well-equipped fitness room and
a small business centre. The hotel has no parking of its own. *Amex,
Diners, Mastercard, Visa.*

Hotel Queen Mary   Map C2.55

| Tel 42 66 40 50   Fax 42 66 94 92 | H |

| 9 rue de Greffulhe 75008 | M⁰ Havre Caumartin |

British-owned (and mainly British-staffed) this small hotel in a
quiet back street near the Madeleine was totally renovated in 1993
and offers good air-conditioned bedrooms that have attractive
matching bedcovers and curtains, often with period plaster-
panelled walls. All rooms have safe, mini-bar and good workspace
with all but five small singles having two telephones. Fully tiled
bathrooms have showers over tubs except for the singles which
have shower & wc only. Nice touches include a welcoming
decanter of sherry, and scrambled eggs and sausages included
in the buffet breakfast (67F), which is served in a bright yellow
basement breakfast room. There is a small bar but no restaurant.
Room service till 10pm. *Amex, Mastercard, Visa.*

Résidence Maxim's de Paris   Map C2.56

| Tel 45 61 96 33   Fax 42 89 06 07 | H |

| 42 ave Gabriel 75008 | M⁰ Concorde/Champs-Elysées-Clemenceau |
| Rooms 39 | Double from 2250F |

Pierre Cardin's name is synonymous with haute couture. Six years
ago he turned his attention to this grand building, which
he purchased and then set about indulging all his design skills and
fantasies. The result has been to create some of the most refined
and elegant bedrooms and suites to be found anywhere, though
the hotel brochure hardly does them justice. Individually
furnished, they differ greatly one from another, ranging in style

from those with an ultra-modern, cool, late 20th-century decor
to those with exquisite original art deco furniture and others with
genuine 18th-century pieces. All except four standard bedrooms
are suites but even the former are spacious and all have almost the
full A to Z of amenities, from full air-conditioning to video
players. Bathrooms feature highly polished fossil stones together
with stunning murals. Hallways too are extraordinary, with their
beautiful antiques and fine paintings. Standards of service are
exemplary and there is valet parking. A hotel of outstanding
quality and merit but with prices to match. *Amex, Diners,
Mastercard, Visa.*

Royal Monceau

Tel 42 99 88 00   Fax 42 56 90 03   **Map B1.57**   **H R**

37 ave Hoche 75008   **M° Etoile**
Rooms 220   Double from 2550F

A huge, arched, marble-floored lobby with trompe l'oeil sky
ceiling is at the centre of things at this luxury hotel in the business
district. Amenities include a sybaritic health centre (pool, steam
bath, sauna, squash, all sorts of beauty treatments), pretty gardens,
news stand and choice of bars. Bedrooms and suites, some quite
grand, are furnished and decorated in traditional style while being
provided with every modern comfort. 24-hour room service.
Amex, Diners, Mastercard, Visa.

Le Jardin
Tel 42 99 98 70
Seats 60 (+ 40 outdoor)   Meal for 2 approx 1000F

Appropriately named restaurant in a circular, glass-walled
conservatory jutting out into the hotel's garden. Bruno Cirino
took over the kitchen here at the beginning of 1994 having
formerly been at the Royal Monceau's sister hotel *Vernet* (*qv*).
He brings the flavours of his native Provence – grilled
Mediterranean bream with a pistou thinned with olive oil, small
Provençal artichokes stuffed with a mushroom mixture – to
a menu that might also include duck foie gras from Landes, saddle
of Pauillac lamb with herbs and a bouillon of lentils and foie gras
with the claws of Breton lobster and quenelles of bone marrow.
No surprises on an expensive all-French wine list. Set L 300F Set
D 420F. *L 12.30-2.30 D 7.30-10.30. **Closed** Sat & Sun.*

Il Carpaccio
Tel 42 99 98 90
Seats 60   Meal for 2 approx 900F

For a complete change of cuisine, though not of decor as this also
has something of a garden theme with trelliswork, mirrors and
large troughs of flowers, the hotel's second restaurant
is thoroughly Italian. Working in the modern idiom chef Angelo
Paraccuchi (here for 11 years) prepares a menu using only the best
of ingredients – buffalo mozzarella for a salad with tomato and
basil, Parma ham that has matured for 22 months – for dishes such
as a risotto of fresh peas, monkfish roasted with rosemary, fish and
vegetable salad with pistou, grilled calf's liver with ceps and
lemon, and tagliatelle with mussels, courgettes and baby onions.
A modest and mostly Italian wine list, presented by region. Set
L 280F. *L 12.30-2.30 D 8-10.30. **Closed** Aug.*

Saint Moritz
Map B1.58

Tel 45 61 02 74   Fax 53 75 03 18   R

33 ave Friedland 75008   M⁰ Etoile
Seats 40   Meal for 2 approx 800F

Panelling creates a warm ambience in a traditional restaurant
whose chef-patron Alain Raichon hails from the Jura. Specialities
from this mountainous region of Eastern France feature on the
menu with some dishes cooked in Jura wines, for example a starter
of duck foie gras and a main dish of Bresse chicken with *vin jaune*
and morilles. Serrano ham with tomato bread, tartare of salmon,
monkfish roasted with mignonette pepper, goujonettes of sole
with artichokes, marquise of bitter chocolate with coffee sauce,
crème brulée and a delicious gingerbread charlotte are among the
other offerings. Some 20 Jura wines are included in an all-French
list. Set L & D 185F. *L 12-2.15 D 7-10.15.* **Closed** *Sat, Sun &*
Public Holidays. Amex, Diners, Mastercard, Visa.

San Regis
Map B2.59

Tel 44 95 16 16   Fax 45 61 05 48   HR

12 rue Jean Goujon 75008   M⁰ Champs-Elysées-Clemenceau
Rooms 44   Double from 2100F

Quietly elegant hotel with an intimate home-from-home
atmosphere in the prestigious 'Golden Triangle' area favoured
by renowned fashion houses like Christian Dior, Valentino and
Ricci. Individually decorated bedrooms combine 17th- and 18th-
century style furniture with well-chosen fabrics, often with
matching wall-coverings, and such modern comforts as air-
conditioning. Good, coloured-marble bathrooms. Day rooms
include a charming lounge with antique, blond-wood panelling
and a clubby bar. Unobtrusive yet attentive service. *Amex, Diners,*
Mastercard, Visa.

Restaurant
Seats 21   Meal for 2 approx 900F

Separated from the bar by a pillared archway, the small, pretty
restaurant is almost like a private dining room. The menu – there's
a version with French on one side and an English translation
on the facing page – is sensibly short (about eight choices at each
stage) but well-balanced: *fond d'artichaut, jus aigre; poèlée de gambas*
et huitres à la favorite and *navarin de lotte et olives au pistou* are
specialities with other dishes including a fricassee of scallops and
veal with morel mushrooms. French list with a couple of wines
served by the glass. *L 12-2.30 D 7.30-10.30.*

Le Sarladais
Map C1.60

Tel & Fax 45 22 23 62   R

2 rue Vienne 75008 Paris   M⁰ Eglise St Augustin
Seats 70   Meal for 2 approx 650F

No one goes away hungry from Jean and Josette Tartrou's
unpretentiously comfortable restaurant near the Gare St Lazare.
The cooking is that of the South-West of France with more than
half the menu devoted to *Spécialités Périgourdines*: neck of goose
stuffed with foie gras, *anchaut Périgord* (fillet of pork confit

in aspic), *tourin à l'ail* (garlic soup), truffle omelette, *salade sarladaise* (confit of duck's gizzard). Particular specialities are foie gras (served with seasonal produce – ceps when we last dined), confit of duck with *pommes sarladaise* (sliced potatoes with onion and garlic), and *cassoulet périgourdin* which arrives in a huge terrine with a proper breadcrumb crust. Other dishes might include ravioli of mussels with saffron, *brandade de morue*, sweetbreads in cider, noisettes of lamb with tarragon, fillet of beef béarnaise and fricassee of veal with leeks. A shortish wine list concentrates on the wines of the South and South-West. The lower part of the split-level dining room is reserved for non-smokers. Set L & D 145F & 200F. *L 12-2.30 D 7.30-10.* **Closed** *L Sat, all Sun & Aug. Amex, Mastercard, Visa.*

Les Saveurs
Map B2.61

Tel 45 63 17 44   Fax 42 25 06 59
R

Hotel Sofitel-Paris-Elysées, 8 rue Jean Goujon 75008
Mᵒ Champs-Elysées-Clemenceau
Seats 60
Meal for 2 approx 650F

On the mezzanine level of the Sofitel-Paris-Elysées hotel, Les Saveurs is a civilised, air-conditioned restaurant with an ambience that is both classic and modern reflecting the innovative style of Didier Lanfray in the kitchen. Scallops marinated in spices from Szechuan, *meurette de ris de veau et queues d'ecrevisses à l'ancienne*, sweet curry of langoustines and John Dory with a lemon risotto, rabbit marinated in thyme with fresh tagliatelle, wild duck with pink peppercorns and noisettes of venison with bilberries featured on an autumn menu along with desserts like *pain perdu* with caramelised pear and apple tart with quince jelly. There's a separate list of the 'foreign' wines and another of wines offered by the glass. Set L & D 160F, 220F & 280F. *L 12.15-2.30 D 7.30-10.30.* **Closed** *Sat, Sun & Aug. Amex, Diners, Mastercard, Visa.*

The best way to get around Paris is by bus or metro – buy a book of tickets (carnet) at any metro station and save money

---

Savy
Map B2.62

Tel 47 23 46 98
R

23 rue Bayard 75008
Mᵒ Franklin D Roosevelt
Seats 80
Meal for 2 approx 650F

Wood panelling adds warmth and character to this informal local bistro. Short Auvergne-based menu (about nine main dishes) on which some dishes – rabbit terrine *en gelée,* calf's liver *à l'auvergnate,* grilled veal kidneys, roast shoulder of lamb, *charlotte au chocolat,* Poire William sorbet – are permanent fixtures while others change regularly. Just four wines offered, a white Macon and one red from each of Bordeaux, Cahors and Morgon; the latter arrives by cask and is bottled by the restaurant. *L 12-3 D 7.30-11.* **Closed** *Sat, Sun, Public Holidays & Aug. Mastercard, Visa.*

Taillevent ★★★

Map B1.63

Tel 45 61 12 90 Fax 42 25 95 18

R

15 rue Lammenais 75008
Seats 95

M⁰ George V
Meal for 2 approx 1350F

Taillevent (Guillaume Tirel) was France's first great chef back
in the 1300s and the great achievement of the restaurant which
bears his name is that of sustained excellence over many years.
Presided over by the urbane second-generation owner Jean-Claude
Vrinat, this is the most civilised of restaurants with wood-panelled
walls and discreet, polished service helping to create an almost
club-like atmosphere relished by the good and the great of the
capital's establishment. Philippe Legendre is now firmly established
in the kitchen and continues in the tradition of his predecessor
(who was head chef here for 30 years) of acknowledging modern
trends but only gradually and from a solidly classical base.
Specialities include a moreish *boudin d'homard breton à la nage,*
poulette de Bresse en cocotte and, among the desserts, a *moelleux*
au chocolat et à thym. Other impeccable dishes might include
courgette flowers with truffle juice, *oeufs en cocotte périgourdine,*
curried langoustines from Brittany, fricassee of Barbary duck with
girolle mushrooms, roast best end of Pauillac lamb, *noix de ris*
de veau en cocotte à l'ancienne, gingerbread ice cream, mille-feuille
of exotic fruits and a hot soufflé flavoured with Columbian coffee.
The legendary wine list is supported by their own wine shop, one
of the best in Paris, in the nearby Rue du Faubourg Saint-Honoré.
Valet parking. *L 12-1.30 D 7.30-10.* **Closed** *Sat, Sun, last week*
July & 1st 3 wks Aug. Amex, Diners, Mastercard, Visa.

Hotel de la Trémoille

Map B2.64

Tel 47 23 34 20 Fax 40 70 01 08

H

14 rue de la Trémoille 75008
Rooms 108

M⁰ Alma-Marceau
Double from 2240F

Forte-owned hotel in a quiet street of a fashionable quarter
of town. Named after a military hero of the 15th century, General
Louis de la Trémoille, it's an excellent base for luxury shopping.
The stylish lobby, with rugs over a marble-tiled floor and
a profusion of fresh flowers and potted palms, sets the tone for
traditionally furnished, period-style suites and rooms above.
Facilities though, are totally up-to-date with air-conditioning,
cable TV, mini-bar and room safe. Valet parking. *Amex, Diners,*
Mastercard, Visa.

Le Val d'Or

Map B1.65

Tel 43 59 95 81

R

28 ave Franklin D Roosevelt 75008
Seats 50

M⁰ St-Philippe-du-Roule
Meal for 2 approx 500F

A modest establishment with 1940s decor offering a short
lunchtime menu in a basement restaurant – salad of chicken livers,
rabbit terrine, simply-roasted duck served on slices of potato,
braised sweetbreads – and charcuterie and sandwiches throughout
the day in the ground floor wine bar/café where some dozen or so
mostly Burgundian wines, including most of the Beaujolais crus,
are available by the glass. Both very popular with local office
workers, and it is advisable to book for the restaurant. Watch out

for the hole-in-the-ground loos. *L only 12-3 (wine bar/café 9-5).*
Closed *Sat (except wine bar/café), Sun & Aug (except wine bar/café).*
Mastercard, Visa.

Vancouver ★   Map A1.66

Tel 42 56 77 77   Fax 42 56 50 52   **R**

4 rue Arsène Houssaye 75008   **M° Etoile**
Seats 45   Meal for 2 approx 900F

After having spent an idyllic holiday in Vancouver, Chantal
Decout and her chef-husband Jean-Louis decided to name their
restaurant accordingly. Set on two levels, the art deco interior
resembles a 30s ocean liner with plenty of wood, sanded glass,
metal and light colours. Opening in October 1991, Jean-Louis
successfully specialises in cooking seafood – velouté of mussels with
saffron or sautéed shrimps sweet sour, followed by sea bream with
cider, *brandade de rouget-barbet* or *bouillabaisse parisienne* (as Jean-
Louis likes it!), and a light *crème brulée* or *Paris-Brest craquelin*
to finish. So Vancouver is worth a visit, and you don't have
to cross the ocean to get there. Set L & D 190F & 380F. *L 12-1.30
D 7.30-10.* **Closed** *Sat, Sun & Aug. Amex, Mastercard, Visa.*

Vernet   Map A1.67

Tel 44 31 98 00   Fax 44 31 85 69   **H R**

25 rue Vernet 75008   **M° Etoile**
Rooms 57   Double from 1850F

In a quiet street just a step away from the Arc de Triomphe and
the bustle of the Champs Elysées, the Vernet, built in the early
1900s, is an elegant hotel with an intimate feel. Tranquil public
areas feature rug-strewn marble floors, antiques and an abundance
of fresh flowers. Bedrooms boast fabric-covered walls and every
modern comfort from air-conditioning to spa baths. The ten
deluxe rooms are largest. Beds are turned down at night and room
service is available 24hrs. Guests have use of the health and beauty
centre of the nearby *Royal Monceau Hotel (qv)*. 24hr room service.
Valet parking. *Amex, Diners, Mastercard, Visa.*

Les Elysées du Vernet   ★
Seats 40   Meal for 2 approx 1000F

Splendid glass-roofed dining room in a style transitional between
art nouveau and the Belle Epoque. Former sous-chef Alain
Solivères hails from Provence, like his predecessor, and having
taken over the top job has reinforced the Mediterranean flavour
of the *carte*: lobster salad with tomato, olive oil, basil and buffalo
mozzarella; potato gnocchi with ham and ceps simmered in the
jus; *lasagnes au pistou* with Brittany lobster and aged Parmesan;
wild duck roasted in vine leaves with a fig and chestnut confit;
breast of pigeon with lentils and foie gras. Patisserie is Alain's
particular forte as evidenced by a delicious ravioli of chocolate
with caramelised nuts and a first-rate nougat ice cream;
a charmingly humorous touch amongst the *mignardises* is a hen's
egg, sitting in an egg cup filled with a mini-tiramisu. Notably
good cheese trolley and home-made bread to accompany. Fairly
comprehensive French-only wine list with a nicely varied selection
of half bottles. Set L 300F, Set D 350F & 450F. *L 12-2.30 D 7.30-
10.* **Closed** *Sat, Sun, 1 week Christmas, some Public Holidays & Aug.*

Virgin Café
Map B2.68

Tel 42 89 46 81   Fax 49 53 50 41
R

52 ave des Champs Elysées 75008
Mº Franklin D Roosevelt

Large bright café on the top floor of the Virgin Megastore. The
trendy darkwood and black decor matches the menu: carpaccio
of beef with *courgettes frites,* salmon steak with vegetable ravioli,
fruit soup with champagne, banana mousse on a passion fruit
sauce. They also offer breakfast, brunch, afternoon teas, cocktails,
children's menu and smiling service. On the drinks front there are
as many cocktails (ten of them alcohol free) as wines. *Open 10am-
midnight.* **Closed** *1 Jan & 1 May. Amex, Mastercard, Visa.*

Warwick
Map B1.69

Tel 45 63 14 11   Fax 45 63 75 81
HR

5 rue de Berri 75008
Mº George V
Rooms 147
Double from 2650F

Luxurious modern accommodation seconds from the Champs-
Elysées. Space and comfort are watchwords in the bedrooms, with
soundproofing and air-conditioning in all rooms. Piano bar;
rooftop terraces; 24-hour room service. *Amex, Diners,
Mastercard, Visa.*

La Couronne
Seats 50
Meal for 2 approx 750F

Smart restaurant where first-class service complements the reliably
good cooking of long-standing chef Paul Van Gassel. There is a
distinct flavour of the South of France to such dishes as rillettes
of John Dory with aubergine, croutons and black olives; pimento
stuffed with baby vegetables; tuna *à la creme* with new season's
garlic; ragout of langoustines, asparagus and baby artichokes, and
shoulder of Pyrenean lamb with savory. There are three set menus
in addition to a short *carte.* Fine wine list covering all French
regions. Set L & D 220F, 270F & 390F. *L 12-2.30 D 7.30-10.30.*
Closed *L Sat, all Sun & Aug.*

Yvan
Map B2.70

Tel 42 89 16 69   Fax 45 63 78 69
R

1bis rue Jean-Mermoz 75008
Mº Franklin D Roosevelt
Seats 75
Meal for 2 approx 700F

Dishes like beef braised in beer and *waterzooi* (fish simmered
in white wine with vegetables) reflect Yvan Zaplatilek's Flemish
origins but share the menu with, for example, ravioli of mussels;
cod with braised lettuce and a vanilla jus; quail roasted with
honey and spices served with pine kernel polenta; veal kidneys
with basil and a galette of vegetables, and fillets of bream with
aubergine and potatoes puréed with saffron that demonstrate his
imaginative modern style. At lunchtime there are four different
set menus, each with three choices at each stage, from which you
can mix and match; at night just one prix-fixe plus an à la carte.
Set L 168F, 188F, 238F & 278F, Set D 178F. *L 12-2.30 D 8-
midnight.* **Closed** *L Sat, all Sun & Public Holidays. Amex, Diners,
Mastercard, Visa.*

9th Arrondissement
Places of Interest

Place de Clichy
Opéra de Paris Garnier, 40 17 33 33, Mº Opéra
Boulevard des Italiens
Olympia, 47 42 25 49, Mº Opéra
Folies Bergères, 44 79 98 98, Mº Cadet/Rue Montmartre
Musée Grévin (waxworks), 47 70 85 05, Mº Rue Montmartre
Trinité
Apollo Casino de Paris, 36 68 01 40, Mº Trinité
Moulin Rouge, 46 06 00 19, Mº Blanche

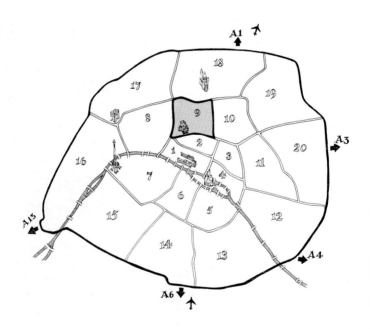

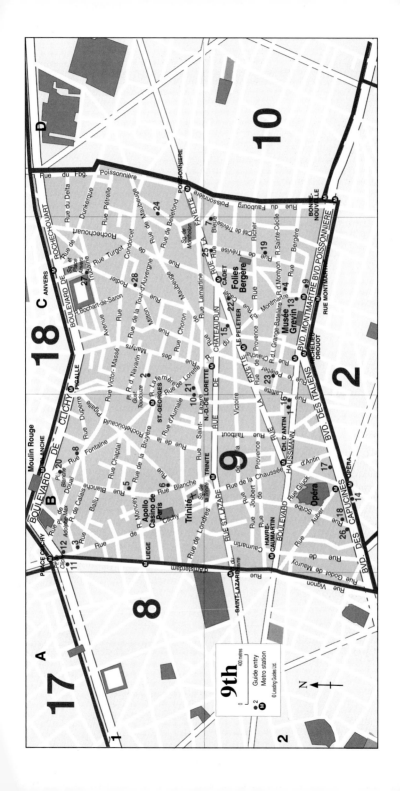

9th

0 ————— 400 metres

● 2   Guide entry

Ⓜ   Metro station

© Leading Guides Ltd.

N

A   B   C   D

18

17

8

1

2

10

9

2

Moulin Rouge

Apollo Casino de Paris

Trinité

Folies Bergère

Musée Grévin

Opéra

BOULEVARD DE CLICHY

BOULEVARD DE ROCHECHOUART

RUE LA FAYETTE

BVD. MONTMARTRE

BVD. POISSONNIÈRE

BVD. DES ITALIENS

BVD. DES CAPUCINES

BOULEVARD HAUSSMANN

Ⓜ PLACE CLICHY

Ⓜ BLANCHE

Ⓜ PIGALLE

Ⓜ ANVERS

Ⓜ POISSONNIÈRE

Ⓜ BONNE-NOUVELLE

Ⓜ RICHELIEU DROUOT

Ⓜ CADET

Ⓜ LE PELETIER

Ⓜ CHAUSSÉE D'ANTIN

Ⓜ TRINITÉ

Ⓜ ST-GEORGES

Ⓜ N.-D.-DE LORETTE

Ⓜ LIÈGE

Ⓜ SAINT-LAZARE

Ⓜ HAVRE CAUMARTIN

Ⓜ OPÉRA

Rue du Fbg. Poissonnière
Rue du Delta
Rue Pétrelle
Rue Dunkerque
Rue de Maubeuge
Rue de Belzunce
Rue de Montholon
Rue Bleue
Rue Richer
Rue Bergère
Rue Sainte-Cécile
Rue du Fbg. Poissonnière
Rue nd Poissonnière
Rue Montmartre
Rue Richelieu
Rue Drouot
Rue de Trévise
Rue du Fg. Montmartre
R. du Faubourg Montmartre
R. de Provence
R. de la Grange-Batelière
Rue Lafitte
Rue Le Peletier
Rue Laffitte
Rue de Châteaudun
Rue Condorcet
Rue Turgot
Rue de Rochechouart
Rue Bochart-de-Saron
Avenue Trudaine
Place d'Anvers
Rue Rodier
Rue Milton
Rue Choron
Rue Lamartine
Rue de Maubeuge
Rue La Fayette
Rue de la Tour-d'Auvergne
Rue des Martyrs
Rue Victor-Massé
Rue Victoire
Rue Rochechouart
Rue de la Bruyère
Rue Chaptal
Rue Fontaine
Rue Blanche
Rue Ballu
Rue Moncey
Rue Mogador
Rue de Clichy
Rue de Londres
Rue de Liège
Rue d'Amsterdam
Rue Saint-Lazare
Rue de la Trinité
Rue Joubert
Rue de Provence
Rue de la Chaussée d'Antin
Rue Taitbout
Rue Laffitte
Rue Caumartin
Rue Godot de Mauroy
Rue Vignon
Rue Scribe
Rue Auber
Rue Glück
Rue Halévy
Rue Meyerbeer
Rue d'Antin
Rue Gaillon
R. Sainte-Anne
Place de la Trinité
Place Saint-Georges
Rue N.-D.-de-Lorette
Rue d'Aumale
Rue La Bruyère
Rue Taitbout
Rue des Martyrs
Rue du Delta
Rue Adolphe Max
Pl. de Clichy
R. de Calais
R. Duperré
Pl. Blanche
R. Douai
Rue Pigalle
Pl. Gust. Toudouze
R. de Navarin
Rue Clauzel
Rue Henry Monnier
Rue La Rochefoucauld
Rue Henner

1 2 3 4 5 6 7 8 9 10 11 12 13 14 15 16 17 18 19 20 21 22 23 24 25 26 27 28

Ambassador

Map B2.1

Tel 44 83 40 40   Fax 40 22 08 74   HR

16 bd Haussmann 75009   M⁰ Richelieu-Drouot/Chaussée d'Antin
Rooms 298   Double from 1510F

Constructed in 1927 and recently entirely renovated, this
traditional and luxurious hotel in the Groupe Concorde
is conveniently located for the Opéra and Paris's major department
stores. Modern comforts and amenities are combined with
an elegant decor. The bedrooms (half of them air-conditioned)
contain period pieces and well-equipped bathrooms. 24hr
reception and room service. Eleven conference and function
rooms (max 200 people). *Amex, Diners, Mastercard, Visa.*

Venantius Restaurant
Tel 48 00 06 38
Seats 50   Meal for 2 approx 900F

Decorated in an opulent 'neo-Pompeian' style, this gastronomic
restaurant in the elegant Ambassador Hotel also has its own street
entrance. Guests sit at round white-clothed tables in ochre-
coloured surroundings to sample such dishes as eggs with lamb
sweetbreads and sorrel sauce; salmon marinated in Russian tea
served with a vegetable 'cake'; sole with braised chestnuts; and
rack of lamb with sesame seeds and haricots with confit tomatoes.
Set menu: L & D 210F D 380F (*dégustation*). *L 12-2.30 D 7-10.30.*
***Closed** Sat, Sun, Aug, 1 week Feb.*

Auberge Landaise

Map C1.2

Tel 48 78 74 40   Fax 48 78 20 96   R

23 rue Clauzel 75009   M⁰ Pigalle/St-Georges
Seats 60   Meal for 2 approx 460F

Block-stone walls give a rustic look to Dominique Morin's
restaurant, which is divided into two dining areas by upright
beams and a small entrance hall. Armagnac dating back to 1800
is displayed on one wall. As the name suggests, the chef-patron
concentrates on dishes and wines from the South-West (Bayonne,
Biarritz and Bordeaux areas). *Hors d'oeuvre landais* (a selection
of meats); salad with artichokes, green beans and goose liver;
pipérade; cassoulet maison, braised duck with ceps and *tarte tatin*
with *crème fraiche* are some of the specialities leaving his kitchen.
Choose a Bordelais, Cahors or Madiran wine to accompany the
meal and one of those 80 armagnacs to finish. Set menu: D 180F.
Two private rooms can cater for 30 people each. *L 12-2.30
D 7-10.30.* ***Closed** Sun, 10 days mid-Aug. Amex, Diners,
Mastercard, Visa.*

Aurore Montmartre

Map B1.3

Tel 48 74 85 56   Fax 42 81 09 54   H

76 rue de Clichy 75009   M⁰ Place Clichy
Rooms 24   Double from 420F

A neat little hotel with well-maintained bedrooms equipped with
mini-bars, televisions and telephones. Breakfast (35F) is taken in a
vaulted room in the basement. A child stays free if sharing parents'
room. *Amex, Diners, Mastercard, Visa.*

Bergère
Map C2.4

| Tel 47 70 34 34   Fax 47 70 36 36 | **H** |

34 rue Bergère 75009
Rooms 136

M° **Rue Montmartre**
Double from 550F

This modern hotel is conveniently located for shopping in the
large department stores or visiting Montmartre. The double-
glazed rooms with en-suite bathrooms are equipped with satellite
TV, mini-bars, direct-dial telephones, safes and hairdryers. *Amex,
Diners, Mastercard, Visa.*

Le Bistrot Blanc
Map B1.5

| Tel 42 85 05 30 | **R** |

52 rue Blanche 75009
Seats 40

M° **Blanche/Trinité**
Meal for 2 approx 550F

A welcome oasis in a fairly unremarkable street. Inside, the decor,
in soft shades of cream, is both inviting and homely. The latter
also aptly describes the food, which is simple and mainly
Provence-inspired. Begin with a garlicky *soupe au pistou*,
langoustine ravioli, stuffed artichokes *à la barigoule* or *brandade de
morue* with garlic croutons. Main dishes include carefully cooked
filets de rouget en tapénade, canette aux épices and *filet de boeuf aux
gousses d'ail roties*. Straightforward, enjoyable desserts. Service
could not be more accommodating. Set menu: L & D 85F. *L 12-2
D 7-10.* **Closed** *Sat, Sun, Aug. Amex, Mastercard, Visa.*

Le Bistro des Deux Théatres
Map B1.6

| Tel 45 26 41 43   Fax 48 74 08 92 | **R** |

18 rue Blanche 75009
Seats 85

M° **Blanche/Trinité**
Meal for 2 approx 330F

The inexpensive fixed-price menu at this friendly corner bistro
gets you an aperitif, three courses, wine and coffee. There's
a choice of ten dishes at each stage, and in spite of the low price
there's no stinting on luxury, with oysters, foie gras, smoked
salmon, rumpsteak and turbot all making appearances.
Set menu: 165F. *L 12-2 D 7.30-12.30am. Mastercard, Visa.*

Le Bistrot Papillon
Map C2.7

| Tel 47 70 90 03 | **R** |

6 rue Papillon 75009
Seats 60

M° **Poissonière/Cadet**
Meal for 2 approx 550F

Jean-Yves Guion's classic cooking is served in the two small dining
rooms of this auberge, whose walls are covered with suede-effect
claret-coloured wallpaper and tables laid with silver cutlery and
crystal glass. Andouillettes are a major speciality, served Vallé
d'Auge-style with caramelised apples, and other great favourites
include foie gras with port jelly, *sole à l'orange*, salmon steak
en papillote, confit de canard, pan-fried lamb cutlets with tarragon
and *chateaubriand béarnaise*. Round things off with a 'symphony
of sorbets'. Loire wines are particularly popular on the 130-strong
wine list. Set menu: L & D 135F. *L 12-2.30 D 7-10. Closed Sat,
Sun, 1 week Easter, 3 wks from 7/8 Aug. Amex, Diners,
Mastercard, Visa.*

Blanche Fontaine
Map B1.8

Tel 45 26 72 32   Fax 42 81 05 52   **H**

34 rue Fontaine 75009   **M° Blanche**
Rooms 49   Double from 557F

Since it's a little way off the busy Boulevard de Clichy, the hotel
is reasonably quiet, though the action at the Moulin Rouge is not
far away. A bar service operates until 8.30pm and breakfast
is served until 11.30am. Double-glazing, cable TV, radio, direct-
dial telephone and hairdryer in all rooms. The room price includes
breakfast. Private parking (40F). *Amex, Mastercard, Visa.*

Brébant
Map C2.9

Tel 47 70 25 55   Fax 42 46 65 70   **H**

32 bd Poissonnière 75009   **M° Rue Montmartre**
Rooms 122   Double from 890F

An early 19th-century building houses this traditional Parisian
hotel, which offers comfortable accommodation in double-glazed
bedrooms decorated in pastel colours with matching curtains and
bedcovers. All have satellite TV, radio, direct-dial phones, mini-
bars and safes and top floors boast slanting ceilings and beams.
Breakfast is served in the **Le Vieux Pressoir** restaurant, which
takes its name from the old Norman cider press which the owner
has installed. Three lifts serve the building. Seven conference
rooms (max 200 people) are available. Laundry and dry cleaning
service. *Amex, Diners, Mastercard, Visa.*

Casa Olympe
Map B1.10

Tel 42 85 26 01   Fax 45 26 49 33   **R**

48 rue Saint-Georges 75009   **M° St-Georges**
Seats 32   Meal for 2 approx 500F

It has become fashionable in Paris for chefs to open a bistro.
Olympe's is an informal restaurant of Mediterranean atmosphere
located in a quiet street in northern Paris. On the well-priced
menu carte, which changes according to seasons, straightforward
basic cooking is lifted by the best quality ingredients. Typical
dishes include salad of lentils and salmon, marinated raw sardines,
spicy pigeon with red and green cabbage, tuna with bacon and
onions, and, for dessert, a bitter chocolate *fondant* or crème brulée
with vanilla. Set L & D: 180F. *L 12-2 D 8-11.* **Closed** *Sat, Sun,
Aug, 25 Dec, 1 Jan. Mastercard, Visa.*

La Champagne
Map B1.11

Tel 48 74 44 78   Fax 42 80 63 10   **R**

10bis place de Clichy 75009   **M° Place Clichy**
Seats 145   Meal for 2 approx 600F

Essentially for fish and shellfish lovers, this large 'brasserie de luxe'
on two floors with a distinctive nautical theme offers oysters, skate
with brown butter or monkfish with green pepper sauce until the
early hours. Wines from Chablis, Loire and Alsace feature. *L 12-3
D 7-2am. Amex, Diners, Mastercard, Visa.*

Charlot Roi des Coquillages

Tel 48 74 49 64 Fax 40 16 11 00

Map B1.12

R

12 place de Clichy 75009
Seats 140

Mᵒ Place Clichy
Meal for 2 approx 600F

Mirrors in the ceiling, 20s furnishings, engraved glass, tiles and
shells make a most attractive setting for Charlot, 'King
of shellfish". Mediterranean seafood specialities such as mussels *à la
provençale, bouillabaisse marseillaise, bourride tropézienne* or a *ragout
of octopus à la niçoise* dominate chef Didier Lizard's menu, which
varies "according to the season, the weather and the fishermen".
Fish such as bass or red mullet might be steamed, grilled, fried,
cooked in foil or poached. Shellfish is in season when the month
of the year includes an 'R', so during winter try the plateau
de fruits de mer (oysters and shellfish). To accompany the
Provençal dishes choose one of several wines from the region.
Desserts vary from a pear crème brulée or a Grand Marnier
soufflé to a lemon tart with blackcurrant sorbet. Set menu: 149F.
L 12-3 D 7-1am. Amex, Diners, Mastercard, Visa.

Chartier

Tel 47 70 86 29

Map C2.13

R

7 rue du Faubourg Montmartre 75009
Seats 300

Mᵒ Rue Montmartre
Meal for 2 approx 150F

The road is largely given over to fast food outlets, but at the end
of a dim courtyard a revolving door leads into another world and
almost another age. Chartier is a much-loved Paris institution with
the look of a grand railway station and a permanent rush-hour
buzz. Clusters of globe lamps shine brightly from the glass roof,
huge panelled mirrors line the walls and tall copper coat racks run
between and above the tables. Waiters, clad classically in black
jackets and white aprons, perform with speed and efficiency,
noting your order on the paper tablecloths and rushing around
with heavily laden trays. The food is, in all honesty, nothing
special, but prices are amazingly low and there's no better place
to watch Paris eating (and no more convivial spot, as you're quite
likely to have to share a table). Starters are priced from 8F for egg
mayonnaise, beetroot salad or andouille with butter to 25F for
half-a-dozen snails. Main courses start at 30F for hachis Parmentier
(shepherd's pie) and stop short of 50F (entrecote with frites 90F
for 2, perch with shallot sauce 48F). Chocolate mousse, compote
of peaches or an ice cream could be your dessert, and with a glass
or two of wine and a cup of coffee the bill for two will hardly
exceed 150F. Another Chartier outlet, with a similar menu but
without the atmosphere, is *Le Drouot* at 103 Rue Richelieu in the
2nd. Tel 42 96 68 23. *L 11-3 D 6-9.30. Mastercard, Visa.*

Chez Clément Opéra

Tel 47 42 00 25 Fax 47 42 94 00

Map B2.14

R

17 bd des Capucines 75009
Seats 200

Mᵒ Opéra
Meal for 2 approx 320F

New and very popular all-day brasserie catering admirably for
a constant stream of hungry shoppers, tourists and office workers.
Oysters, shellfish, spit-roasted meats and profiteroles are the house
specialities, along with hare terrine, bone marrow with salt,

See over

moules marinière and knuckle of pork with lentils. The oysters, meats and profiteroles are served *à volonté* for, respectively, 135F, 73F and 38F, and if you order the excellent Camembert, you can help yourself from a board left on the table. Other Chez Cléments are in the 8th (123 ave des Champs Elysées Tel 47 20 01 13 – opening Feb 95) and 17th (99 bd Gouvion-St-Cyr Tel 45 72 93 00). *Meals noon-1am. Amex, Mastercard, Visa.*

Cidotel Lafayette   Map C2.15
Tel 42 85 05 44   Fax 49 95 06 60   **H**

49 rue Lafayette 75009   **Mᵒ Cadet/Le Peletier**
Rooms 75   Double from 850F

A practical hotel located between Opéra and the Sacré Coeur. One floor is designated no-smoking. Bedrooms are practical and well equipped, with little balconies and grey and white tiled bathrooms, most of which have tubs. As we went to press, a new wing of 28 suites, a conference room, reception room and bar was near completion. The hotel offers laundry, dry cleaning and photograph developing services. *Amex, Diners, Mastercard, Visa.*

Copthorne Commodore   Map C2.16
Tel 42 46 72 82   Fax 47 70 23 81   **H**

12 bd Haussmann 75009   **Mᵒ Richelieu-Drouot**
Rooms 162   Double from 1450F

Enjoying a prime location midway between the Opéra and the Bourse (Stock Exchange) near the major department stores, this Copthorne hotel, built in 1927 in Italian rococo style, offers a high standard of comfort and service. Bedrooms have pastel blue walls, grey carpet and green or pink floral curtains and antique-style furniture; all have well-appointed en-suite bathrooms. The glass-domed Carvery is open for breakfast and a buffet lunch. The *Cancans* bar/brasserie is an alternative option for lunch or dinner à la carte. Three meeting rooms, maximum capacity 28. There's a parking arrangement with the Drouot park – 70F for 24 hours. *Amex, Diners, Mastercard, Visa.*

Le Grand Café Capucines   Map B2.17
Tel 47 42 19 00   Fax 47 42 74 22   **R**

4 bd des Capucines 75009   **Mᵒ Opéra**
Seats 240   Meal for 2 approx 500F

An elegant brasserie with a breathtaking art deco interior of enormous mirrors and walls covered with tiles painted with Mucha drawings, sculpted stair railings and lights in the form of giant shells. It's open day and night, and fish and shellfish are a major draw – the options, both à la carte and fixed-price, are many and varied; the shellfish platter (192F) is a meal in itself, and other specialities include carpaccio of monkfish and salmon with dill, seafood tagliatelle, veal kidney with Meaux mustard, rump steak with shallots, champagne sorbet and chocolate mousse. After 11pm and until dawn, 'à l'heure des violons', there's a fixed price menu of 119F offering two courses and a drink. Set menu 185F. *Meals 24 hours. Amex, Diners, Mastercard, Visa.*

Grand Hotel Inter-Continental

Map B2.18

| Tel 40 07 32 32   Fax 42 66 12 51 | **HR** |

2 rue Scribe 75009   **M⁰ Auber Opéra**
Rooms 514   Double from 2100F

On the corner of Place de l'Opéra and facing the opera house itself,
this luxurious and tastefully decorated hotel dating back to the
Napoleon III era has twenty-five spacious suites amongst its 500+
rooms. The hotel's central reception room, the **Cour d'Honneur**,
is a marble-floored lounge with a vast glass and steel dome. There
are 18 conference rooms and a health club. There's valet parking
and they're building a hotel car park opposite. Take your breakfast
in the **Brasserie du Café de la Paix**, which runs along two sides
of the building, your lunch at **La Verrière** and for a more
gastronomic meal, try the **Opéra** restaurant (see below for **Opéra**
and **Café de la Paix**). Conference rooms (max 500). *Amex,
Diners, Mastercard, Visa.*

Restaurant Opéra

Tel 40 07 30 10   Fax 40 07 33 75
5 place de l'Opéra 75009
Seats 75   Meal for 2 approx 1000F

The Grand Hotel Inter-Continental is home to a very grand
gastronomic restaurant. It has its own entrance on the Place
de l'Opéra – an elegant restaurant decorated in blue and gold, with
original gold leaf mouldings, and famous painted ceiling of stylised
cherubs and clouds. Dishes are often luxurious and quite elaborate:
ravioli of langoustines and coriander cooked in a shellfish
bouillon; beignets of frogs' legs with confit tomatoes and
cauliflower à la grecque; baked turbot with young spinach,
tarragon and béarnaise sauce; roast pigeon accompanied by a
'tourte' of cabbage with lardons and foie gras; feuilleté with
arabica and pecan nuts; poached figs with cinnamon and a
fromage blanc sorbet. Comprehensive wine list. Set menus: L and
D 285F, 385F, 450F. *L 12-3 D 7-11.* **Closed** *Sat, Sun & Aug.*

Brasserie du Café de la Paix

Tel 40 07 30 20
12 bd des Capucines 75009
Seats 220   Meal for 2 approx 350F

Taking up two sides of the hotel, one on the boulevard and the
other on the Place de l'Opéra, this famous brasserie has been
a popular meeting place for 130 years. With its 19th-century
frescoes on ceiling and walls and stylised winter garden decor, the
interior of the brasserie is an appropriate setting for traditional
French cuisine. Oysters are something of a speciality, with six
types available in season. The glass-roofed pavement plus six types
of oyster while the glass-roofed pavement terrace is an ideal spot
for cocktails, coffee, simple meals and elite people-watching! Set
menu: 135F. *Meals 12-1.15am.*

Hotel du Léman

Map C2.19

| Tel 42 46 50 66   Fax 48 24 27 59 | **H** |

20 rue de Trévise 75009   **M⁰ Cadet**
Rooms 24   Double from 440F

A small modernised hotel with double-glazing and a cosy cellar-
like breakfast room with an all-day brunch menu. Bedrooms,   *See over*

some with beams, are neatly decorated and useful extras provided
include video, stereo, cassettes and a mini-bar. Dry cleaning and
laundry service. Parking (80F for 24 hours) in a nearby garage.
Amex, Diners, Mastercard, Visa.

Hotel du Moulin Rouge

Map B1.20

Tel 42 81 93 25   Fax 40 16 09 90   **H**

30 rue Fontaine 75009
M° Blanche
Rooms 50
Double from 785F

Attractive modern hotel that's part of a small group. Located
a short distance from the Moulin Rouge in a pleasant street,
it features smartly decorated bedrooms, some with terraces but all
with mini-bars and up-to-date marble-lined shower/bathrooms.
Breakfast, available up to midday, is in the form of a buffet (60F).
Laundry and dry cleaning service. *Amex, Mastercard, Visa.*

L'Oenothèque

Map C1.21

Tel 48 78 08 76   **R**

20 rue St Lazare 75009
M° Notre Dame de Lorette
Seats 40
Meal for 2 approx 650F

Wine and cognac merchant Daniel Hallé runs this splendid
'restaurant à vins', which is divided into two rooms. The first
is full of bottle-laden shelves, while the second is decorated with
paintings (for sale) by contemporary artists. There are 350
references on the all-French wine list, while the short menu
changes on a daily basis according to what's best in the market.
Marinated raw sardines, *terrine de volaille*, fried *céteaux* (like small
soles) or *bavarois de poivrons* could precede rack of lamb, grilled
veal kidney, andouillette in red wine or fillet of rascasse with
lemon butter. Roast pigeon is something of a speciality. To finish,
perhaps a fruit tart, chocolate marquise or crème brulée. *L 12-2.30
D 7.30-10.30.* **Closed** *Sat, Sun, last 3 weeks Aug, 1 week Feb.
Mastercard, Visa.*

Opéra Cadet

Map C2.22

Tel 48 24 05 26   Fax 42 46 68 09   **H**

24 rue Cadet 75009
M° Cadet
Rooms 85
Double from 740F

A modern hotel in a building located in a semi-pedestrianised
street. The buffet breakfast is served in a conservatory overlooking
a plant-filled garden. The air-conditioned rooms offer en-suite
bathrooms, satellite TV, direct-dial telephones and mini-bars.
A lounge bar is open all day and there are two conference rooms.
Private parking (60F a day). Laundry service. *Amex, Diners,
Mastercard, Visa.*

Au Petit Riche

Map C2.23

Tel 47 70 68 68   Fax 48 24 10 79   **R**

25 rue Le Peletier 75009
M° Richelieu-Drouot
Seats 110
Meal for 2 approx 490F

Engraved glass, mirrors and wood give the correct period look
to this 19th-century bistro, where good food is matched by fine
wines (the Loire features very strongly). A plate of oysters, *terrine
de lapin*, leeks in *sauce ravigote*, a salad of goat's cheese or mixed

smoked fish are typical starters, while the main-course
choice might include poached haddock *à l'aigre-doux,* cod with
basil, *magret* or *confit de canard,* andouillette with Vouvray
or grilled entrecote with three mustards. End with farmhouse
cheeses, *choco-menthe* or the speciality *tarte fine aux pommes tièdes.*
There are four private rooms upstairs for 8-45 people. Set menu:
L & D 160F. *L 12-2.15 D 7-12.15am.* **Closed** *Sun. Amex, Diners,
Mastercard, Visa.*

Hotel du Pré   Map D1.24

Tel 42 81 37 11 Fax 40 23 98 28	**H**

10 rue Pierre Sémard 75009   M° Poissonnière/Cadet
Rooms 41   Double from 520F

1900 building renovated ten years ago. Peaceful, comfortable and
family-run with big beds and good bathrooms. Buffet breakfast
50F. 24hr reception. No room service. No restaurant. Madame
du Pré also owns, in the same street, the *Relais du Pré* (Tel 42 85
19 59 Fax 42 85 70 59) and the *Résidence du Pré* (Tel 48 78 26 72
Fax 42 80 64 83). The hotels are between Gare du Nord and
Opéra. *Amex, Diners, Mastercard, Visa.*

Riboutté-Lafayette   Map C2.25

Tel 47 70 62 36 Fax 48 00 91 50	**H**

5 rue Riboutté (corner 82 rue Lafayette) 75009   M° Cadet
Rooms 24   Double from 450F

A small, inexpensive and tastefully decorated hotel in a tiny street
well placed for the area's department stores. The rooms are
individually decorated with en-suite facilities (some with showers
only) and a few have a view of Square Montholon nearby. 24hr
reception. Special parking tariff at a nearby garage. *Amex,
Mastercard, Visa.*

Scribe   Map B2.26

Tel 44 71 24 24 Fax 42 65 39 97	**HR**

1 rue Scribe 75009   M° Opéra
Rooms 217   Double from 2200F

A major corner site, formerly the Jockey Club, whose Napoleon
III façade today conceals a busy, cosmopolitan hotel in the Sofitel
group. Refurbishment over recent years has extended from the
spacious lobby with its Baccarat crystal chandeliers and the
luxurious, softly-lit cocktail bar to the bedrooms. Things like air-
conditioning, double-glazing (for streetside rooms) and endless
TV channels provide the modern comforts for rooms that are
mainly traditionally furnished in Louis Philippe or Louis XVI
style. Some rooms are in 'English' style and there are some suites,
featuring mezzanine bedroom floors, that are more contemporary
in concept. Conference rooms have a maximum capacity of 100.
Valet parking. This is the place where the Lumière brothers first
showed their moving picture images on a screen, an event whose
centenary this year is being celebrated at the Centre Pompidou
and elsewhere. *Amex, Diners, Mastercard, Visa.*   *See over*

Les Muses
Tel 44 71 24 26
Seats 30   Meal for 2 approx 800F

In elegant panelled surroundings guests enjoy a fine variety
of dishes prepared by Philippe Pleuën and his team. Top-quality
produce is sought in the markets and many dishes are enhanced
by subtle use of herbs and spices: fresh coriander with a medley
of vegetables, wild purslane with a 'fantaisie' of calf's sweetbreads
and Challans chicken and lavender infusing an iced fondant served
with Guanaja chocolate sauce. Game has an autumn/winter menu
to itself ('carte de la chasse'), as do coffees and teas. Fine
cheeseboard and some alluring desserts. Set menus: L &
D 210F/270F. *L 12-2.30 D 7.30-10.30.* **Closed** *Sat, Sun, Aug &
Public Holidays.*

La Table d'Anvers   ★   Map C1.27
Tel 48 78 35 21   Fax 45 26 66 67   R
2 place d'Anvers 75009   M° Anvers
Seats 50   Meal for 2 approx 900F

Christian Conticini is the *cuisinier* and his brother Philippe the
patissier at this restaurant overlooking the square. Christian
is known for the original way in which he mixes spices,
condiments, oils and vinegars in dishes that regularly feature
vegetables, mushrooms and pastas. Foie gras is accompanied by
quince, spices and *trompettes*; John Dory by *mousserons*, orange and
coriander; wild duck by *girolles* and Jerusalem artichokes; scallops
by gnocchi and Provençal tomatoes. Philippe's crafted desserts
may include some irresistible chocolate creations and a *passion
créole* (soaked biscuit, vanilla ice cream, rum, pineapple, pepper
and coconut). On arriving at your table, choose as an aperitif
a glass of one of fifteen regional wines and to clean the palate
between courses the Conticini brothers offer unusual 'parfums
à boire' (hot or cold drinks flavoured with hibiscus, star anise, sage
or cinnamon). The extensive wine list includes a number of Italian
wines and several vins de pays. Set menus: L 160F, D (Mon-Thur)
190F. *L 12-2.45 D 7-11.30.* **Closed** *L Sat, all Sun.* Amex,
Mastercard, Visa.

Wally le Saharien   Map C1.28
Tel 42 85 51 90   Fax 45 86 08 35   R
36 rue Rodier 75009   M° Anvers
Seats 45   Meal for 2 approx 575F

Wally Shouaki has moved lock, stock and camel from the 4th
to the 9th, where he now entices old friends and new with his
unique *menu dégustation*. There are three choices for starter – *harira*
(a hearty vegetable soup), pigeon pastilla and sardines stuffed with
herbs and onion; next comes the main-event couscous
accompanied by méchoui and excellent merguez but with
no bouillon and no vegetables; dessert is a delicate gateau with
a fresh orange coulis, and as much mint tea as you want. Wines
from North Africa naturally accompany the food at this splendid
oasis in a gastronomic semi-desert. Set menu: 240F. *L 12-2.30
D 7.30-12. Closed Sun, 1-2 weeks Jan, 1-2 weeks early Sept.
No credit cards.*

10th Arrondissement
Places of Interest

Musée de Cristalleries de Baccarat, 47 70 64 30, Mº Chateau d'Eau
Place de la République

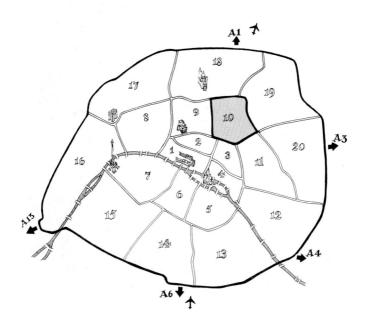

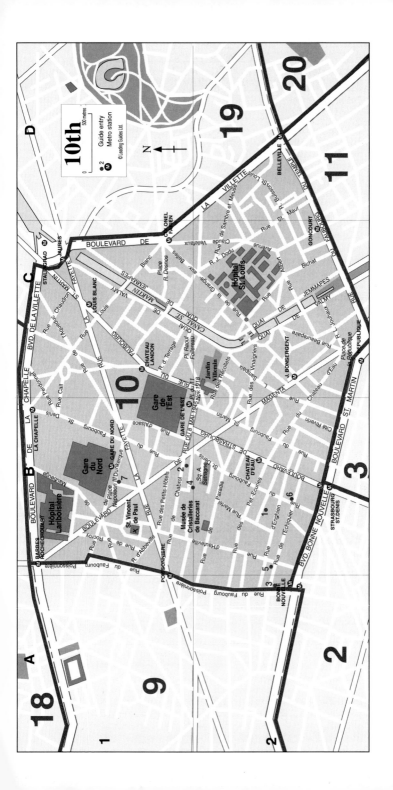

10th

0 500 metres

● 2 Guide entry
Ⓜ ● Metro station
© Leading Guides Ltd.

N

18
9
1

A

BARBES
ROCHECHOUART Ⓜ

BOULEVARD DE LA CHAPELLE

Hôpital
Lariboisière

St. Vincent
X de Paul

Rue de Maubeuge

Rue de la Place Napoléon III Dunkerque

Rue de Rocroy

Rue d'Abbeville

Gare du Nord
Ⓜ GARE DU NORD

7

Rue de Dunkerque

Rue du Faubourg St Denis

RUE LA FAYETTE

BOULEVARD DE LA CHAPELLE Ⓜ

Rue Philippe de Girard

Rue Cail

Rue du Faubourg St Denis

C
STALINGRAD Ⓜ

BOULEVARD DE LA VILLETTE

Rue Chaudron

Rue Louis Blanc

Ⓜ LOUIS BLANC

RUE DU FAUBOURG ST MARTIN

Rue Louis Blanc

VALMY

QUAI DE VALMY

QUAI DE JEMMAPES

Place
R. Desnos R. Blanc

COLONEL FABIEN Ⓜ

BOULEVARD DE LA VILLETTE

de Sambre et Meuse

Avenue Claude Vellefaux

Rue R.T. Dodu

Rue Bichat

Rue Albert

Hôpital
St. Louis

Rue de la Grange-aux-Belles

10

Gare
de
l'Est

Ⓜ GARE DE L'EST RUE DU 8 MAI 1945 PL DU 11 NOV 1918

Ⓜ CHÂTEAU LANDON

R. d Terrage

Pl Raoul
Follereau

Jardin
Villemin

Rue des Récollets

Rue du Faubourg St Martin

Rue des Vinaigriers

Rue du Château d'Eau

Rue des Récollets

D

19

20

11
Ⓜ BELLEVILLE

Rue Simon-Bolivar

Rue des Buissons-St-Louis

Rue du Temple

GONCOURT Ⓜ

Rue St Maur

Rue Bichat

JEMMAPES

J. BONSERGENT Ⓜ

Rue Beaurepaire

Place de
la République

Rue de la République

RUE DU FAUBOURG DU TEMPLE

BOULEVARD DE MAGENTA

Rue du Château d'Eau

Cité Riverin

BOULEVARD ST MARTIN

3

Musée de
Cristalleries
de Baccarat

Rue de Chabrol

2

Sq A
Satragne 4

Rue des Petits-Hôtels

Rue d'Hauteville

Rue de Paradis

Rue de Paradis

Rue Martel

Rue des Petites-Écuries

Rue du Faubourg St Denis

CHÂTEAU D'EAU Ⓜ

Rue des Messageries

Rue de Paradis

BOULEVARD DE STRASBOURG

Rue d'Enghien

Rue de l'Échiquier

1

6

Rue Beauregard

BOULEVARD ST DENIS

STRASBOURG
ST DENIS Ⓜ

Rue d'Hauteville

5

Rue du Faubourg Poissonnière

3

BONNE NOUVELLE Ⓜ

BVD BONNE NOUVELLE

POISSONNIÈRE Ⓜ

Rue Poissonnière

Rue du Faubourg Poissonnière

9
1

2

2

Brasserie Flo
Map B2.1

Tel 47 70 13 59   Fax 42 47 00 80   R

7 cour des Petites-Ecuries 75010   M° Chateau d'Eau/Strasbourg St Denis
Seats 140   Meal for 2 approx 450F

The site has been a tavern/brasserie since 1886 and to the present
day parquet flooring, leather banquettes, the original darkwood
panelling and coffered ceiling remain. The decor sets off the
colourful pictures and frescoes that evoke scenes related to the
brewing of beer and landscapes of the Alsace region. Once called
Hans, it changed its name after passing into the hands of the
Floderer family, who owned it until 1964. Seafood is a major
speciality – oysters, clams, crab, mussels, prawns, langoustines –
which you can order piecemeal or in various platters. Grilled
lobster flamed with whisky is currently very popular. The menu
changes on a very regular basis, but *foie gras gelée au Riesling*,
terrine of skate with tomato coulis, *petit salé*, steak tartare, grills
and choucroute are among the favourites. The entrance to the
courtyard is at 63 Rue du Faubourg St Denis. Valet parking in the
evening. Set menus: L 109F, D 185F (and 109F after 10pm). *L 12-
3 D 7-1.30am. Closed D 24 Dec. Amex, Diners, Mastercard, Visa.*

Au Chateaubriant
Map B1.2

Tel 48 24 58 94   R

23 rue de Chabrol 75010   M° Poissonnière/Gare de l'Est
Seats 40   Meal for 2 approx 550F

A fine collection of modern prints fills the walls of this warm,
stylish little restaurant, where owner-chef Guy Bürkli belies its
name by offering Italian cuisine both traditional and adventurous.
In the first category come garlic mushrooms, *penne all'arrabbiata*,
osso buco and *tournedos Rossini*, in the latter lasagne with
aubergines and sardines, cod steak with confit tomatoes,
millefeuille of veal and *croustillant de tete de veau* with capers.
Charming service by Madame Bürkli. Set menu: 149F (including
aperitif). *L 12.15-2.30 D 7.20-10.15. **Closed** Sun, Mon & Aug.
Amex, Mastercard, Visa.*

Aux Deux Canards
Map A2.3

Tel 47 70 03 23   R

8 rue du Faubourg Poissonnière 75010   M° Bonne Nouvelle
Seats 50   Meal for 2 approx 410F

A stable door (opened from the inside) leads from the busy street
into a little haven of brass and mirrors and traditional French
cooking by Bernard Ferec, a chef who rarely leaves his kitchen.
The menu, which changes daily, is written on a blackboard and
the voluble patron Gérard Faesch uses an extending blackboard
pointer to explain at length what is on offer. (The prelude is a
demonstration – sniffing included – of how they make and mature
the orange honey which is an integral part of their *Barbary duck
à l'orange* and chocolate mousse.) Foie gras makes regular
appearances and other choices run from *pétoncles* (little scallops)
and dill-marinated salmon to *salade lyonnaise* (pork, onions,
potatoes, leaves), duck terrine, veal kidneys, pig's trotters with
mustard, *moules de Bouchot*, sardines with pistou, *andouillette* and
faux filet béarnaise. Salmon is served with two sauces – beurre

blanc and beurre rouge. Munster and other cheeses, crème brulée and pears in syrup with hot chocolate sauce could round off the meal – or, of course, that chocolate mousse. This is a strictly non-smoking restaurant, and your reward for abstaining is the offer of a cigar on the way out. A place full of atmosphere, run by a real enthusiast who personally oversees the ordering of wines – look for some blackboard bargains. Conviviality is guaranteed not only by the patron but also by the piano, which guests can play when the mood takes them. Set menus: L & D 95F & 120F. *L 12-2 D 7-10. (Fri & Sat to 10.30). **Closed** L Sat, all Sun and Aug. Amex, Diners, Mastercard, Visa.*

Flora

Map B1.4

Tel 48 24 84 84   Fax 48 00 91 03   H

**1-3 cour de la Ferme-Saint-Lazare (corner 79 bd
Magenta) 75010**   **M° Gare de l'Est**
Rooms 45   Double from 595F

Being close to both the Gare du Nord and the Gare de l'Est, there's easy access to areas to the north and east of Paris (especially airports and ferries). The hotel is pleasantly decorated in pastel colours and offers functional accommodation. There's no restaurant, but breakfast is served in a vaulted stone cellar. *Amex, Diners, Mastercard, Visa.*

L'Horset Pavillon

Map B2.5

Tel 42 46 92 75   Fax 42 47 03 97   H

38 rue de l'Echiquier 75010   **M° Strasbourg St Denis/Bonne Nouvelle**
Rooms 92   Double from 810F

In 1593, when the building was in forested land outside the city walls, it was used as a hunting lodge by Henry IV. He then gave it to a religious order who were forced to hand it over to the State during the French Revolution. From the basement, subterranean passages led to the town. In 1850 it became a hotel. Located in a quiet street in the area known as 'Les Grands Boulevards', this is one of five L'Horset hotels in Paris. Genuine Belle Epoque stained glass, frescoes and wooden panelling fill the reception rooms and the fully-equipped bedrooms are done out in keeping with this era. *Amex, Diners, Mastercard, Visa.*

Julien

Map B2.6

Tel 47 70 12 06   Fax 42 47 00 65   R

16 rue du Faubourg St Denis 75010   **M° Gare de l'Est**
Seats 180   Meal for 2 approx 450F

Built in 1889 but not opened until 1903; the public had a long wait to appreciate Fournier's art nouveau interior for which the establishment has now been classified a historic monument. The artist Louis Trezel, who was passionate about the theatre and modern art, painted an astonishing decor of women and flowers in the style of Mucha on *pates de verre* panels on the walls of the entire brasserie; another eye-catching feature is a magnificent mahogany counter. In the same family as *Brasserie Flo* (see above), with a daily-changing menu virtually the same but without the choucroute and shellfish specialities. Popular orders include   *See over* smoked salmon, foie gras, terrine of skate with tomato coulis, grills, confit and cassoulet. Set menus: L 109F D 109F (after 10). *L 12-3 D 7-1.30am. Amex, Diners, Mastercard, Visa.*

Terminus Nord

Map B1.7

Tel 42 85 05 15   Fax 40 16 13 98   **R**

23 rue Dunkerque 75010   **M° Gare du Nord**
Seats 200+   Meal for 2 approx 450F

A railway journey to or from the channel ports or Le Tunnel is all that brings most visitors to this part of Paris, but this classic, rambling 1925 brasserie in the Flo group is very well worth a visit. A vast bank of shellfish is on eye-catching display all year round, and is the subject of a separate menu. Other specialities include asparagus in its brief season, choucroute and steaks, and the daily specials such as veal Marengo, navarin of lamb or salmon with sorrel are always in demand. Serious service from well-drilled, smartly attired waiters and waitresses, who dash around with trayloads of food and drink. Child-friendly. Set menu 109F. Also open for breakfast, teas and coffees. Pavement terrace. *Meals 11.30am-12.30am. Amex, Diners, Mastercard, Visa.*

CHAMPAGNE

FONDÉE EN 1827

G.H. MUMM & Cᴵᴱ

REIMS~FRANCE

11th Arrondissement
Places of Interest

Place de la Bastille/Opéra Bastille
Place de la République
Musée Edith Piaf, 43 55 52 72, M° Ménilmontant

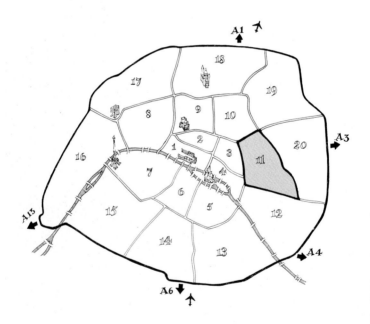

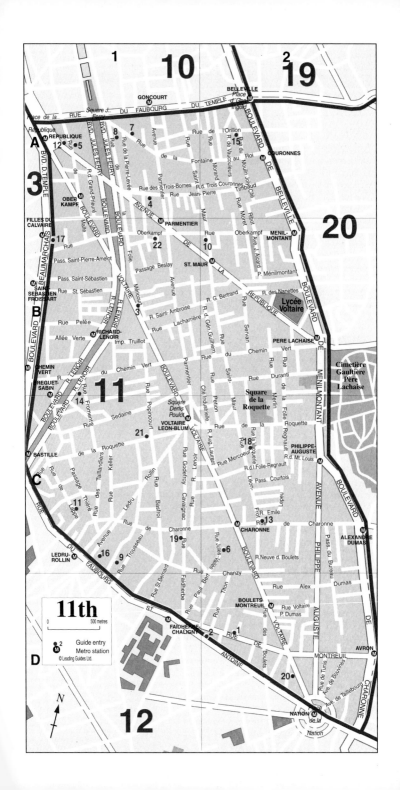

L'Aiguière   Map D2.1

Tel 43 72 42 32   Fax 43 72 86 36   **R**

37bis rue de Montreuil 75011   Mᵒ Nation/Faidherbe-Chaligny
Seats 80   Meal for 2 approx 650F

Aiguières were originally pewter receptacles for water until Louis
XIII had them made in glass and used them for wine when
he dined here with his musketeers. To this day, *grands crus* wines
are served in them at L'Aiguière. In this comfortable and elegant
restaurant neatly decorated in grey and white with plenty
of flowers, chef Pascal Viallet adapts traditional recipes to modern-
day tastes in dishes which show many innovative touches. The
foie gras is home-prepared and one of the main-course specialities
is Tournedos Yella (fillet of Charolais beef with fresh foie gras,
sweetbreads and a Périgourd sauce with truffles) which could
be followed by another speciality, *feuillantine de poire en chaud froid*.
On the fish front, try steamed cod with fried vegetables, or
gourmandise of turbot with roasted pistachios and an infusion of
turmeric. A la carte and set menus: L 125F, L & D 175F & 248F.
The last (248F) menu offers a complementary glass of wine with
each course. *L 12-2.30 D 7.30-10.30.* **Closed** *L Sat, all Sun. Amex,
Diners, Mastercard, Visa.*

Les Amognes   Map D2.2

Tel 43 72 73 05   **R**

243 rue du Faubourg St Antoine 75011   Mᵒ Faidherbe-Chaligny
Seats 35   Meal for 2 approx 460F

Chef/owner Thierry Coué describes his cuisine as "du terroir" but
slightly lighter than usual. His generous menu is a four-course
affair with six choices of starters, main courses and puddings. Start
with *beignets de brandade de morue* with fried sage leaves and confit
tomatoes or boudin noir in filo pastry, and move on to tuna with
artichokes, peppers and coriander or oxtail-stuffed cèpes or a very
special *cote de boeuf* with *truffade auvergnate*. For dessert, perhaps
a feuilleté of pears with a spiced wine granita, or roast figs stuffed
with red berries. French-only wine list with fair prices that match
the cost of the food. *Menu carte:* L & D 170F. *L 12.30-2.30
D 7.30-11.* **Closed** *Sun & Mon. Mastercard, Visa.*

Anjou-Normandie   Map B1.3

Tel 47 00 30 59   **R**

13 rue de la Folie Méricourt 75011   Mᵒ St Ambroise
Seats 23 (+30 for lunch)   Meal for 2 approx 400F

A setting of auberge quaint-cosiness: old beams, flowery curtains,
assorted landscapes, seascapes and foodscapes on the walls, crisp
white table linen, candles in old pewter holders. Speciality meat
dishes ("all seasoned with sea salt and ground pepper") are
andouillettes (grilled plain, grilled and flambéed with Calvados,
grilled with shallots, baked with Comté cheese), *confit de canard*,
tripe and *filet de boeuf*. Start with feuilleté of mussels or Roquefort,
or *terrines maison* – you help yourself from three king-size terrines.
Tarte tatin is the recommended dessert. Coffee is served with
a Valrhona chocolate and a cracked fresh hazelnut –a charming
touch to end a satisfying meal. Good sound cooking by Alain
Langevin, service led by his wife Monique. They've been here

nearly 20 years. Set L & D 140F, 165F & 60F *(menu enfant)*. *L 12-1.45 D 7.30-9.15.* **Closed** *D Mon, all Sat & Sun, Aug. Amex, Diners, Mastercard, Visa.*

Astier

Map A1.4

R

Tel 43 57 16 35

44 rue Jean-Pierre Timbaud 75011   **M⁰ Oberkampf/Parmentier**
Seats 80   Meal for 2 approx 360F

A very popular and convivial neighbourhood bistro on two floors with a particularly appealing 130F menu for lunch or supper. The cooking is in traditional bistro style, and some of the most popular dishes are fresh pasta with basil, *terrine de poisson beurre blanc,* whelks with aïoli, salmon with tarragon, *tete de veau vinaigrette,* sautéed lamb with flageolets, and *saucisse de Morteau* with lentils. The ravenous will help themselves from an excellent 20-strong cheese tray before rounding off with pears in red wine, clafoutis or a very refreshing terrine of orange and grapefruit. A very comprehensive and reasonably-priced wine list features many of the best growers – quite exceptional for such an unassuming place. This is a really good traditional restaurant, where the staff want you to have a jolly time whether you're a regular or a first-timer. *L 12-2 D 8-11.* **Closed** *Sat, Sun, 2 wks Easter, all Aug, 2 wks Christmas. Amex, Mastercard, Visa.*

Cartet

Map A1.5

R

Tel 48 05 17 65

62 rue de Malte 75011   **M⁰ République**
Seats 18   Meal for 2 approx 550F

Raymond Nouaille, chef-owner of this tiny bistro with its 1930s' decor of wood-panelled walls, mirrors, pictures and floor tiles, specialises in regional dishes from the Lyons area. *Pieds de mouton sauce poulette* or *sauce rémoulade,* crab soufflé, *quenelles de brochet, gras-double flambé,* monkfish *sauce Nantua, cote de veau aux morilles* and *boeuf à la ficelle* are typical choices. Choose from the six classic desserts (lemon tart, crème caramel and floating islands are some examples) displayed on the small bar. *L 12-2 D 7.30-9.30.* **Closed** *Sat, Sun, 8 days Mar, all Aug, 8 days Christmas. No credit cards.*

Chardenoux

Map C2.6

R

Tel 43 71 49 52

1 rue Jules-Vallès 75011   **M⁰ Faidherbe-Chaligny/Charonne**
Seats 40   Meal for 2 approx 500F

Owner/chef Bernard Passavant produces traditional bistro cuisine in his beautiful and genuine, listed 1900s' bistro with its etched glass doors separating the two dining rooms, mirrors, intricately moulded ceilings and a gleaming zinc bar. The menu may feature salad of St Jacques with hazelnut oil, cod florentine, veal kidneys cooked whole with Meaux mustard, *onglet* with mushrooms, game in season and a dark chocolate mousse with orange purée. Wines from the South-West are prominent on the list. *L 12-2.15 D 8-10.* **Closed** *Sat, Sun, 1 week Feb, all Aug. Amex, Mastercard, Visa.*

Chez Fernand (Les Fernandises)   Map A1.7

Tel 43 57 46 25   **R**

17 rue de la Fontaine-au-Roi 75011   **M° République**
Seats 70   Meal for 2 approx 440F

All the regional products for which Normandy is famous – cider,
butter, milk, Camembert, apples, Calvados – feature on the menu
in chef-owner Fernand Asseline's inexpensive restaurant. Typical
dishes may include skate with Camembert, fillet of duck in a cider
sauce with apples, and *crêpes flambés au calvados*. Drink Normandy
cider as an alternative to wine. Set menu: L & D 130F. *L 12-2.30
D 8-11.30*. **Closed** *Sun, Mon & Aug. Mastercard, Visa.*

Chez Philippe (Auberge Pyrénées-Cevennes)   Map A1.8

Tel 43 57 33 78   **R**

106 rue de la Folie Méricourt 75011   **M° République**
Seats 65   Meal for 2 approx 650F

Rustic best describes the good food and cosy decor of this bistro
specialising in the food of the South-West and with a chef
(Philippe Serbource) of 25 years standing. Alongside several
Bayonne hams are cartwheels hanging from the ceiling with lights
attached which illuminate a setting of exposed stone walls, beamed
ceilings, red tiled floor, wooden tables covered in white linen and
cane-seated chairs. Home-prepared foie gras is available every day
as a starter, and there's always a hearty *plat du jour*, with a tart
or clafoutis to finish. *L 12-2 D 7.30-10.30*. **Closed** *Sat, Sun, Aug &
Public Holidays. Amex, Mastercard, Visa.*

Cormillot Bistro Lyonnais   Map C1.9

Tel 48 05 77 10   **R**

8 rue de la Main d'Or 75011   **M° Ledru-Rollin**
Seats 45   Meal for 2 approx 300F

In a quiet, somewhat neglected little street of carpenters and
cabinet-makers, Patrick Cormillot's bar is a touch seedy but also
a bit special. It's basically, in looks at least, a typical down-at-heel
bar, and the name Cormillot does not appear on the outside.
Patrick used to combine his cooking with a coal-delivery service,
and that side of the business, though no longer in operation, is still
advertised on the frontage. The locals drop in for snacks
at lunchtime, and in the evening the blackboard menu of Lyonnais
specialities comes into play: *saucisson*, *terrine maison*, *cervelle des
canuts* (not brains, but fromage blanc, shallots, wine, herbs),
quenelles de brochet, several veal dishes (liver, sweetbreads,
andouillette) and *civet de porc* (like a *civet de lièvre*, the meat
simmered with wine, lardons, onions and potatoes). Finish with
a fine St Marcellin cheese and chestnut gateau. This is the sort
of place which should not be allowed to fall victim to the brash,
bright, fast food operations that are now such a feature of many
parts of Paris (including the main streets in this area). Put on your
third best outfit, go along to M. Cormillot and tuck into his
hearty Lyonnais food at very low prices. *L snacks 12-2.30 D 8-
10.30 Tues-Fri*. **Closed** *Sat, Sun, Aug, Christmas-New Year.
No credit cards.*

Les Folies – Chez Rosine

Map B2.10

Tel 43 38 13 61

R

101 rue St Maur 75011
Seats 48

M⁰ St Maur
Meal for 2 approx 400F

Rosine Ek came to Paris from Cambodia in 1974 and set up her
unique restaurant three years ago serving very traditional
Cambodian cuisine. In a long and fairly seedy street hers is an
evocative setting of ancient sculptured doors, wood columns and
further sculptures on the walls, Rosine produces from the kitchen
mainly grilled seafood adding lots of herbs and roots. A speciality
starter is *natang* (chopped chicken, prawns, coconut milk and
crispy rice) and two of her popular main courses are grilled catfish
with tamarind and sautéed mussels with spices and roots. She
makes a *gateau maison* with jackfruit, coconut milk and palm
fruit. French wine or Chinese beer to drink (the Cambodians
do not yet brew beer). Set menus: L and D 98F (incl. wine), 138F.
L 12-2.30 D 7.30-11. **Closed** *L Sat, all Sun, last 3 weeks Aug.*
Amex, Mastercard, Visa.

La Galoche d'Aurillac

Map C1.11

Tel 47 00 77 15

R

41 rue de Lappe 75011
Seats 52

M⁰ Bastille
Meal for 2 approx 400F

If you haven't visited the Auvergne region of France, here's your
chance to do it in Paris, in one of the most ancient of streets (now
taken over mainly by clubs and tapas bars). You can come to these
authentic surroundings (hams and musical instruments hang from
the walls) simply to sample the wines of the region or eat some
of the regional specialities such as kidney beans cooked in goose
fat, a selection of charcuterie or salad of cured country ham and
Cantal cheese, followed by sausage with lentils, stuffed breast
of veal, mutton tripe or a steak, and a plum tart to finish. All
wines available by the glass. Wine, ham and cheese can
be purchased to take home. Set menu: L & D 150F. *L 12-2.30
D 7-11.30.* **Closed** *Sun, Mon, 6 weeks Jul-Sep. No credit cards
(Mastercard, Visa soon).*

Holiday Inn République

Map A1.12

Tel 43 55 44 34   Fax 47 00 32 34

HR

10 place de la République 75011
Rooms 318

M⁰ République
Double room from 1465F

Both the 'standard' and 'luxurious' categories of air-conditioned
bedroom at this large chain hotel are well equipped. The building,
which dates back to 1850, is now a listed historic monument and
the original attractive courtyard is popular for sitting out in or for
hiring for private functions. The hotel is exceptionally well served
with restaurants – La **Belle Epoque** restaurant for gastronomic
food, and for a lighter meal the **Folies Brasserie**, which has
an interior garden. The largest of nine conference rooms can hold
280 theatre-style. *Amex, Diners, Mastercard, Visa.*   *See over*

La Belle Epoque
Seats 50   Meal for 2 approx 700F

Recently renovated, the Belle Epoque has abandoned its set menus
and now offers à la carte and various buffets, including Italian
specialities on Thursday evening, seafood Friday and Saturday
evenings and a family Sunday lunch. On the à la carte selection
look for cassolette of escargots, paupiettes of sole, veal chop with
sorrel and baked pear with pistachio sabayon. Wines from
Australia and Spain as well as France. *L 12-2.30 D 7-10.30.*

Jacques Mélac	**Map C2.13**
Tel 43 70 59 27 Fax 43 70 73 10	**R**
42 rue Léon-Frot 75011	**M⁰ Charonne**

The wooden beams, stone floor tiles and the thousands of empty
wine bottles covering the wall space give Jacques Mélac's *bistrot
à vins* a distinct but understated charm. His own Domaine des
Trois Filles (appellation Lirac) is the only wine which is always
included in the list of thirty, chosen every fortnight. A good
selection of simple dishes is available to accompany the chosen
wine, such as *andouillette au vin blanc de chez Duval, crépinettes
de porc* or Auvergne cheeses served with Aveyron charcuterie. The
cooking is unpretentious and the host amiable and enthusiastic.
Open for drinks outside meal times. *L 12-3 D 5.30-10.30.*
***Closed** D Mon, all Sat and Sun, Aug & Pub Hols. Mastercard, Visa.*

Méridional	**Map B1.14**
Tel 48 05 75 00 Fax 43 57 42 85	**H**
36 bd Richard Lenoir 75011	**M⁰ Bréguet-Sabin**
Rooms 36	Double room from 600F

Modern hotel conveniently located for visiting the recently-
revived Bastille and Marais areas. Double-glazed rooms are
equipped with en-suite bathroom, direct-dial telephone, radio
alarm, TV, mini-bar and hairdryer. No restaurant. *Amex, Diners,
Mastercard, Visa.*

Nioullaville	**Map A2.15**
Tel 43 38 30 44 Fax 43 38 58 48	**R**
32 rue de l'Orillon 75011	**M⁰ Belleville**
Seats 500	Meal for 2 approx 300F

An operation rather similar to London's Chinatown giants – a vast
restaurant with an equally vast menu ('un voyage gourmand
en Asie') covering Hong Kong, Szechuan, Cambodia, Vietnam and
Thailand. The Parisians have really taken this place to their hearts,
and it's especially popular at weekends, but a week-long feature
is the dim sum, wheeled round on metal wagons (if you miss one
wagon, don't worry, because another one will come along soon –
the service is as reliable as Paris buses!). The menu choice really
is enormous, with many dishes found hardly anywhere else
in Paris – sea cucumber and jellyfish are just two examples.
Belleville, east of Place de la République, is a major centre
of ethnic eating, with China, North Africa, the Middle East and
Kosher all represented. Nioullaville has its own parking in the
basement (for 150 cars). *L 12-3.30 D 7-1am. Amex, Diners,
Mastercard, Visa.*

Le Passage

Tel 47 00 73 30   Fax 47 00 14 00

Map C1.16

R

18 passage de la Bonne-Graine 75011   **Mᵒ Ledru-Rollin**

Do not be deceived by the rather drab little alleyway which leads off Rue du Faubourg-Saint-Antoine to this bright and modern wine bar/restaurant. An international selection of wines stretches to around 270 references (only twenty of which, however, are available by the glass). Perhaps the most outstanding feature of the menu is the selection of andouillettes (an entire page!), all served with a gratin dauphinois and either peas or lentils (with a 10F optional extra of mustard sauce). Other choices may include ricotta with confit aubergines, whole baby artichokes with olive oil and marinated peppers, duck rillettes or smoked and matjes herrings served together with a warm potato salad. At the time of going to press plans to create a second outlet were well under way (Café du Passage, 12 Rue de Charonne). Open for drinks outside meal times. *L 12-2.30 D 7.30-10.30.* **Closed** *Sun. Amex, Diners, Mastercard, Visa.*

Le Repaire de Cartouche

Tel 47 00 25 86

Map B1.17

R

8 bd des Filles-du-Calvaire 75011   **Mᵒ St Sebastien-Froissart**
Seats 45   Meal for 2 approx 600F

A cosy country-style neighbourhood restaurant opened in the 1940s. One translation of *cartouche* is cartridge, and indeed there are a few weapons on the walls, alongside frescoes, dark panelling and scorched lampshades. But this *Cartouche* remembers a French version of Robin Hood whose lair (*repaire*) was nearby. Unusually, the restaurant is on two levels with small-paned windows and entrances on the main République-Bastille road and on the parallel Rue Amelot behind. Specialising in all manner of duck (magret is served *saignant*), the chef offers sweet music for *abats* fans in *l'assortiment du terroir*, which includes giblets, heart, neck and *graisseround*. There's also duck terrine and foie gras, and elsewhere on the varied menu could appear cassolette of snails, carpaccio of monkfish with a pepper mousse, chicken with tarragon sauce and salmon served with an asparagus sauce. For dessert, choose *crepe soufflé, a tourtière landaise* flamed with armagnac, *nougat glacé* or one of the excellent sorbets. Good coffee comes with pieces of dark bitter chocolate. Some decent country wines in bottles or pewter *pichets*, and over 100 armagnacs. Fixed-price menu at 150F and (D Sat) 220F. *L 12-2.30 D 7-10.30.* **Closed** *L Sat, all Sun, last week Jul-last week Aug. Amex, Diners, Mastercard, Visa.*

Le Roudoulié

Tel 43 79 27 46

Map C2.18

R

16 rue de La Vacquerie 75011   **Mᵒ Voltaire**
Seats 40   Meal for 2 approx 350F

A Chilean artist has painted the eye-catching ceiling in Madame Vilar's restaurant, formerly a bistro. Also vying for attention is the food, which comes from the South-West: *salade de Roudoulié* (confit of quails, smoked magret of duck and fresh foie gras), duck pot-au-feu, rabbit stuffed with vegetables or wing of skate with Meaux mustard, followed by a raspberry clafoutis or chocolate   *See over*

tart. Accompanying wines like Madiran are also from the area.
A daily-changing lunch menu of 62 francs (starter and main
course) provides outstanding value for money. Set menus: L 62F,
L & D 92F & 210F. *L 12-2.30 D 7.30-10.30.* **Closed** *L Sat, all Sun.
Amex, Mastercard, Visa.*

A Sousceyrac   ★   Map C1.19

| Tel 43 71 65 30   Fax 40 09 79 75 | R |

35 rue Faidherbe 75011   · M° Charonne/Faidherbe-Chaligny
Seats 60   Meal for 2 approx 650F

One of the culinary delights of the little town of Soucceyrac in the
Lot region of France is its cassoulet. This dish therefore features
as one of the South-Western specialities served in this typical
1920s-30s' bistro with its tiled floors, wood panelling and
diplomas on the walls. Others might be their foie gras (goose
or duck), terrine of lobster and foie gras in jelly, hare à la royale
(in season) or coquilles St Jacques with sorrel, followed by an apple
feuilleté with armagnac or crème brulée maison. Patrick Asfaux
is the third generation of the founding family. 260-long wine list.
Set menu: L and D 175F. *L 12-2 D 7.30-10.* **Closed** *L Sat, all
Sun & Aug. Amex, Diners, Mastercard, Visa.*

La Table Richelieu   Map D2.20

| Tel 43 72 31 23 | R |

276 bd Voltaire 75011   M° Nation
Seats 50   Meal for 2 approx 600F

La Table Richelieu is a gastronomic restaurant where the pictures
on the wall are for sale and menus change four times a year.
Seafood is perhaps the predominant ingredient in the classic
cooking of owner-chef Daniel Rousseau with dishes depending on
the catch: lobster with Sauternes and fresh pasta, salmon and
Normandy oysters with a ballotine of cabbage, bass steamed over
seaweed. Seafood platters range up to the mighty *plateau des quatre
mousquetaires* (800F) with a cascade of oysters, clams, whelks,
winkles, prawns, langoustines and crabs. Meat dishes, too, and
some splendid desserts. Private room (max 35). Set menus:
L (Mon-Fri) 145F inc wine, L & D 200F & 260F. *L 12-2.30, 7-11.*
Closed *L Sat. Amex, Diners, Mastercard, Visa.*

Thai Elephant   Map C1.21

| Tel 47 00 42 00   Fax 47 00 45 44 | R |

43-45 rue Roquette 75011   M° Bastille
Seats 200   Meal for 2 approx 600F

Resembling a Thai village, this elegant restaurant on different
levels with teak furnishings, exotic plants and flowers, roofs over
the tables and centrepiece of a water fountain, bridge and pond,
has recently changed its name from Blue Elephant. Nothing else
has changed, and it still serves authentic 'Royal Thai cuisine'.
Starters include the *Kiss du Golfe du Siam* (giant stuffed prawns),
chicken or pork satay and mussels with celery and basil, whilst
among the main courses are *Coco Cabane* which originates from
Phuket (curried beef served in a fresh coconut shell accompanied
with noodles) and a chicken soufflé (presented within a banana
leaf, steam-cooked and seasoned with curry, coconut and

citronella). Wines are taken very seriously here, and the Alsatian house wine in particular complements the cooking. Fair prices, even a champagne at around 250F – cheap for France! Set menus: L 150F D 265F & 295F. *L 12-2.30 D 7-12 (Sun to 11).*
Closed *L Sat, 3 days Christmas. Amex, Diners, Mastercard, Visa.*

Le Villaret

Map B1.22

`Tel 43 57 89 76`   **R**

13 rue Ternaux 75011   **Mᵒ Oberkampf/Parmentier**
Seats 45   Meal for 2 approx 400F

No name on the door outside, and a very modest handwritten menu, but enough people know about this place to keep it full each evening, so don't turn up without booking. Decor is 'new old' – beams, bricks, stones, tiled floor, long-backed kitchen-style chairs. Chef Olivier Gaslain changes his menu with the seasons (St Jacques and mushrooms were appearing on an autumn visit). Everything on the list is worth trying, including *soupe de rougets*, *friture de céteaux* (a small sole-like fish), *oeufs cocotte* in a foie gras cream, langoustines in a saffron-infused lobster sauce, veal sweetbreads and kidneys, fresh *morue* with a creamy garlic sauce and purées of broccoli and potatoes, quenelles of chocolate with *griottes* and a vanilla sauce. Small, personal wine list. *D only 7.30-1am.* **Closed** *Sun, Aug. Mastercard, Visa.*

12th Arrondissement
Places of Interest

Opera de Paris Bastille, Reservations 44 73 13 00, Enquiries 40 01 17 89, Mº Bastille

Musée National des Arts d'Afrique et d'Océanie, 44 74 84 80, Mº Porte Dorée

Palais Omnisports de Paris Bercy, 43 42 01 23 (43 46 12 21), Mº Bercy

Bois de Vincennes (pleasure garden, zoo, boating), 44 75 20 00, Mº Porte Dorée

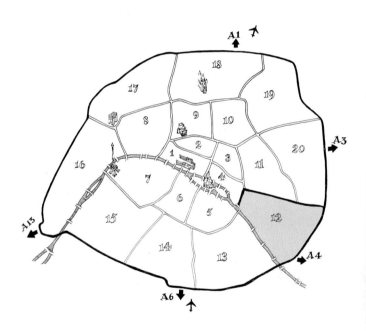

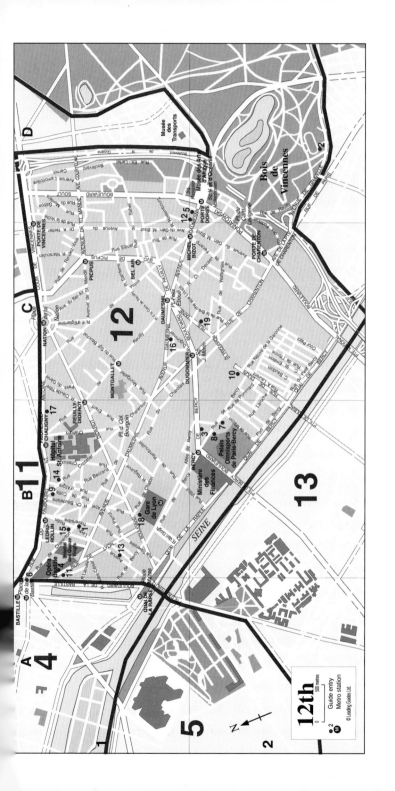

Belle Epoque   Map B1.1

| Tel 43 44 06 66   Fax 43 44 10 25 | **H** |

66 rue de Charenton 75012   **M° Ledru Rollin**
Rooms 29   Double from 590F

Built around a garden courtyard, the rooms in this art deco hotel
are numbered from 1900 upwards! The reproduction furniture
was made by craftsmen using the same woods and the original
designs of two famous French designers of that period, Printz and
Ruhlmann. Three suites however have genuine pieces from the
early 1900s. Modern comforts include marble bathrooms, double-
glazed windows, mini-bars, direct-dial telephones, and TVs. The
bar is open from noon to 10pm and tea is served at around 5pm
with a selection of cakes. No restaurant. Three meeting rooms
(max 50). *Amex, Diners, Mastercard, Visa.*

La Cipale   Map D2.2

| Tel 43 75 54 53 | **R** |

49 ave de Gravelle 75012   **M° Charenton Ecoles**
Seats 32   Meal for 2 approx 500F

'Cipale' is an abbreviation of 'piste municipale' – in other words,
the local cycling stadium! Bruno Frédéric and his new chef Marc
Dufosée run this small restaurant, with its own outside entrance,
within the ancient stadium (dates back to 1896). In summer, guests
sit out on the terrace. Menus change according to the seasonal
availability of produce – *escargots au vin de Sancerre, papillote
de rouget au vermouth blanc, gigotin d'agneau à la fleur de thym, canette
rotie à l'ananas et mangues,* various hot soufflés and a fig tart with
fig ice cream. Bruno's contact with Vendome *cavistes* produces
a wine list on which he has personally tasted each reference. Set
menus: L & D 160F, 190F. *L 12-2 D 7.30-9.30.* **Closed** *L Sat,
D Sun, all Mon & Aug. Mastercard, Visa.*

Hotel Claret   Map B2.3

| Tel 46 28 41 31   Fax 49 28 09 29 | **H** |

44 bd de Bercy 75012   **M° Bercy**
Rooms 52   Double from 450F

Formerly a post office and then a police station, the building now
houses a family-run, rustic hotel where all rooms have TV and
either bath or shower, with wc. Some rooms are quite small and,
in the absence of air-conditioning, can become rather warm.
Buffet breakfast 45F. Italian restaurant. The hotel is close to the
POPB (the futuristic Bercy sports complex) and Gare de Lyon.
Pronounce the t in Claret. *Amex, Diners, Mastercard, Visa.*

Fouquet's Bastille   ★   Map B1.4

| Tel 43 42 18 18 | **R** |

place de la Bastille 75012   **M° Bastille**
Seats 130   Meal for 2 approx 850F

Immediately beneath the ultra-modern edifice of the Opéra
Bastille, the restaurant shares its cool, sophisticated lines with
frosted glass screens, stone floors and smart, if rather
uncomfortable chairs. Walls are in attractive distressed fresco-style
as if executed by some artist from ancient Rome. The menu has

elements of both tradition and modernity with a good section
of generous salads including one with halved fresh artichoke
bottoms, mixed salad leaves and a super vinaigrette. Main dishes
include the crispiest of duck confits served with paper-thin
triangles of exceptionally good sautéed potatoes with more than
a hint of garlic or else a generous rolled piece of beautifully
trimmed monkfish served with a very light, creamy *dugléré* sauce.
A popular place for post-theatre dining. *Set L 97F (inc wine &*
coffee). L 12-3 D 6-11.30. **Closed** *L Sat, all Sun & Aug. Amex,*
Diners, Mastercard, Visa.

La Gourmandise
Map D2.5

| Tel 43 43 94 41 | R |

271 ave Daumesnil 75012   M^o Porte Dorée
Seats 45   Meal for 2 approx 680F

Alain Denoual has been serving his "personalised classic cuisine"
to his clients for more than 10 years in this warm and intimate
restaurant with flowers and flowery fabrics. A choice of around
140 wines is listed to accompany fixed-price menus (including one
for children) as well as the *à la carte*. Fish is predominant: salad
of langoustines and artichokes, mullet with olive oil and balsamic
vinegar dressing, monkfish with mushrooms and red wine, lobster
ravioli. On the meat side, veal kidneys and sweetbreads, lamb with
honey and cider vinegar, and *faux filet* with two peppers are
typical, and mango charlotte remains a popular dessert. Only three
non-French wines on an excellent list – one of them, a Californian
Opus One 1985, is very fairly priced at 400F. Set menus: L &
D 92F (child), 140F, 170F, 300F. *L 12-2 D 7.15-10.30.*
Closed *D Mon, all Sun, 3 weeks Aug. Amex, Mastercard, Visa.*

Les Grandes Marches
Map A1.6

| Tel 43 42 90 32   Fax 43 44 80 02 | R |

6 place de la Bastille 75012   M^o Bastille
Seats 200   Meal for 2 approx 600F

The first floor of this large *brasserie de luxe* dominating one section
of Place de la Bastille is a little more intimate (leather armchairs
and wall-to-wall carpeting) than the ground floor, where the
atmosphere is that of a genuine brasserie. The decor nevertheless
is as contemporary as the adjacent new Opéra Bastille building.
The long menu offers something for everyone – oysters, fish soup,
foie gras, *bavarois* of vegetables with a tomato coulis, millefeuille
of smoked salmon, grilled sole, turbot and giant prawns, baked
John Dory, calf's kidney, andouillette, *magret de canard*,
chateaubriand, raspberry tart, *ile flottante*, orange mousse. Each
section of the *carte* has a couple of recommended wines. Set menu:
L & D 168F (ground floor only). *Meals noon-1am.* **Closed** *10 days*
Aug. Amex, Diners, Mastercard, Visa.

Ibis Paris-Bercy
Map B2.7

| Tel 43 42 91 91   Fax 43 42 34 79 | H |

77 rue de Bercy 75012   M^o Bercy
Rooms 364   Double from 450F

A large, modern, functional and inexpensive hotel of the Ibis
chain with the Bercy gardens opposite. Children under 12 stay   *See over*

free if sharing parents' room. Amenities include parking, well-equipped conference rooms (among them 4 new rooms on the first floor) and a 70-seat restaurant with an outdoor terrace (cold snacks are available 24hrs from reception). Laundry service. This is one of several Ibis hotels within the Paris area. See Around Paris section for Ibis airport hotels. *Amex, Mastercard, Visa.*

Novotel Paris-Bercy

Map B2.8

| Tel 43 42 30 00   Fax 43 45 30 60 | **H** |

85 rue de Bercy 75012 **Mᵒ Bercy**
Rooms 129 Double from 760F

One of the chain's hotels, built in 1987 and located opposite the lawns and gardens of the Palais Omnisports de Paris-Bercy. Well-equipped, soundproofed and air-conditioned, pastel-coloured rooms with en-suite bathrooms. Two children under 16 stay free if sharing parents' room. Six conference rooms (the largest holds 120 theatre-style). This is one of several Novotels in the Paris region – call 60 77 51 51 for central reservations. *Amex, Diners, Mastercard, Visa.*

D'Oggi

Map B1.9

| Tel 43 41 33 27 | **R** |

27 rue Cotte 75012 **Mᵒ Ledru-Rollin**
Seats 40 Meal for 2 approx 320F

The exposed stone-walled basement with paper-clothed tables and candles is the main dining room of Madame Cartier's Italian restaurant. She insists on not cooking pizzas and concentrates instead on pasta and other specialities such as *caponata* (similar to ratatouille) or carpaccio for starters, followed by *tagliatelle al salmone, tortellini* with cream, lardons and mushrooms, saltimbocca or *gambas San Daniel* (prawns rolled in ham with the chef's special 'red' sauce) and finally, a traditional *tiramisu.* A tiny wine list: six Italian and two French. Set menus: L 60F & 80F (3 courses plus wine). *L 12-2.30 D 7-11.* **Closed** *D Mon, all Sun, 2 weeks Aug, 1 week Christmas-New Year. Diners, Mastercard, Visa.*

L'Oulette   ★

Map C2.10

| Tel 40 02 02 12 | **R** |

15 place Lachambeaudie 75012 **Mᵒ Bercy/Dugommier**
Seats 50 (+ 30 outdoor) Meal for 2 approx 650F

A modern restaurant, square-shaped, with a wood block floor and picture windows opening on to the terrace. Bold fabric on the chairs and banquette seating contrast with the pale yellow tablecloths, plants, central flower arrangements, small earthenware table pots with dried flowers, English china, and Villeroy & Boch loos! The back wall has a shelf displaying copper cooking pans and jars of home-made preserves, pickles and fruit. Mostly cooking from the South West, as in the *menu du marché* (150F) and *menu de saison* (230F) which includes an excellent French country wine. Dishes are both interesting and satisfying, typified by *tartine à la moelle et au foie gras*, squid escabèche with warm potatoes, *petits-gris* snails with Banyuls wine and a salad of rocket and walnuts, *confit de canard*, cassoulet with Tarbais beans, bream with celery blinis and saddle of hare with ginger and grilled chestnuts.

Regional cheeses and some hard-to-resist desserts like *tourtière* with apples and medlars or parfait-glacé with caramelised hazelnuts. As in most Parisian restaurants, precious few non-French wines on the list, though one here is just that: Opus One Robert Mondavi 1988 from California at a fair 400F. All-in-all, a good list with a trio of monthly suggestions. Choice of seven arabica coffees served with *madeleines* and mini-chocolate marquises. Set menus: 150F, 230F (incl wine). *L 12-2.15 D 8-10.15.* **Closed** *L Sat, all Sun. Amex, Mastercard, Visa.*

Le Pavillon Bastille   Map B1.11

| Tel 43 43 65 65   Fax 43 43 96 52 | **H** |

65 rue de Lyon 75012   **M⁰ Bastille**
Rooms 24   Double from 925F

This 19th-century building surrounds a 17th-century courtyard and fountain. The yellow and blue air-conditioned rooms are comfortably furnished and offer international TV channels, mini-bars (soft drinks are free) and en-suite bathrooms with bathrobes, magnifying mirrors and hairdryers. Breakfast is served in the vaulted basement and the entrance hall becomes a relaxed bar area later in the day. No restaurant. Laundry service. *Amex, Diners, Mastercard, Visa.*

Au Pressoir   ★   Map D2.12

| Tel 43 44 38 21   Fax 43 43 81 77 | **R** |

257 ave Daumesnil 75012   **M⁰ Michel Bizot**
Seats 50   Meal for 2 approx 1100F

In an ancient former wine warehouse (hence the name), the restaurant was entirely renovated three years ago including the wood panelling in light oak and the leather banquette seating. This is a gastronomic restaurant in traditional terms, relying very much on fresh produce including truffles. *Truffe en croute de gros sel, gazpacho de homard* or *terrine de foie gras et d'artichauts* could be followed by baked turbot with spinach, *St Pierre aux oignons confits* or hare *à la royale* (a big seasonal speciality). 500 references on a mainly French wine list. Two private rooms upstairs (max 12 & 20). Valet parking. Set menu: L and D 390F. *L 12-2.30 D 7.30-10.30.* **Closed** *Sat, Sun, Aug, 1 wk in Feb (school hols). Mastercard, Visa.*

Le Quincy   Map B1.13

| Tel 46 28 46 76 | **R** |

28 ave Ledru-Rollin 75012   **M⁰ Gare de Lyon**
Seats 35   Meal for 2 approx 600F

Country cooking, in particular from the Ardeche area of France, predominates in this bistro – *terrine fermière avec chou à l'ail, foie gras, écrevisses pates rouges, queue de boeuf braisée, dorade à l'ancienne* and an assortment of desserts from which diners may choose. Wines of the region accompany (you pay by the measure and the owner drinks what you don't!) and it's all served in rustic, country-style surroundings. *L 12-2 D 7-10.* **Closed** *Sat, Sun, Mon, mid-Aug to mid-Sep. No credit cards.*

Le Relais de Lyon   Map B1.14

Tel 43 44 22 50   Fax 43 41 55 12   **H**

64 rue Crozatier 75012   **M⁰ Ledru-Rollin**
Rooms 34   Double from 530F

A very quiet modern hotel with comfortable, light bedrooms.
Breakfast 40F. *Amex, Diners, Mastercard, Visa.*

Sipario   Map B1.15

Tel 43 45 70 26   **R**

69 rue Charenton 75012   **M⁰ Ledru-Rollin/Bastille**
Seats 48   Meal for 2 approx 400F

Giant vegetables painted in pastel colours are the decorative
highlights of this very good Italian restaurant. Southen Italian
cuisine is the summer speciality, while hearty dishes from the
North keep the customers full and happy in winter. Post-opera-
goers come here for *vitello tonnato* followed by rascasse ravioli
with fresh tomato, with a vanilla ice cream in a 'bath' of hot coffee
sauce to finish. Set menu: L 100F. *L 12-2 D 7.30-12. **Closed** Sun,
15 days mid-Aug. Amex, Diners, Mastercard, Visa.*

La Sologne   ★   Map C2.16

Tel 43 07 68 97   **R**

164 ave Daumesnil 75012   **M⁰ Daumesnil**
Seats 45   Meal for 2 approx 450F

Didier Maillet, whose previous experience includes a spell
in Chicago, presents a seasonal menu in his comfortably appointed
terrasse restaurant near Place Félix Eboué. Sologne is a major
hunting area south of Paris, and game features prominently
in winter. Mushrooms and coquilles St Jacques also find their place
in season, and other house specialities include a fine, delicate *terrine
de lapereau* (all rabbit, with no pork or chicken 'boosters'), calf's
foot terrine with *sauce aigrelette, blanquette de veau à l'ancienne,*
roast cod with cabbage confit and tartare of salmon. Among the
desserts note *tarte fine aux pommes, nougat glacé* with dried fruit
and pistachios and a splendid *crème brulée* subtly sharpened with
lemon zest. There's plenty of interest, too, on the wine list,
including a Morgon 'Marcel Lapierre', Chateau Meylet St Emilion
1989 and a 'Branger' Muscadet which is hand-produced by old-
fashioned methods and comes in a 'satin-finish' bottle. The
connoisseur with longer pockets will consult the list of *crus
millésimés.* Virginie Maillet is a charming, concerned hostess in this
really excellent little restaurant. Set L 150F. *L 12-2.30 D 7.30-
10.30 (Sat to 11.30). **Closed** L Sat, all Sun, 2 weeks Aug. Amex,
Diners, Mastercard, Visa.*

Le Temps des Cerises   Map B1.17

Tel 43 67 52 08   Fax 43 67 60 91   **R**

216 rue du Faubourg St Antoine 75012   **M⁰ Faidherbe Chaligny/Nation**
Seats 58 (+ 15 terrace)   Meal for 2 approx 650F

The paintings change on the walls in each of the three dining
rooms as and when a new artist is invited to put on a show in this
restaurant, which stays in fine form. Credit has to go to chef

Bernard Bergounioux, a former sous-chef to Alain Dutournier (of *Carré des Feuillants* fame) who continues to attract customers with his *cassoulet d'escargots aux noix*, duck foie gras, fillet of beef with a truffle sauce, saddle of lamb with tarragon, skate with red butter and calf's kidneys with a mustard sauce. To finish, perhaps *tarte fine aux pommes* or *nougat glacé*. The reliable quality, good-value menus and modestly priced wine list make this an excellent address in the area. Set menus: L & D 95F, 145F, 185F & 220F. *L 12-2.30 D 7.30-10.30 (Fri & Sat to 11). Amex, Mastercard, Visa.*

Le Train Bleu   Map B1.18

Tel 43 43 09 06   Fax 43 43 97 96   **R**

Gare de Lyon 75012   **M° Gare de Lyon**
Seats 200   Meal for 2 approx 600F

The station itself, with a facade over 100 yards long, is an impressive monument to late 19th-century architectural grandeur, but the restaurant is absolutely stunning. Thirty painters were commissioned to paint the walls and ceilings, their theme being the towns and regions served by the PLM (Paris-Lyon-Méditerranée) railway company. Complementing the paintings are myriad handsome ornaments and statues, sculptures and gilt mouldings, as well as some unique furniture including a remarkable cash desk which dominates the **Salle Dorée**. The restaurant was declared a historic monument, with the official protection that entails, in 1972. From the kitchen comes a good variety of traditional French cooking, with some specialities from the Lyons area: sausages hot and cold, brill soufflé with mushrooms, fish quenelles with crayfish butter sauce, *gigot*, *confit* of goose leg. There are also regional bottles among the 150,000 kept in stock. Set menus: L&D 195F & 260F. *L 12-2 D 7-10. Amex, Diners, Mastercard, Visa.*

Au Trou Gascon   ★   Map C2.19

Tel 43 44 34 26   Fax 43 07 80 55   **R**

40 rue Taine 75012   **M° Daumesnil**
Seats 45   Meal for 2 approx 800F

Maitre-chef Alain Dutournier made his name in this 1900 bistro-style setting at the top of Rue Taine before going on to greater glory at his *Carré des Feuillants* (see entry in 2nd arrondissement). His wife Nicole now runs Au Trou Gascon, a traditional haven of South-Western cuisine, but it's chef Jacques Fassat who actually delivers the goods. His cassoulet is among the finest in all Paris, with home-made sausages and beans from Tarbes. Top-quality produce is very much the keynote, all the game being guaranteed wild and all the poultry coming from farms in Chalosse. Other signature dishes are pheasant consommé with fresh chestnuts, warm paté of ceps in parsley *jus*, foie gras, *confit de canard* and hare *à la royale*. Desserts, some of which should be ordered at the start of the meal, include *tourtière chaude landaise*, *crème brulée cannelle et moka* and *croustade* of figs with *nougat glacé*. The long wine list covers France comprehensively and also has a fair Spanish showing. *L 12-2 D 7.30-10.* **Closed** *Sat, Sun, Aug, 1 week Christmas. Amex, Diners, Mastercard, Visa.*

13th Arrondissement
Places of Interest

Gobelins (tapestry factory), 43 37 12 60, M° Gobelins
Place d'Italie

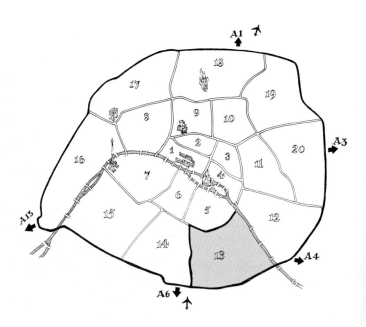

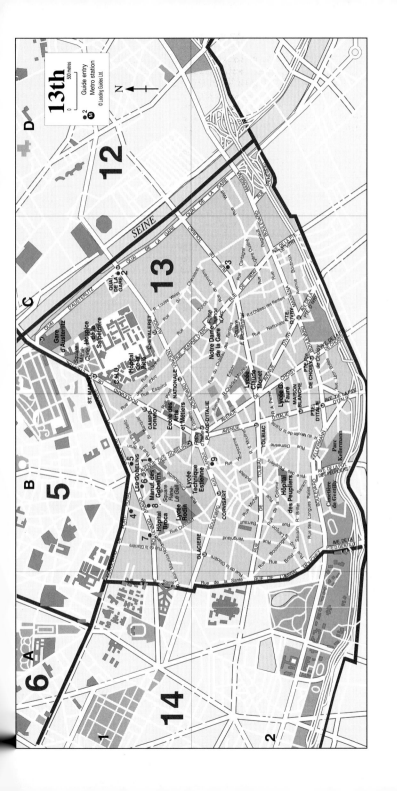

13th

0   500 metres

● 2   Guide entry
Ⓜ 2   Metro station

© Leading Guides Ltd.

N

SEINE

QUAI D'AUSTERLITZ
Gare d'Austerlitz
Square Marie-Curie
Hospice de la Salpêtrière
QUAI DE LA GARE 2
QUAI DE LA GARE

13

Hôpital de la Pitié
C.H.U.
CHEVALERET
ST. MARCEL
BOULEVARD
R. Louise Weiss
R. Jeanne d'Arc
Rue Esquirol
CAMPO-FORMIO
Ecole des Arts et Métiers
NATIONALE
PLACE D'ITALIE
Notre Dame
Rue Jeanne d'Arc
Square E. Brunetour
PTE. D'IVRY
DIVRY
MASSENA
12

D

C

B

5
● 5
● 1
● 6 ● 3
Manuf. des Gobelins
● 8
Lycée Technique Estienne
● 9
Square René-Le Gall
Lycée des Gobelins
AVENUE DES GOBELINS
TOLBIAC
CORVISART
GLACIÈRE
Hôpital Broca
● 7
● 4
Lycée Rodin
Rue de la Glacière
Rue de la Santé
RUE DE LA SANTÉ
Rue de la Santé
14
6
A

Lycée Claude Monet
Lycée G. Faure
AVE. D'ITALIE
PTE. DE CHOISY
PTE. D'ITALIE
BLANCHE
Hôpital des Peupliers
BOULEVARD KELLERMANN
Parc Kellermann
Cimetière de Gentilly
AVE. DE LA PTE. DE GENTILLY
PIED GENTILLY

1

2

Equinoxe
Map B1.1

| Tel 43 37 56 56   Fax 45 35 52 42 | **H** |

40 rue le Brun 75013
Rooms 49

M° Gobelins
Double from 480F

Well-appointed, practical hotel in a modern (1981) building. Tubs
in all bathrooms, ever-open bar and private parking (50F per day
– lift access) are among the pluses. Work continues on the
building of 36 additional rooms. *Amex, Diners, Mastercard, Visa.*

Mercure Paris-Bercy
Map C1.2

| Tel 45 82 48 00   Fax 45 82 19 16 | **H** |

6 bd Vincent Auriol 75013
Rooms 89

M° Quai de la Gare
Double from 580F

Not far from the Bibliothèque Nationale which is currently under
construction, this ultra-modern functional hotel offers comfortably
furnished, air-conditioned and sound-proofed bedrooms. Private
parking for 10 cars. Restaurant and bar. Buffet breakfast 60F.
Conference room for 40 delegates theatre-style. *Amex, Diners,
Mastercard, Visa.*

Mercure Paris-Tolbiac
Map C2.3

| Tel 45 84 61 61   Fax 45 84 43 38 | **H** |

21 rue de Tolbiac 75013
Rooms 71

M° Nationale
Double from 580F

Another of fifty Mercure hotels located inside the Périphérique
offering modern, comfortably furnished rooms with en-suite
bathrooms, direct-dial phones, mini-bars, satellite TV, radio (with
speakers in bathroom) and a room service providing light meals
from Monday to Thursday, 7-11 pm. Buffet breakfast 60F.
Parking for 13 cars (reserve your place). *Amex, Diners,
Mastercard, Visa.*

Le Petit Marguery
Map B1.4

| Tel 43 31 58 59 | **R** |

9 bd du Port-Royal 75013
Seats 80 (+ 20 terrace)

M° Gobelins
Meal for 2 approx 700F

The three Cousin brothers, Michel, Jacques and Alain, create
a very friendly ambiance at this authentic Parisian bistro. Michel
and Jacques spend most of their time in the kitchen, occasionally
coming out to greet customers or join in conversation. Alain
makes sure all runs smoothly in the two dining rooms with their
ancient tiled floors and aged pink walls covered with mirrors. The
brothers specialise in game, offal, fresh fish and regional dishes:
hure de sanglier, terrines of hare, partridge and pheasant, escalope of
lightly smoked salmon in a cabbage leaf, veal kidney with
mustard, tripe, fricassee of lamb with baby vegetables, hare *à la
royale*, noisettes of venison *à la romaine*. To finish, perhaps a bitter
chocolate cake with moka sabayon, Grand Marnier soufflé or
cherry soup with prunes in armagnac. Set menus only: L 160F,
L & D 200F (menu carte), 320F, 450F. *L 12-2.15 D 7.30-10.30.*
Closed *Sun, Mon, Aug & 8 days Christmas. Amex, Diners,
Mastercard, Visa.*

Pizza César
Map B1.5

Tel 43 31 68 60 | R

81 bd St Marcel 75013 | Mº Les Gobelins

Near the old Gobelins factory, Pizza César offers a Franco-Italian menu with the emphasis on pizzas cooked in a wood-fired oven. Best bet for the hungry is the 69F three-course menu with pizza or pasta as the centrepiece. Open for lunch and dinner every day. *Mastercard, Visa.*

Résidence des Gobelins
Map B1.6

Tel 47 07 26 90   Fax 43 31 44 05 | H

9 rue des Gobelins 75013 | Mº Gobelins
Rooms 32 | Double from 400F

Well located hotel with clean, straightforward accommodation. The breakfast room looks out on to a charming courtyard with creeping ivy. *Amex, Mastercard, Visa.*

Le Rhône
Map B1.7

Tel 47 07 33 57 | R

40 bd Arago 75013 | Mº Gobelins
Seats 50 (+ 30 outdoor) | Meal for 2 approx 300F

Bright, simply appointed restaurant whose scope extends in summer on to a wide pavement terrace. Jean Reuschlein and his wife seem to take turns in the kitchen, where they specialise in the cooking of Lyons. Andouillettes, tripe, stuffed neck of goose, *quenelles de brochet, magret de canard au poivre vert* and *pavé* of beef with a Meaux mustard sauce are the principal central dishes, with marinated herrings a favourite starter and *tarte tatin* a popular finale. Plenty of simpler choices too, like egg mayonnaise, *céléris rémoulade* and *crème caramel*. There's always a daily special or two, perhaps *pot au feu* or *rascasse provençale*. Cotes du Tarn (Gamay) is a recommended tipple. Set Menus: L & D 75F, 105F & 160F. *L 12-2 D 7-10.* **Closed** *Sat, Sun, Aug, Public Holidays. Mastercard, Visa.*

La Table d'Honfleur
Map B1.8

Tel 47 07 01 15 | R

21 bd Arago 75013 | Mº Gobelins
Seats 43 | Meal for 2 approx 320F

Pascal Besnard is the dedicated chef-patron at this little bit of Normandy in Paris – quite simple in its appointments, with a mixture of banquettes and comfortable round-backed chairs, prints and paintings on the walls and planks on the ceiling. It's most popular at lunchtime, when the 75F menu is much in demand. There's also a seafood 'composition' menu at 95F (Normandy oysters, whelks, prawns, mussels, fish soup, hake mayonnaise, salmon tartare) plus a pud; and the gourmet menu at 145F which often features Normandy specialities, including *tripes à la mode de Caen, oeufs cocotte* with Pont L'Eveque and various dishes using apples, cider or Calvados – pork *à la normande, tarte flambée au Calvados,* whole apple cooked in pastry. Many dishes have a personal stamp – note lamb terrine served warm on a bed of salad leaves with walnuts and olives; and foie gras

See over

on buckwheat galettes with raisins, honey and glacé paw paw.
Set menus: L 75F L & D 95F (inc glass of wine) 145F (inc wine
or cider). *L 12-2.30 D 7.30-10.30.* **Closed** *Monday, 1 week
Christmas, 2 weeks Jul (phone for exact dates). Amex, Diners,
Mastercard, Visa.*

Les Vieux Métiers de France   Map B2.9

| Tel 45 88 90 03   Fax 45 80 73 80 | R |

13 bd Auguste Blanqui 75013   **M° Place d'Italie**
Seats 60   Meal for 2 approx 700F

Neo-medieval is the style of this restaurant just off Place d'Italie. Its
name means 'the old tradesmen of France' and various crafts are
depicted on the facade. Slate floor, mock stone walls and heavy
tapestries are other features. Owner-chef Michel Moisan updates
classical dishes, as shown by casserole of snail and pig's trotters
in Suresnes wine, brill in a sorrel sauce, papillote of foie gras with
cabbage, braised breast of veal with a Provençal compote and
Bresse chicken with morels. Long, interesting wine list. Two
private rooms for parties of up to 16. Set menus: L & D 165F,
300F (8-dish *dégustation*). *L 12-2 D 7.30-10.30.* **Closed** *Sun, Mon.
Amex, Diners, Mastercard, Visa.*

CHAMPAGNE
FONDÉE EN 1827

G.H. MUMM & CIE
REIMS~FRANCE

14th Arrondissement
Places of Interest

Montparnasse (Boulevard)
Cimetière du Montparnasse (Baudelaire, Sartre, A.Citroën,
Maupassant, Serge Gainsbourg, César Frank, Saint-Saens)
Catacombes, 43 22 47 63, M° Denfert-Rochereau
Observatoire, 40 51 22 21, M° Denfert-Rochereau

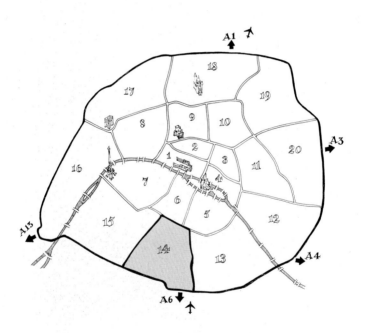

L'Amuse Bouche

Map B1.1

Tel 43 35 31 61   **R**

186 rue du Chateau 75014   Mº Gaité/Mouton-Duvernet
Seats 24   Meal for 2 approx 600F

Gilles Lambert, former sous-chef of Jacques Cagna, set up this tiny
restaurant in May 1990 and continues in fine form. The elegant
dining room has apricot walls and attracts a rather well-heeled
clientele to his 'classique mais renouvelée' cuisine. Dishes are kept
light with distinct flavours as in langoustine ravioli with basil,
salad of *pissenlit* and confit quails, red mullet in a potato crust
with rosemary butter, or rabbit fricassee with sage. Interesting
desserts too: *croustillant* with a lime mousse, soup of medlar and
cinnamon with vanilla ice cream, crème brulée with bergamot
tea. The three-course fixed-price menus offer particularly good
value and the short wine list is well chosen. Set menus: 125F (inc.
wine) & 160F *L 12.15-2.15 D 7.15-10.30.* **Closed** *L Sat, all Sun &
1st 2 wks Aug. Amex, Mastercard, Visa.*

Les Armes de Bretagne

Map B1.2

Tel 43 20 29 50   Fax 43 27 84 11   **R**

108 ave du Maine 75014   Mº Gaité
Seats 120   Meal for 2 approx 800F

From the moment of arrival at this luxurious restaurant, the
impeccable service takes care of your every need, including valet
parking. There are two dining rooms – one to the front with
an enclosed terrace and the other at the back with a fresco
by Zuber on the wall. Upstairs a large salon can be divided into
several small individual rooms for private parties. Tables are
widely-spaced and the decor is Napoléon III-style. Seafood is the
speciality, including oysters, clams, sea urchins, grilled sardines,
salmon *à l'unilatéral,* fish soup and *petite marmite. Confit de canard,
caneton à l'orange,* Lyons sausage with pistachios, *tournedos béarnaise*
and saddle of lamb with truffled risotto are among the classic
main courses. Set menu: L & D 200F. In the same ownership
as *Pierre 'à la Fontaine Gaillon'* in the 2nd arrondissement. *L 12-3
D 7-11.* **Closed** *L Sat, all Sun & Aug. Amex, Diners,
Mastercard, Visa.*

Bar à Huitres

Map C1.3

Tel 43 20 71 01   Fax 43 21 35 47   **R**

112 bd de Montparnasse 75014   Mº Vavin
Seats 150   Meal for 2 approx 500F

A great way to get things under way here is the *apéri-huitre* – one
belon oyster, one claire, one spéciale and a glass of Pineau des
Charentes. The Bar à Huitres offers a lot more than just oysters!
Sit in the glassed-over terrace or at the busy bar in this bright and
pleasant brasserie for a plate of velvet swimming crabs, sea urchins,
barnacles or sea squirts followed perhaps by skate with caper sauce,
turbot curry with wild rice or 'kaleidoscope' of salmon, scorpion
fish and smoked cod with three sauces. The lengthy dessert list
offers almost as much choice! Non-fish eaters are also catered for.
Set menus: L & D 98F, 128F, 198F. Also at 33 bd Beaumarchais
75003 Tel 48 87 98 92 and 33 rue St Jacques 75005 Tel 44 07 27
37. *Meals noon-2am. Amex, Mastercard, Visa.*

Le Bistrot du Dome

Map C1.4

Tel 43 35 32 00

R

1 rue Delambre 75014
Seats 60 (plus terrace 16)

M⁰ Vavin
Meal for 2 approx 500F

Very near its famous progenitor *Le Dome* (see below), the Bistrot
is solely fish-orientated. The menu is renewed daily according
to availability and written on slate boards which are passed around
the tables. All is simply cooked – start with a tuna and salmon
tartare, brandade-stuffed peppers or pan-fried shrimps, move on to
roasted John Dory with herbs or skate with a vinaigrette sauce
(hot) and finish with *pommes miettes* (apple crumble). All wines
are 98F per bottle and are available by the glass. *L 12-2.30 D 7.30-
11.* **Closed** *Sun (Aug only), Mon (Aug only). Amex,
Mastercard, Visa.*

La Cagouille   ★

Map B1.5

Tel 43 22 09 01   Fax 45 38 57 29

R

Face 23 rue de l'Ouest, 12 place Constantin-Brancusi 75014
Seats 70 (+ 40 Terrace)

Mo Gaité
Meal for 2 approx 700F

Best described as a classy bistro with attentive service,
La Cagouille offers an exclusively seafood menu which changes
constantly with the markets and the chef's inspiration. Cockles
from Granville, Bouchot mussels, grilled mackerel with mustard
sauce, cod with cabbage, turbot grilled or steamed, *pavé* of tuna
and ratatouille, saffron-sauced plaice, salmon *à l'unilatéral, matelote*
of eels . . .. these are among the tempting choices you might find
on the board. Diners eat at round marble tables in surroundings
decorated with items of marine interest; there's also an agreeable
terrace. Note the large collection of cognacs. Set menus:
L & D 150F, 250F (with wine). *L 12-2 D 7.30-10.30.*
Closed *1 wk Christmas. Amex, Mastercard, Visa.*

Le Caroubier

Map B1.6

Tel 43 20 41 49

R

122 ave du Maine 75014
Seats 60

M⁰ Gaité
Meal for 2 approx 400F

Among the best couscous restaurants of the hundreds in Paris,
Le Caroubier has been run for 20 years by the ex-colonial
husband-and-wife team of Michel and Adrienne Yaga. The
couscous comes with merguez, chicken, lamb (brochette, boulette,
méchoui) and the other main-course choice is tagines – chicken,
olives and preserved lemons; lamb, prunes, almonds and
cinnamon; or lamb with broad beans and artichokes. Brik
or pastilla to start, exotic patisserie to finish, robust North African
wines to accompany. Set menu: 130F. *L 12-2 D 7.30-10.30.*
Closed *D Sun, L Mon, Aug. Mastercard, Visa.*

La Chaumière des Gourmets

Map C1.7

Tel 43 21 22 59

R

22 place Denfert-Rochereau 75014
Seats 40

M⁰ Denfert-Rochereau
Meal for 2 approx 700F

Adjacent to the Denfert cinemas, the wooden frontage secluded
by curtains hides a cosy spring-like dining room with a strong   *See over*

provincial atmosphere. A rare restaurant when it comes to warmth and attention, shown for example in the *amuse-bouche* of *mousse de saumon* served in a precious coloured glass. Famous for his *civet de lièvre* and *chartreuse de perdreau au coulis de truffes*, Jean-Paul Huc also offers speciality fish dishes – sole grilled or meunière, *marmite dieppoise*, braised *turbotin* with mustard. *Nougat glacé* with acacia honey, *tarte fine aux pommes tièdes* or splendid *crème brulée* to finish. Interesting wine list. Set menus: L & D 165F & 240F. *L 12-2.30 D 7-10.15.* **Closed** *L Sat, all Sun, 1-20 Aug. Amex, Mastercard, Visa.*

La Coupole
Map B1.8

| Tel 43 20 14 20   Fax 43 35 46 14 | R |

102 bd de Montparnasse 75014 — M⁰ Vavin
Seats 450 — Meal for 2 approx 440F

Good, honest food is served by very professional staff in this vast brasserie, beloved of Parisians and visitors alike, and busy since the day it opened in 1927. Reservations are only taken up to 8.30pm, so should there be a wait for a table, order a drink at the bar to the left of the entrance and watch the comings and goings to pass the time. If you've arranged to meet friends, allow plenty of time just to find their table, so big is the place! Oysters, choucroute, snails and onion soup, grills and steak tartare are favourite choices, along with *carré d'agneau* and *curry d'agneau*, goat's cheese salad and seasonal specialities like pheasant terrine and *civet de bison St Hubert* served with fresh pasta. Tabouleh with marinated raw sardines, whitebait and stuffed squid with a sauce of their ink are interesting fishy starters, while among the main courses are sole (meunière or curried fillets), turbot hollandaise, mackerel steak with *pommes miettes* and fillet of brill with *champignons des bois*. A simpler menu is available on the terrace. Set menus: 85F (till 3, not Sun), 109F (before 6 and after 10). *Open 7.30am-2am (lunch served from noon). Amex, Diners, Mastercard, Visa.*

Le Dome
Map B1.9

| Tel 43 35 25 81   Fax 42 79 01 19 | R |

108 bd de Montparnasse 75014 — M⁰ Vavin
Seats 140 — Meal for 2 approx 700F

Bouillabaisse for two, oysters, clams and lobster remain among the traditional specialities at this most durable of Montparnasse institutions, and the *coquillages* can be enjoyed as a feast in the *plateau de fruits de mer*. Fruit is put to excellent use in many desserts, and Roquefort is the speciality cheese. *L 12-3 D 7-12.30. Open for coffee and snacks from 8am.* **Closed** *Mon, also Sun in Aug. Amex, Diners, Mastercard, Visa.*

Le Duc
Map C1.10

| Tel 43 22 59 59   Fax 43 20 46 73 | R |

243 bd Raspail 75014 — M⁰ Raspail
Seats 40 — Meal for 2 approx 1000F

A fashionable rendezvous for seafoodies, with the look of a classic luxury yacht. The *à la carte* is extremely varied within the fishy realm, with raw fish (sardines, bass, *poissons des iles* and coquilles St Jacques) as speciality starters. Alternatives could be *friture*

of squid with garlic, *moules madras,* warm crab mayonnaise or a
selection of home-smoked fish with a vodka and *fines herbes* sauce.
Main courses feature lobster (*sauté à l'orange* is a house special),
langoustines, plain grills and more elaborate white fish
preparations – *rougets au pistou en vessie, filet de bar au basilic, lotte
à la bohémienne, pavé de cabillaud* steamed in seaweed. The cheese
is Roquefort, the desserts Berthillon ices or *patisserie maison. L 12-
2.30 D 8-10.30.* **Closed** *Sun, Mon & Public Holidays.
Mastercard, Visa.*

Friant
Map C2.11

Tel 45 42 71 91   Fax 45 42 04 67 H

8 rue Friant 75014   **M° Alésia**
Rooms 27   Double from 370F

Situated in a quiet street, this inexpensive hotel offers small,
adequately-equipped bedrooms with compact en-suite bathrooms.
Breakfast is taken in a glass-roofed courtyard. *Mastercard, Visa.*

Aux Iles Marquises
Map B1.12

Tel 43 29 93 58 R

15 rue de la Gaité 75014   **M° Edgar Quinet/Montparnasse**
Seats 40   Meal for 2 approx 640F

Mathias Théry, a 'disciple' of the Troisgros brothers, presents a
modern adaptation of classic cuisine in his marine-decorated
restaurant lying between an Italian theatre and a naughty
book/video shop. Creamy crab and parsley soup, *gelée de
grenouilles et langoustines,* veal sweetbreads with a gratin of
artichokes, mustard rabbit with a pipérade jus, turbot with ginger,
red mullet with rosemary – this is the esoteric Théry style, which
extends to desserts such as a hot kiwi fruit soufflé. Set menus: L &
D 130F, 150F. *L 12-2 D 7-11.30.* **Closed** *L Sat, all Sun, 1-16 Aug.
Amex, Mastercard, Visa.*

Istria
Map C1.13

Tel 43 20 91 82   Fax 43 22 48 45 H

29 rue Campagne-Première 75014   **M° Raspail**
Rooms 26   Double from 520F

Located not far from the attractions of Montparnasse and the
Luxembourg Gardens, the small Hotel Istria offers comfortable,
inexpensive accommodation (showers only in the majority
of rooms, four with bath tubs). Breakfast is served in a charming
vaulted room with exposed stone walls. No restaurant. 24hr
reception. *Amex, Diners, Mastercard, Visa.*

Lenox
Map B1.14

Tel 43 35 34 50   Fax 43 20 46 64 H

15 rue Delambre 75014   **M° Vavin**
Rooms 52   Double from 580F

The discreetly decorated Hotel Lenox with its antique furniture,
paintings and old mirrors is an appealing place to stay. All rooms
are double-glazed and equipped with en suite bathrooms (shower
or bath), satellite TV, radio, direct-dial telephone and hairdryer.
There's no restaurant, but light snacks and drinks are served   *See over*

in rooms, or the small bar from 5pm to 2am. Another Lenox, with the same caring owner, is in the 7th arrondissement at 9 rue de l'Université Tel 42 96 10 95 Fax 42 61 52 83. It has 34 rooms, price starts at 680F and amenities are similar to this one. *Amex, Mastercard, Diners, Visa.*

Lous Landès   Map B1.15

Tel 45 43 08 04	R

157 ave du Maine 75014   M⁰ Mouton Duvernet
Seats 45 (+ Terrace 15)   Meal for 2 approx 600F

The convivial owner-chef of this auberge, Hervé Rumen, concentrates on the 'grande cuisine du Sud-Ouest' with such specialities as *foie gras de canard* ('pour apprécier 150F, pour gouter 80F'), *matelote* of eel, *magret* with Guérande salt and of course, *cassoulet*, followed by a caramelised pastry case of armagnac-soaked prunes or a mousse with red berries. The interior of the restaurant is what the French would describe as *style anglais* with decorated wallpaper and widely spaced white-clothed tables laid with silver cutlery. Madiran, Cahors and Buzet (all from the South-West) are some of the 200 wines in stock. The more expensive set menu ('notre menu confiance 300F') is a *dégustation* of six dishes to be ordered for whole parties. Set menus: L & D 190F, 300F. *L 12-2.30 D 8-10.30.* **Closed** *L Sat, all Sun, Aug. Amex, Diners, Mastercard, Visa.*

Mercure Paris-Montparnasse   Map B1.16

Tel 43 35 28 28	H

20 rue Gaité 75014   M⁰ Gaité
Rooms 185   Double from 820F

This hotel of the large Mercure chain is very centrally located for those who prefer to stay within a short distance of the Latin Quarter. Well-equipped bedrooms include 6 suites and 5 rooms adapted for disabled guests. There's a restaurant (**Le Bistro de la Gaité**), bar and three conference rooms with a combined capacity of 120. Private parking for 45 cars (64F for 24 hrs). *Amex, Diners, Mastercard, Visa.*

Méridien Montparnasse   Map B1.17

Tel 44 36 44 36 Fax 44 36 49 00	HR

19 rue Cdt-Mouchotte 75014   M⁰ Montparnasse
Rooms 953   Double from 1200F

In what is one of the few skyscraper buildings (25 floors and 8 lifts) in the centre of Paris, the view from the top floors is exceptional. In the heart of Montparnasse guests here are perfectly located for a stay in Paris, whether on business or pleasure. The comfortable bedrooms include 29 suites and 6 'pied à terre' rooms with offices. All rooms are air-conditioned and soundproofed, and room equipment includes 20-channel TVs, radios, mini-bars, hairdryers and automatic alarms. The business centre offers a multilingual secretarial service 8.30 to 6.30 Monday to Friday, and the hotel caters superbly for conferences and banquets. Day rooms include the **Platinum Bar** (open noon-2am) and the **Café Atlantic** piano bar. *Amex, Diners, Mastercard, Visa.*

Montparnasse 25
Tel 44 36 44 25   Fax 44 36 49 03
Seats 90   Meal for 2 approx 700F

The decor emphasises the mid-1920s – photos of stars of the stage
and screen of the period hang on the walls next to reproductions
of Modigliani paintings. This is an elegant restaurant where tables
are well spaced and service is discreetly efficient. The cuisine
is classical French with well-crafted, often fairly elaborate dishes
such as *tian de langouste aux rattes confites et marinière de légumes
à l'huile vierge; joue de boeuf braisée, parmentier de queue et croquette
de pied de veau;* and *col vert* duck in two services – *aiguillette* with
autumn fruits and ceps, the thigh *en civet* with polenta. Desserts are
in the same vein – baked figs with a purée of bitter oranges and
ice cream made with almond milk is a good example. California,
Italy and Spain are represented on the wine list, as well as France.
Set menus: L 230F, D 290F & 380F. *L 12-2.30 D 7.30-10.30.*
Closed *Sat, Sun, Aug, 1 wk Christmas and Public Holidays.*

Justine
Tel 44 36 44 00
Seats 240   Meal for 2 approx 500F

On the first floor of the hotel, overlooking a 100 square metre
terrace of garden with trees, plants, shrubs and flowers, this
brasserie resembles an enclosed verandah. It opens for breakfast
at 7am and the buffet menu (195F, children 100F) operates from
midday offering a table of hors d'oeuvre, three *plats du jour*, cheese
and sweets. From the *carte* come the likes of mullet served with
pistou and tabouleh, monkfish with saffron and olive oil mash,
boned pig's trotter with Puy lentils, entrecote with bone marrow
and gratin dauphinois, and a low-calorie dish of steamed chicken
with a walnut oil emulsion. Among the 'gourmandises' are fruit
salad with Sauternes, meringues with caramel and fondant cottage
cheese with a raspberry coulis. Justine regularly holds theme
evenings – for example New Orleans, Chinoise and the 60s.
On Sundays, the 'Bébé Brunch' menu, especially geared towards
families and with frequent special events, is a roaring success –
you'll need to book a week ahead. The interior reflects the terrace
garden theme with a pastel green and pink decor. Guests at tables
by the large windows enjoy a view of the greenery. **Open** 7-10.30
for breakfast and noon-11pm. *L (buffet) 12-2.30 D 7-11.*

Hotel de l'Orchidée   Map B1.18
Tel 43 22 70 50   Fax 42 79 97 46   H
65 rue de l'Ouest 75014   M° Gaité
Rooms 40   Double from 490F

The reception area of this simply appointed family-owned hotel
in the heart of Montparnasse has a small bar and lounge area with
cane furniture, green plants and contemporary paintings and
it looks out on to an open terrace and garden. Basic comforts
in the bedrooms. Conference room (capacity 20) in the basement.
Sauna and jacuzzi available, like reception, 24 hours a day. Just
two, reservable, parking places (70F for 24 hours). *Amex, Diners,
Mastercard, Visa.*

Orléans Palace Hotel
Tel 45 39 68 50   Fax 45 43 65 64

Map C2.19

H

185-187 bd Brune 75014
Rooms 92

M⁰ Porte d'Orléans
Double from 550F

Virtually at Porte d'Orléans, the hotel has well-equipped bedrooms
which are modern and functional; many overlook an interior
garden. The piano bar serves light snacks and drinks until 1am.
Two adjoining conference rooms (max 70), the larger holding 60
people theatre-style. *Amex, Diners, Mastercard, Visa.*

Hotel du Parc Montsouris
Tel 45 89 09 72

Map C2.20

H

4 rue du Parc Montsouris 75014
Rooms 35

M⁰ Porte d'Orléans/Cité Universitaire
Double from 370F

Close to the delightful Parc Montsouris with its lawns, trees, lake
and flowerbeds. There are seven apartments that sleep four (480F).
Rooms are equipped with baths or showers and have satellite TV,
desk and direct-dial telephone. The hotel's breakfast is a better bet
than those at nearby cafés. There's limited street parking. *Amex,
Mastercard, Visa.*

Pavillon Montsouris
Tel 45 88 38 52   Fax 45 88 63 40

Map D2.21

R

20 rue Gazan 75014
Seats 160 (+ Terrace 100)

M⁰ Cité Universitaire
Meal for 2 approx 660F

The L-shaped restaurant in this delightful Belle Epoque house
looking out over the charming Parc Montsouris provides an ideal
setting for either a romantic dinner or a family occasion.
In summer, seats on the outdoor terrace are sought after to enjoy
the view while eating from one of the *carte-menus* compiled
by chef Stéphane Ruel, whose training included spells with
Guérard and Chibois. The choice of his 'cuisine d'aujourd'hui'
could include *terrine d'anguille aux champignons, eau de tomates 'bio';
foie gras de canard aux cinq poivres; ballotine de morue fraiche aux
pieds de cochon sauce vin rouge;* tournedos of tuna with braised
chicory; *supreme de canette aux épices.* And Bernard Vatel's *douceurs*
provide an appropriate finale – *crème brulée, gateau mi-cuit aux
chocolats, feuilleté de raisins au fromage blanc.* Over 100 French
wines. Two private rooms (max 20). Set menus: 189F, 255F.
L 12-2.30 D 7.30-10.30. Amex, Diners, Mastercard, Visa.

Note: from April 16 1995 the
international dialling code 010 changes to 00

CHAMPAGNE
FONDÉE EN 1827
G.H. MUMM & CIE
REIMS~FRANCE

15th Arrondissement
Places of Interest

Montparnasse, M⁰ Montparnasse-Bienvenue
Tour Montparnasse (panoramic view from 56th & 59th storeys),
45 38 52 56, M⁰ Montparnasse-Bienvenue
Héliport de Paris, 45 54 95 11, M⁰ Balard
Parc A. Citroën (Futurist), M⁰ Balard
Parc George Brassens, M⁰ Convention
Porte de Versailles (Parc des Expositions de Paris), 43 95 37 00,
  M⁰ Porte de Versailles
Musée Bourdelle, 45 48 67 27, M⁰ Falguière/Montparnasse-
Bienvenue
Musée de la Poste, 42 79 23 45, M⁰ Montparnasse-Bienvenue

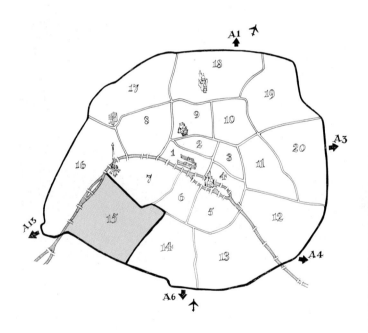

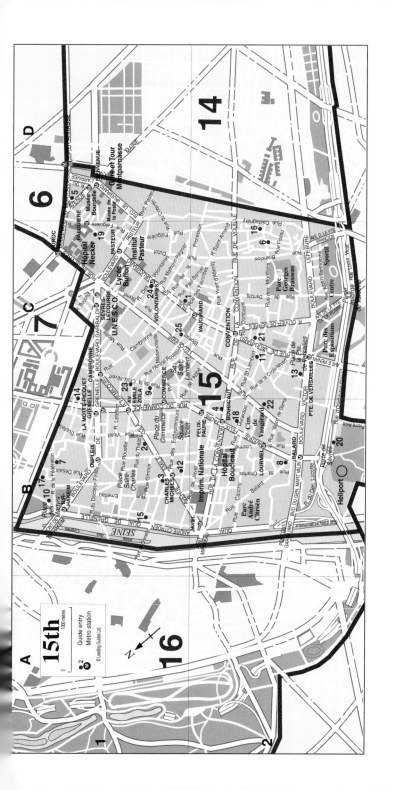

Adagio

Map C1.1

Tel 40 45 10 00   Fax 40 45 10 10   H

257/263 rue de Vaugirard 75015   M° Vaugirard
Rooms 187   Double from 840F

Recently purpose-built, it is the only hotel in the Adagio group
to be centrally located. Public rooms are airy and agreeable. The
bar extends on to a flowery terrace in summer. Bedrooms are
small but functional with air-conditioning and efficient double-
glazing. Bathrooms are built with separate toilets. Conference
facilities are versatile and most have daylight. Good-value
weekend breaks but note also a surcharge of 110F during major
exhibitions at the nearby Parc des Expositions. *Amex, Diners,
Mastercard, Visa.*

Alizé Grenelle

Map B1.2

Tel 45 78 08 22   Fax 40 59 03 06   H

87 ave Emile Zola 75015   M° Charles Michels
Rooms 50   Double from 502F

An inexpensive and pleasantly furnished hotel with soundproofed
en-suite bedrooms which are all equipped with hairdryer, trouser
press, cable TV, telephone, alarm clock and mini-bar. *Amex,
Diners, Mastercard, Visa.*

Beaugrenelle St Charles

Map B1.3

Tel 45 78 61 63   Fax 45 79 04 38   H

82 rue St Charles 75015   M° Charles Michels
Rooms 51   Double from 420F

A modern hotel where the reception rooms have a distinctive art
deco style and the bedrooms have bath or shower, toilet, satellite
TV, direct-dial telephone, mini-bar, digital alarm, hairdryer and
trouser press. Meeting room (max 20). *Amex, Diners,
Mastercard, Visa.*

Bistro 121

Map B2.4

Tel 45 57 52 90   Fax 45 55 14 69   R

121 rue de la Convention 75015   M° Javel/Boucicaut
Seats 80   Meal for 2 approx 650F

Jean Moussié is no longer in the kitchen of his 30-year-old bistro
but he does still greet customers alongside his wife and daughter.
The Slavik-designed interior – mirrored ceiling and walls, pictures
of life in Russia, claret-coloured carpet, leather banquettes – seems
to be from another era. The cuisine nevertheless keeps evolving,
though some classic bourgeois dishes like hare *à la royale* remain
on the menu. Game and fish predominate here and both the three-
course menus (which include wine, coffee and service) are good
value at 200F & 280F. Why not try the '121'-style leek vinaigrette
before moving on to langoustine and citrus fruit salad or whole
grilled calf's kidneys with dauphinoise potatoes. Extensive wine
list. *L 12-3 D 7.30-12. Amex, Diners, Mastercard, Visa.*

Chez Yvette   Map D1.5

Tel 42 22 45 54   **R**

1 rue d'Alencon 75015   **Mᵒ Montparnasse/Duroc**
Seats 40   Meal for 2 approx 350F

Traditional and simple cooking in an old Parisian restaurant
complete with mirrors, wooden chairs and red tablecloths:
chicken liver paté, chateaubriand steak with pepper or mustard
and chocolate mousse. Family atmosphere and jovial ambience.
*L 12-2 D 7-10. **Closed** Sat, Sun & Aug. Mastercard, Visa.*

Le Clos Morillons   Map C2.6

Tel 48 28 04 37   Fax 48 28 70 77   **R**

50 rue des Morillons 75015   **Mᵒ Convention/Porte de Vanves**
Seats 30   Meal for 2 approx 600F

Colonial-style surroundings of ceiling fans, wooden blinds, large
mirrors, bamboo furniture, papyrus plants and photos of Cannes
at the beginning of the century set the stage for gastronomic food
perked up with spices. Starters and main courses on the *carte* are
priced at 75F & 125F respectively, while the set menus (165F
menu d'affaires and 285F *découverte*) are further options at both
sessions. Specialities include a pressed paté of potato and foie gras
with Szechuan pepper, fillet of venison with spice loaf and celery
compote followed by a good selection of cheeses (priced at 45F).
Wines from the Loire take precedence. *L 12-2 D 7.45-10.*
***Closed** L Sat, all Sun. Amex, Mastercard, Visa.*

Erawan   Map B1.7

Tel 47 83 55 67   Fax 47 34 85 98   **R**

76 rue de la Fédération 75015   **Mᵒ La Motte-Picquet-Grenelle/Dupleix**
Seats 85   Meal for 2 approx 400F

Prawn fritters with a soya galette (*thon ngan*) and Thai-style
stuffed mussels (*hoy men phon song kreung*) and seafood brochettes
(*pinh xi sahay*) are only a few of the many Thai seafood specialities
served up in the three bustling dining rooms of this distinctively
Thai restaurant. French wine and Thai beer. Set menus: L 75F
(min 2 people), also L & D 106F, 138F, 146F, 172F. *L 12-2.30
D 7-10.30. **Closed** Sun, Aug. Amex, Mastercard, Visa.*

La Farigoule   Map B2.8

Tel 45 54 35 41   **R**

104 rue Balad 75015   **Mᵒ Balard**
Seats 25   Meal for 2 approx 550F

Behind a somewhat unprepossessing exterior, at the Balard metro
end of the road, this is quite a smart little restaurant with panelled
walls and large golden orange 'dish' lights lending a warm glow,
matched by the friendly welcome. Only some 'chocolate box'
pictures spoil the effect. Nothing spoils the cooking, however,
which is firmly based in Provence; Jean and Thierry Gras hail
from Toulon and specialise in seafood: delicious roulade-like herby
stuffed sardines, fish soup with a potent rouille, *brandade de morue
fraiche*, seafood gratin, simple grilled fish (depending on the
market). Particular specialities are *bouillabaisse du pecheur* and
a *bourride provençale*, both for minimum of two persons. Just a few
desserts – *marquise au chocolat, oeuf à la neige*, pears poached

See over

in wine, sorbets and a feuilleté of apples with cinnamon – the last
needing to be ordered at the beginning of the meal. *L 12-2
D 7.30-10.* **Closed** *D Mon, all Sun & last 2 weeks Aug. Amex,
Mastercard, Visa.*

Fellini

Map C1.9

Tel 45 77 40 77

R

58 rue Croix-Nivert 75015
Seats 40

Mᵒ **Commerce/Cambronne**
Meal for 2 approx 460F

Home-made pasta is served in at least fourteen different ways
by the Neapolitan chef-owner Giuseppe Feleppa: macaroni may
be served with a sausage, tomato and fennel sauce, fettucine with
ham and mushrooms, spaghetti with egg and smoked belly
of pork. Giuseppe also prepares a number of regional fish and meat
specialities from his native southern Italy for non-pasta eaters. Set
menu: L 130F. *L 12-2.30 D 7-10.45.* **Closed** *L Sat, all Sun, Aug.
Mastercard, Visa.*

Frantour Paris Suffren

Map B1.10

Tel 45 78 50 00   Fax 45 78 91 42

H

20 rue Jean Rey 75015
Rooms 407

Mᵒ **Bir Hakeim**
Double from 880F

A programme of renovation began three years ago in this modern
chain hotel a few yards from the Eiffel Tower, commencing with
the now fully-equipped bedrooms located on different colour-
coded floors. The American-style bar **Les Quatres Saisons** is an
impressive feature. Ten meeting rooms (max 170) have recently
been refurbished. *Amex, Diners, Mastercard, Visa.*

Le Gastroquet

Map C2.11

Tel 48 28 60 91

R

10 rue Desnouettes 75015
Seats 50

Mᵒ **Convention**
Meal for 2 approx 550F

A *restaurant du quartier*, but chef-patron Dany Bulot's reputation
(he was in charge of the kitchen at *Benoit* (*qv*) for more than
a decade) also brings customers from further afield to enjoy his
robust, flavourful country cooking: *soupe de moules paysanne*
(served from a terrine with 'seconds' offered); an autumn salad
with nuts, ham and cheese; confit of duck; *joue de boeuf
bourguignonne*; cassoulet; skate with capers and nut brown butter;
veal kidneys Grand-Mère; crème brulée with apples and Calvados.
Straightforward but professional service – they never have to ask
who is having what – is supervised by Madeleine Bulot. Just down
the road from the Parc des Expositions at Porte de Versailles, they
sometimes open on winter weekends when there is a major
exhibition. Set Menus: L 99F L & D 149F. *L 12-3 D 7-10.30.*
Closed *Sat, Sun & Aug.*

Kim Anh

Map B1.12

Tel 45 79 40 96   Fax 40 59 49 78

R

15 rue de l'Eglise 75015
Seats 20

Mᵒ **Charles-Michels**
Meal for 2 approx 500F

A husband and wife team run this small, intimate and quietly
elegant Vietnamese restaurant which is open in the evenings only.

While he is organising the dining room, she works alone in the kitchen to produce specialities such as stuffed oven-baked crab, fish stew, fish brochettes *à la tonkinoise* or chicken, ginger and rice casserole – all of which remind many of their clients of days spent in Saigon. Reservations essential. Set menu: D 220F. *D only 7.30-11.30. Amex, Diners, Mastercard, Visa.*

Mercure Paris-Vaugirard   Map C2.13

| Tel 44 19 03 03   Fax 48 28 22 11 | **H** |

69 bd Victor 75015   **M⁰ Porte de Versailles**
Rooms 91   Double from 864F

Right in front of the Porte de Versailles exhibition centre, this Mercure hotel is ideally suited for exhibitors and visitors alike. The comfortable, spacious, soundproofed and well-equipped bedrooms have en-suite marble bathrooms and have been recently renovated. Conference room (max 200). Private parking under the hotel (50F for 24 hrs). *Amex, Diners, Mastercard, Visa.*

Morot-Gaudry   ★   Map B1.14

| Tel 45 67 06 85   Fax 45 67 55 72 | **R** |

6 rue de la Cavalerie 75015   **M⁰ La Motte-Picquet-Grenelle**
Seats 70 (+ 26 Terrace)   Meal for 2 approx 900F

Situated on the 8th floor of a 1930s' building, the two greatest assets of this restaurant are the panoramic view and the fixed-price four-course lunch menu at 220F (wine and service included). A recent choice included *terrine tiède de lièvre aux pommes*, *dos de saumon sauté aux endives au porto*, and *crème brulée à la noisette*. Another set menu (390F) is also available to parties at both lunch and dinner: with a different glass of wine with each course it costs 550F. Ring 2-3 days in advance for a window table in the octagonal dining-room decorated with wood panelling and a large chandelier of Murano glass. Sample dishes from the à la carte menu are a scallop and langoustine salad in vanilla oil followed by *col vert* duck in two styles, with figs and with ripe apples, and pan-fried fillets of red mullet with celery chips and a langoustine vinaigrette. After cheese comes the luxuriant decadence of 'confidentiel pour chocophile'. Set menus: L 220F L & D 390F, 550F. *L 12-2 D 7.30-10.30. **Closed** Sat & Sun. Amex, Mastercard, Visa.*

Hotel Nikko de Paris   Map B1.15

| Tel 40 58 20 00   Fax 45 75 42 35 | **H R** |

61 quai de Grenelle 75015   **M⁰ Javel/Charles Michels**
Rooms 779   Double from 1690F

On the banks of the Seine between the Eiffel Tower and Mirabeau Bridge, the Nikko is a tall (31 floors), strikingly modern Japanese-owned hotel. Public areas are bright, cool, smart and spacious. **La Seine Bar** shows a more classic side, with well-upholstered light wood furniture, splendid Japanese murals and a nightly pianist. The majority of the bedrooms offer good views and are modern in style and design, each with cable TV and mini-bar among the up-to-date facilities provided. Executive rooms are on the top floor. There are 17 conference rooms, the largest with room for 900 theatre-style. Indoor swimming pool, gym, sauna. *Amex, Diners, Mastercard, Visa.*   *See over*

Les Célébrités
Tel 40 58 21 29   Fax 40 58 16 03
Seats 70   Meal for 2 approx 1000F

A table by the window looking out over the Seine must be the
best location to sit in this spacious, modern restaurant. As a starter
you could choose sautéed clams in garlic or home-smoked salmon
in a creamy chive sauce and then perhaps a salad of grilled scallops
with parmesan shavings or pan-fried escalopes of duck foie gras
with ceps and chestnuts as main courses. Open for breakfast
7-9.30am. Set menus: L and D 280F, 370F. *L 12-2.30 D 7-10.*
Closed Aug.

Benkay
Seats 120   Meal for 2 approx 1200F

The decor may be contemporary but essentially this is a traditional
Japanese restaurant offering a variety of set meals as well as a short
but comprehensive *carte*. For a 100F supplement on the evening
menu diners can eat at a teppanyaki counter where their food
is prepared in front of them. Lunchtime is best for lower-priced set
menus: L from 110F, D from 540F. *L 12-2 D 6.30-10.*

L'Oie Cendrée   Map C2.16
Tel 45 31 91 91   **R**
51 rue Labrouste 75015   M⁰ Plaisance
Seats 30   Meal for 2 approx 400F

Duck and goose totally dominate the menu here and are prepared
in ways typical of the South-West region of France: *aiguillettes*
of duck in a Madeira sauce, slowly-cooked goose and morel stew,
duck confit with sorrel purée and so on. This is a neighbourhood
restaurant with a rustic, provincial decor. Set menus: L 95F, L &
D 125F. *L 12-2 D 7.30-10. Closed L Sat, all Sun, Aug.*
Mastercard, Visa.

Paris Hilton   Map B1.17
Tel 42 73 92 00   Fax 47 83 62 66   **H**
18 ave de Suffren 75015   M⁰ Bir Hakeim
Rooms 456   Double from 1590F

Only a few yards from the Eiffel Tower, the Paris Hilton
overlooks the Palais de Chaillot and Trocadéro Gardens. All
rooms are equipped with air-conditioning, cable TV (18 channels)
in stereo with remote control, radio, mini-bar and direct-dial
telephone. Light meals are served in the **Terrasse Restaurant**
7am to 11pm while the **Western Restaurant** reflects the
American Southwest in its choice of food. The **Toit de Paris Bar**
on the 10th floor has a panoramic view of Paris. Conference
centre and meeting rooms (max 800). *Amex, Diners,
Mastercard, Visa.*

Pierre Vedel   Map B2.18
Tel 45 58 43 17   **R**
19 rue Duranton 75015   M⁰ Boucicaut
Seats 45   Meal for 2 approx 600F

A typical Parisian bistro with cream walls, plenty of mirrors,
leather bench seating, green plants and smart waiters. Owner

Pierre Vedel buys his produce directly from the market and his wine from vineyards thus assuring fresh food and reasonably priced, personally chosen wines. Roasted partridge may be preceded by celery and aubergine millefeuille with a herb vinaigrette. From a choice of several desserts, choose a Catalan *crème brulée* or chocolate charlotte. *L 12-2 D 8-10.15.* **Closed** *Sat & Sun. Mastercard, Visa.*

Rascasson
Map C1.19
R

Tel 47 34 63 45   Fax 47 34 39 45

148 rue de Vaugirard 75015
M° Pasteur
Seats 80
Meal for 2 approx 400F

This neighbourhood Parisian eatery with its nets hanging overhead transports one to the South of France. The bargain 135F menu offers three courses: salmon carpaccio or fresh anchovy escabèche to start, silver sea bream with fresh thyme or grouper fish in lemon to follow, with floating islands to finish. Both à la carte dishes and menu are written on a blackboard. *L 12-2.15 D 7-10.* **Closed** *L Sat, all Sun, Aug. Mastercard, Visa.*

Le Relais de Sèvres   ★
Map B2.20
R

Tel 40 60 33 66   Fax 45 57 04 22

Hotel Sofitel 8-12 rue Louis-Armand 75015
M° Balard
Seats 45
Meal for 2 approx 800F

This classic-style restaurant in pastel blue and grey with yellow tablecloths, mirrors and paintings (often a current exhibition) in a large hotel is the setting for a gastronomic experience. After nine years as sous-chef the capable Bruno Turbot has moved up the scale to become big fish in the kitchen. Choose from the à la carte menu or the four-course Menu Club (320F including aperitif, wine and coffee), both of which change every Wednesday: soft-boiled egg with crab and horns of plenty followed by smoked Norwegian salmon or *canon d'agneau de Pauillac, polenta aux pousses d'epinards*, and liquorice and chocolate millefeuille to finish. Turbot-charged cuisine. International wine list. Set menu: L and D 320F. *L 12-2 D 7.30-10.* **Closed** *Sat, Sun, Aug, 1 wk Christmas and Public Holidays.*

Résidence Saint-Lambert
Map C2.21
H

Tel 48 28 63 14   Fax 45 33 45 50

5 rue Eugène-Gibez 75015
M° Convention
Rooms 48
Double from 550F

Conveniently located for visitors to the Porte de Versailles exhibition halls. Bedrooms were refurbished in the winter of 1992. All have en-suite bathrooms (35 with showers only), radios, televisions, mini-bars and direct-dial telephones. Small courtyard garden. *Amex, Diners, Mastercard, Visa.*

Aux Senteurs de Provence
Map B2.22
R

Tel 45 57 11 98   Fax 45 58 66 84

295 rue Lecourbe 75015
M° Lourmel
Seats 40 (+ Terrace 10)
Meal for 2 approx 600F

All the favourite and best known Provençal dishes (with the emphasis on seafood) appear on the menu in this comfortable   *See over* restaurant. Depending on the day's market, *bouillabaisse* or *bourride* might precede monkfish roasted with truffles and anchovy fillets or pan-fried skate with mushrooms. If the appetite then permits, choose from the enticing selection of desserts, such as white cheese mousse with raspberry coulis. Wines from the South-East predominate. Set menu: L and D 198F. *L 12.15-2 D 7.15-10.30. Closed L Sat, all Sun, 2-3 wks Aug. Amex, Diners, Mastercard, Visa.*

Wallace   Map C1.23

| Tel 45 78 83 30   Fax 40 58 19 43 | H |

89 rue Fondary 75015   M° Emile Zola/Cambronne/La Motte-Picquet-Grenelle
Rooms 35   Double from 550F

Some bedrooms overlook the plant-filled courtyard at this two-storey hotel. The pastel-coloured rooms have colourful bedspreads and are equipped with all the essential facilities for a comfortable stay. *Amex, Diners, Mastercard, Visa.*

Yllen   Map C1.24

| Tel 45 67 67 67   Fax 45 67 74 37 | H |

196 rue de Vaugirard 75015   M° Volontaires
Rooms 40   Double from 560F

The neo-classical architecture of the building conceals a tastefully decorated hotel with a marble entrance hall, leather chairs, oak panels and original paintings. Rooms are fully equipped with marble bathrooms, direct-dial telephones, satellite TVs, mini-bars and individual electronic safes. *Amex, Diners, Mastercard, Visa.*

Yves Quintard   Map C1.25

| Tel 42 50 22 27 | R |

99 rue Blomet 75015   M° Vaugirard
Seats 40   Meal for 2 approx 700F

Yves Quintard's bright and colourful restaurant is a refreshing stop in rather austere residential surroundings. His lively and enthusiastic wife takes great care of her clientele, whether regulars or tourists. Equally colourful is the cooking, full of inventive and refreshing ideas like warm paté of roast hare with a blackcurrant coulis, fillet of brill in a creamy mussel and white wine sauce, salad of smoked scallops in hazelnut oil or light tart of wild duck and honey with a turnip confit. Desserts like the *trio de gratins – orange, poire, figue à la vanille* – or fluffy coffee Bavarois with grilled nuts and whisky biscuit are equally successful. Set L & D 160F, 280F. *L 12.15-2.30 D 7.30-10.30. Closed L Sat, all Sun, Aug. Mastercard, Visa.*

16th Arrondissement
Places of Interest

Trocadéro
Palais de Chaillot, M⁰ Trocadéro
Musée de la Marine, 45 53 31 70, M⁰ Trocadéro
Musée du Cinéma, 45 53 74 39, M⁰ Trocadéro
Palais de Tokyo (modern art), 47 23 61 27, M⁰ Iéna
Parc des Princes, 42 88 02 76, M⁰ Porte de Saint Cloud
Stade Roland Garros, 47 43 48 00, M⁰ Porte d'Auteuil
Maison de Radio-France, 42 30 22 22, M⁰ Ranelagh/Passy
Musée d'Ennery (China/Japan objets d'art), 45 53 57 96,
   M⁰ Porte Dauphine
Maison Honoré de Balzac, 42 24 56 38, M⁰ La Muette/Passy
Bois de Boulogne
   Jardin d'Acclimatation
   Musée National des Arts et Traditions Populaires, 44 17 60 00,
   M⁰ Les Sablons
Hippodrome d'Auteuil (steeplechase), M⁰ Porte d'Anuteuil
Hippodrome de Longchamp (flat racing)

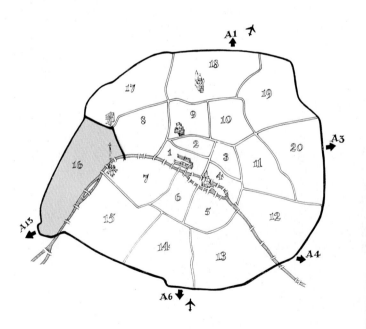

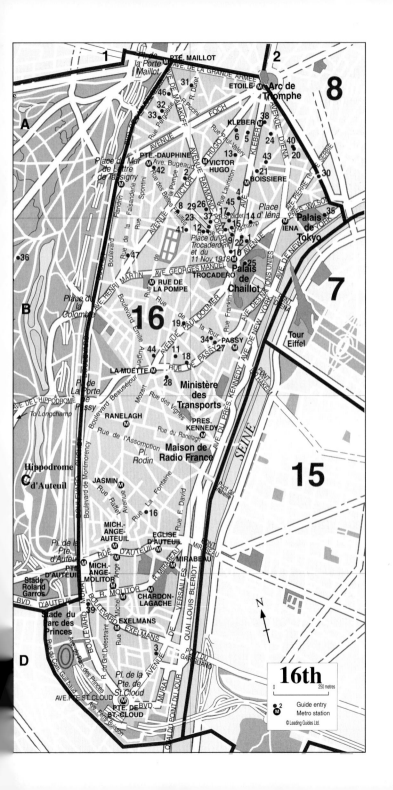

Al Mounia   Map B2.1
Tel 47 27 57 28   **R**
16 rue Magdebourg 75116   **M° Trocadéro**
Seats 60   Meal for 2 approx 500F

Moorish decor – carved wood, mosaics, copper-topped tables –
and a moreish menu of couscous, tagines and pastillas. The owners,
who hail from Casablanca, have two other restaurants, one there
and one in Madrid. *L 12.15-2 D 8-11.* **Closed** *Sun & last 2 weeks
Aug. Amex, Mastercard, Visa.*

Alexander   Map A1.2
Tel 45 53 64 65   Fax 45 53 12 51   **H**
102 ave Victor Hugo 75016   **M° Victor Hugo**
Rooms 62   Double from 1190F

A renovated 1900 building by Place Victor Hugo. The bedrooms,
including three apartments, are comfortable, stylish (Louis XVI)
and well equipped, the ones looking on to the courtyard being the
most desirable. Room service till 9.30pm. *Amex, Diners,
Mastercard, Visa.*

La Baie d'Ha Long   Map D1.3
Tel 45 24 60 62   Fax 42 30 58 98   **R**
164 ave de Versailles 75016   **M° Porte St Cloud**
Seats 40 (+8 outside)   Meal for 2 approx 400F

Catherine Deneuve is among the many showbiz fans of Roger
Leroy's excellent little Vietnamese restaurant, whose decor
includes ethnic *objets* and paintings and a number of aquaria.
Nathalie Leroy is in charge in the kitchen, producing dishes
to rouse and delight the palate: *lac xa* – soup with prawns and
coconut milk, *ga gung* – chicken caramelised with ginger, *nuong
nuong* – pork with lemon grass, *tom chien* – prawn fritters.
Vietnamese fondue for two is a speciality as are various grills.
Wines include an interesting Bordeaux rosé *biologique.* Set L: 99F.
L 12-2.30 D 7-10. **Closed** *Sun, 25 Jul-30 Aug, 24 Dec & 1 Jan.
Amex, Mastercard, Visa.*

Baltimore   Map A2.4
Tel 44 34 54 54   Fax 44 34 54 44   **HR**
88 bis ave Kléber 75116   **M° Boissière**
Rooms 105   Double from 1900F

Gustave Eiffel is reputed to have been one of the designers of this
hotel, built over 100 years ago, and recently renovated to its
present luxury standard. It only became a hotel in 1920 and took
its name from one of its first and most famous clients, Lord
Baltimore. It's an attractive corner building with green awnings
and wrought-iron balustrades, in an enviable position between the
Champs Elysées and Trocadéro. From the impressive marble-
floored foyer with its modern sculptures on plinths to the elegant
panelled library and intimate bar, the hotel oozes charm and
elegance. Throughout, there are some 700 works of contemporary
art dotted around, making this a showcase for talented artists.
Individually decorated bedrooms are air-conditioned, with deep-
pile carpets, quality fabrics and cherrywood furniture, and offer
as standard mini-bar, cable TV, bathrobes and decent toiletries

in the smart bathrooms. In addition, 19 luxury bedrooms provide
a safe, facilities for making tea and coffee, and a telephone
extension in the bathroom. There's a non-smoking floor and cots
are available. Secure parking (150F per 24hrs). *Amex, Diners,
Mastercard, Visa.*

Bertie's
Tel 44 34 54 34
Seats 60   Meal for 2 approx 600F

A change of name (formerly L'Estournel) heralds a complete
change of style here. Black and white photos of British royals past
and present around the cherrywood-panelled walls give the clue
that everything here is now thoroughly British. Cullen skink,
steak and kidney pie, Lancashire hot pot, bread-and-butter
pudding, Bakewell tart and lemon posset are all here along with
British farmhouse cheeses, served with celery of course, and
savouries like Welsh rarebit and Scotch woodcock. There's a daily
roast from the trolley at both lunch and dinner (except D Sat) –
Scottish lamb with mint sauce on Monday, English ham braised
in sherry with roast peaches on Tuesday, duck with sage and
onion stuffing on Wednesday – and Sunday brings a traditional
lunch centred around roast rib of Aberdeen Angus beef complete
with Yorkshire pudding and horseradish sauce. The main *carte*
is written in English with French translations. If they had looked
a little harder it would surely have been possible to find more than
two English wines to add to an otherwise all-French list but
to compensate there is an impressive list of single malt whiskies.
Set menus: L 250F (Sun) L & D 195F (Mon-Fri). *L 12.30-2
D 7.30-10.30.*

Bistrot de l'Etoile   Map A2.5
Tel 40 67 11 16   Fax 45 00 99 87   **R**
19 rue Lauriston 75016   M⁰ Etoile
Seats 52   Meal for 2 approx 500F

One of Guy Savoy's 'other' restaurants: there are about half
a dozen with the man himself at the one that carries his name
in the 17th (*qv*). Dark green outside and with foodie pictures
decorating the interior, this little bistro offers a short *carte* (about
six main dishes) along the lines of *moules marinière* with
chanterelle mushrooms; fricassee of guinea fowl with a potato and
sweetcorn galette; sea bream roasted in its skin with cabbage,
black radish, lemon and capers; roast figs with green apple sorbet
and warm apple tart. William Ledeuil cooks with invention that
avoids gimmickry. Pleasant service. *L 12-2.30 D 7.30-12.*
Closed L Sat, all Sun. *Amex, Mastercard, Visa.*

Hotel du Bois   Map A2.6
Tel 45 00 31 96   Fax 45 00 90 05   **H**
11 rue du Dome 75116   M⁰ Etoile
Rooms 41   Double from 540F

Small, neatly kept hotel on the corner of Rue du Dome and
Avenue Victor Hugo, just a few steps away from the Arc
de Triomphe. Bedrooms have a Laura Ashley look. Continental
breakfast is served in rooms or in the little lounge with 1930s style
leather chairs, opposite reception. No room service. Sister hotel
to the *Queen Mary* in the 8th (*qv*). *Amex, Mastercard, Visa.*

Brasserie de la Poste

| Tel 47 55 01 31   Fax 42 25 94 31 | R |

54 rue de Longchamp 75016   **M° Trocadéro**
Seats 64   Meal for 2 approx 400F

Map B2.7

Opposite a post office, hence the name and the logo (a franking
mark) on the menu and on the paper table covers. This is an old-
style neighbourhood brasserie both in looks – marbled paint
in nicotine colour, ceiling fans, mirrors, a show or two of flowers
– and in its menu of simple classics. Specialites include *choucroute*
(the cabbage happily without the frequent over-pickled taste),
cassoulet, *confit de canard* and pig's trotters. Other regulars include
goose foie gras in a Riesling aspic, snails, whole veal kidneys with
an excellent *sauce béarnaise* and *tripes à la mode de Caen*. Daily
specials widen the choice still further – *navarin d'agneau, coquilles
St Jacques Provençale*. Honest, reliable cooking at moderate prices,
with affable, efficient service. Hot winkles are served as appetisers,
and the pins would come in useful if you don't know what
to order. Set menu: L & D 120F (including wine). *L 12-3 D 7-1.*
Amex, Mastercard, Visa.

Brasserie Stella

| Tel 47 27 60 54   Fax 47 27 11 82 | R |

133 ave Victor Hugo 75016   **M° Victor Hugo**
Seats 120   Meal for 2 approx 450F

Map A1.8

Forming a wedge where Avenue Victor Hugo meets Rue de la
Pompe, Stella looks like an archetypal cheap and cheerful brasserie.
It's certainly cheerful, but your bill very much depends
on whether you prefer egg mayonnaise to oysters, or sardines
to sea urchins. *Fruits de mer* are a speciality (there's also a roaring
take-away trade) and others include *andouillette*, tripe, *petit salé*,
choucroute and the very popular steak tartare, the last deftly
composed by the waiters in between their other duties. Daily
dishes are also worth considering – *pot au feu* and *paupiettes
de veau* are typical. Book (but you might still have a wait at the
bar) or arrive early, because it sometimes seems as though most
of the 16th is in the queue. An all-French wine list favours the
Loire. Most wines are also sold by the glass or 45cl carafe. *Meals
noon – 1am.* **Closed 4 or 5 days mid-Aug.** *Amex, Mastercard, Visa.*

La Butte Chaillot ★

| Tel 47 27 88 88   Fax 47 04 85 70 | R |

112 ave Kléber 75116   **M° Trocadéro**
Seats 90   Meal for 2 approx 650F

Map B2.9

On the ground floor and basement of a luxurious modern
development, this is the grandest of the Guy Savoy 'other'
restaurants (the rest are called Bistrot de l'Etoile – see 16th and
17th arrs). Decorative features include iron girders and columns
and turquoise for seats, matching the shirts of the hard-working
yuppy waiters. Cooking is in most cases highly innovative, but
never outlandish, exemplified by *raviolis au pistou et à la crème
de mascarpone,* warm oysters *en feuilleté* with coriander, steamed
brill with a vanilla jus and wild mushrooms, salmon grilled with
red wine and bone marrow, and saddle of lamb stuffed with goat's
cheese. Short, reasonably priced list of wines. Very much a place

of the moment, especially for business lunches and social evenings.
Set menu: L & D 210F. *L 12-2.30 D 7-12.* **Closed** *25 Dec & 1 Jan.*
Amex, Mastercard, Visa.

Carette
Map B2.10

| Tel 47 27 88 56 | R |

4 place du Trocadéro 75116   **M⁰ Trocadéro**

The redoubtable Mme Letard-Carette is the third generation
to run this old-fashioned *salon de thé*/patisserie/restaurant –
established in 1927 and still a popular meeting place – bang on the
Place Trocadéro, opposite the Parvis and Chaillot. It's open all day
for coffee, tea, cakes and light savouries, and there are a few more
substantial daily specials at lunchtime. Fresh fish from the Rungis
market – feuilleté of langoustines, fillet of hake *dieppoise* – are
a speciality. There's also a busy take-away trade – all the patisserie
is first-class, with macaroons the house speciality. Sandwiches are
less recommendable. *Meals 8-6.45.* **Closed** *Tue. No credit cards.*

Chez Géraud
Map B1.11

| Tel 45 20 33 00 | R |

31 rue Vital 75016   **M⁰ La Muette**
Seats 40   Meal for 2 approx 600F

The carte changes with the seasons, the fixed-price menu daily
according to the market, at this restaurant in a former bakery with
marble floor, oak bar and an eye-catching faïence fresco. Daniel
Vacher's cooking is fairly traditional with the likes of baby leek
vinaigrette with shavings of foie gras, fricassee of wild
mushrooms, tuna steak with green peppercorns, saddle of hare
with sauce poivrade and entrecote steak either *persillée, nature*
or with a wine sauce. About 100 entries on the all-French wine list
– all their Beaujolais are bought in casks direct from the producer
and bottled on the premises. Set menu: L & D 200F. *L 12-2
D 7.30-10.* **Closed** *L Sat (Mar-Sep), all Sun & Aug. Amex,
Mastercard, Visa.*

The best way to get around Paris is by bus or metro – buy a
book of tickets (carnet) at any metro station and save money

Chez Ngo
Map B2.12

| Tel & Fax 47 04 53 20 | R |

70 rue de Longchamp 75116   **M⁰ Trocadéro**
Seats 90   Meal for 2 approx 400F

There are two styles of cooking here – Chinese and Thai. The
specialities only feature fish as in the steamed bass with Chinese
mushrooms and soya sauce, sautéed mussels with Thai basil leaves,
or sautéed lobster with ginger and chives. Meat-eaters are not
neglected, however, and may like to try the sautéed beef Peking-
style. A ten-metre long fresco of Chinese landscape and plenty
of wood create a realistically authentic old Chinese decor. Drink
French wines or Oriental beers. Set L 98F (Mon-Fri including
wine) Set menus: L & D 97F & 398F (for two). *L 12-3 D 7-11.45.
Amex, Diners, Mastercard, Visa.*

Conti   ★

Tel 47 27 74 67   Fax 47 27 37 66   **R**   Map A2.13

72 rue Lauriston 75116   M° Boissière
Seats 45   Meal for 2 approx 750F

In intimate, quietly luxurious surroundings a civilised clientele
enjoys the high-quality Italian cooking of Frenchman Michel
Ranvier. The produce and inspiration of both countries combine
in a delightful menu whose specialities include *carpaccio d'artichauts
poivrades, assiette Toscane;* lasagne of lobster; *caciucco à la
livournaise; bollito misto, moutarde de Cremone, biscuit
léger* 'tiramisu', and roast pear with honey and sweet lemon oil.
Lunchtime menu at 265F includes wine and coffee. 300-strong
wine list includes all areas of Italy and most of the 'grand vins'
of France. Set L 265F. *L 12-2.30 D 7.30-10.30. **Closed** Sat, Sun,
3 weeks Aug & Christmas-New Year. Amex, Diners,
Mastercard, Visa.*

Fakhr el Dine   Map B2.14

Tel 47 27 90 00   Fax 47 27 11 39   **R**

30 rue de Longchamp 75016   M° Trocadéro
Seats 110   Meal for 2 approx 500F

Good classic and modern Lebanese cuisine is guaranteed in the
warm surroundings of two large dining rooms decorated with
large frescoes. Begin with *fatayers* (spinach rissoles) or *sojok* (spicy
sausages flambéed with lemon juice) and move on to *chiche taouck*
(chicken brochettes marinated in lemon, oil and garlic) or lamb
cutlets, followed by one of a variety of sweet Lebanese desserts.
Lebanese and French wines, the latter including a Beaujolais
bought by the cask and bottled on the premises. Also at Rue
Quentin Bauchart in the 8th (Tel 47 23 44 42) and the Institute
du Monde Arabe in the 5th (Tel 46 33 47 70). Set menu: L &
D 160F. *Meals noon-midnight. Amex, Diners, Mastercard, Visa.*

Faugeron   ★★★   Map B2.15

Tel 47 04 24 53   Fax 47 55 62 90   **R**

52 rue de Longchamp 75116   M° Trocadéro
Seats 50   Meal for 2 approx 1000F

It was in 1972 that Henri Faugeron first put puréed truffles
together with a simple soft boiled hen's egg and brioche 'soldiers'
to create his famous signature dish *oeufs croque Faugeron,* as popular
now as it was then to judge by the number being eaten all around
us on a recent lunchtime visit. But there are many other
wonderful dishes to be enjoyed here: tournedos of lobster with
raviolis of ceps was stunning and a dish of fresh foie gras with figs
and caramelised butter lacked only "the sound of trumpets" – both
from the day's *Grand Menu Dégustation.* What you will not find
here is asparagus in autumn or strawberries in winter as Henri is a
stickler for using ingredients only in their natural season when
they are at their very best. Game is a particular speciality in season
– noisettes of venison with autumn fruits, *croustillant et salmis
de faisane aux jus de truffes* – and amongst the desserts a *mille-feuille
'Amadéus' en duo de chocolats,* the creation of Gerlindé Faugeron,
who is the charming hostess overseeing the discreetly cosseting
service. The immaculately hand-written wine list is outstanding

and wine waiter Jean-Claude Jambon was voted the 'best sommelier in the world' a couple of years ago. Each month there is a selection of three or four wines by the glass, a recent selection included Chateau Margaux 1980 at 135F the glass. Everything about this fine restaurant combines to make it a most deserving winner of our first Paris Restaurant of the Year Award. Set L 290F Set L & D 650F (dégustation) Set D 550F (with wine). *L 12-2 D 7.30-10.* **Closed** *Sat (except D Oct-Apr), Sun, Aug & Christmas-New Year. Amex, Mastercard, Visa.*

La Fontaine d'Auteuil

Map C1.16

Tel 42 88 04 47   R

35bis rue la Fontaine 75016   M° Jasmin
Seats 40   Meal for 2 approx 700F

A former brasserie, with dark wood and lots of flowers, this high-class neighbourhood restaurant is situated near the Maison de la Radio. Xavier Grégoire's style is traditional, lightened for today's tastes, and many of his best dishes are based on fish and shellfish: warm lobster salad with Sauternes and ginger vinaigrette, tournedos of salmon with bacon and green lentils. Other specialities include aiguillettes of pigeon marinated in soya and lemon and served with a herb salad, parmentier of hot foie gras with celery and an oxtail jus and, amongst the desserts, a trilogy of bitter chocolate. No wines by the glass shown on the wine list but they will happily come up with something on request. Set L 170F Set L & D 350F (*dégustation*) Set D 230F. *L 12-2.15 D 7.30-10.* **Closed** *L Sat, all Sun, 1 week Feb & 3 weeks Aug. Amex, Diners, Mastercard, Visa.*

Garden Elysée

Map A2.17

Tel 47 55 01 11   Fax 47 27 79 24   H

12 rue St Didier 75116   M° Boissière
Rooms 48   Double from 1450F

Spacious air-conditioned bedrooms with satellite TV, individual room-safes and whirlpool baths in a modern building set back from the street. Gardens front and rear. Room service till 11pm. Private parking for five cars. *Amex, Diners, Mastercard, Visa.*

For a glossary of menu terms see page 293

Hameau de Passy

Map B1.18

Tel 42 88 47 55   Fax 42 30 83 72   H

48 rue de Passy 75016   M° Passy/La Muette
Rooms 32   Double from 540F

Glass-enclosed spiral staircases either side of the main entrance are an unusual feature at this peaceful hotel opposite a private garden in a cul de sac near Trocadéro. Bright, modern, straightforward accommodation; pleasant staff. Room rates include breakfast, served in your room or in the lounge. Room service, provided from outside the hotel, is available between 5pm and 3am. *Amex, Diners, Mastercard, Visa.*

Jean-Claude Ferrero

Map B1.19

| Tel 45 04 42 42   Fax 45 04 67 71 | R |

38 rue Vital 75016   **M° La Muette**
Seats 50   Meal for 2 approx 850F

In a grand Second Empire *hotel particulier* the grandest way
to celebrate is to work through the seasonal truffle or mushroom
menus. If those are earthier than your taste, try the *bouillabaisse*
raphaëloise, herb-stuffed bass *en croute* (both for 2 persons),
noisettes of venison with bilberries, the fish of the day with olive
oil and a gratin of fennel or one of the traditional dishes like
brandade de morue salée and *blanquette de veau à l'ancienne*. Set
L 200F Set L & D 280F & 350F. Three private rooms. *L 12-2.30
D 6-10.30.* **Closed** *Sat, Sun (except D Nov-Feb) 1st 2 wks May &
last 3 wks Aug. Amex, Mastercard, Visa.*

Kambodgia

Map A2.20

| Tel 47 23 31 80   Fax 47 20 41 22 | R |

15 rue Bassano 75016   **M° George V**
Seats 54   Meal for 2 approx 600F

Oriental wood panelling and embroideries lend a clubby
atmosphere to this intimate restaurant just off the Champs Elysées.
There are some Thai and Vietnamese dishes but the cooking
is mainly Cambodian: spicy beef with coconut milk, fish with
ginger cooked in banana leaves, chicken with honey and lemon
in a crisp pastry case. For afters there are exotic fruits and sorbets
along with various fritters (apple with caramel, flambéed banana)
and an iced mango soup with coconut milk. Short list of French
wines and a couple of beers, one Thai and one Chinese. Set
L 170F. *L 12-2.30 D 7-11.* **Closed** *L Sat, all Sun. Amex,
Mastercard, Visa.*

L'Hotel Kléber

Map A2.21

| Tel 47 23 80 22   Fax 49 52 07 20 | H |

7 rue Belloy 75116   **M° Etoile**
Rooms 23   Double from 590F

A second Empire building between Etoile and Trocadéro in the
business and embassy district. Small and comfortable with friendly
staff and bedrooms that are well equipped with multi-channel TV,
direct-dial phones and hairdryer. All bathrooms have both shower
and tub. The bar, which also serves snacks, is open 24hrs a day.
Amex, Diners, Mastercard, Visa.

Kléber Palace

Map B2.22

| Tel 44 05 75 00   Fax 44 05 74 74 | H |

81 ave Kléber 75016   **M° Trocadéro**
Rooms 83   Double from 1300F

A prestigious, ultra-modern *résidence hotelière* inaugurated
in October 1993. Bedrooms (no suites) vary in size and a little
in their appointments, but all have kitchenettes (sometimes just
a sink and hob in a cabinet) which provide the possibility of life
without the hotel's considerable facilities; these include a bright
breakfast room and a full-scale restaurant. The hotel is built round
an atrium in which a jungle of plants is gaining height by the day.

All bedrooms overlook either this or the street, and the latter also
get a look at greenery, in this case bamboo plants in a dramatic
vertical greenhouse clinging to the facade. Bedroom furniture
is simple, stylish and practical, and some inside rooms have
terraces with wooden outdoor furniture. All rooms have
individual air-conditioning, fax points and marble bathrooms. Day
rooms include a long, long lounge beyond the always-manned
reception desk, a bar with a crescent counter and a fitness centre
in the basement with mini-gym, sauna, turkish bath, solarium and
a jacuzzi the size of a small swimming pool. Room service can
provide snacks at any time. Parking 60F per day. *Amex, Diners,
Mastercard, Visa.*

Hotel de Longchamp

Map B2.23

Tel 47 27 13 48   Fax 47 55 68 26   H

68 rue de Longchamp 75116   **M⁰ Trocadéro**
Rooms 23   Double from 620F

Quiet, comfortable and welcoming hotel near Place de Mexico.
Modernised behind its traditional facade, it offers all the necessities
in bedrooms done out in pastel shades. TV includes English
channels. Private parking 100F per day. *Amex, Diners,
Mastercard, Visa.*

Majestic

Map A2.24

Tel 45 00 83 70   Fax 45 00 29 48   H

29 rue Dumont-d'Urville 75116   **M⁰ Kléber**
Rooms 32   Double from 950F

Recently installed air-conditioning has added to the comfort
of traditionally furnished bedrooms at this charming hotel not far
from the Arc de Triomphe. Some of the atmosphere of old France
remains in the civilised public areas. Pick of the accommodation
is the penthouse suite (1900F) with a flowery balcony. Double
glazing keeps things peaceful. Sister hotel to the *Raphael* (just
around the corner) and the *Regina* (*qv*) in the 1st. *Amex, Diners,
Mastercard, Visa.*

Les Monuments

Map B2.25

Tel & Fax 44 05 90 00   R

1 place du Trocadéro 75016   **M⁰ Trocadéro**
Seats 40   Meal for 2 approx 700F

Part of the main concourse of the Musée de Monuments Français
within the Palais de Chaillot, a big plus is the view of the Eiffel
Tower, especially in summer when tables spill out on to the
terrace. Les Monuments was fairly recently opened by
chocolatier/patissier Christian Constant (see entry in the 7th), so it
is not surprising that desserts – *tarte fondante du chocolat, millefeuille
aux poires* – are a highlight of a menu that might also include
a salad of lobster and langoustines with lime and ginger, duck
with mango and a ragout of veal sweetbreads. In the afternoon (4-
6pm) the restaurant becomes a *salon de thé* with snacks like ham
quiche and salad of white cabbage with Bayonne ham plus,
of course, Monsieur Constant's patisserie and chocolate creations.
Set L & D 180F. *L 12-2.30 D 7-10.30.* **Closed** *Tues.
Mastercard, Visa.*

Le Parc Victor Hugo
Map A2.26

Tel 44 05 66 66   Fax 44 05 66 00

HR

55 ave Raymond Poincaré 75016
M° Trocadéro

Rooms 120
Double from 2300F

A discreet hotel, between the Place Victor Hugo and the
Trocadéro, which aims to combine English refinement with
French hospitality, and does so with great charm. The English
'country house' feel is achieved with wood panelling and brass
chandeliers in the lobby and Nina Campbell interiors featuring
her hallmark dark green and red plaid fabrics in the bar-lounge.
Bedrooms, in five buildings set around a delightful courtyard full
of trees and flowers, come in nine different colour schemes
ranging from light and summery to rich and warm. Some beds
are four-posters and many of the others canopied, and all have
padded headboards that gain muslin anti-macassars in the evening
when beds are turned down, lights lit and curtains drawn. Air-
conditioning, two direct telephone lines, room safe, mini-bar and
Bang & Olufsen cable television are standard. Both room service
(24hrs) and breakfast are overseen by Joël Robuchon. Valet
parking. *Amex, Diners, Mastercard, Visa.*

Joël Robuchon   ★★★
Tel 47 27 12 27   Fax 47 27 31 22
59 ave Raymond Poincaré 75016

Seats 50
Meal for 2 approx 2400F

To describe this establishment as a restaurant is like calling Joël
Robuchon a cook: both are accurate but equally inadequate
descriptions. To begin with, you cannot just walk in, but have
to ring the door bell (actually a doorman does the ringing for
you) to gain admittance, as if at some ultra-expensive jewellers
shop, having reserved a table several months in advance. Once
inside, the setting is that of a turn-of-the-century private house
where you dine in one of three first-floor rooms, each retaining
the atmosphere of an *haute bourgeois* private residence: the
mahogany-panelled former Smoking Room (also used as a *salle
privée*), the Library (where *trompe l'oeil* tomes now fill the shelves),
or the original dining room of the house with its beamed ceiling
and massive, heavily carved fireplace and overmantel. All are
equally comfortable (the latter perhaps best at lunchtime as it has
most natural light) rooms in which to enjoy the most sought-after
cooking in Paris. Robuchon's masterly modern cuisine includes
specialities of *gelée de caviar à la crème de chou-fleur, ravioli
de langoustines au chou, agneau pastoral aux herbes en salade* and
canette rosée aux épices en cocotte lutée, navets au foie gras. Desserts
such as *crousillant aux noix* and a 'jubilee' of fruit *flambé* with
caramel ice cream supplement the sweet trolley. A good plan,
to avoid some agonizing choices, is to go for one of the two set
menus (both served only to the whole table), one at 890F a tasting
menu of seven courses, the other concentrating on shellfish.
Service is extremely professional. Set menus: L & D 890F &
1200F. *L 12-2 D 8-10. **Closed** Sat, Sun & 4 weeks July-Aug.*

Le Relais du Parc   ★
Tel 44 05 66 10
Seats 80 (+90 Outside)   Meal for 2 approx 600F

The hotel's main restaurant – because staying at the hotel does not
overcome the need to book months in advance for **Joël
Robuchon** (above). Two rooms running by the side of a leafy
courtyard, into which the tables spill out in summer, are decorated
in a colonial style that includes old photographs of safaris.
Redwood is used for the bar, the tables and the chairs, whose grey-
and-white upholstery takes up the colour of the tiled floor.
Managers are smartly and soberly suited, and the waiters wear
distinctive silk waistcoats. Overseen by Joël Robuchon, Gilles
Renault's menu has an immediate, straightforward appeal: country
terrine with thyme, warm mackerel tart with aromatic herbs,
roast monkfish with fresh curried tagliatelle, calf's liver with
rosemary and a gratin of white onions, black pudding with
creamed potatoes and *hachis parmentier de canard* – a duck confit
version of shepherds pie! Desserts range from fresh fruit salad and
petits pots de crème vanille et chocolat to wild strawberry tart and
a *feuilleté* of pears with honey. Booking advisable. *L 12-2.30
D 7.30-10.30.*

Passy Eiffel   Map B2.27
Tel 45 25 55 66   Fax 42 88 89 88   **H**
10 rue de Passy 75016   **Mᵒ Passy**
Rooms 50   Double from 580F

The rooms here are spread over five floors, and one or two are
large enough for family occupation. Traditionally-styled bedrooms
boast fresh-cut flowers and about half are air-conditioned.
No restaurant but a conservatory breakfast room with a couple
of tables out on a patio when the weather allows. The hotel is just
across the river from the Eiffel Tower. *Amex, Diners,
Mastercard, Visa.*

Passy Mandarin   Map B1.28
Tel 42 88 12 18   Fax 42 60 33 92   **R**
6 rue Bois le Vent 75016   **Mᵒ La Muette**
Seats 90   Meal for 2 approx 500F

Three handsomely appointed dining areas, with walls and
furniture in dark wood and Chinese artwork in traditional style,
make up one of the capital's leading Chinese restaurants. Cooking
is Cantonese, with a short list also of Vietnamese dishes. Dim sum,
available lunchtime and evening, are particularly good, and as well
as the familiar varieties there are prawn-stuffed courgette rings,
shark's fin ravioli and buns (*bau*) with a filling of curried chicken.
Elsewhere, prawns, crab, monkfish, chicken, pork and beef are all
well prepared in straightforward style, along with six ways with
duck – lacquered is a speciality. A Chinese fondue for a minimum
of two diners is for special occasions. Another branch, more
sumptuously decorated, is in the 2nd arrondissement (*qv*). That
one is closed on Sundays. Staff at both are friendly and attentive.
Set L & D 460F (for two). *L 12-2.30 D 7-11. Amex,
Mastercard, Visa.*

Paul Chene
Map B2.29

Tel 47 27 63 17   **R**

123 rue Lauriston 75116   M^o Trocadéro
Seats 55   Meal for 2 approx 800F

Classic dishes make up the majority of the menu at this elegantly
appointed, formal restaurant just up from Trocadéro. *Vichyssoise,*
terrine de canard, filets of sole *'tout Paris',* whole baby turbot with
hollandaise sauce, *daube de boeuf à l'ancienne, confit d'oie,* chocolate
profiteroles and fresh pineapple with Kirsch will appeal
to traditional tastes, and along with this style of cooking goes
smart, correct and efficient service. It's a quiet, civilised place with
a jolly maitre d'hotel who's a past master at filleting and presenting
fish dishes. The wine list majors on Bordeaux, and there's
a selection of grand and expensive digestifs. A Sauternes and
a Muscadet are served by the glass and a champagne by the goblet.
Set L & D: 200F. *L 12.30-2.45 D 7.30-10.30.* **Closed** *L Sat, all Sun,*
28 Jul-21 Aug & 23 Dec-2 Jan. Amex, Diners, Mastercard, Visa.

Note: from April 16 1995 the
international dialling code 010 changes to 00

Pavillon Noura
Map A2.30

Tel 47 20 33 33   Fax 47 20 60 31   **R**

21 ave Marceau 75116   M^o Alma-Marceau/George V
Seats 105   Meal for 2 approx 500F

The Middle East, especially Lebanon, is very much in evidence
on entering the large dining room. Frescoes of Tyre and Sidon
taken from 17th-century drawings cover two walls. The exotic
interior of wood and ceramic surfaces, chandeliers and banquette
seating sets the stage perfectly for some authentic Lebanese food.
Tabouleh (cracked wheat with parsley, mint, lemon, olive oil and
onions) and *falafel* (bean croquettes with garlic, chick peas and
sesame oil) are cold and hot starters respectively which could
be followed by charcoal-grilled skewered lamb or *kofta korfalyeh*
(lamb meatballs with tomato). The Patisserie Noura a few doors
up the road supplies the sweet pastries (also to take away) and the
Noura Traiteur, on the opposite corner to the Patisserie, is a less
formal, snackier version of the Pavillon. Set L 156F & 190F Set
D 220F, 270F & 320F. *L 12-3.30 D 8-12. Amex, Diners,*
Mastercard, Visa.

Hotel Pergolèse
Map A2.31

Tel 40 67 96 77   Fax 45 00 12 11   **H**

3 rue Pergolèse 75116   M^o Porte Maillot/Argentine
Rooms 40   Double from 960F

Ultra-modern behind its fin-de-siècle facade, the Pergolèse offers
comfort, service and a style (Rena Dumas) all its own. Half the
bedrooms are on the street side, the others over the courtyard, and
all feature ash bedheads. TVs and mini-bars are hidden away
in the furniture; bathrooms gleam in glass, marble and chrome.
Amex, Diners, Mastercard, Visa.

Le Pergolèse

Map A1.32

Tel 45 00 21 40   Fax 45 00 81 31   **R**

40 rue Pergolèse 75116   M° **Porte Maillot**
Seats 45   Meal for 2 approx 700F

A pastel-pretty restaurant with some delightful paintings and
flower displays. Chef-patron Albert Corre's style is classic, suitably
lightened, and there are some interesting combinations on his
menu: frog's legs sautéed with *pleurottes*, ravioli of langoustines
with duxelle of mushroom, scallops cooked in little jacket
potatoes, red mullet with fresh pasta, olive oil and basil. Desserts
are equally appealing, and there's a good regional French wine list.
Set L & D: 230F & 300F. *L 12.2.30 D 8-10.30.* **Closed** *Sat, Sun &
Aug. Amex, Mastercard, Visa.*

Le Petit Bedon

Map A1.33

Tel 45 00 23 66   Fax 45 00 15 19   **R**

38 rue Pergolèse 75016   M° **Argentine**
Seats 38   Meal for 2 approx 750F

Small and chocolate-box pretty, with walls in polished oak, round
tables, paintings and candles. The cuisine is 'bourgeoise mais
royale', with dishes served in generous portions: eggs poached
in wine with a ragout of onion, *soupe au pistou* with herbs, *croquant*
of shellfish with fennel, roast bream, shoulder of milk-fed lamb
with grilled aubergines, chocolate tart, *baba au rhum.* Good, wide-
ranging selection of wines. Set L & D 240F. *L 12-2.30 D 7.30-11.*
Closed *Aug. Amex, Diners, Mastercard, Visa.*

La Petite Tour   ★

Map B2.34

Tel 45 20 09 31   **R**

11 rue de la Tour 75116   M° **Passy**
Seats 40   Meal for 2 approx 850F

Christine Israël's flower displays are one delight at this friendly
little restaurant with its rough-painted walls and red plush
upholstery, another is Freddy Israël's excellent cooking. A menu
of classic dishes acknowledges the season but otherwise does not
change much – quite deliberately: *bisque de homard*, brochette
of scallops, *cassolette d'escargots aux aromates*, escalopes of salmon
with sorrel, *magret* of duck with fresh ceps, veal kidneys with
mustard sauce, *tete de veau sauce ravigote*, jugged hare with fresh
pasta, *crème brulée, vacherin glacée*, chocolate gateau, *ile flottante aux
pralines.* Well-balanced, all French wine list. *L 12-2.30 D 7.30-
10.30.* **Closed** *Sun, & 2 weeks mid-Aug. Amex, Diners,
Mastercard, Visa.*

Port Alma

Map A2.35

Tel 47 23 75 11   **R**

10 ave de New York 75116   M° **Alma-Marceau**
Seats 50   Meal for 2 approx 700F

A quayside seafood restaurant (air-conditioned in summer) which
is more or less an enclosed terrace with large picture windows
offering views across the Seine to the Eiffel Tower. Next door
to the Musée de l'Art Moderne, it's decorated in blue and white
with well-spaced round tables and period-style chairs. The
restaurant, run by a husband and wife team with Paul Canal in the   *See over*

kitchen and Sonia at front of house, is popular with the business community at lunchtime when booking is advisable. Changing daily, according to the market, a typical menu might include a warm lobster salad, feuilleté of scallops with wild mushrooms and squid *à l'encre* amongst the staters and the likes of bream cooked in salt, roast turbot with hollandaise, fricassee of sole with foie gras and grilled lobster with tarragon in the main-course section. Short but well-balanced list of desserts such as *tarte au pommes,* chocolate soufflé, fresh figs *chantilly,* ice cream and sorbets. Set L 200F. *L 12.30-2.30 D 7.30-10.30. Closed Sun, Aug. Amex, Diners, Mastercard, Visa.*

Le Pré Catelan   ★★   Map B1.36

Tel 45 24 55 58   Fax 45 24 43 25   **R**

route de Suresnes, Bois de Boulogne 75016   M⁰ Porte Dauphine (2km)
Seats 80 (+80 outside)   Meal for 2 approx 1400F

A magical spot in the Bois de Boulogne, and perhaps the most beautiful restaurant in all Paris, superbly restored to its 18th-century elegance by Christian Benais. The dining rooms are magnificent, and in summer terraces make the most of the marvellous setting. Chef-director Roland Durand loves cooking and remains in the kitchen creating such dishes as oyster and cep soup, terrine of hare with bilberries and a mushroom chutney, langoustines cooked in their shells with a tomato and banana sauce, turbot with parsley jus and cheese ravioli, shoulder of venison lightly curried with chestnuts and prunes, pig's trotters with truffle juice, and *aiguillettes* of duck with lemon and pear. A remarkable wine list covering all the French classics kicks off with over 40 champagnes. Le Pré Catelan is also a venue for seminars and business meetings. Set L 260F Set D 550F. *L 12-2.30 D 7.30-10.30.* **Closed** *D Sun, all Mon, 2 wks Feb. Amex, Diners, Mastercard, Visa.*

Quach   Map B2.37

Tel 47 27 98 40   **R**

47 ave Raymond Poincaré 75016   M⁰ Trocadéro
Seats 60   Meal for 2 approx 500F

A comfortable room jutting out on to a broad pavement, exotic but sober in style, with large tropical fish paddling around in a couple of aquaria. Cantonese and Vietnamese dishes make up the bulk of the menu, which numbers steamed dim sum, mussels with basil, lamb grilled with five spices and lacquered duck among its specialities. Some 20 French wines plus beer from Thailand, China and the Netherlands. Set L & D 109F. *L 12-2.30 D 7-11. Amex, Diners, Mastercard, Visa.*

Raphael   Map A2.38

Tel 44 28 00 28   Fax 45 01 21 50   **H**

17 ave Kléber 75116   M⁰ Etoile/Kléber
Rooms 90   Double from 1950F

Opened as a hotel in 1925, the Raphael has ever since that time been synonymous with opulence, elegance, calm and high levels of service. Luxury is all around, from Oriental rugs on marble floors to oak-panelled meeting rooms, gilt and elaborate marquetry in the **salon bleu**, treasured books and magical tapestries in the library and crimson plush and amberwood in the **English Bar**. Spacious bedrooms offer the highest levels of comfort, with rich, solid furnishings, mainly in rococo style, magnificent wardrobes and vast bathrooms. The bar and about one third of bedrooms are now air-conditioned. Every possible accessory is included, and 24-hour room service is provided. *Amex, Diners, Mastercard, Visa.*

Relais d'Auteuil ★ Map D1.39

Tel 46 51 09 54   Fax 40 71 05 03   **R**

31 bd Murat 75016   M° Porte d'Auteuil
Seats 40   Meal for 2 approx 1100F

From the moment that a member of staff appears and parks the car for you, it is apparent that this is a 'serious' restaurant. Situated in a well-to-do part of Paris, its equally well-heeled customers reflect the increasing reputation of charismatic young chef Patrick Pignol, who is on hand, dressed in his immaculate whites, first to welcome diners and then to explain the day's special dishes not on the printed menu. Contemporary decor, a covered terrace, peach-coloured walls, impressionist paintings, expensive floral arrangements and beautiful Italian tableware, backed up by a team of extremely professional and smartly-dressed staff, create the perfect backdrop for some really splendid cooking. Current specialities – some are seasonal – include grilled langoustines with coriander, *armandine de foie gras de canard et sa terrine,* poached oysters with a shallot confit, young partridge *en cocotte* with sage, *compote de liévre en crépinette* with fresh pasta, scallops meunière *au sel de Guerlande,* desserts like a bitter chocolate tart with Grand Marnier butter and *soufflé cacao et chicorée.* The wine list has some quite reasonably priced bottles and a few halves among more than 800 listings and, unusually for a restaurant of this class, there are also some available by the glass. Fine coffee comes with both petits fours and chocolates. Set L 230F Set L & D 390F & 480F. *L 12.15-2.30 D 7.15-10.30.* **Closed** *L Sat, all Sun, 1st 3 weeks Aug & 10 days Christmas. Amex, Mastercard, Visa.*

La Résidence Bassano Map A2.40

Tel 47 23 78 23   Fax 47 20 41 22   **H**

15 rue Bassano 75016   M° George V
Rooms 31   Double from 750F

The building is Haussmann vintage, but inside all is neatly contemporary. Bedrooms, all with marble-clad bathrooms, include three suites, two of which have kitchenettes. The hotel has two restaurants, one French, the other Vietnamese (see Kambodgia). A programme of bedroom refurbishment was due to commence in November '94. *Amex, Diners, Mastercard, Visa.*

Hotel du Rond-Point de Longchamp Map B1.41

Tel 45 05 13 63   Fax 47 55 12 80   **H**

86 rue de Longchamp 75116   M° Trocadéro
Rooms 57   Double from 730F

Double glazing keeps the traffic noise away from this comfortable hotel, whose other assets include air-conditioning, billiard room and internal communication with a branch of the popular tea shop **Angelina**. *Amex, Diners, Mastercard, Visa.*

Saint James Paris
Map A1.42

Tel 44 05 81 81   Fax 44 05 81 82   H

5 place du Chancelier Adenauer, ave Bugeaud 75116   **M⁰ Porte Dauphine**
Rooms 48   Double from 1500F

Built in 1892 by a charitable foundation to house outstanding
scholars studying in the capital, the Saint James has all the
appearance of a country chateau (fronted by a fountain and
complete with landscaped grounds) transplanted to this residential
area of Paris near the Avenue Foch. Air-conditioned bedrooms,
ten of which on the third floor open on to a winter garden, were
designed by Andrée Putman and have an uncluttered 1930s
elegance. Day rooms include a well-stocked library bar where
a pianist plays each evening except Friday when it is the turn of a
jazz trio. Other amenities include a health club and free secure
parking. See photos page 21. *Amex, Diners, Mastercard, Visa.*

Hotel de Sévigné
Map A2.43

Tel 47 20 88 90   Fax 40 70 98 73   H

6 rue de Belloy 75116   **M⁰ Kléber/Boissière**
Rooms 30   Double from 700F

The 30 rooms all have little lobbies, and some rooms interconnect
for family use. Colour schemes vary from floor to floor, but
fittings are standard, including 20-channel TVs and telephone
extensions in the bathrooms. *Amex, Diners, Mastercard, Visa.*

Le Toit de Passy   ★
Map B1.44

Tel 45 24 55 37   Fax 45 20 94 57   R

94 ave Paul Doumer (6th floor) 75016   **M⁰ La Muette**
Seats 70 (+30 outside)   Meal for 2 approx 1000F

A rooftop restaurant filled with plants and with a terrace
affording fine views of the city. Dedicated chef Yannick Jacquot's
cooking is as elevated as his restaurant, with subtle combinations
of flavours and textures evident in such specialities as foie gras –
either hot with polenta, raisins, passion fruit and a sweet and sour
sauce or cold in a light Graves and port jelly –fillets of red mullet
and its liver with potato 'scales' and *sauce antiboise*, and pigeon
baked in salt and served with a garnish of cabbage and foie gras
en feuillatage. Desserts include a caramelised apple tart; roast figs
with honey sorbet and a dark chocolate soufflé perfumed with
rum. The 495F menu is a *dégustation* of seven courses (served only
to the whole table) with a choice only for the principal course.
A predominantly French wine list majoring in reds from
Bordeaux and whites from Burgundy. Set L 195F Set L &
D 295F, 380F & 495F. *L 12.30-2.30 D 7.30-10.30.* **Closed** *L Sat &
all Sun. Amex, Mastercard, Visa.*

Trocadéro
Map A2.45

Tel 45 53 01 82   Fax 45 53 59 56   H

21 rue St-Didier 75116   **M⁰ Trocadéro**
Rooms 23   Double from 570F

A smiling welcome and all the usual comforts in a well-run hotel
just north of Trocadéro. Recently refurbished bedrooms boast

mini-bars and multi-channel TV. Children under 12 are
accommodated free in their parents' room. Room service is limited
to breakfast. *Amex, Diners, Mastercard, Visa.*

La Villa Maillot
Map A1.46

| Tel 45 01 25 22   Fax 45 00 60 61 | **H** |

143 ave de Malakoff 75116
Rooms 42

M⁰ Trocadéro
Double from 1700F

Handily situated for visitors, whether on business or for pleasure,
a five minute walk from the Arc de Triomphe and the Champs
Elysées, this is an elegant and quiet art deco-style hotel of much
charm. Behind the white facade (illuminated at night) the public
areas are quite striking, from the marble-floored foyer and pastel-
coloured lounge with sofas aplenty to the boldly decorated bar
and garden conservatory restaurant, the setting for an inviting
buffet breakfast. Comfortable and restful bedrooms in soft colours,
with queen-size beds and floor-length curtains, are soundproofed,
air-conditioned and offer satellite TV, mini-bar, kitchenette and
trouser press. Modern bathrooms, in rose-coloured marble,
provide excellent hotel-monogrammed toiletries. There are three
suites, named after Picasso, Chagall and Modigliani. Garage
(6 cars), garden. *Amex, Diners, Mastercard, Visa.*

Vivarois   ★
Map B1.47

| Tel 45 04 04 31   Fax 45 03 09 84 | **R** |

192 ave Victor Hugo 75116
Seats 50

M⁰ Rue de la Pompe
Meal for 2 approx 1200F

Colourful fabric panels in abstract designs bring some warmth
to this well-lit restaurant done out in grey marble with 60s style
moulded plastic chairs behind its plate glass windows on the
ground floor of a modern block near the Place Tattergrain. Here
for over 25 years, chef-patron Claude Peyrot's presents a shortish
written menu that does not change much and is somewhat poetic
in style so that some explanation from Claude's wife Jacqueline
is often required. *Poupre de turbot Sylvestre* for example is so called
because tomato in the sauce tends to give a purple colour to the
fish and *soufflé de l'écureuil* is not squirrel soufflé but made with
nuts, the squirrel's favourite food. Ravioli Rastellini is made with
lobster and proved an excellent beginning to a recent meal.
In addition to the written menu there are always a number
of verbally described specials of the day that are dependent upon
the market (Claude places great importance on using only the best
of ingredients) such as *crépinette* of skate stuffed with onions and
ceps. Desserts might include *mousse de cassis Cote de Nuits, parfait
de marrons d'Ardeche* and a delicious, melt-in-the-mouth chocolate
tart. The unwritten fixed-price lunch changes daily and offers
several choices at each stage; the à la carte is also available. On our
last visit the dining room seemed to be a bit understaffed. Set
L 345F. *L 12-2 D 8-9.45. Closed Sat, Sun, 1 Nov & Aug. Amex,
Diners, Mastercard, Visa.*

17th Arrondissement
Places of Interest

Arc de Triomphe, M° Charles de Gaulle-Etoile
Palais des Congrès (Porte Maillot), 40 68 22 22, M° Porte Maillot
Place de Clichy
Parc Monceau, M° Monceau

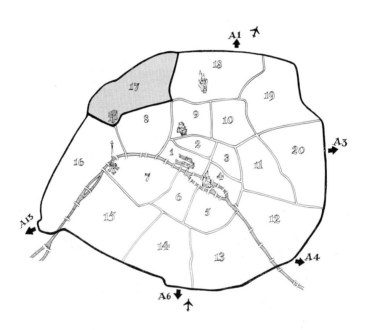

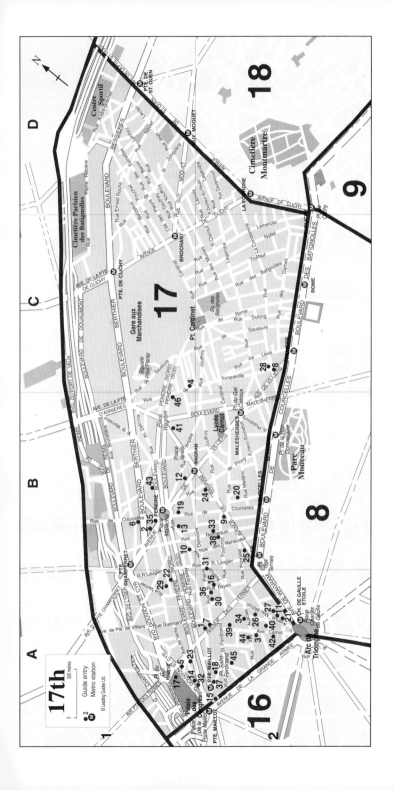

Amphyclès   ★   Map A2.1

Tel 40 68 01 01   Fax 40 68 91 88   R

78 ave des Ternes 75017   M° Porte Maillot
Seats 42   Meal for 2 approx 1500F

A pretty restaurant with ribbon-hung etchings of classical urns,
trellis-work against mirrors and a little 'garden' on the pavement
outside to create a pleasant view. It's a bit cramped though, with
barely room for the various trolleys, including those for the
tempting desserts and impressive cheese selection, to wend their
way between the tables; Philippe Groult's seriously good cooking
deserves a more expansive setting. Unfussy but sophisticated dishes
such as his *fumet* of truffles in aspic with a foie gras 'cream',
steamed foie gras served whole in a 'stew' of white beans, and
scallops grilled with slices of chestnut served with a salad featuring
white truffles from Piémont are intense flavour experiences. Other
specialities include *araignée de mer en carapace flanquée
de langoustine, torteau et homard* in which the seafood is served
in the shell of a spider crab, Challans duck roasted with orange
and coriander, and *joue de boeuf braisée aux carottes confites.*
In season there is a special game and mushroom menu in addition
to the *Menu Tradition Amphyclès (dégustation)*, shellfish menu and
carte. The service aims to match the high standards of the kitchen
but can occasionally lack co-ordination, although wife Cathy is an
unfailingly charming hostess. Extensive (within France) and
expensive, the wine list finds room for only a single page of nine
'foreign' wines and was overdue for reprinting when we last
visited to judge by the number of deletions. Set menus: L 260F
L&D 580 & 820F. *L 12-2.30 D 7-10.30.* **Closed** *L Sat & all Sun.*
Amex, Diners, Mastercard, Visa.

> The best way to get around Paris is by bus or metro – buy a
> book of tickets (carnet) at any metro station and save money

---

Apicius   ★★   Map B1.2

Tel 43 80 19 66   Fax 44 40 09 57   R

122 ave de Villiers 75017   M° Péreire
Seats 60   Meal for 2 approx 1400F

Jean-Pierre Vigato's cooking is firmly grounded in the classics, but
many of his superb dishes have a contemporary ring. *Terrine glacé
de concombres au raifort et caviar,* tempura-style langoustines, salmon
cooked *en vessie* and a speciality dish of escalopes of duck foie gras
sautéed in a sweet-sour sauce with confit of horseradish are
examples of his modern thinking, while at the other end of the
scale are still fashionable classics such as 'la belle cote de boeuf' for
2 (*saignant* only). Desserts based on chocolate are definitely worth
leaving space for (*le grand dessert au chocolat amer; le soufflé
au chocolat noir, chantilly mousseuse et peu sucrée; les feuilles
de chocolat 'passion choco'*). Wide-ranging French wine list. The
restaurant itself is divided into three areas by eye-catching
bouquets and floral sculptures. Valet parking. L & D: 520F
(*dégustation*). *L 12.30-2.30 D 8-10.* **Closed** *Sat, Sun & Aug. Amex,
Diners, Mastercard, Visa.*

Astrid
Map A2.3

Tel 44 09 26 00   Fax 44 09 26 01   H

27 ave Carnot 75017   M⁰ Etoile
Rooms 42   Double from 425F

Run with quiet efficiency by a long-standing team, the Astrid,
a hotel of traditional charm, benefits from a splendid location
literally one minute from the Arc de Triomphe (Place de l'Etoile).
Rooms are fairly simple in their appointments but perfectly
comfortable; four of them are triples/quadruples designated
'chambres familiales'. A large underground car park is nearby.
Room service operates for breakfast only. *Amex, Mastercard, Visa.*

Augusta
Map C1.4

Tel 47 63 39 97   Fax 42 27 21 71   R

98 rue de Tocqueville 75017   M⁰ Villiers/Malesherbes
Seats 40   Meal for 2 approx 850F

The warm blue dining room is the setting for some excellent
seafood cuisine. Main courses on the menu are divided into
Atlantic fish and Mediterranean fish, and all can be served
poached, grilled or meunière. From the Atlantic come lobster,
turbot baked with rhubarb, and sweet and sour skate with langoustines
on a bed of puréed parsley, while on the Mediterranean team you
could find bass *à la niçoise*, *Saint-Pierre* with ginger, monkfish
with grapefruit and a tea-scented *jus*, and *bouillabaisse* (for two).
A couple of meat dishes are available, plus some tempting desserts
like nectarine soup 'thym-citron' and *truffe glacée* with warm
chocolate. **Closed** *Sat, Sun (except D Oct-Apr), 2 wks mid Aug.
Mastercard, Visa.*

Le Ballon des Ternes
Map A1.5

Tel 45 74 17 98   Fax 45 72 18 84   R

103 ave des Ternes 75017   M⁰ Porte Maillot
Seats 120 (+24 outside)   Meal for 2 approx 450F

Traditional brasserie with a traditional menu majoring on fish and
shellfish, choucroute and grills. Oysters, cod provençale, John
Dory grilled with dill, steak tartare, *andouillette*, veal kidneys
with Meaux mustard, *confit de canard* and fricassee of chicken
with morels are among the favourite choices, with *sablé aux fraises*
a popular dessert. Wines come direct from the owners and include
a section of grands crus Beaujolais. *L 12-4 D 7-12.30.* **Closed** *1-20
Aug. Amex, Mastercard, Visa.*

Hotel de Banville
Map B1.6

Tel 42 67 70 16   Fax 44 40 42 77   H

166 bd Berthier 75017   M⁰ Porte de Champerret
Rooms 39   Double from 700F

A family-run hotel offering abundant charm and peace in its quiet
location near Place Maréchal Juin (Place Péreire). Bedrooms differ
in detail – some in country style, some with marble bathrooms –
but all are cheerful and comfortable. A lift serves all but the top
(8th) floor, whose little rooms have sloping ceilings and great
views. Three or four bedrooms are renovated each year,
so everything is in good order; safes have recently been installed.   *See over*

24hr room service includes snacks and light meals. Three kinds of breakfast are available – Continental, diet and English-style with eggs and sausages. No restaurant. *Amex, Mastercard, Visa.*

Baumann Ternes   Map A2.7

| Tel 45 74 16 66   Fax 45 72 44 32 | R |

64 ave des Ternes 75017   **Mᵒ Porte Maillot/Ternes**
Seats 100   Meal for 2 approx 500F

The pavement terrace is the place to be in the summer, but inside, on two levels, is equally inviting, with handsome panelling, leather banquettes or wicker-backed chairs, and a large bar which dominates the ground floor. Choucroute is the main speciality of this Alsatian institution (seven versions include *aux poissons,* a Baumann invention), and other popular choices take in shellfish, grills, four ways with steak tartare and desserts based on seasonal fruits. Pleasant staff are a bonus. A sister restaurant *L'Etage Baumann* is in the 8th (*qv*) and another in Strasbourg. Set menus: 118F/150F. *Meals noon-midnight. Amex, Diners, Mastercard, Visa.*

Note: from April 16 1995 the
international dialling code 010 changes to 00

Le Bistrot d'à Coté   Map C2.8

| Tel 47 63 25 61 | R |

16 ave de Villiers 75017   **Mᵒ Villiers**
Seats 65   Meal for 2 approx 500F

Michel Rostang's brilliant restaurant in Rue Rennequin (see *Michel Rostang* in this arrondissement) has, in the current fashionable trend, spawned several less formal offspring, including this marvellous bistro at the eastern end of Avenue de Villiers. The cramped little tables fill up quickly at every session, and the reason is very evident. Not only is the food of very high quality, but the prices are reasonable and the place has a great bustle, assisted in no small measure by the attentive manager and his cheerful, hard-working staff. Everything on the 'menu carte' (135F for 2 courses, 178F for 3) is a model bistro dish – nothing too elaborate and everything extremely well prepared: *terrine de foies de volaille* with onion marmalade, salad of lentils and *chicago de Lyon,* or confit tomatoes with marinated anchovies and tarragon cream to start; andouillette with an onion fondue and *pommes purées,* fricassee of guineau fowl with cider, *pain d'épices* and pasta, or pavé of salmon with coco beans and *sauce vierge* for a main course; and to complete a memorable meal *crème brulée à la vanille Bourbon, poire Belle Hélène* or figs baked in red wine with vanilla ice cream. Best value among the wines is the house selection – Cotes du Lubéron white and rosé, Cotes du Ventoux red – at 56F for a 46cl fillette. *L 12.30-2 D 7.30-11.* **Closed** *L Sat, all Sun. Amex, Mastercard, Visa.*

The Neuilly branch, at 4 rue Boutard 92200 Tel 47 45 34 55, has the same menu, while the other branch in the 17th (10 rue   **Map B2.9**
Gustave-Flaubert Tel 42 67 05 81) has an à la carte menu of similar inspiration. See also entry in the 5th.

Bistrot de l'Etoile

Map B1.10

Tel 42 27 88 44   Fax 42 27 32 12   R

75 ave Niel 75017   **M° Péreire**
Seats 70   Meal for 2 approx 450F

One of Guy Savoy's very successful restaurants serving a menu
of modernised bistro dishes. Vincent Berthamaux is the chef at this
one, an old 'bistro de l'époque' with attractive woodwork and
mirrors. The main menu changes with the seasons, with additional
plats du jour adding to the choice. Creamy soup of mussels and
pumpkin, tagliatelle with gambas and a mild paprika jus, chicken
fricasseed with vinegar accompanied by garlic and *pommes purées*,
and entrecote with herb butter and macaroni gratin are typical
choices, joined each day by 'bonnes habitudes du Bistrot' – *pot
au feu* on Monday, skate with capers on Wednesday, beef with
carrots on Saturday. Set D (Sun only – 'retour de weekend'): 170F.
*L 12-2 D 7.30-12. **Closed** L Sun. Amex, Mastercard, Visa.*

Bistrot de l'Etoile

Map A2.11

Tel 42 67 25 95   R

13 rue Troyon 75017   **M° Etoile (Wagram exit)**
Seats 25 (+10 outside)   Meal for 2 approx 450F

Guy Savoy's first bistro, a tiny, cheerful little place with a huge
mirror running along one wall. The same high-quality produce
as at the Avenue Niel outlet is the basis of a different menu, the
regular choice being supplemented by daily suggestions. A la carte
only. The third Bistrot de l'Etoile is in the 16th (see entry).
*L 12.30-2 L 7.30-11.30. **Closed** L Sat, all Sun. Amex,
Mastercard, Visa.*

Bistro du 17e

Map B1.12

Tel 47 63 32 77   R

108 ave de Villiers 75017   **M° Péreire**
Seats 105   Meal for 2 approx 330F

A great formula – kir with sparkling wine, $\frac{1}{2}$ a bottle of wine,
three courses and coffee – keeps this roomy bistro at Place Péreire
very busy for most of the time. The cooking is, in truth, nothing
out of the ordinary, but to walk into a restaurant knowing what
the final bill will be is in itself a delight. The menu offers plenty
of choice, and the moderate price does not preclude some luxury
items: smoked salmon, foie gras, warm salad of scallops,
rémoulade of crab with avocado, rack of lamb, langoustines and
salmon with virgin olive oil, calf's liver with raspberry vinegar,
magret à la landaise, and skate with tomato vinaigrette typify the
dishes on offer. Set L & D: 165F. *L 12-2.30 D 7.30-11.
Mastercard, Visa.*

Cave Pétrissans

Map B1.13

Tel 42 27 52 03   Fax 40 54 87 56   R

30bis ave Niel 75017   **M° Ternes/Péreire**
Seats 40 (+30 outside)   Meal for 2 approx 450F

For generations a gathering place for serious wine buffs, this classic
wine bar with the look of the 30s was actually opened by the
great-grandfather of the current owners. Its role as an emporium
of fine wines has recently been expanded (as have the

See over

premises) to include a restaurant serving traditional French dishes. Simple classics are prepared with a sure touch by chef Jacques Bertrel – *terrine et sa confiture d'oignons, oeufs en gelée* or *meurette, poulet à l'estragon,* kidneys flamed in armagnac, *saumon aux petits légumes, pruneaux à l'Armagnac, nougat glacé* are all likely to appear on the set menus, while there are some slightly more elaborate dishes on the *carte*. The chef has a particularly good way with the less glamorous cuts of pork – *palette, travers, échine* served with cabbage. The splendid list of wines (all available in the shop) includes an inexpensive house selection of some 20, served in the restaurant by bottle or glass. You can still turn up just for a drink at the bar, where you will join half-a-dozen punters raising plenty of chat and a fair amount of smoke. Set L & D: 155F. *L 12-2.30 D 7.45-10.30.* **Closed** *Sat, Sun, last week Feb, last Sat Jul. Amex, Mastercard, Visa.*

Charly de Bab-el-Oued   Map A1.14

| Tel 45 74 34 62   Fax 45 74 35 36 | **R** |

95 bd Gouvion Saint-Cyr 75017   **M° Porte Maillot**
Seats 200   Meal for 2 approx 450F

In an exotic setting of palms and cedarwood and colourful tiles and fountains diners feast on splendid, generously served dishes from North Africa. *Bestelles* and *briks,* sardines and *chakchouka* are among the starters, while the main courses are mainly couscous (eight varieties) and tagines. The nice but naughty way to end a meal is with the *mosaïque de patisseries orientales* – a selection of 10 at 52F per person. A set menu (200F) is available for all at a table, otherwise it's à la carte. Note for kidney-lovers: *rognons blancs* are not kidneys. All the pastry, bread and sorbets are made on the premises. Wines from France, Algeria and Morocco. Take-away and delivery service available. *L 12-2.30 D 7-11.30. Amex, Diners, Mastercard, Visa.*

Chez Georges   Map A2.15

| Tel 45 74 31 00   Fax 45 74 02 56 | **R** |

273 bd Péreire 75017   **M° Porte Maillot**
Seats 130 (+30 outside)   Meal for 2 approx 600F

A classic bistro-brasserie with a large and loyal clientele. Sunday lunchtime sees it at its busiest and most 'Parisian', but at any time customers can enjoy the comforting dishes which have made it so popular since its opening nearly 70 years ago. A new chef has made no changes, and the cooking remains very sound and reliable. Speedy, professional waiters bear the main meat dishes from the kitchens and carve them by the table: *petit salé* with cabbage, *gigot d'agneau* with flageolets and ribs of beef with excellent *gratin dauphinois* are the ever-present stars of the show, but salmon tartare and steak tartare play an increasingly important support role. Lyonnais sausage, *terrine de foies de volaille,* foie gras, salad of *museau de boeuf* and marinated herrings are popular starters, and giant éclairs make a splendid end to a meal. The only cheese on the menu is a very good Brie de Meaux, which is served with a help-yourself platter of *crottins de chèvre.* An easy-drinking Brouilly is a favourite accompaniment to the consistently good food. Set L & D: 170F. *L 12-2.30 D 7-11.30.* **Closed** *Aug. Mastercard, Visa.*

Le Col Vert

Tel 45 72 02 19

R

Map A2.16

18 rue Bayen 75017
Seats 60

M⁰ Ternes
Meal for 2 approx 600F

The young chef from Martinique offers both 'traditional' and 'créole' menus at this quiet, refined restaurant, whose gentle lightwood, pink and green decor is interspersed with appetising montages of plaster-cast vegetables. From the *menu gourmand* come smoked salmon with dill, steamed cod with mini-ratatouille and braised pork knuckle with a lentil ragout, while flying the Creole flag are the likes of *Christophines* (an African vegetable resembling a small pear), *ouassous* (large crayfish), *lambis* (conch), *cabri* (wild goat) and *mérou* (a large white Mediterranean fish). Round things off with *confitures créoles* and warm *pain d'épices*, apricot *délice* and sorbet, or a gratin of bananas with coconut milk. Sunday lunchtime brings a brunch menu of international provenance. Quiet, charming service puts the seal on a very civilised meal. Set menu: L & D 160F. *L 12-2.30 D 7.30-10.30.* **Closed** *L Sat, all Sun. Amex, Mastercard, Visa.*

Concorde Lafayette

Tel 40 68 50 68   Fax 40 68 50 43

H R

Map A1.17

3 place Général Koenig 75017
Rooms 970

M⁰ Porte Maillot
Double from 1420F

The last six of the 33 floors of this building are called 'Le Top Club' where the 157 Executive bedrooms have butler service and use of a business support centre as well as a health club located in the basement of the hotel (not part of the establishment). It has its own check-in area and private lounge. The hotel is part of the Palais des Congrès, where exhibitions, conventions, congresses, trade fairs and concerts are held and eighty shops plus four cinemas are located. The hotel itself has a gigantic conference room, which can be sectioned off as necessary; it can hold 4000 delegates. There's also a fully-manned business centre. The view across Paris from the standardised, comfortable and well-equipped bedrooms is exceptional. It can be even better appreciated from the panoramic bar 'Plein Ciel' on the 33rd floor. 24hr room service and reception. *Amex, Diners, Mastercard, Visa.*

Etoile d'Or
Tel 40 68 51 28
Seats 60

Meal for 2 approx 850F

Tucked away on the first floor of the hotel is a modern, comfortable restaurant with lightwood panelled walls and ceiling and claret-coloured carpet and chairs. Diners are serenaded by a harpist in the evenings whilst enjoying Jean-Claude Lhonneur's classic but inventive cuisine: quail parcels with asparagus tips, pan-cooked perch with spinach, sweetbread lasagne, grilled shoulder of lamb with savory-scented mustard, escabèche of fish with artichokes, hot chocolate soufflé or carpaccio of mango with lime. Plenty of half bottles on a good wine list. Set menu: 250F. *L 12-2.30 D 7-10.30.* **Closed** *Sat, Sun, Aug & Public Holidays.*

La Coquille   Map A2.18

| Tel 45 74 25 95 | R |

6 rue de Débarcadère 75017   M° Argentine/Porte Maillot
Seats 45   Meal for 2 approx 750F

Let's do the time warp again! It's just a jump to the left (from
Place St Ferdinand, M° Argentine) or a step to the right (from
Bd Péreire, M° Porte Maillot). Almost nothing has changed here;
the decor, elegant and intimate in greens and orangey-pinks,
is regularly refreshed, but this menu – no criticism – remains more
or less as we've always known it. Sip your champagne cocktail
with pineapple ring while choosing from among the Coquille
classics: coquilles St Jacques, *escargots* (*en coquille!*), foie gras
or *jambon persillé* to start, then sole with noodles, boudin with
apples, chicken fricassee with morels or veal kidney with mustard;
and finally the renowned hazelnut soufflé with Grand Marnier.
Clément Lausecker is the chef, his wife the business-like but
charming hostess. Set menu: L & D 230F. *L 12-2.30 D 7-10.30.*
Closed Sun, Mon, Aug, 10 days Christmas-New Year. Amex,
Diners, Mastercard, Visa.

Courcelles   Map B1.19

| Tel 47 63 65 30   Fax 46 22 49 44 | H |

184 rue de Courcelles 75017   M° Péreire
Rooms 42   Double from 750F

Comfort and modern convenience just by Place Péreire. All the
bedrooms have mini-bars, TVs with satellite channels, radios and
hairdryers. There's a bar in an interior 'winter-garden', and a small
meeting room. Paid parking nearby. 24hr reception, no room
service or restaurant. *Amex, Diners, Mastercard, Visa.*

Eber Monceau   Map B2.20

| Tel 46 22 60 70   Fax 47 63 01 01 | H |

18 rue Léon-Jost 75017   M° Courcelles
Rooms 18   Double from 580F

Jean-Marc Eber's little hotel in a quiet side street near the
charming Parc Monceau has 13 rooms all with bath or shower
and wc, and five apartments. All include mini-bars and cable
TVs among their appointments. Day rooms include a bar and two
small sitting rooms. In summer breakfast can be served out on the
patio. A popular spot with the worlds of fashion and cinema. Car
park (paying) at 150m from the hotel. 24hr reception.
No restaurant. *Amex, Diners, Mastercard, Visa.*

Etoile Park   Map A2.21

| Tel 42 67 69 63   Fax 43 80 18 99 | H |

10 ave Macmahon 75017   M° Etoile
Rooms 28   Double from 683F

Double-glazed bedrooms are decorated and furnished in unfussy
modern style, and each has its own bath or shower room with
hairdryer, plus safe, mini-bar, dial-out phone, radio and cable TV.
There's a little bar at reception, and a breakfast room below stairs.
The Air France bus from Charles de Gaulle airport stops just
around the corner. Laundry and dry cleaning services. *Closed 1 wk*
Christmas. Amex, Diners, Mastercard, Visa.

Etoile Péreire
Map A1.22

Tel 42 67 60 00 Fax 42 67 02 90 H

146 bd Péreire 75017   **Mᵒ Péreire**
Rooms 26   Double from 700F

Run in friendly, cheerful style, the Etoile Péreire is on two levels
in a quiet courtyard. Bedrooms have a contemporary elegance,
with decor inspired by New York or Italy. All rooms have
hairdryers, and all but the little singles with showers have mini-
bars. Room service (minimum 150F; hot dishes available)
is offered between 7pm and 3am. A notable feature at the
breakfast table is a range of 40 jams and honeys. Private parking
is available 300 metres away at 100F for 24 hours. *Amex, Diners,
Mastercard, Visa.*

La Famiglia Fuligna
Map A1.23

Tel 45 74 20 28   Fax 45 72 15 87 R

2 rue Waldeck-Rousseau 75017   **Mᵒ Porte Maillot**
Seats 48 (+40 outside)   Meal for 2 approx 600F

The combined talents of the Fuligna family have made
a considerable success of their comfortable Italian restaurant
behind the Méridien Hotel at Porte Maillot. The pasta
is outstanding – every thread and every twirl made individually –
and accompanied by mamma's secret sauces, and other notable
dishes are *involtini* with mozzarella (also made on the premises),
mixed grill of fish, steak with mushrooms, tiramisu and
zabaglione. Plenty of Italian wines, and a few French. *L 12-3
D 7-11.30. Mastercard, Visa.*

Faucher   ★
Map B2.24

Tel 42 27 61 50 Fax 46 22 25 72 R

123 ave de Wagram 75017   **Mᵒ Ternes**
Seats 50 (+ Terrace 30)   Meal for 2 approx 600F

Nicole and Géraud Faucher's bright, elegant restaurant, with
a terrace looking out on to a quiet street, lies in one of Paris'
residential quarters. With Monsieur in the kitchen and Madame
at the front of house, this is very much a family-run operation –
witness the fresh flower arrangements and choice of pictures
on the walls. The cooking is in the modern fashion with a good
à la carte choice – millefeuille of spinach and raw beef, rémoulade
of celery, peppers and smoked salmon, haddock with lentils, cod
with virgin olive oil and stuffed macaroni, ribs done *pot au feu-*
style with a truffled jus, mixed cuts of lamb with marjoram. Finish
with spicy apple cake, or a warm chocolate tart and ice cream.
L 12-2 D 8-10. **Closed** *L Sat, all Sun. Amex, Mastercard, Visa.*

Goldenberg
Map B2.25

Tel 42 27 34 79 Fax 42 27 98 85 R

69 ave de Wagram 75017   **Mᵒ Ternes**
Seats 45 (+ 50 outdoor)   Meal for 2 approx 400F

Open from noon till midnight every day except Yom Kippur,
this is both shop and restaurant, with the capital's best-known
kosher kitchen run for 25 years by Patrick Goldenberg. Zakouski,
blinis, stuffed poultry neck, gefilte fish, pojarski and Wiener

See over

schnitzel are among the classics, and salamis and pastramis are
other specialities. Grills include King David, with lamb chops,
merguez and steak. Various set menus (98F for Russian, Yiddish,
Romanian, Turkish, 150F 'formule schnaps'), 20 vodkas, kosher
wines (and others). Popular at all times, including Saturday &
Sunday brunch (120F, children 100F). Cold food is available
outside meal times. *L 12-3 D 7-11. Mastercard, Visa.*

Graindorge
Map A2.26

Tel 47 54 00 28   Fax 44 09 84 51
R

15 rue Arc de Triomphe 75017
M° Etoile
Seats 45
Meal for 2 approx 500F

Two rooms in 30s style make up this appealing restaurant, whose
name derives from a variety of beer (there's a very interesting list
of beers). Before setting up on his own, Bernard Broux spent six
years as chef at Alain Dutournier's *Au Trou Gascon*. Many of his
dishes originate in Flanders, Broux's birthplace, and the 250F
menu is his Flanders speciality menu, with dishes such
as *potjevleesch* (a long-cooked terrine of veal, chicken, rabbit and
pork), *waterzooi* of plaice and shellfish, and stuffed tomatoes
à l'ostendaise. Eels in a herby green sauce remain a great favourite,
and raspberry sabayon with a raspberry-flavoured beer is a dessert
worth saving room for. Set menus: L 130F, 160F D 185F, 250F.
L 12-2.30 D 7.30-11. **Closed** *L Sat, all Sun. Amex,
Mastercard, Visa.*

Guy Savoy   ★★★
Map A2.27

Tel 43 80 40 61   Fax 46 22 43 09
R

18 rue Troyon 75017
M° Etoile
Seats 90
Meal for 2 approx 1400F

Close to the Arc de Triomphe, Guy Savoy's air-conditioned
restaurant is one of *the* gastronomic temples in a city that's not
short of good tables! It's an intimate restaurant with columned
lightwood screens sectioning off areas, pastel colours, quite bold
wallpaper, modern paintings, exquisite china and table settings,
plants and fresh flowers all combining to create a sophisticated
atmosphere. Since opening here in 1986, Guy Savoy has become
one of the top chefs in Paris – his secret of success can perhaps
be put down to his refreshingly simple style and just cooking for
sheer pleasure – and is backed up throughout his empire by a very
bright, efficient team. This bold, relatively straightforward
approach relies on an amazing talent which shows at every stage
in the constantly changing menus. *Everything*, absolutely
everything should be tried, not just 'specialities' such as *foie gras
de canard* with sea salt; 'croustillants' of calf's trotter with
horseradish, a herby salad and a parsley dressing; bass grilled with
a marvellously subtle combination of gentle spices; pigeon *'poché-
grillé'* with vegetables in a vinaigrette with giblets; and *'craquant-
moelleux' vanille et pomme* or the stunning grapefruit terrine with
a tea sauce. Unusually for a French restaurant, there's a good
selection of wines from outside France, with Italy, Spain and
California making a respectable show. Some own label house
wines. Guy Savoy is a man of many talents, and a man of many
restaurants. For details of his excellent, less formal and less
expensive offshoots, see entries for *Bistrots de l'Etoile, Les Bookinistes*

and *Butte Chaillot*. Set menu: L & D 750F *dégustation*. Private
rooms 6/35. Valet parking. *L 12-2 D 7.30-10.30.* **Closed** *L Sat,
all Sun. Amex, Mastercard, Visa.*

Le Madigan   Map C2.28
Tel 42 27 31 51   Fax 42 67 70 29   R
22 rue de la Terrasse 75017   **M° Villiers**
Seats 40 (+36 outside)   Meal for 2 approx 750F

Concerts of classical music are a unique finale to a meal in this
intimate little restaurant just north of Metro Villiers. The
programme is planned six weeks in advance and is published in the
weekly guide *Pariscope*. A deal of thought, planning and skill also
go into Jean-Michel Descloux's cooking, which produces a wide
variety of enjoyably different dishes. Salad of quail or smoked eel,
aïoli of sole, foie gras with a port aspic or hot with a salad, rascasse
grilled Norwegian-style, braised sweetbreads with Parma ham and
pink champagne sorbet are typical dishes on his menu. *Grenadin*
of veal with baby onions and artichokes, a duo of lobster and
salmon in a 'pistou' salad and *florentin de sésame méli-mélo de fruits
rouges* are speciality dishes. Separate lists of French and foreign
wines. Set menus: L 150F, 250F D 180F, 280F. *L 12-2.15 D 7.30-
9.30.* **Closed** *L Sat, all Sun & Aug. Amex, Diners, Mastercard, Visa.*

Magellan   Map A1.29
Tel 45 72 44 51   Fax 40 68 90 36   H
17 rue Jean-Baptiste Dumas 75017   **M° Péreire/Porte de Champerret**
Rooms 75   Double from 584F

Renovation took place in 1992, and the bedrooms are done out
in practical, contemporary style. Satellite TV, radios and
hairdryers are standard, and the bathrooms all have baths, showers
and bidets. There's a large bar in the lobby and in the summer
guests can sit out in the garden for drinks or breakfast. Secure
parking is available for 4 cars (80F per day). 24hr reception. Room
service offers a menu from an outside caterer. *Amex, Diners,
Mastercard, Visa.*

Le Manoir de Paris   ★   Map B2.30
Tel 45 72 25 25   Fax 45 74 80 98   R
6 rue Pierre Demours 75017   **M° Ternes/Etoile**
Seats 70   Meal for 2 approx 900F

Carved wood, wall mirrors, pillars and abundant flowers and
greenery make a splendid setting for the superb, sunny cooking
of Gilles Méry. Dishes, often elaborate, many with a
Mediterranean influence, are typified by risotto of salt cod with
chorizo, hare terrine with Garrigues herbs, velouté of white beans
and coquilles St Jacques perfumed with pistachio oil, long-cooked
wild boar with chestnuts and sweet potatoes, and grilled bass steak
with fried onions, sweet pepper croquettes and anchoïade jus.
Equally exotic sweets, fine wines. Set menus: 265F, 295F, 380F.
L 12-2.30 D 7.30-10.30. **Closed** *L Sat, all Sun. Amex, Diners,
Mastercard, Visa.*

Les Marines de Pétrus
Map B2.31

Tel 47 63 04 24   Fax 44 15 92 20
R

27 ave Niel 75017   **M° Ternes**
Seats 50   Meal for 2 approx 500F

The name and the bright, nautical decor tell you that this
is indeed a seafood restaurant. Small blackboards list the likes
of oysters Roquefort, tuna tartare, bream or salmon *à l'unilatéral*
(cooked on one side only till the skin is crisp and served with
olive oil, rock salt and a timbale of courgettes), gigot of monkfish
with olives, squid in its ink and plaice with a cream of
langoustines. Just one or two meat dishes – terrine of guinea fowl
with onion confiture, filet mignon with mushrooms. Madame
Barrié also owns the more formal *Pétrus* (*qv*) just along the road
at Place Péreire (aka Place Maréchal Juin). *L 12-2.30 D 7-11.*
Closed *Sun, Mon & Aug. Amex, Diners, Mastercard, Visa.*

For a glossary of menu terms see page 293

Le Méridien Paris Etoile
Map A2.32

Tel 40 68 34 34   Fax 40 68 31 31
HR

81 bd Gouvion Saint-Cyr 75017   **M° Porte Maillot**
Rooms 102   Double from 1450F

The city's largest hotel, opened in 1972, stands on nine floors
at Porte Maillot and the Palais des Congrès, where the Air France
shuttle bus leaves for Charles de Gaulle airport every 15 minutes.
Day rooms are a hive of activity, from power breakfasts at 7.30
through Sunday jazz brunch to dinner in one of several restaurants
then dancing till dawn in the **Ecume des Nuits** discothèque.
There's also a most impressive conference centre with facilities for
up to 1000 attendees. A multilingual secretarial service is offered
8.30-7.30pm on weekdays. Bedrooms, though not notable for
their spaciousness, are quiet, comfortable and well equipped, and
room service operates 24 hours a day. There are 17 suites. Two
floors of rooms offer the new *Club Président* service, which
includes speedy check-in and check-out, a lounge with terrace,
a day-long bar availability and priority booking in the **Clos
Longchamp** restaurant and the Lionel Hampton Jazz Club.
Private parking. *Amex, Diners, Mastercard, Visa.*

Le Clos Longchamp   ★
Tel 40 68 00 70   Fax 40 68 30 81
Seats 60   Meal for 2 approx 1200F

The hotel boasts a Japanese restaurant, a Beaujolais buffet and the
Café Arlequin, but gastronomic pride of place undoubtedly goes
to the refined and elegant Clos Longchamp with its central
garden. Chef Jean-Marie Meulien's seasonal menus add
Mediterranean and Oriental influences to classic French cuisine,
shown in such dishes as prawns with Thai herbs, tandoori navarin
of lamb and fricassee of sole and artichokes with pine nut oil.
Marbré de foie de canard au Beaumes de Venise is a home-grown
speciality! Didier Bureau is as dab a hand in the cellar as is Jean-
Marie in the kitchen. Set menus: L 250F L & D 470F. *L 12-2.30
D 7.30-10.30.* **Closed** *Sat, Sun & Aug.*

Michel Rostang   ★★   Map B2.33

| Tel 47 63 40 77   Fax 47 63 82 75 | R |

20 rue Rennequin 75017   M° Ternes
Seats 65   Meal for 2 approx 1200F

Michel Rostang comes from a family of chefs and arrived in Paris in 1977, having taken over from his father Jo at their restaurant in Grenoble. Here in north-west Paris is his 'headquarters' restaurant, strikingly and boldly decorated, almost Oriental, with a cream and red ceiling, deep red lacquered woodwork and matching walls, carpets and chairs, complemented by beautiful flower arrangements. Mirrors abound, as do staff, all very professional, who glide effortlessly around the room. Michel's cooking is full of life and invention, and his menu goes far beyond the borders of France, incorporating ideas and ingredients from the East: langoustines could be prepared sushi-style, with celery rémoulade and a subtle hint of *anis*. His menu is constantly evolving, but current classics include quail's eggs served in sea urchins; sole with shallots, olives and swiss chard; Bresse chicken in a garlic and mustard crust, with confit tomatoes and a gratin of Noirmoutier potatoes; and duck served *saignant*, its sauce laced with blood and foie gras. Jo is credited with a couple of dishes – *soufflé de quenelle de brochet au homard comme le faisait 'Jo Rostang'*, *gratin de queues d'écrevisses façon 'Jo Rostang'*. There's a marvellous selection of cheeses (especially goat's cheese) and some absolutely unmissable desserts, including Rostang's own favourite warm bitter chocolate tart, or vine peach with amaretti. As in many Parisian restaurants, fixed-price menus offer the best value and the chance to enjoy some of the à la carte dishes at a lower price. The wine list carries some 600 bins, mostly French. Private rooms 8/20. Set menus: L 298F D 520F & 720F. Michel is very often present here but not always –he has quite an empire to oversee, including the popular *Bistrot d'à Coté* quartet (see entries). *L 12-2 D 7.30-10.30.* **Closed** *Sat (except D Sep-Jun), all Sun and two wks early Aug. Amex, Mastercard, Visa.*

Le Petit Colombier   ★   Map A2.34

| Tel 43 80 28 54   Fax 44 40 04 29 | R |

42 rue des Acacias 75017   M° Etoile
Seats 80   Meal for 2 approx 1000F

Bernard Fournier's provincial-style auberge has remained for 60 years a bastion of classic French cooking with each day's menu depending on the pick of the markets. Amid the woodwork and the flowers and the copper ornaments an appreciative clientele tucks into hare terrine boosted with foie gras, saffrony mussel soup, *confit de canard*, milk-fed veal braised en cocotte with mushrooms, or the day's superb roast, carved at the table. Seasonal game is a great speciality, and pigeon cooked in a salt crust served with truffled jus remains one of the Bernard's signature dishes. Crème caramel with muscat grapes and a cassis sorbet is a tempting dessert. The 200F four-course *menu carte* is a real bargain. There's a great cellar, with bottles selected from all round the world. Set D: 350F. *L 12.15-2.30 D 7.30-10.30.* **Closed** *L Sun, all Sat, 1st 2wks Aug. Amex, Diners, Mastercard, Visa.*

Pétrus
Map B1.35

| Tel 43 80 15 95 | R |

12 place du Maréchal Juin 75017   M⁰ Péreire
Seats 60   Meal for 2 approx 900F

Smart, well-established seafood restaurant with a corner site on the
Place du Maréchal Juin (sometimes known as Place Péreire): limed
oak panelling, 1920s-style light fittings, mirrors painted with
appropriately fishy motifs. *Bar de ligne en terre d'Argile de Vallauris*
is a newly instituted dish in which a line-caught bass, plus lemon
grass and thyme, is wrapped in unfired pottery 'paste' fashioned
into the shape of a fish before both fish and pottery are cooked
together in the oven to be broken open at the table. Each one, for
two persons, comes with a numbered pottery plaque to be kept
as a souvenir – chef Jacky Louaré spent a year working at the *Tour
d'Argent* (*qv*), where they have been giving out numbered
certificates with their duck *à la presse* for over a hundred years.
Other specialities are *tournedos de thon Rossini* (the tuna cooked
pink, topped with fresh foie gras and served with a truffle sauce)
and John Dory with spices 'Marco Polo'. Scallops with chicory
and orange, monkfish with cumin and fennel and a galette
of sardines *à la provençale* are other offerings from a menu that
changes according to the market. Just a couple of meat dishes for
determined carnivores. Shortish wine list with the emphasis
on whites along with a good selection of champagnes. See also *Les
Marines de Pétrus* above. *L 12-2.30 D 7-11.* **Closed** *Aug. Amex,
Diners, Mastercard, Visa.*

Quality Hotel
Map B1.46

| Tel 44 01 04 90   Fax 44 40 25 54 | H |

51 bd Péreire 75017   M⁰ Malesherbes
Rooms 44   Double from 650F

Modern accommodation in an old building on the south side of a
boulevard which straddles RER line C. Satellite TV, mini-bar,
hairdryer, safe, computer points in all bedrooms. Continental
breakfast served in the rooms, buffet in the breakfast room.
No restaurant. *Amex, Diners, Mastercard, Visa.*

Regent's Garden
Map A2.36

| Tel 45 74 07 30   Fax 40 55 01 42 | H |

6 rue Pierre Demours 75017   M⁰ Etoile/Ternes
Rooms 39   Double from 690F

Built by Napoleon III for his private physician and since 1920
a hotel of abundant charm and personality with a delightfully
peaceful garden at the back. Bedrooms are generally of a good size,
with furnishings mainly of original inspiration. There's space for
a few cars in the courtyard at the front of the hotel. 24hr reception
but no room service. *Amex, Diners, Mastercard, Visa.*

Le Relais de Venise (l'Entrecote)
Map A2.37

| Tel 45 74 27 97 | R |

271 bd Péreire 75017   M⁰ Porte Maillot
Seats 100   Meal for 2 approx 320F

The queues outside this bustling, close-tabled restaurant at Porte
Maillot testify to our belief that is one of the very best 'formula'

restaurants of its kind in Paris. That formula is simple: salad with
walnuts, entrecote with an excellent 'secret' sauce and splendid
little chips 104F. And that's the only option until the selection
of pastries and the wines. No bookings. No cheques. See photo
page 20. *L 12-2.30 D 7-11.45.* **Closed** *Good Fri, all July.*
Mastercard, Visa.

Il Ristorante   Map B2.38

`Tel 47 63 34 00`   **R**

22 rue Fourcroy 75017   M⁰ **Wagram**
Seats 40   Meal for 2 approx 900F

Popular with the well-heeled residents of a smart neighbourhood
off Avenue Niel, the restaurant has a very French atmosphere and
staff, though the menu (with French translations) is strictly Italian.
Familiar classics are given marginally modern treatment (mainly
as smaller portions – particularly the vegetables!) Cooking is to a
generally enjoyable, if unexciting standard, considering the prices.
Set menu: L 165F. *L 12.15-2.15 D 7.30-11.* **Closed** *Sun, 5-20 Aug.*
Amex, Mastercard, Visa.

Rotisserie d'Armaillé   Map A2.39

`Tel 42 27 19 20`   **R**

6 rue d'Armaillé 75017   M⁰ **Etoile/Ternes**
Seats 85   Meal for 2 approx 500F

Jacques Cagna's Rotisserie in a street of restaurants is a very
handsome place with lightwood panelling, a spot-patterned green
carpet, paintings and prints of food and animals, fuchsia for
upholstery and green stripes in the banquettes. The menu is 150F
for two courses, 195F for three and what you get is a good choice
(plus daily specials) of classics and updated classics prepared
by Lionel Delage and his team: sea trout soufflé with lemon
butter, aubergine gateau with a tomato coulis, *croustillant* of bream
with sorrel, roast partridge with stuffed cabbage (game attracts a
supplement), spit-roasted calf's kidney with a compote of onions
and lime, *soufflé praliné noisette*, steamed chocolate cake with a
heart of hot melted chocolate. Sister restaurant to *Rotisserie d'en
Face* (qv) in the 6th. *L 12.15-2.30 D 7.15-11.* **Closed** *L Sat, all Sun.*
Amex, Mastercard, Visa.

Sormani   ★   Map A2.40

`Tel 43 80 13 91`   **R**

4 rue du Général-Lanrezac 75017   M⁰ **Etoile**
Seats 65 (+12 outside)   Meal for 2 approx 1000F

Owner-chef Jean Pascal Faiget's Piedmontese grandmother sowed
the seeds of his love of Italian cooking, and his luxuriously
appointed restaurant is undoubtedly one of the best of its kind
in all Paris. He has put a highly personal French stamp on the
cooking, which produces dishes of great allure like salad of pasta
and *langoustines à l'orange,* grilled mullet with a gratin
of aubergines and courgettes, beef carpaccio (*à la vénitienne*, with
scampi or with truffle oil and parmesan shavings), veal escalope
with lemon and spinach, and medallions of lamb on polenta
crostini with Tuscan beans. A dozen pasta choices, some familiar
(*spaghetti alle vongole*), others less so (mullet-filled ravioli, tagliatelle
with bacon, beans and truffles); fish arrives daily from the   *See over*

market; desserts include bouchées of ricotta with a bitter
chocolate sauce and rhubarb millefeuille with vanilla ice cream.
Wines are mainly from Italy, with a leaning to Tuscany and
Piedmont. *L 12.30-2.30 D 7.30-10.30. Closed Sat, Sun, 1 week
Easter, 3wks Aug, 1 wk Christmas. Mastercard, Visa.*

La Soupière   Map B1.41

Tel 42 27 00 73   Fax 46 22 27 09   **R**

154 ave de Wagram 75017   **Mᵒ Wagram**
Seats 30 (+10 outside)   Meal for 2 approx 550F

Trompe l'oeil decor, pink tablecloths, crystal glass and silver
cutlery add up to a picture of elegance in Camille and Christian
Thuillart's splendid little restaurant. Market-led menus show both
classic and modern elements, and Christian's passion for
mushrooms means that they have their very own menu at the
appropriate time of year. A la carte suggestions could be tartare
of fish with lime, salad of brains and capers, terrine maison or a
red pepper mousse to start, then maybe turbot with chive butter,
veal knuckle with herb vinaigrette or a fricassee of guinea fowl,
broad beans, onions and mushrooms; and finally caramelised apple
tartlet, coffee parfait or rhubarb feuillantine with a red fruit coulis.
There's also a bistro menu with cheaper dishes such as salad
of goat's cheese, stuffed aubergine with smoked duck, scrambled
eggs with smoked salmon and minute steak. Set menus: 130F to
280F. *L 12-2.30 D 7.30-10.30. Closed L Sat, all Sun, 3rd wk Aug.
Amex, Mastercard, Visa.*

Splendid Etoile   Map A2.42

Tel 45 72 72 00   Fax 45 72 72 01   **H**

1bis ave Carnot 75017   **Mᵒ Etoile (ave Carnot exit)**
Rooms 57   Double from 980F

A solidly handsome building on the corner of Ave Carnot and
Rue de Tilsitt, just a few paces from the Arc de Triomphe.
Bedrooms are comfortable and generally spacious, with pink
or blue decor, reproduction furniture, air-conditioning and
double-glazing. Day rooms include an English-style bar and
a small restaurant, the **Pré Carré**. There's also a 20-seat conference
room. 24hr reception. *Amex, Diners, Mastercard, Visa.*

La Table de Pierre   Map B1.43

Tel 43 80 88 68   **R**

116 bd Péreire 75017   **Mᵒ Péreire**
Seats 45 (+20 in a conservatory)   Meal for 2 approx 700F

The kitchen and the front of house are both Basque-run, the
furniture is Basque and the picture on the walls of this cheerful,
good-looking restaurant have a theme of the Basque country. So of
course does the menu, with specialities such as Serrano ham,
pipérade, foie gras with potatoes and cinnamon, calamares cooked
in olive oil, pimentos stuffed with salt cod, *chipirons* (baby squid)
in their ink, roast shoulder of baby lamb and a fine *gateau Basque
de cerises* to to round things off. Some dishes must be ordered
24hours in advance, for a minimum of four diners; *ttoro* (a Basque
soup), *paella Valenciana, cassoulet, poule au pot Henry IV*. *L 12.30-
2.45 D 7.30-10.45. Closed L Sat, all Sun. Amex, Mastercard, Visa.*

Taïra

Map A2.44

Tel 47 66 74 14   R

10 rue des Acacias 75017   **M° Argentine**
Seats 34   Meal for 2 approx 650F

Chef Taïra Kurihara has put his personal stamp on dishes from
both East and West in his bright, cosy little restaurant, whose
green and grey decor is highlighted by striking paintings by a
contemporary Romanian artist. Salmon *tataki*, tuna carpaccio,
St Jacques with ginger and brochette of langoustines with Chinese
herbs show the Oriental influence, while other dishes are from the
current French mainstream, and, like so many Paris chefs, Tara
prepares his own *foie gras de canard*. Fillet of bream grilled under
a stout shell of sea salt is a speciality. The set menu (150F/170F)
offers excellent value for money; there's also a *menu dégustation*
at 320F. Taïra is a few steps south of Avenue de la Grande Armée.
*L 12-2.30 D 7.30-10.30. **Closed** L Sat, all Sun. Amex, Diners,
Mastercard, Visa.*

Timgad

Map A2.45

Tel 45 74 23 70   Fax 45 74 11 16   R

21 rue Brunel 75017   **M° Argentine**
Seats 70   Meal for 2 approx 700F

The best couscous in town? Probably, and it's certainly served
in the plushest, most exotic Moorish surroundings. Timgad has
been in business since 1971, and it remains a very popular spot not
only for its dishes based on hand-rolled couscous but also for its
briks (crisp-fried pastry enveloping lamb, tuna, eggs, brains,
prawns or salmon), its tagines (lamb with prunes is a speciality)
and its beautifully succulent spit-roasted meats. There are several
'party' dishes for 4 or more (lamb or chicken tagine with quinces,
stuffed chicken, stuffed gigot, pastilla). Wines from Algeria,
Morocco, Tunisia (all the same price) and France. *L 12-2.30
D 7.30-11. Amex, Diners, Mastercard, Visa.*

18th Arrondissement
Places of Interest

Marché aux Puces (Porte de Clignancourt)
Montmartre (Sacré Coeur, Place du Tertre), 42 51 17 02,
 Mº Anvers/Abbesses
Cimetière de Montmartre (Stendahl, Berlioz, Nijinsky)
Moulin Rouge, 46 06 00 19, Mº Blanche

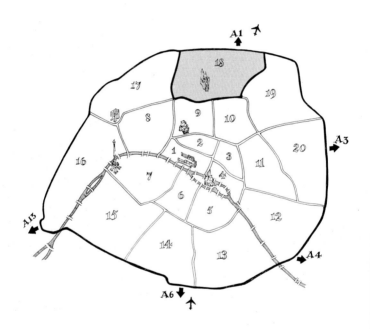

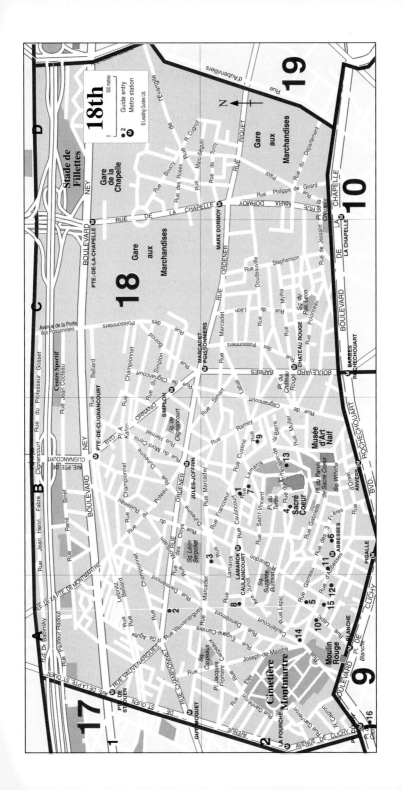

A. Beauvilliers   Map B2.1

| Tel 42 54 54 42   Fax 42 62 70 30 | **R** |

52 rue Lamarck 75018   **M° Lamarck Caulaincourt**
Seats 86 (plus terrace 40)   Meal for 2 approx 1100F

Entering Edouard Carlier's former bakery is like walking into
another century (the 19th)! Three dining rooms are filled with
enormous bouquets of flowers, gold-leafed framed mirrors, old
furniture, portraits in oil, spectacular chandeliers, elegant china and
glass all set against a blue background. In summer, guests can sit
out on the leafy terrace and savour such elaborate specialities
as *millefeuille de pétoncles et tomates confites, filets de rouget
en escabéche, filet d'agneau en croute* and *tourte de pigeon de grain* with
haricot beans and broad beans. *Gateau aux deux chocolats*
or millefeuille with Grand Marnier *crème patissière* to finish. Set
menus: L 185F, 300F (wine incl) L & D 320F. *L 12-2 D 7.30-
10.45. Closed L Mon, all Sun. Amex, Mastercard, Visa.*

Chez Frézet   Map A1.2

| Tel 46 06 64 20   Fax 46 06 10 79 | **R** |

181 rue Ordener 75018   **M° Jules-Joffrin**
Seats 90 (plus interior courtyard 30)   Meal for 2 approx 600F

Chef Robert Antoine, here for 20 years, concentrates on regional
dishes that are traditional bistro fare. His menus are dominated
by seafood: hot oysters with a champagne sabayon, salmon raw or
smoked, bream with ratatouille, crab in cabbage, *choucroute de la
mer*. There's also foie gras, beef steak béarnaise, and an autumn
fricassee of veal sweetbreads and kidneys. In summer, sit at a table
in the covered plant-filled interior courtyard away from the street
noise for a more tranquil meal. Set menus: L & D 145F & 180F.
*L 12-2.30 D 7.30-10.30. Closed L Sat, all Sun. Amex,
Mastercard, Visa.*

Le Cottage Marcadet   Map B2.3

| Tel 42 57 71 22 | **R** |

151bis rue Marcadet 75018   **M° Lamarck Caulaincourt**
Seats 22   Meal for 2 approx 750F

A cosy, comfortable little restaurant on the ascent up to Butte
Montmartre. Jean-François Canot puts a modern slant on classic
cuisine with dishes like creamy pumpkin soup with a pheasant
quenelle, fricassee of lobster with herb butter and fillet of beef
with a creamed grape sauce. *Crème brulée* or moneybag of apple
caramelised with Calvados to finish. Set menus: L 115F L &
D 200F. *L 12-2.15 D 8-10. Closed Sun, Aug. Mastercard, Visa.*

La Crémaillère 1900   Map B2.4

| Tel 46 06 58 59   Fax 42 64 08 57 | **R** |

15 place du Tertre 75018   **M° Abbesses/Anvers**
Seats 300   Meal for 2 approx 550F

A short distance from the Sacré Coeur basilica and in a very
Parisian square, the restaurant dates back to the 1900s and still
retains the original decor including paintings by Mucha. Other
attractive features include an internal courtyard garden and
a terrace on the square. The comprehensive menu, served
throughout the day, is of classic, familiar dishes, the simpler ones

being best. Sole, salmon, John Dory and prawns are grilled
to order, and each day brings a speciality (Monday andouillette,
Thursday choucroute or cassoulet). Knuckle of pork braised with
beer is a special dish of chef Henri Boulard. This is a restaurant
popular with group bookings. Set menus: 60F, 80F, 140F. *Meals
11am-12.30am. Amex, Mastercard, Visa.*

La Galerie
Tel 42 59 25 76

Map A2.5

R

16 rue Tholozé 75018
Seats 28

M⁰ Abbesses/Blanche
Meal for 2 approx 360F

On a steep street just away from the touristy part of Montmartre,
this is a particularly cosy and inviting little restaurant, its walls
a mini-gallery of artwork. At lunchtime, when the cheapest of the
set menus offers quite remarkable value for money, it's generally
quieter than in the evening, when locals and tourists dine by soft
music and candle-light. Seafood is the favourite medium of chef-
partner Eric Callait, who puts a personal stamp on dishes such
as *raie* (skate) *aux pistaches et au curry,* mackerel in Sauvignon
wine, and a prawn, courgette and tarragon tart. *Terrine de foies
de volaille aux amandes et au cognac* is also a house speciality and
other dishes enjoyed on an autumn visit were *oeuf poché aux
épinards,* sauté of turkey in red wine with brussels sprouts and
a crisp potato galette, and a first-rate *crème caramel.* Set menus: 68F
(L only), 115F, 149F. *L 12-2 D 7-10.30. Closed Sun, 1 week Feb
(school holidays), 1st 2 weeks Aug. Mastercard, Visa.*

Au Grain de Folie
Tel 42 58 15 57

Map B2.6

R

24 rue La Vieuville 75018
Seats 20

M⁰ Abbesses
Meal for 2 approx 275F

A tiny, relaxed vegetarian restaurant with a particularly cheerful
owner. Vegetable paté, avocado with Roquefort sauce, houmus
and taramasalata are simple starters, while composite main items
include baked goat's cheese with crudités, grains, lentils or beans
and cooked vegetables. Set menus: 65F, 80F, 100F (with wine).
L 12-2.30 D 7-10.30 (Sat & Sun all day). No credit cards.

Langevin "Au Poulbot Gourmet"
Tel 46 06 86 00

Map B2.7

R

39 rue Lamarck 75018
Seats 30

M⁰ Lamarck Caulaincourt
Meal for 2 approx 600F

Jean-Paul Langevin's little restaurant in Montmartre is decorated
with painter Poulbot's pictures and there are also interesting scenes
outside from the glass enclosed terrace. Jean-Paul's creativity
is noticeable not only in his food but also in its presentation. The
carte changes two to three times a year and is always full of
temptations: try his tomato stuffed with curried snails; cockles and
mussels in *mouclade* style; duck foie gras with a glass of Jurançon;
wild salmon steak with ceps; mustardy veal kidneys cooked *en
cocotte*; and Barbary duck in a cider sauce. Iced charlotte with
chestnuts is a hard-to-resist dessert. Set menus: L 115F, L and
D 198F (incl. wine). *L 12-2 D 7-10. Closed Sun (except L Sun Oct-
May). Mastercard, Visa.*

Le Maquis
Map A2.8

Tel 42 59 76 07   **R**

69 rue Caulaincourt 75018   **M⁰ Lamarck Caulaincourt**
Seats 50 (plus terrace 15)   Meal for 2 approx 400F

A Montmartre bistro with a small pavement terrace which
is delightful in summer. A varied choice of classic bistro-style
dishes is offered. Fish soup or *feuilleté au Roquefort* to start, and
skate with capers or rabbit with mustard as a main course are
some examples. Set menus: L 63F (with wine) L & D 159F (incl
apéritif, wine, coffee). *L 12-2 D 7.30-10.30.* **Closed** *Sun.*
Mastercard, Visa.

Aux Négociants
Map B2.9

Tel 46 06 15 11   **R**

27 rue Lambert 75018   **M⁰ Chateau Rouge**
Seats 40   Meal for 2 approx 300F

Begin the day in Montmartre by dropping by for a glass of wine
at the Naviers' *bistro à vins* or linger longer to taste one of Jean's
chicken terrines, rillettes or *paté de campagne*. The *plat du jour* could
be stuffed cabbage, *boudin, andouillettes* with a white wine sauce,
cassoulet or sauté d'agneau. The Naviers have made many friends
in the area following on from the previous owners, who were
there for 36 years! The Loire region is particularly well
represented on the wine list. *L 12-2.30 D 8-10.30.*
Closed *D Mon & Fri, all Sat & Sun, Aug. No credit cards.*

Prima Lepic
Map A2.10

Tel 46 06 44 64   Fax 46 06 66 11   **H**

29 rue Lepic 75018   **M⁰ Blanche**
Rooms 38   Double from 380F

While potted plants feature in the reception rooms, flowery
wallpaper decorates the bedrooms. All rooms have en-suite
bathrooms and direct-dial telephones. No restaurant. Sacré Coeur
is five minutes away. *Mastercard, Visa.*

Regyn's Montmartre
Map B2.11

Tel 42 54 45 21   Fax 42 23 76 69   **H**

18 place des Abbesses 75018   **M⁰ Abbesses**
Rooms 22   Double from 465F

Clean, very modest accommodation is offered here with the added
advantage to those on the 4th and 5th floors of superb views over
Paris. The hotel's chief attribute, however, is the staff, who are
extremely pleasant and helpful – they'll book tickets, obtain all the
tourist concessions and provide information packs. Continental
breakfast is available all day. *Amex, Mastercard, Visa.*

Le Restaurant
Map A2.12

Tel 42 23 06 22   **R**

32 rue Verou 75018   **M⁰ Blanche/Abbesses**
Seats 50   Meal for 2 approx 400F

A bright and modern restaurant with a short, imaginative *carte*
and a choice of fixed-price menus. Typical dishes in Yves Pelado's
repertoire include sautéed baby squid with a sweet pepper confit

and saffron, a bone marrow tart with softened cabbage, bream
with fennel and a leek cream, and roast sliced pork served with
sauerkraut and spiced fruit chutney. Delicious sweets too such
as *crème brulée* with spiced vinegar or a bitter chocolate *sablé*.
Several wines are available by the glass. They've recently opened
a traiteur called *Aspic* at the same address. Set menus: L 70F, L &
D 120F. *L 12-3 D 8-12.* **Closed** *L Sat-Mon. Amex, Mastercard, Visa.*

Le Sagittaire

Map B2.13

Tel 42 55 17 40

R

77 rue Lamarck 75018
Seats 50

Mᵒ Lamarck Caulaincourt
Meal for 2 approx 320F

This is a small, lived-in restaurant, about ten minutes' walk away
from Sacré Coeur, with a horseshoe bar and lacy tablecloths. It has
recently changed hands, but the new owner – a close friend of the
previous incumbent – has no plans for changing much. A largely
familiar choice of mainstream dishes makes up the 160F menu,
which also includes an aperitif and half a bottle of wine. Terrine
with confiture of onions, salad of sweetbreads deglazed with
vinegar, *confit de canard, duo de la mer* with lobster sauce, *tartare
maison* (a speciality) and noisettes of chicken with morels show
the style. *L 12-2.30 D 7-10.30.* **Closed** *Sun & Mon.*
Mastercard, Visa.

Terrass

Map A2.14

Tel 46 06 72 85   Fax 42 52 29 11

H

12-14 rue Joseph-de-Maistre 75018
Rooms 101

Mᵒ Place de Clichy
Double from 1085F

Sacré Coeur, Place du Tertre and Rue Lepic's market are all
within walking distance and thanks to its location at the foot
of the Butte Montmartre, the view on a clear day from the roof
terrace over to the Eiffel Tower and beyond is exceptional. This
is a sobrely decorated, comfortable hotel offering every amenity
to overnighting guests as well as seminar attendees. There's
a private car park directly opposite the hotel (100F a day). Valet
parking. Porter. Laundry service. *Amex, Diners, Mastercard, Visa.*

The best way to get around Paris is by bus or metro – buy a
book of tickets (carnet) at any metro station and save money

Utrillo

Map A2.15

Tel 42 58 13 44   Fax 42 23 93 88

H

7 rue Aristide Bruant 75018
Rooms 30

Mᵒ Abbesses
Double from 400F

Within walking distance of the Sacré Coeur Basilica and Place
du Tertre, Hotel Utrillo is halfway up the Butte Montmartre.
Renovated in 1991, rooms have modern furniture, white-painted
walls, blue curtains and bedcovers, TV, radio, direct-dial
telephone, hairdryer and mini-bar. Reproductions of Utrillo's
works adorn the walls. Buffet breakfast 40F. *Amex, Diners,
Mastercard, Visa.*

Wepler

Map A2.16

Tel 45 22 53 24   Fax 44 70 07 50

R

14 place de Clichy 75018   **M° Place Clichy**
Seats 250 (plus terrace 50)   Meal for 2 approx 475F

A great place for watching the action in Place Clichy. At this 100-year-old brasserie with tiled floor, red banquettes, mirrors and pictures, there's also plenty going on inside with waiters swiftly passing between the tables, balancing precariously above their heads large platters of shellfish, *magret* of duck with prunes and fillet of salmon with a fricassee of girolles. Set menu: L & D 150F. *Meals noon-1am. Amex, Diners, Mastercard, Visa.*

19th & 20th Arrondissements
Places of Interest

Parc de la Villette
Cité des Sciences et de l'Industrie-La Villette, 40 05 70 00,
  Mº Porte de la Villette
Parc des Buttes Chaumont (Haussmann-designed),
  Mº Botzaris/Buttes Chaumont
Cimetière Père Lachaise (Héloise & Abelard, La Fontaine, Chopin,
Dumas, Proust, Jim Morrisson, Wilde, Piaf), Mº Père Lachaise

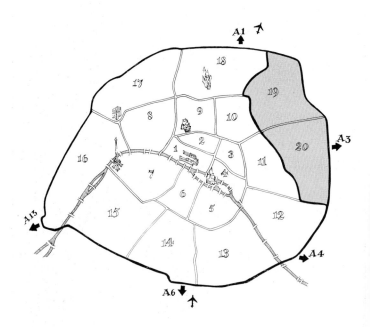

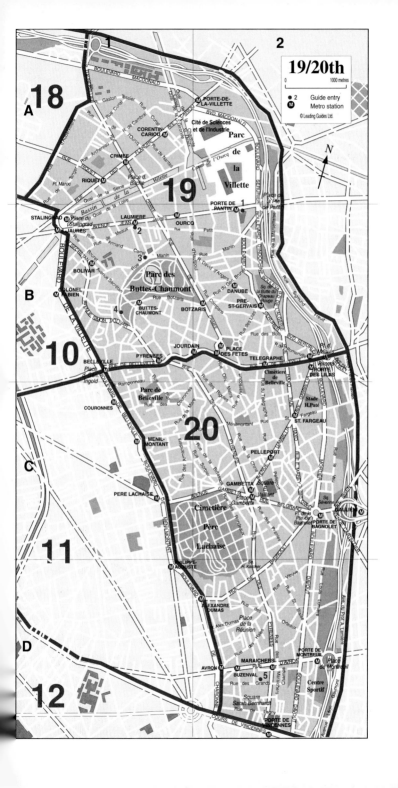

19/20th

0   1000 metres

● **2**   Guide entry

Ⓜ   Metro station

© Leading Guides Ltd.

N

A

18

1

2

BOULEVARD MACDONALD

PORTE-DE-LA-VILLETTE Ⓜ

BVD. MACDONALD

CORENTIN-CARIOU Ⓜ

Cité de Sciences et de l'Industrie

Parc de la Villette

CRIMÉE Ⓜ

RIQUET Ⓜ

Pl. Maroc

Place d. Bitche

19

STALINGRAD Ⓜ
Place de Stalingrad

LAUMIÈRE Ⓜ

JAURÈS Ⓜ

PORTE DE PANTIN Ⓜ

1

Place de la Pte de Pantin

OURCQ Ⓜ

AVENUE JEAN •**2**

•**3**

B

BOLIVAR Ⓜ

Parc des Buttes-Chaumont

DANUBE Ⓜ

COLONEL FABIEN Ⓜ

•**4**

BUTTES-CHAUMONT Ⓜ

BOTZARIS Ⓜ

PRÉ-ST-GERVAIS Ⓜ

Sq. de la Butte du Chapeau Rouge

10

JOURDAIN Ⓜ

PYRÉNÉES Ⓜ

PLACE DES FÊTES Ⓜ

TÉLÉGRAPHE Ⓜ

Cimetière de Belleville

PORTE DES LILAS Ⓜ

BELLEVILLE Ⓜ
Place Ingold

Parc de Belleville

COURONNES Ⓜ

MÉNIL-MONTANT Ⓜ

20

Stade H.Paté

ST. FARGEAU Ⓜ

PELLEPORT Ⓜ

C

PÈRE LACHAISE Ⓜ

GAMBETTA Ⓜ
Place Gambetta
Square E. Vaillant

Cimetière Père Lachaise

SAINT-FARGEAU

ST GALLIÉNI Ⓜ

PORTE DE BAGNOLET Ⓜ

Place de la Pte de Bagnolet

11

PHILIPPE AUGUSTE Ⓜ

ALEXANDRE DUMAS Ⓜ

Place de la Réunion

D

PORTE DE MONTREUIL Ⓜ

Place de Montreuil

MARAICHERS Ⓜ

AVRON Ⓜ

BUZENVAL Ⓜ

•**5**

12

Centre Sportif

Square Sarah Bernhardt

COURS DE VINCENNES

PORTE DE VINCENNES Ⓜ

Les Allobroges   ★   Map D2.5

Tel 43 73 40 00   **R**

71 rue des Grands-Champs 75020   **M° Maraichers**
Seats 30   Meal for 2 approx 600F

Olivier Pateyron has been here for 10 years, but a sea change
occurred during the summer closure. The decor took on a
'modern country' look – with light browns, greys and greens
in the decor, wallpaper made to look like panelling, large poppies
in the upholstery, rustic pictures (farm animals) on the walls,
terracotta vases, wheatsheafs decorating the central bread table,
spotless white linen, straw tying the napkins. Madame Pateyron
and a helper take charge of front of house, while Olivier and
a small team do great work in the kitchen. Signature dishes
marked by care without undue elaboration include *galette de foie
gras*, confit tomatoes with a cream of green olives, roast Bresse
chicken, Barbary duck with spices and dried fruit with Madeira,
and cocotte of lobster and monkfish with tarragon. Raw salmon,
the current rave in Paris, here comes marinated with bacon and
juniper. Galette of potato, wrapped in bacon and topped with
meltingly delicious foie gras, calls for a 20-minute wait and is
worth all 1200 seconds. *Sandre* – a chunky fillet of a generally not
all that exciting fish – is accompanied by discs of grilled celeriac
and fried onion rings. *Marquise au chocolat* is all that it should be.
Les Allobroges is a real gem – a romantic little spot in the far-
flung limits of the 20th arrondissement, not usually associated
with excellent or fashionable eating. Well worth a detour – Cours
de Vincennes is the nearest landmark, and the 26 bus almost passes
the door. Set L & D 81F & 150F (4 courses). *L 12-2 D 7.30-10.*
Closed Sun, Mon, Public Holidays. Mastercard, Visa.

Au Cochon d'Or   Map B2.1

Tel 42 45 46 46   Fax 42 40 43 90   **R**

192 ave Jean-Jaurès 75019   **M° Porte de Pantin**
Seats 105   Meal for 2 approx 800F

The old abattoirs of Villette are opposite this appropriately-named
restaurant, which has a tradition for good-quality meat served
in copious portions. In particular, try *tete de veau* with a mustard
sauce, grilled andouillette, toast with marrow, pig's trotters with
sauce choron, veal sweetbreads and kidneys served with chanterelle
mushrooms, *grillade de boeuf spéciale Cochon d'Or, pommes soufflés*
(for 2) and finish with a *nougat glacé* or a speciality soufflé. Plenty
of fish options, too. Dating from 1924 and barely altered since, the
decor is typical of a bistro of that era with mirrors and some
wood panelling. The restaurant is divided into several rooms.
Next door is **La Mer**, a seafood restaurant with the same phone
number. Valet parking. Set menu: L & D 240F. *L 12.30-2.30
D 7.30-10.30. Amex, Diners, Mastercard, Visa.*

Le Laumière   Map B1.2

Tel 42 06 10 77   Fax 42 06 72 50   **H**

4 rue Petit 75019   **M° Laumière**
Rooms 54   Double from 340F

A modern hotel built in 1968 and entirely renovated in 1991,
offering inexpensive, simple accommodation with a courtyard
garden overlooked by some bedrooms and the breakfast room.
Parking for a few cars (43F per night). *Mastercard, Visa.*

Le Palais de l'Inde   Map B1.3

| Tel 42 39 31 14 | R |

65 rue Manin 75019   **Mᵒ Laumière**
Seats 64 (plus terrace 20)   Meal for 2 approx 500F

An agreeably lit, intimate Indian restaurant specialising in tandoori dishes of chicken, giant prawns and quail plus lamb and chicken tikka served with vegetable beignets. Set menus: L 92F, L & D 125F & 150F. *L 12-2.30 D 7-11.30. Mastercard, Visa.*

Le Pavillon Puebla   Map B1.4

| Tel 42 08 92 62 | R |

Parc Buttes-Chaumont 75019   **Mᵒ Buttes-Chaumont/Pyrénées**
Seats 60   Meal for 2 approx 860F

To reach Le Pavillon Puebla, enter the Buttes-Chaumont park through the gate at the corner of Avenue Simon Bolivar and Rue Botzaris. Established five years ago in an 1890s house, the interior decor is that of Napoleon III with an impressive chandelier in one of the dining rooms and large bouquets of flowers everywhere. Three sides of the restaurant have plate-glass windows with floral drapes and in summer the outdoor terrace is set up with large parasols. Owner-chef Christian Vergès' Catalan origins are made evident in his cuisine in the way he adds spices and herbs to his light sauces. Amongst the starters are squid in ink, a cold version of saddle of stuffed rabbit with onion confit or chopped marinated fillets of duck *à la tapénade*, and braised bream with artichokes or grilled pigeon with foie gras and galette of potato to follow. Crown a splendid meal with a first-rate *crème brulée* or figs and pears in wine. Car parking is available in the Parc. Set menus: L & D 180F (Catalan speciality), 230F. *L 12-2.30 D 7.30-10.* **Closed** *Sun & Mon, 8 days Mar, 2 wks mid-Aug. Amex, Mastercard, Visa.*

CHAMPAGNE
FONDÉE EN 1827

G.H. MUMM & Cⁱᴱ
REIMS~FRANCE

Around Paris
Places of Interest

La Defense: Grande Arche, 49 07 27 57,
  Mº Grande Arche de la Defense
Versailles (Chateau, musée), 30 84 74 00, RER line C
Eurodisney, 64 74 43 06, Info Hotel 49 41 49 41, RER line A Chessy-
Marne-La-Vallée
Musée National de la Céramique Sèvres, 45 34 99 05,
  Mº Pont de Sèvres
Fontainebleau (Chateau, musée), 64 22 27 40/64 22 34 39,
  SNCF from Gare de Lyons
Basilique St Denis (tombs of the kings of France), 48 09 83 54,
  Mº St Denis-Basilique
Vincennes (Chateau), 43 28 15 48, Mº Chateau de Vincennes,
  RER line A
Musée des Transports Urbains, St Mandé, 43 28 37 12
Mº Porte Dorée (bus 46 passes entrance). Open weekends pm.

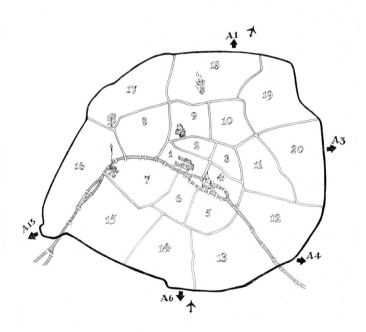

La Barrière de Clichy

| Tel 47 37 05 18   Fax 47 37 77 05 | **R** |

1 rue de Paris 92116 Clichy   **Mᵒ Porte de Clichy**
Seats 50   Meal for 2 approx 700F

Air-conditioned comfort on the Clichy side of the Périphérique.
Gilles de Gallès' cooking combines traditional and adventurous
elements, typified by vinaigrette of oysters and salmon with herbs,
fillet of John Dory with artichokes, fricassee of sole and
sweetbreads with thyme, and rack of lamb with garlic. Don't
forget to order the splendid apple tart with the rest of your meal.
Set menus: L 220F D 190F *L&D 300F (dégustation)*. *L 12-2 D 8-
10*. **Closed** *L Sat, all Sun, two wks Aug. Amex, Diners,
Mastercard, Visa.*

Bistrot d'à Coté

| Tel 47 45 34 55 | **R** |

4 rue Boutard Neuilly 92200   **Mᵒ Pont de Neuilly**

See 17th arrondissement Bistrot d'à Coté for details.

Ibis

| Tel 47 78 15 60   Fax 47 78 94 16 | **H** |

4 bld de Neuilly 92400 Courbevoie   **Mᵒ Esplanade de La Défense**
Rooms 284   Double from 450F

Sharing the same building as the *Novotel* (see below), the Ibis
offers budget accommodation in the business district with
excellent public transport connections to the rest of town.
At weekends (Fri, Sat & Sun nights) the price drops to 310F per
room if you ring on the day or just turn up – this rate is not
available for prior bookings. *Amex, Diners, Mastercard, Visa.*

Novotel

| Tel 47 78 16 68   Fax 47 78 84 71 | **H** |

2 bld de Neuilly 92400 Courbevoie   **Mᵒ Esplanade de La Défense**
Rooms 280   Double from 750F

Mid-range chain hotel overlooking the Seine on the La Défense
side of the Pont de Neuilly. All rooms have air-conditioning,
mini-bar and bathroom with separate loo. *Amex, Diners,
Mastercard, Visa.*

Sofitel CNIT

| Tel 46 92 10 10   Fax 46 92 10 50 | **HR** |

2 pl de La Défense 92053   **Mᵒ Grand Arche de La Défense**
Rooms 147   Double from 1350F

There are two Sofitel hotels at La Défense; this one is within the
extraordinary CNIT building next to the even more striking
Grande Arche. Practical bedrooms are notably spacious and come
with good bathrooms, all having both power and hand-held 'hair-
washing' showers over tubs and polished red granite vanity units.
A live pianist brings atmosphere to the modern open-plan bar each
evening. 24hr room service. Ample free parking. *Amex, Diners,
Mastercard, Visa.*

Les Communautés
Tel 46 92 10 30
Seats 110   Meal for 2 approx 650F

The hotel's restaurant has moved up to the 5th-floor space
formerly occupied by *Fouquet's Europe*. On one side windows look
into the vast interior space of the CNIT building, on the other the
view is of the Place de La Défense and Mitterrand's Grande Arche.
The same menu is differently priced at lunch (270F for a four-
course meal that includes the excellent cheese trolley) and dinner
when starters are all 60F, mains 110F, cheese 40F and desserts 50F.
There is also a short (two choices) 160F table d'hote dinner that
is aimed at hotel guests but is available to all. Dishes have
a modern slant and tend to feature bold flavours – stewed
artichokes with tomato and fresh coriander, oxtail ravioli with
a fricassee of girolle mushrooms, sea bream with lentils and
a green curry sauce, roast lamb chops with courgette and tapénade,
magret of duck with polenta and sweet and sour sauce. A large
room with well-spaced tables and plenty of bustling waiters,
particularly at lunchtime when it is usually full of business folk.
The wine list is not over-long but offers something to suit most
pockets. Set Menus: L 270F D 160F. *L 12.15-2 D 7.30-10.30.*
***Closed** Sat & Sun, 25 Dec & Public Holidays.*

Sofitel

Tel 47 76 44 43 Fax 47 73 72 74	**H**

34 Cours Michelet 92060 La Défense   **M⁰ Esplanade de La Défense**
Rooms 150   Double from 1250F

The other Sofitel hotel at La Défense. Exceptionally good work
space, with phone at the desk as well as at the bedside, and
excellent bathrooms are features of comfortable if rather blandly
decorated bedrooms. Room service is 24hrs and all rooms have
mini-bar and room safe. Private parking (75F per night). *Amex,
Diners, Mastercard, Visa.*

Trianon Palace

Tel 30 84 38 00 Fax 39 49 00 77	**HR**

1 bd de la Reine 78000 Versailles   **RER Line C**
Rooms 94   Double from 1914F

Now Japanese owned, and having just completed a major
refurbishment, the Trianon Palace is a happy marriage
of traditional elegance and modern convenience. Surrounded
by parkland, and adjacent to the Palace of Versailles, the hotel
is nevertheless just a few hundred of metres from the town. Public
rooms include a long gallery with faux-marble columns and
glittering chandeliers and a high-ceilinged bar with pale wood
panelling highlighted with a dash of gilt. If you have to work,
there is a state-of-the-art business centre with multi-lingual staff
and video-conferencing facilities, while for relaxation the sybaritic
Givenchy Spa includes a splendid, galleried swimming pool,
traditional Moroccan hammam, gymnasium, hairdressing salon
and every beauty treatment imaginable. Bedrooms, which all have
air-conditioning and second phone line for personal fax machines,
vary from spacious suites to some rooms of rather more modest
size but all are traditionally furnished, have stylish matching
bedcovers and curtains, and plaster-panelled walls adding a period   *See over*

feel. Fine bathrooms, most with twin washbasins and many with separate shower cubicles, offer enveloping towelling robes and Givenchy toiletries.

Connected to the *Palace* by an underground passageway, the newly built **Trianon Residence** offers an additional 96 bedrooms that are less luxurious, although still spacious and comfortable, than those in the *Palace*, and without such pampering touches as having your bed turned down in the evening, but they do come at the lower price of 1214F per night for a double. Guests here have use of the facilities at the *Palace*, including the Spa, and for guests at the *Palace* it offers a change of mood with live jazz three nights a week in its mirror-ceilinged bar and a less formal dining option in the **La Fontaine** brasserie. *Amex, Diners, Mastercard, Visa.*

Les Trois Marches   ★
Tel 39 50 13 21   Fax 30 21 01 25
Seats 60 (+60 outside)   Meal for 2 approx 1500F

Added when the hotel was refurbished, the restaurant is in the style of an orangery with black and white tiled floor, numerous potted trees and high windows looking out on to a terrace (ideal for summer dining). Whether choosing from the *carte* or one of the four set menus (which include one for vegetarians and one called *printemps-été* – regardless of the time of year), every meal begins with a slice of ham, carved at the table, that comes from Caune in the South of France – not far from chef Gérard Vié's home town. Next comes the day's complimentary starter, a soft pheasant purée in a light, frothy sauce on our last visit. The main *carte* includes no less than five different ways with foie gras – from a whole liver served cold with pepper to a foie gras soup with oysters – along with such dishes as a galette of potatoes with bacon and caviar, *ravigote de tete de veau,* turbot with a meat jus and ragout of broad beans, duck with cider vinegar and honey, *cassoulet à la saucisse de Couïza* and veal chop with truffle juice and curried fruits. Opt for cheese to follow and three separate, fully laden trolleys arrive offering a vast selection – a little too vast perhaps as a few appeared not to be in absolutely perfect condition. Set menus: L 260F (not Sat), L & D 395, 495, 595 & 795F. *L 12.30-2 D 7.30-10.* **Closed** *Sun, Mon & Aug.*

La Truffe Noire "Jenny Jacquet"
Tel 46 24 94 14   Fax 46 37 27 022   **R**
2 place Parmentier Neuilly-sur-Seine 92200   **M° Porte Maillot**
Seats 50   Meal for 2 approx 700F

Although in Neuilly, Jenny Jacquet's restaurant is only 150 metres from Porte Maillot metro station. Or, if you journey by car, a valet will park it for you. Diners sit at widely-spaced tables in four small dining rooms in a warm and comfortable atmosphere. The three-course *menu-carte* (185F) provides the best value for money, with dishes such as artichoke rémoulade with Bouchot mussels, hare terrine with *trompettes* and cranberry jelly, old-fashioned *blanquette de veau* with semolina pasta, pot-au-feu of ox cheek and oxtail, and quenelles of vanilla ice cream and chocolate sorbet. The truffle season runs from mid-December to mid-March. Wines from the Loire region predominate. Set menus: L & D 185F, 320F. *L 12.30-2 D 7.30-10.* **Closed** *Sat, Sun & 3 wks end Aug. Amex, Mastercard, Visa.*

Airports

Ibis

| Tel 48 62 49 49   Fax 48 62 54 22 | H |

Roissypole, Aéroport Charles de Gaulle Roissy-en-France 95701
Rooms 556   Double from 375F

Practical accommodation at a keen price just 200 metres from the
airport's new Terminal 9. No room service. Secure parking (50F
per 24hrs for residents). *Amex, Mastercard, Visa.*

Maxim's

| Tel 48 62 16 16   Fax 48 62 45 96 | R |

Aéroport Charles de Gaulle 95713 Roissy-en-France
Seats 40   Meal for 2 approx 800F

By far the best of the airport eating is provided at this cool,
elegant restaurant, where the skills of the chef are matched
by service from a large and efficient team. Alain Bariteau,
previously at the *Jules Verne* restaurant on the Eiffel Tower,
presents a mouthwatering menu of superb dishes: Vendée pigeon
roasted with honey and spices, and red sea bream with crispy
courgettes are two specialities, and look out too for duck and
goose foie gras in two cookings, braised sole with a shellfish
stuffing and hare *à la royale*. Fine wine list with plenty of half
bottles. The *Grill* has gone – it's now two private salons with
a combined capacity of 70. Set menus: 210F, 280F. *L 11.30-2.30
D 6.30-10. Closed Sat, Sun, Aug. Amex, Diners, Mastercard, Visa.*

Sofitel

| Tel 48 62 23 23   Fax 48 62 78 49 | H |

Aéroport Charles de Gaulle Roissy-en-France 95713
Rooms 352   Double from 800F

Handily situated right in the middle of the airport complex. All
rooms have two phones plus mini-bar and multi-channel TV.
Leisure facilities include an indoor swimming pool, sauna and
tennis. Parking for 180 cars. *Amex, Diners, Mastercard, Visa.*

Orly Hilton

| Tel 45 12 45 12   Fax 45 12 45 00 | H |

Orly Sud 267 94544 Orly
Rooms 360   Double from 1100F

Practical modern accommodation with the Hilton style, a short
shuttle from Orly Sud and Orly Ouest, and half an hour from the
city centre. The bedrooms are air-conditioned and soundproofed,
and all the expected up-to-date amenities are standard. There are
rooms adapted for handicapped guests and rooms designated non-
smoking. Public areas include two restaurants (the less formal
is open from 6am to midnight), a bar and shops. There's a business
centre and no fewer than 25 conference and function rooms,
whose various configurations permit up to 500 to be seated
together theatre-style. 24hr reception and room service. Plans for
1995 include a fitness centre. *Amex, Diners, Mastercard, Visa.*

Ibis

| Tel 46 87 22 45   Fax 48 87 84 72 | **H** |

1 rue Mondétour Rungis 94656
Rooms 119   Double from 350F

One of the Ibis budget chain. This one is in a complex of hotels,
called the 'Delta Zone', about 10 minutes from Orly airport,
halfway to the town of Rungis. No room service. Own parking.
Amex, Mastercard, Visa.

Maxim's

| Tel 46 87 16 16   Fax 46 87 05 39 | **R** |

94546 Aéroport d'Orly Ouest
Seats 40   Meal for 2 approx 700F

Classically based cuisine marked by restrained innovation in a
restaurant on the second floor of the west terminal. Gil Jouanin's
menus combine international favourites like smoked salmon,
caviar and foie gras with seasonal specialities such as fricassee
of scallops and frogs' legs with autumn flavours and sweet garlic;
or hare *à la royale* prepared with cream, mustard, mushrooms and
confit'd pear. The wine list is almost exclusively French. Set
menu: L & D 290F. The *Grill*, at the same address, is open both
sessions, seven days a week including August. Restaurant statistics:
L 12-2.30 D 7-10. **Closed** *Sat, Sun, Aug. Amex, Diners,
Mastercard, Visa.*

FOR THE WIDEST RANGE OF SERVICED APARTMENTS WORLDWIDE

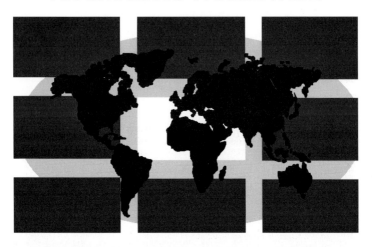

CALL THE SPECIALISTS

Serviced Apartments are the ideal alternative to hotel accommodation for holidays, business or as an interim housing solution.

Cost-effectively priced, all our apartments are serviced by maids, fully equipped and offer unrivalled luxury, space, privacy and security.

With over 25 international partners, The Apartment Service has unique representation in local markets who can help you choose the property that best suits your needs from the thousands of quality apartments throughout the World, from London to New York, from Paris to Sydney.

The Guide to Serviced Apartments containing details of over 3,000 apartments in Europe is available free of charge on request.

SERVICES APARTMENTS HAVE:-

- Lounges
- Kitchens
- Bathrooms
- Maid Service
- Baby Sitting Service
- Direct Dial Telephones

IDEAL FOR:-

- Holidays
- Training Courses
- Relocation
- Temporary Assignments
- Workbases
- Exhibitions
- Conference Presentations

CALL TODAY FOR MORE DETAILS OF OUR FREE SERVICE AND OUR BROCHURE

THE APARTMENT SERVICE
66 Dalling Road, London W6 0JA, U.K. Telephone: 081 748 4207 Facsimile: 081 748 3972

Serviced Apartments

Paris is rivalling London in providing the advantages that serviced apartments can offer over hotels – privacy, security, freedom, cooking facilities, in short 'a place of your own' for individuals, pairs or even family groups. The apartments that are reviewed on the next few pages afford a wide choice of accommodation, from studios to grand penthouse suites, and the addresses vary from the fashionable heart of Paris to the quiet suburbs. Maid services are provided, and many boast well-equipped kitchens (all have at least rudimentary kitchenettes). Some apartments are effectively hotels, where guests have the choice of using the full hotel amenities or living an independent life. That choice naturally determines the level of service and the price (the latter is liable to vary greatly according to the season, the length of stay and of course the number of occupants in the apartment).

All the locations listed have been independently assessed by the Guide's inspectors, and all are highly recommendable.

Citadines Paris Opéra

18 rue Favart 75002   **Mᵒ Richelieu-Drouot**
Apartments 76   From 590F to 1170F per night

Established in Paris for ten years, Citadines expanded in 1994 with the opening of Opéra, République and Prestige Haussmann residential hotels, bringing the total to nine. Paris Opéra, just off Boulevard des Italiens and handy for the Opéra and the Bourse, is part of a handsome redevelopment and opened its doors in June 1994. Accommodation comprises small studios (studettes), studio-flats and two-room apartments including some grand duplexes. Furnishings combine quiet good looks with solid practicality, and all rooms have air-conditioning, private telephone with message service, TV with Sky News, Eurosport and Canal+, a hob, oven, dishwasher and a full range of kitchen essentials. WCs are separate from bathrooms, which are provided with hairdryers. The résidence boasts a private underground car park, billiard room, keep-fit equipment, laundrette, American bar and a meeting room for 20. Entrance is through a peaceful courtyard into a large reception area manned from 6am to midnight. The price quoted is per night from mid-July to end August, 1994 rate. Slightly higher tariff at other times; discounts for stays of more than 10 nights and more than 20 nights. Separate quotes for regular hotel services.

JRH Prestige Champs Elysées

20-22 rue de Berri 75008   **Mᵒ George V/St Philippe du Roule**
Apartments 50   From 840F to 3000F per night

A superb location near the glamour of the Champs Elysées and the fashion shops of Faubourg St Honoré, this is a very modern building occupying two blocks and comprising 36 studios, 7 one-bedroom apartments and 7 two-bedroom apartments. Lifts ply between the basement parking and all but the top (8th) floor. Furnishings are both practical and stylish, and each unit has a well-equipped kitchen, private-line phone and, with security in mind, armoured door and video-entry phone. Iron and vacuum cleaner are standard, and the apartments also have washing machines. Apartments are cleaned, with change of towels and bed linen every other day. A welcome/information office is manned daily from 8.30 to 7. Most rooms overlook the garden at the back of the building. Minimum stay 3 nights.

Citadines Paris République

75 ave Parmentier 75011   **M⁰ Parmentier**
Apartments 75   From 400F to 910F per night

The 11th arrondissement, on the Eastern side of Paris, has seen massive redevelopment in recent years, and this Citadines is a fine example of new building. Opened in June 1994, it has studettes, 2-person studios and 2-room suites with room for 4. Private phone line with message service, kitchen facilities, multi-channel TV (with CNN) in all rooms, with regular hotel services offered as optional extras. Reception is manned from 7am to 10pm. Laundry, breakfast room, private parking. The nightly rate quoted (1994 prices) is the lowest (mid-July to end August). Slightly higher tariff at other times; discounts for stays of more than 10 and more than 20 days.

JRH Prestige Gobelins

5 rue Michel Peter 75013   **M⁰ Gobelins**
Apartments 20   From 395F to 880F per night

Just off the Ave des Gobelins, to the north of Place d'Italie, this Haussmann-style town house has just been totally refurbished to provide 20 comfortable apartments from compact studios with simple kitchenettes in a curtained alcove to more spacious one-bedroom apartments with separate sitting room and fully equipped kitchen. Clean-cut modern decor features black-stained wood furniture and folding chairs. All have the usual amenities such as remote-control television, direct phone line, iron and ironing board, washing machine vacuum cleaner and all necessary kitchen and tableware. Security is taken care of by the digitcode access system and strengthened doors to each individual apartment. Service with cleaning and a change of linen takes place every eight days. Minimum stay 5 nights.

JRH Prestige Auteuil

49 rue Chardon Lagache 75016   **M⁰ Chardon Lagache**
Apartments 30   From 395F to 960F per night

Accommodation in this quiet residential area on the western edge of Paris ranges from studios for 1 or 2 with open kitchens to two-bedroom apartments. The building, dating from 1930, has been completely renovated, with lifts serving all seven floors. All the necessities for independent living are provided, and the welcome/information desk is open from 8.30 to 6 from Thursday to Saturday, with minimum service on Sunday and Monday. Sheets and towels are changed every eight days. These apartments are of particular appeal to sports fans, being close to Auteuil racecourse, the Parc des Princes and Roland Garros stadium. Minimum stay 5 nights.

JRH Prestige Trocadéro

104-106-108 rue de Longchamp 75116   **M° Rue de la Pompe**
Apartments 31   From 690F to 3000F per night

104, 106 and 108 Rue de Longchamp face one of the leading lycées in the arrondissement. There's no noise from the almost grown-up children, and in any case most of the bedrooms overlook the courtyard at the back of the block. All the accommodation, from 35 sq metre studios to large duplexes with 2 bathrooms, is in pristine condition, furnished in practical modern style and equipped with everything from excellent kitchens to private-line phone and video-entry phones. The offices, at 106, are open from 8.30 to 6 Monday to Friday, and at the weekend according to particular needs. Towels and sheets are changed every 4 days. The Trocadéro Esplanade and Chaillot Palace are within a five minute walk. Minimum stay 5 nights.

Kléber Palace – see entry in 16th arrondissement

Résidence Times Square Alma Marceau

5-7 rue Jean-Giraudoux 75016   **M° Alma-Marceau**
Apartments 10   From 1700F to 4500F per night

Luxurious modern accommodation in a prestigious part of Paris, as quiet and private as you like, but also just a short walk from the bright lights and high life of the Champs Elysées. The Alma Marceau Residence offers all the essentials for comfortable, elegant living in apartments that range from 2-room (1-bedroom) to 6-room duplex flats. Furnishings in carved light wood are of a very high standard, beds large and comfortable, kitchens luxuriously equipped, videophone, private telephones, car parking and daily cleaning/caretaker services provided. The living and kitchen areas are particularly spacious, with plenty of standard lamps, parquet floors and mirrors fronting generous storage space. 22-channel TVs, one in the living area, one in the bedroom.

There are three other Times Square Residences. On a similar level of luxury to Alma Marceau is Times Square St Honoré at 218 Rue du Faubourg St Honoré. All the apartments here overlook a courtyard, most have a private balcony or terrace and the full services of the adjacent hotel are available. Also on the premises is the marine centre Villa Thalgo with a seawater pool. On a more modest scale are Times Square Pascal at 71 Rue Pascal 75013, with 44 studio apartments, and Times Square Montparnasse at 121 Boulevard du Montparnasse 75006, with studios and duplexes. Prices at Pascal start at 540F per night, at Montparnasse 750F.

Bookings at the above serviced apartments may be made through the Apartment Service in London, freecall 0800 243 163.

Late Eating – Last Orders 11.30pm or later

1st Arr

Brasserie Munichoise
Chez Clovis
Fellini
Joe Allen
Au Pied de Cochon
La Tour de Montlhéry

2nd Arr

Arco Tapas y Vinos
Gallopin
Le Grand Colbert
Aux Lyonnais
Pierre "A La Fontaine Gaillon"
Café Runtz
Vaudeville

3rd Arr

Bar à Huitres
La Guirlande de Julie

4th Arr

Brasserie Bofinger
Le Bistrot de Bofinger
Le Coude Fou

5th Arr

Bar à Huitres
Brasserie Balzar
La Bucherie
Le Départ de Saint-Michel
La Gueuze (Fri, Sat)

6th Arr

L'Arbuci
Bistro de la Grille
Les Bookinistes
Brasserie Lipp
Café de Flore
Café des Deux Magots
Aux Charpentiers
L'Hotel, Le Belier
Le Muniche
La Palette
Le Petit Vatel
La Petite Cour
Polidor
La Vigneraie

7th Arr

Chez Françoise
Thoumieux

8th Arr

Al Ajami
L'Apport
L'Avenue
Le Boeuf sur le Toit
Caviar Kaspia
Le Cercle Ledoyen
Chez André
Chez Edgard
Chez Francis
L'Etage Baumann
Fakhr el Dine
La Fermette Marbeuf
Fouquet's
La Maison d'Alsace
La Maison du Valais
Le Pichet
Plaza Athénée, Relais Plaza
Virgin Café
Yvan

9th Arr

Le Bistro des Deux Théatres
La Champagne
Charlot Roi des Coquillages
Chez Clément
Le Grand Café Capucines
Grand Hotel Inter-Continental,
    Brasserie du Café de la Paix
Au Petit Riche
Wally le Saharien

10th Arr

Brasserie Flo
Julien
Terminus Nord

11th Arr

Chez Fernand
La Galoche d'Aurillac
Nioullaville
Thai Elephant
Le Villaret

12th Arr

Fouquet's Bastille
Les Grandes Marches
Sipario

13th Arr

Pizza César

14th Arr

Bar à Huitres
La Coupole
Aux Iles Marquises

15th Arr

Bistro 121
Kim Anh

16th Arr

Bistrot de L'Etoile
Brasserie de la Poste
Brasserie Stella
La Butte Chaillot
Chez Ngo
Fakhr el Dine
Pavillon Noura

17th Arr

Le Ballon des Ternes
Baumann Ternes
Bistrot de l'Etoile (both restaurants)
Charly de Bab-el-Oued
Chez Georges
La Famiglia Fuligna
Le Relais de Venise (l'Entrecote)

18th Arr

La Crémaillère
Le Restaurant
Wepler

19th Arr

Le Palais de l'Inde
Les Allobroges

Restaurants Open Throughout the Weekend

1st Arr

Hotel Inter-Continental, Terrasse
Fleurie
Joe Allen
Le Meurice
Au Pied de Cochon
Ritz, L'Espadon
Willi's Wine Bar

2nd Arr

Drouant
Le Grand Colbert
Les Noces de Jeanette
Vaudeville

3rd Arr

Ambassade d'Auvergne
Bar à Huitres
Chez l'Ami Louis
La Guirlande de Julie

4th Arr

Bistrot du Dome
Brasserie Bofinger
Le Bistrot de Bofinger
Coconnas
Le Vieux Bistro

5th Arr

Restaurant A
Bar à Huitres
Le Bistro du Port

Brasserie Balzar
La Bucherie
Le Départ de Saint-Michel
E Marty
La Rotisserie du Beaujolais
La Tour d'Argent

6th Arr

L'Arbuci
Bistro de la Grille
Brasserie Lipp
Café de Flore
Café des Deux Magots
Le Caméléon
Dominique
L'Hotel, Le Belier
Mariage Frères
La Méditerranée
Le Muniche
La Petite Cour
Polidor

7th Arr

La Cantine des Gourmets (La Bourdonnais)
Chez Françoise
Christian Constant
Foc-Ly
Jules Verne
Montalembert Restaurant
Thoumieux

8th Arr

Al Ajami
L'Appart
L'Avenue
Le Bristol
Chez André
Chez Francis
Hotel de Crillon, Les Ambassadeurs
Hotel de Crillon, L'Obelisque
L'Etage Baumann
Fakhr el Dine
La Fermette Marbeuf
Fouquet's
George V, Les Princes Restaurant
La Maison d'Alsace
Plaza Athénée, Le Régence
Plaza Athénée, Relais Plaza
Royal Monceau, Il Carpaccio
San Regis
Virgin Café

9th Arr

Le Bistro des Deux Théatres
La Champagne
Charlot Roi des Coquillages
Chartier
Chez Clément
Le Grand Café Capucines
Grand Hotel Inter-Continental,
Brasserie du Café de la Paix

10th Arr

Brasserie Flo
Julien
Terminus Nord

11th Arr

La Belle Epoque
Nioullaville

12th Arr

Les Grandes Marches
Le Temps des Cerises
Le Train Bleu

13th Arr

Pizza César
La Table d'Honfleur

14th Arr

Bar à Huitres
La Cagouille
La Coupole
Le Méridien Montparnasse, Justine
Pavillon Montsouris

15th Arr

Bistro 121
Kim Anh
Hotel Nikko de Paris, Les Célébrités
Hotel Nikko de Paris, Benkay

16th Arr

Baltimore, Berties
Brasserie de la Poste
Brasserie Stella
La Butte Chaillot
Carette
Chez Ngo
Fakhr el Dine
Les Monuments
Le Parc Victor Hugo, Le Relais du
Parc
Passy Mandarin
Pavillon Noura
Le Petit Bedan
Quach

17th Arr

Le Ballon des Ternes
Baumann Ternes
Bistro du 17e
Charly de Bab-el-Oued
Chez Georges
La Famiglia Fuligna
Goldenberg
Pétrus
Le Relais de Venise (L'Entrecote)
Timgad

18th Arr

La Crémaillère
Au Grain de Folie
Wepler

19th Arr

Au Cochon d'Or
Le Palais de l'Inde

Restaurants Open Throughout August

1st Arr

Armand au Palais-Royal
Brasserie Munichoise
Les Cartes Postales
Le Caveau du Palais
Chez Clovis
Chez Elle
Chez Pauline
Au Cochon d'Or des Halles
Fellini
Gérard Besson
Goumard-Prunier
Hotel Inter-Continental, Terrasse Fleurie
Joe Allen
Juveniles
Kinugawa
Mercure Galant
Le Meurice
Pharamond
Au Pied de Cochon
Ritz, L'Espadon
Willi's Wine Bar

2nd Arr

Arco Tapas y Vinos
Country Life
Coup de Coeur
Drouant
Gallopin
Aux Lyonnais
Le Moï
Les Noces de Jeanette
Passy Mandarin
Vaudeville

3rd Arr

Bar à Huitres
Chez l'Ami Louis
La Guirlande de Julie

4th Arr

Bistro du Dome
Brasserie Bofinger
Le Bistrot de Bofinger
Coconnas
Le Coude Fou
Le Fond de Cour
Au Gourmet de L'Isle
Le Grizzli
Jo Goldenberg
Au Monde des Chimères

Le Vieux Bistro
Wooloomooloo

5th Arr

Restaurant A
Bar à Huitres
Le Bistrot d'à Coté
La Bucherie
Campagne et Provence
Chez Toutoune
Le Départ de Saint-Michel
E Marty
La Gueuze
Au Pactole
La Rotisserie du Beaujolais
La Timonerie
La Tour d'Argent

6th Arr

L'Arbuci
Bistro de la Grille
Le Bistrot d'Alex
Les Bookinistes
Brasserie Lipp
Le Caméléon
Aux Charpentiers
Chez Maitre Paul
L'Ecaille de PCB
L'Hotel, Le Belier
La Méditerranée
Le Muniche
Le Petit St Benoit
Le Petit Vatel
La Petite Cour
Polidor
La Rotisserie d'en Face

7th Arr

L'Arpège
La Boule d'Or
La Cantine des Gourmets (La Bourdonnais)
Chez Françoise
Christian Constant
Foc-Ly
Jules Verne
Montalembert Restaurant
Le Récamier
Thoumieux

8th Arr

Al Ajami
Androuët

L'Appart
L'Avenue
Le Boeuf sur le Toit
Le Bristol
Caviar Kaspia
Le Cercle Ledoyen
Chez André
Chez Francis
Hotel de Crillon, Les Ambassadeurs
Hotel de Crillon, L'Obélisque
Le Crétois
Fakhr el Dine
La Ferme St Hubert
La Fermette Marbeuf
Fauchon-Le 30
Fouquet's
George V, Les Princes Restaurant
Les Georgiques
Hédiard
Laurent
La Maison d'Alsace
La Maison du Valais
Maxim's
Plaza Athénée, Le Régence
Plaza Athénée, Relais Plaza
Royal Monceau, Le Jardin
Saint Moritz
San Regis
Virgin Café
Yvan

9th Arr

Le Bistro des Deux Théatres
La Champagne
Charlot Roi des Coquillages
Chartier
Chez Clément
Le Grand Café Capucines
Grand Hotel Inter-Continental,
Brasserie du Café de la Paix
Au Petit Riche
La Table d'Anvers
Wally Le Saharien

10th Arr

Brasserie Flo
Julien
Terminus Nord

11th Arr

L'Aiguière
Les Amognes
Holiday Inn République
Nioullaville
Le Passage
Le Roudoulié
La Table Richelieu
Thai Elephant

12th Arr

L'Oulette
Le Train Bleu

13th Arr

Pizza César
Les Vieux Métiers de France
La Table d'Honfleur

14th Arr

Bar à Huitres
Le Bistrot du Dome (not Sun & Mon
in Aug)
La Coupole
Le Dome
Le Duc
Méridien Montparnasse, Justine
Pavillon Montsouris

15th Arr

Bistro 121
Le Clos Morillons
Kim Anh
Morot-Gaudry
Hotel Nikko de Paris, Benkay
Pierre Vedel

16th Arr

Baltimore, Bertie's
Bistrot de l'Etoile
Brasserie de la Poste
La Butte Chaillot
Carette
Chez Ngo
Fakhr el Dine
Kambodgia
Les Monuments
Le Parc Victor Hugo, Le Relais du
Parc
Passy Mandarin
Pavillon Noura
Le Pré Catelan
Quach
Le Toit de Passy

17th Arr

Amphyclès
Baumann Ternes
Le Bistrot d'à Coté
Bistrot de l'Etoile (both restaurants)
Bistro du 17e
Cave Pétrissans
Charly de Bab-el-Oued
Le Col Vert
La Famiglia Fuligna
Goldenberg
Graindorge

Guy Savoy
Le Manoir de Paris
Le Relais de Venise (L'Entrecote)
Rotisserie d'Armaillé
La Table de Pierre
Taïra
Timgad

18th Arr

A Beauvilliers
Chez Frézet
La Crémaillère 1900
Au Grain de Folie

Langevin "Au Poulbot Gourmet"
Le Maquis
Le Restaurant
Le Sagittaire
Wepler

19th Arr

Au Cochon d'Or
Le Palais de l'Inde

Around

Bistrot d'à Coté
Sofitel CNIT

MENU GLOSSARY

Words in italics also have their own entries

AAAAA – Association Amicale des Amateurs d'Andouillettes Authentiques
abats – offal, including head meat, heart, liver, kidneys, tripe, feet
acajou – cashew nut, as in **noix d'acajou**
acidulé – sour
affiné – refined – a description used for cheeses
agneau – lamb (**agneau de lait** – milk-fed lamb)
agrume – citrus fruit
aiglefin – haddock (sometimes also **aigrefin** and **églefin**)
aigo – Provençal garlic soup
aigre – sour, bitter
aigre-doux – sweet-sour
aiguillette(s) – long, thin slices, usually duck breast. Also cut of beef from the sirloin
ail – garlic
aile – wing (as in chicken or skate)
aïoli – garlic mayonnaise
airelle – **airelle myrtille** – bilberry
airelle rouge – cranberry
albertine – poached fish in white wine sauce with mushrooms, truffles and parsley
albigeoise – meat garnish of stuffed tomatoes and potato croquettes. Also a rich meat soup
alcide – white wine sauce with chopped shallots and grated horseradish
algérienne – steak garnish of tomatoes and sweet peppers. Also with sweet potatoes
algues – seaweed
aligot – puréed potatoes with cheese and garlic
aloyau – sirloin of beef
aileron – fin of fish or wing of fowl
allemande – *velouté* sauce blended with egg yolks. Also a beef *consommé* with red cabbage
allumettes – matchstick fried potatoes. Also puff pastry sticks
alsacienne – garnish of noodles, foie gras and truffles. Also of sauerkraut and slices of ham
amande – almond, **amandine** – almond flavoured
ambassadeur – meat garnish of *duchesse* potatoes, artichoke hearts with mushrooms and horseradish. Also a chicken *consommé* with truffles and mushrooms
ambassadrice – sauce of pounded chicken and cream. Also a chicken *consommé* with truffles, chicken and mushrooms
amer – bitter
américaine – also **armoricaine** – a sauce of pounded lobster with truffles, chicken and mushrooms. Also a garnish of lobster tails and truffles (see *homard*)
amourettes – spinal marrow
amuse-gueule – complimentary pre-starter or appetiser, also **amuse-bouche**
ananas – pineapple
anchoïade – anchovy paste
anchois – anchovy

ancienne – traditional or old-fashioned, also a cream sauce with small onions and mushrooms

andalouse – garnish of mayonnaise with sweet peppers stuffed with rice and sauted aubergines. Also a *consommé* with rice and ham

andouille, andouillette – sausage of chopped chitterling and stomach, see also *AAAAA*

aneth – dill

anglaise – usually of fish fried in egg and breadcrumbs. Also applied to simple boiling and steaming. See also *crème anglaise*

anguille – eel

animelles – testicles, also known as *rognons blancs*

anis – aniseed

anis étoilé – star anise, also *badiane*

anna – as in pommes anna: cake of sliced potatoes cooked in butter

antiboise – mayonnaise for fish, of tomato, anchovy and tarragon

arachide – groundnut, peanut

ardoise – slate, blackboard

aretes – fish bones

argenteuil – dish or garnish with asparagus

aromates – *velouté* sauce of mixed herbs. Also the name given to distinctly flavoured herbs and roots

assiette anglaise – plate of assorted cold meats

aubépine – hawthorn

aurore – white sauce tinged with tomato

automne – autumn

baba – yeast cake usually flavoured with rum or kirsch

badiane – see *anis étoilé*

ballotine – meat, fowl, game or fish boned, stuffed and rolled, served either hot or cold. Similar to a *galantine*, which is always cold

bar – bass

barbue – brill

barigoule – mushroom found in the South of France. Also the name given to globe artichoke stuffed with *duxelles* mixture

barquette – small, boat-shaped pastry shell filled with sweet or savoury mixture

basilic – basil

basquaise – usually *poulet* basquaise: cooked with tomatoes, onions and sweet peppers. Also a meat garnish of fried wild mushrooms and moulds of *pommes anna* or a beef *consommé* with tomato and sweet peppers

baudroie – monkfish, also *lotte*

bavarois – cold custard cream with gelatine and often flavoured and garnished with fruits, nuts or chocolate

bavaroise – hollandaise sauce flavoured with crayfish butter and chopped crayfish tails

béarnaise – warm sauce of butter, egg yolks, shallots, wine vinegar, pepper, tarragon and chervil

bécasse – woodcock

bécassine – snipe

béchamel – basic white sauce, made from a roux of flour and butter with milk added

beignet – sweet or savoury batter fritter

belle hélène – Pears poached in vanilla syrup and served with vanilla ice cream and hot chocolate sauce. Also a meat garnish of grilled mushrooms stuffed with tomato, peas or carrots

belons – flat oysters

bercy – *velouté* sauce with fish stock, white wine, shallots and butter. Also a meat sauce made with white wine, shallots and butter garnished with beef marrow and meat glaze

betterave – beetroot

beurre à l'anglaise – melted butter

beurre blanc – reduction of white wine vinegar and shallots beaten vigorously with butter until white

beurre colbert – see *maitre d'hotel* but with added tarragon and meat glaze

beurre maitre d'hotel – butter mixed with chopped parsley, salt, pepper and lemon juice

beurre marchand de vin – a reduction of shallots and red wine to which meat glaze, butter, parsley and lemon juice is added

biche – venison (the doe)

bigarade – sauce of reduced duck gravy mixed with zest and juice of orange and lemon

bigorneaux – winkles

billy by – cream of mussel soup

bisque – creamy shellfish soup: usually *homard* (lobster), *crevettes* (shrimps) or *crabes* (crab)

blanchailles – whitebait

blanquette – white meats mixed with vegetables and served with button onions and mushrooms in a cream sauce

blé – corn, wheat

blette – chard

bleu – used to describe very rare steak

au bleu – as in **truite au bleu** – trout plunged into a vinegar court *bouillon* immediately it has been killed and cleaned causing the skin to take on a blueish hue

blonde – sauce, as *allemande*

boeuf – beef

bois – wood

bombe – shaped ice cream dessert

bonne femme – fillets of sole poached and served with a white wine sauce with mushrooms, parsley and shallots added. Also meat or poultry cooked in a casserole with button onions, mushrooms and ham

bordelaise – sauce of chopped shallots, thyme, bay leaves and red wine with meat glaze and garnished with bone marrow

bordure – in the form of a ring or crown

bouché(e) – a 'mouthful', usually a delicate pastry or small vol au vent

boudin blanc – white sausage of chicken, pork, veal and sometimes *foie gras* and truffles

boudin noir – black pudding but without the cereal content

bouillabaisse – Mediterranean fish stew with saffron, tomato, garlic and olive oil. For authenticity it should contain John Dory, *rascasse*, gurnard and eel as well as monkfish, red mullet, sea bass and various shellfish

bouillon – broth

boulangère – sliced potatoes and onions on which a joint, usually lamb, is baked

bouquetière – meat garnish of potatoes and vegetables sometimes arranged in the shape of a bouquet

bourdaloue – *consommé* with garnish of tomato, asparagus or carrots. Also a pastry tart filled with almond custard and topped with poached pears

bourgeoise – meat garnish of carrot, onion and bacon. Also a beef *consommé* with diced root vegetables and chervil

bourguignon(ne) – Usually beef, braised with red burgundy wine, mushrooms, small onions and carrots. Also a sauce similar to *bordelaise*

bourride – similar to *bouillabaisse* but with no saffron and *aïoli* added instead

boutargue – a paste of dried salt mullet or tuna roe; also *poutargue*

brandade de morue – pounded salt cod, olive oil, milk and garlic served warm

bretonne – onion, white wine, garlic and tomato sauce. Also of leeks, celery, onions and mushrooms served with fish *velouté*

Brillat-Savarin – a cheese as well as the name given to several preparations. A garnish for game or a soufflé of snipe or woodcock and truffles. A garnish for *noisettes* of *duchesse* potatoes with *foie gras*, truffles and asparagus. Also two chicken *consommés*, one thickened with tapioca and with chicken breast, pieces of *crepe*, lettuce, sorrel and chervil, the other thickened with arrowroot and with mushrooms, truffles and carrots

brioche – light yeast dough made with eggs, milk and sugar. Both sweet and savoury uses

brochet – pike. **Quenelles de brochet** is a dish of poached pike mousseline

brochettes – skewered pieces of meat or fish which are grilled

brouillé – scrambled (eggs)

brulé(e) – burnt

brunoise – diced mixed vegetables for flavouring or garnish

bruxelloise – seasoned butter and lemon juice sauce with hard boiled egg, for asparagus. Also a garnish of brussels sprouts, *fondantes* potatoes and light gravy

bulots – whelks

byron – thickened red wine sauce garnished with truffles

cabillaud – fresh cod

café complet – Continental breakfast

café de Paris – garnish of truffles, asparagus, mushrooms, prawns, oysters and a lobster sauce

caille – quail

calamars/calmars – squid, also *encornets*

campagne – country, rustic

camus – type of artichoke

canard/caneton/canette – duck, duckling

cancalaise – oyster garnish

cannelle – cinnamon

capucine – chicken *consommé* with shredded spinach and lettuce. Also a garnish of cabbage leaves, or mushrooms, stuffed with forcemeat and masked with a Madeira sauce

carbonnade – rich stew. Also rapid grilling or frying over high heat. **carbonnade à la flamande** is a Belgian national dish of beef with beer

cardinal – preparations with lobster

Careme – chicken and veal *consommé* garnished with carrots, turnips, lettuce and asparagus. Also a fish garnish of fish *quenelles*, truffles, cream sauce and *fleurons* and a garnish (for *tournedos* and *noisettes*) of olives stuffed with ham forcemeat with a Madeira sauce and potato croquettes

carmélite – *Bourguignonne* sauce with ham and button onions. Also a thickened fish *consommé* garnished with rice and fish forcemeat balls

carré – rack from the best end of lamb, pork or veal neck cutlets
carrelet – plaice or flounder
cassis – blackcurrant
cassolette – small flameproof containers of sweet and savoury dishes. Also a moulded fried batter case with a savoury filling
cassoulet – traditional Languedoc long-cooked stew with haricot beans, goose (sometimes duck), pork, mutton, sausages, onions and garlic
céleri-rave – celeriac
cèpe – boletus mushroom
cerfeuil – chervil
cerise – cherry
cervelas – pork sausage
cervelles – brains
cervelles des canuts – not brains, but fromage frais, shallots, white wine herbs and vinegar
céteaux – tiny sole-like fish
chanterelle – also known as a *girolle* – a small, yellow, trumpet-shaped mushroom
chantilly – With a sweet course *chantilly* means whipped cream sweetened with vanilla sugar. Also a sauce of mayonnaise and cream or a hot sauce of *béchamel* with whipped cream added
chapelure – breadcrumbs
chapon – capon
charbon de bois – wood charcoal
charlotte – filled moulded sponge dessert. *Charlotte* russe – *génoise*-lined mould filled with either *bavarois* or *crème chantilly*
chartreuse – name of a liqueur, a moulded dessert, a dish of cabbage cooked with partridge. Also a beef *consommé* thickened with tapioca and garnished with ravioli stuffed separately with *foie gras*, spinach and mushrooms
chataigne – chestnut
chateau, pomme – potatoes cut into small barrel shapes and sautéed in butter
chateaubriand – large centre cut of beef fillet garnished with pommes *chateau* and **chateaubriand** sauce (quite usual now to serve this with *béarnaise* sauce and *allumettes* potatoes). **Chateaubriand** sauce is one of white wine, meat glaze with shallots, butter and tarragon with cayenne and lemon juice added
chatelaine – artichoke bottoms with either tomatoes, braised celery and *chateau* potatoes or *soubise*, chestnuts and *noisette* potatoes.
chaud-froid – *velouté* sauce with aspic, cream and egg yolks. Quite often flavoured and coloured
chaudrée – fish soup
chausson – turnover filled with apples or fruit or savoury items
chemise – similar to *papillote*. To cook en *chemise* is to bake or roast in a case which can be greased paper, pastry, batter or a vegetable leaf, such as lettuce, spinach or cabbage. Also means unpeeled
cheval – horse
chèvre – goat (**fromage de chèvre** – goat's cheese)
chevreuil – roe deer, venison. Also a reduced red wine sauce for venison
chiboust – choux pastry filled with *crème patissière* mixed with *crème chantilly* or Italian meringue flavoured with bitter almond liqueur or other flavourings
chicorée – curly endive lettuce

chiffonade – vinaigrette with parsley, hard-boiled egg and beetroot. Also strips of sorrel or lettuce cooked in butter

chipirons – baby squid

chips – potato crisps

chivry – chicken *velouté* sauce with white wine, shallots, tarragon, chervil, chives and burnet

choron – *béarnaise* sauce blended with tomato juice

choux – type of pastry of butter, sugar, salt and water boiled in a pan before adding flour and when cool, eggs. Pastry used for éclairs, profiteroles, gateau *Saint Honoré*. Fillings can be sweet or savoury. Also a cabbage (plural **choux**)

choucroute – sauerkraut. **Choucroute garnie** is with ham, bacon or pickled goose, frankfurter sausage and boiled potatoes first braised in white wine or wine vinegar

chou-fleur – cauliflower

choux de bruxelles – brussels sprouts

christ-marine – samphire

ciboulette – chives

cigale – variety of flat lobster

citron – lemon

citron vert – lime

citronelle – lemon-grass, also a lemon liqueur

civet – red wine stew of game garnished with small onions, bacon and mushrooms, classically thickened with the blood of the animal. (Hare is the most usual meat, as in **civet de lièvre**.) In the Languedoc spiny lobster is used

clafoutis – thick moist batter pudding with cherries. Sometimes other soft fruit is used

claires – the best oysters from the Marennes region

clapoton – lamb trotter

clouté – garnished by studding

clovisse – type of clam

cochon de lait – suckling pig

cochonailles – pork charcuterie, from **cochon** – pig

cocos – small white beans

cocotte – small round or oval ovenproof dish used for cooking and serving

coeur – heart

coing – quince

colbert – light chicken stock to which lemon juice and parsley are added. Also applies to fried fish coated in egg and breadcrumbs

colère – **merlan en colère** – whiting cooked with its tail in its mouth

colin – hake

colinot – codling also *merluchon*

col vert – wild duck

compote – slow cooked stew, also stewed fruit

concassé – coarsely chopped

confit – fruit or vegetables preserved in sugar, vinegar or brandy. Also game, pork or duck cooked in its own fat and preserved in it

confiture – jam, **confiture d'oranges**, marmalade

contre filet – see *faux-filet*

consommé – rich, concentrated clear soup served hot or cold

coq, coquelet – cockerel; **coq au vin** – stewed in red wine with mushrooms and onions

coque – as in **oeuf à la coque** – soft boiled egg
coques – cockles
coquillages – shellfish
cornichons – gherkins
cote – rib, chop
cotelette – cutlet
cote première – loin chop
cotriade – Breton fish soup quite similar to *bouillabaisse* but using
Atlantic fish
cou – neck
couennes – pork rind
coulibiac – puff pastry roll filled with salmon or sometimes chicken.
Originally a Russian dish
coulis – liquid purées of fruit, vegetables and sometimes game, poultry
and fish
courge – marrow, pumpkin
court bouillon – broth made with either wine, vinegar or milk in which
fish or meat is cooked
couteaux – razor shells
crapaudine – spatchcocked ie split and flattened
crécy – puréed carrot soup and the name given to preparations with
carrots
crème anglaise – custard
crème chantilly – see chantilly
crème épaisse – thick or double cream
crème patissière – confectioner's custard
crépinette – small, flat sausage
cressonette – cress
cretes de coq – cockscombs
crevettes – shrimps
cromesquis – croquettes of meat, fish, poultry or eggs bound in a thick
cream sauce and fried in batter
croquant(e) – crunchy, crisp
croque-madame – toasted cheese sandwich with ham and fried egg
croque-monsieur – ham-filled toasted cheese sandwich
crottins – ball-shaped, usually applies to goat's cheese
croustade – hollowed-out loaf or any similar case filled with the same
mixture as a vol-au-vent
croustillant(e) – very crisp pastry case, with a caramelised topping
in sweet applications or brushed with egg white for savoury items
croute – crust, as in pastry, also a slice of bread
croutons – small dice of fried or toasted bread used to garnish soup
cru – raw (**mi cru-mi cuit** means half raw-half cooked)
crustacés – generic name for crabs, langoustines, lobsters, shrimps etc
cuisine du (de) terroir – rustic, country cooking
cuisse – leg (thigh)
cuit(e) – cooked
cul – rump
curcuma – turmeric

daim – fallow deer (venison)
dariole – small cylindrical mould and the name given to anything cooked
or prepared in such a mould
darne – thick slice of fish, usually salmon
darphin – a flat cake of grated potatoes

daube – meat, poultry or game braised in stock with wine and herbs.
daube de boeuf is a slow-cooked casserole of larded beef in red wine
with salt pork, bacon, onions, carrots and herbs

dauphine – duchesse potatoes mixed with choux paste, shaped into small
rounds and deep fried. Also sole fillets, stuffed, folded and poached and
rolled in a *villeroy* sauce, egged and crumbed and deep fried, served with
a cream sauce

dauphinois(e) – thinly sliced potatoes baked with cream, Gruyère cheese
and a hint of garlic

daurade – sea bream

daurade royale – gilt-head bream

délice – delicious, name give to a dessert or ice cream, also to a fillet
of fish folded over on itself wide end up

demi-deuil – poultry larded under the breast skin with truffles then
poached in a cream sauce. Garnished with pastry cases of sweetbreads and
mushrooms

demi-glace – basic brown sauce with meat stock added then reduced

demi-sec – lightly salted

demi-tasse – small cup, usually of coffee

demoiselle – very small lobster

désossé – boned

diable – devilled; a sauce of shallots, white wine and wine vinegar
reduced, with the addition of *demi-glace*, herbs and cayenne pepper

diane – a method of preparing steak, usually at the table, by sautéeing
it with the addition of Worcestershire sauce, cream and butter. Also
a partridge *consommé* garnished with truffles, game *quenelles* and Madeira
or a thickened sauce *poivrade* flavoured with game extract

dieppoise – fish garnish of shrimps, mussels and mushrooms simmered
in stock or butter. Also a fish *velouté* blended with shrimp butter, or a dish
of brill cooked in white wine, with the above garnish and masked with
the thickened fish stock and cooked mussels

dinde, dindonneau – turkey

diplomate – classic cold pudding of liqueur-soaked sponge layered with
bavarois and currants and sultanas soaked in warm syrup. Also a sauce
made from sauce *normande* mixed with lobster and mushroom extract and
garnished with truffles and lobster. Also a garnish of calf's sweetbreads,
cockscombs, cock's kidneys and mushrooms bound in a Madeira sauce

dodine de canard – rich duck stew with onions, herbs and red wine.
Also a duck *galantine*

dorée – John Dory also called *St Pierre*. Also means golden as in **pommes
dorées** – potatoes cooked golden brown

doria – garnish of cucumber cooked slowly in butter. Also a chicken
consommé garnished with chicken *quenelles*, cucumber pieces, puff pastry
fried cheese balls and chervil

doux/douce – mild, sweet

Dubarry – soup of cauliflower, stock and cream. Also a garnish
of cauliflower with mornay sauce and grated cheese

duchesse – as in **pommes**

duchesse – pureed potato blended with egg yolks, either piped as a
border or made into various shapes as a garnish

dugléré – method of preparing fine white fish. It is poached in white
wine and butter with shallots, parsley and seasoning with cream, tomatoes
and lemon juice added

dur – hard

duxelles – a preparation of finely chopped mushrooms with shallots, parsley and butter. The sauce of the same name is a white wine, onion and shallot reduction to which *velouté* sauce is added and into this is blended some of the above

eau–de–vie – usually applies to a colourless fruit spirit
eau plate – still water
eau gazeuse – sparkling water
échalote – shallot
Echiré – renowned butter from Echiré in Poitou
écossaise – *consommé* of mutton broth with pearl barley and a *brunoise* of carrot, celery and leek
écrasé(e) – crushed
écrevisses – freshwater crayfish
effilochées – long threads, especially of fish and vegetables
embeurré(e) – buttered
émincé – a dish of leftover toasted or braised meat slices heated in a sauce. Also applies to fruit or vegetables thinly sliced
encornet – squid
encre – ink, in cooking, the ink of octopus or squid
entier – whole
entremets – desserts
épaule – shoulder
éperlan – smelt, whitebait
épicé(e) – spicy, hot
épices – spices
épigramme – slice of breast or lamb chop breaded and fried
épinards – spinach
escabèche – fried small fish such as sardines, anchovy or mullet, marinaded for 24 hours in olive oil, herbs and wine vinegar and served cold
escargot – snail
espagnole – one of the basic sauces along with *velouté* (cream) and *béchamel* (white); this is a brown sauce. Also a garnish of sweet red peppers, tomatoes and garlic
espadon – swordfish
estouffade – highly seasoned beef broth used as base for sauces, soups and casseroles. Also the name of a dish in which the ingredients are stewed slowly
estragon – tarragon
été – summer
étrille – small crab
étuvée – as *estouffade* but also a dish of meat, poultry or vegetables stewed slowly with little or no liquid except butter or oil
éventail – arranged in a fan-shape

façon – in the style of (as in **du chef** – of the chef)
faisan – pheasant
faisandé – well-hung, gamey
farineux – farinaceous or starcy
farci(e) – stuffed
faubonne – thick soup based on *St Germain* soup with a *julienne* of sautéed vegetables and chervil. Also a pheasant purée garnished with pheasant strips and truffles
faux-filet – steak cut from the top of the sirloin

faverolles – name given to many kinds of haricot beans
favorite – a garnish of *foie gras*, truffles and asparagus tips for *tournedos* and *noisettes*, or for meat slices one of artichoke bottoms with celery and small *anna* or *chateau* potatoes. Also a *consommé* thickened with tapioca garnished with artichoke bottoms and mushrooms, small potato balls and chervil
fenouil – fennel
fermière – garnish for meats of carrots, turnips, onions, potatoes and celery
feuillantine – sweet puff pastry strips. Also larger rectangles of puff pastry split and filled with either savoury or sweet fillings
feuille – leaf
feuilletage – puff pastry in general
feuilleté – flaky puff pastry used in the making of pies and tarts
feuilleton – thin slices of veal layered with various stuffings or *salpicons* and braised. Also a mixture of chopped pork, veal and herbs encased in flaky pastry
fèves – broad beans
ficelle – beef fillet, browned and then cooked in *consommé*. Also a thin baguette
figue – fig
fillette – bottle (usually of house wine)
financière – poultry and sweetbread garnish of chicken quenelles, cockscombs, cock's kidneys, truffles, mushrooms and olives. Also a brown sauce flavoured with truffles, mushrooms and Madeira
fine de claire – a Morenne oyster see *claires*
fines herbes – a mixture of many herbs but also sometimes only parsley
flamande – meat garnish of cabbage, carrots, turnips and bacon. Also a method of poaching fish with light beer or a butter sauce seasoned with French mustard, lemon juice and parsley. Can be a beef *consommé* with puréed brussels sprouts, peas and chervil – see also *carbonnade à la flamande*
flammekueche – pizza-like Alsatian bacon, cream and onion flan
flan – sweet or savoury egg and milk mixture similar to a custard
flétan – halibut
fleur de sel – highest quality sea salt
fleurons – small, usually crescent-shaped, puff pastry garnishes
florentine – a garnish with spinach as a main constituent
foie (**foie-gras** – the term applied to fattened duck or goose liver)
fondant – an icing for cakes and gateaux. Also to cook until meltingly tender, eg apples, goat's cheese and **pommes fondant**
fondants – small fried croquettes
forestière – a meat garnish of sautéed *cèpes* or morels with bacon and *noisette* potatoes. Also a *demi-glace* sauce flavoured with sherry with sautéed mushrooms added
fouetté(e) – whipped
four – oven, as in **au four** – baked
fraiche – fresh also **frais**
fraise – strawberry
fraise des bois – wild strawberry
framboise – raspberry
frangipane – a moist mixture of butter, eggs and ground almonds used as a tart filling. Also a mixture of flour, butter, milk and egg used to bind forcemeat for stuffing
frémi(e) – simmered in water

friandises – see *petits fours*
frisée – curly endive (often **frisée aux lardons** – a salad with bacon bits and sometimes a poached egg)
froid(e) – cold, chilled
fromage blanc – cream cheese
fromage de tete – similar to brawn, a cold dish of pig's head, simmered then baked with spices
friandises – *petits fours*
frivolités – mixed hors d'oeuvre of moulded creams, *barquettes*, tartlets
fruits de mer – seafood
fumé – smoked
fumet – highly concentrated meat, fish or vegetable extract

galantine – similar to a *ballotine* but always served cold; the meat, poultry or fish is cooked, stuffed and set in jellied stock
galette – round flat pastry, pancake or cake, also roundels of potato
gambas – giant prawns
garbure – a thick stew of cabbage, bacon, preserved goose and/or pork simmered for several hours
garenne – rabbit warren, also used for wild rabbit
gaufrettes – lattice potato crisps
gelée – in jelly, usually aspic
genevoise – a sauce of white roux with fish stock, parsley, mushrooms, shallots and white wine
genièvre – juniper
génoise – classic sponge of equal measures of flour, sugar and butter with vanilla and eggs
germiny – creamy sorrel soup with egg yolks
gésiers – gizzards
gibier – game
gigot – leg of lamb or mutton
gigue – haunch of venison or other game animal
gingembre – ginger
girofles – cloves, also *reinettes giroflées*
girolle – see *chanterelle*
glacé(e) – ice or iced
gougère – large choux pastry filled with a cheese mixture, served hot or cold
gousse – clove, as in **gousse d'ail** – clove of garlic
gout – taste
grand–duc – a fish and fowl garnish of truffles and asparagus. For fish, crayfish is also used with a mornay sauce
grand'mère – old-fashioned, homely cooking
grand veneur – sauce *poivrade* to which has been added venison extract, redcurrant jelly and cream. Served only with venison and furred game
granité – coarse crystalline water ice
gras–double – tripe
gratin – crusty topped dish that has been browned, also a baked casserole
grecque – mushrooms or artichokes usually, cooked with lemon or wine vinegar with olive oil, onion, fennel, celery, thyme and coriander. Served cold
grenadine – pomegranate syrup
grenadins – small slices of braised meat
grenouille – frog (**cuisses de grenouilles** – frogs' legs)

gribiche – cold sauce of hard-boiled egg yolks blended with olive oil, wine vinegar, gherkins, capers, parsley, chervil and tarragon
griottes – bright red bitter morello cherries
groseille – currant (white or red)
groseille à maquereau – gooseberry
gros sel – salt crystals

haché, hachis – chopped
hachis parmentier – chopped cold meat, usually roast beef, mixed with demi-glace and sometimes served in scooped out baked potatoes. Shepherd's pie
hareng – herring
haricot blanc – white bean
haricot vert – french bean
hiver – winter
homard – lobster
houblon – hops, **jets de houblon** – hop shoots
huile – oil
huitre – oyster: see *belons, claires, marennes*
hydromel – mead

ile flottante – floating islands of soft poached meringue on custard
impératrice – sweet dishes and cakes with a rice base
impérial – garnish of *foie gras*, truffles, mushrooms and *quenelles* with a Madeira sauce
italienne – a garnish of artichoke bottoms, mushrooms and macaroni croquettes. Also a sauce of mushrooms, parsley, shallots in white wine. There is a cold sauce too of mayonnaise with mixed herbs and puréed calf's brains

jalousies – small flaky pastry cakes covered with almond paste and apricot jam
jambon – ham
jambon persillé – chopped ham with parsley in aspic
jardinière – a garnish as well as a sauce of mixed vegetables
jarret – shin or knuckle
jésus de Morteau – pork sausage from Franche-Comté
joinville – sauce *normande* with a *coulis* of crayfish and shrimps. Also a fish garnish of mushrooms, shrimps and truffles
joue – cheek
julienne – finely shredded vegetables
jus – meat juices, gravy (unthickened) also fruit or vegetable juice
jus lié – veal stock thickened with arrowroot

koulibiac – see *coulibiac*
kugelhopf – Alsatian brioche with candied fruits (many other spellings e.g. kougelhopf)

lait – milk
laitance – soft roe
laitue – lettuce
langouste – crawfish or spiny lobster
langoustines – Dublin Bay prawn, large Mediterranean prawns, scampi
langue – tongue

languedocienne – dishes from the Languedoc region. Accompanying sauces are flavoured with garlic. Also a meat garnish of aubergines, *cèpes*, tomatoes and parsley
lapereau – young rabbit
lapin – rabbit
lard, lardons – bacon, fried bacon bits
laurier – bay (leaf)
léger, légère – light
légume – vegetable
lentilles du Puy – tiny bluish-green lentils from Puy
liégeois – **café liégeois** is a dessert of coffee, ice cream and whipped cream. Also cooking with juniper berries
lièvre – hare
limande – lemon sole, dab
limousine – red cabbage with bacon fat and chestnuts used as a garnish
lisette – small mackerel
longchamp – soup of shredded sorrel, vermicelli and peas
longe – loin
lotte – monkfish, also *baudroie*
loup de mer – sea bass
lyonnaise – name for specialities of the Lyons region – tripe, omelettes, sausages. A region also famed for its onions and potatoes. Methods of preparation with fried or braised onions the major constituent

macédoine – mixture of diced raw or cooked fruit or vegetables
mache – lamb's lettuce
maconnaise – meat dish flavoured with red wine
madeleine – small oval cake with a shell-like bottom. Also a garnish for meat of artichoke bottoms, sauce *soubise* and puréed white haricot beans, or a garnish for fish of cream sauce with crayfish butter and celeriac
Madère – Madeira
magret – breast fillet of duck
maigre – lean
maintenon – sauce *soubise*, *béchamel*, egg yolks and mushrooms. Also a garnish of sliced mushrooms in a thick onion purée with cream and truffles
maïs – sweetcorn
maison – house, refers to home-made as in **de la maison** – of the house
maitre d'hotel – butter blended with parsley, lemon juice, salt and pepper
malakoff – an almond pastry
maltaise – name given to preparations using the juice of oranges, especially blood oranges
mangue – mango
maquereau – mackerel, also *lisette* when small
maraichère – market-garden style. A garnish for roasted and braised meats of braised small onions, stuffed cucumber, salsify and artichokes. Also a dish of veal cutlets sautéed in butter served with salsify and brussels sprouts
marbré(e) – marbled
marc – strong spirit distilled from grape pips and skins etc
marcassin – young wild boar
marchand de vin – similar to *bordelaise* sauce. See also *beurre marchand de vin*
Marengo – veal or chicken stewed with tomato, olives, white wine and mushrooms

marennes – oysters from the port of the same name, see *claires*

marguéry – hollandaise flavoured with a purée of oysters and fish extract

mariné – marinated

marinière – fish or shellfish, particularly mussels, cooked in white wine with shallots and herbs

marjolaine – marjoram. Also a multilayered chocolate and nut cake

marmelade – thick, sweetened fruit purée (or onion purée)

marmite – metal or earthenware covered pot used for serving soups. Also, as in **petite marmite**, a clear, strong broth which should contain oxtail, poultry, root vegetables and bone marrow. Garnished with diced bread and grated cheese

marquise – a very rich chocolate mousse with or without a thin plain sponge casing, or a garnish of calf's marrow with asparagus, truffles and sauce *suprème*. Also a hollandaise with caviar added just before serving

marron – chestnut. Also *chataigne*

marseillaise – mayonnaise mixed with sea-urchin purée. Also a meat garnish of olives, anchovy stuffed tomatoes, potato chips and *provençale* sauce

massepain – marzipan

matelote – a rich fish stew made with red or white wine. Freshwater fish is more usual although matelote à la *normande* uses sea fish with cider instead of wine. Not to be confused with a matelot!

mélange – mixture or blend

menthe – mint

merluchon – see *colinot*

merlan – whiting

merle – blackbird

merguez – spicy lamb sausage

merlu/merluche – hake, see *colin*

mesclun – salad of many different salad leaves

meurette – dish of eggs poached in red wine, garlic, onions and bacon bits served with fried bread

mi cru-mi cuit – half raw – half cooked

miel – honey

mignonette – coarsely ground white pepper or a mixture of white and black pepper

mignons – small cuts from the ends of fillet

mijoté – simmered

mirabelle – small, golden yellow plum used in cooking and the manufacture of an *eau de vie*

mirepoix – very small dice of vegetables sometimes with ham or belly pork

miroir – name given to dishes with a polished, mirror-like finish

mitonné – simmered under cover in an oven

mocha, moka – name given to any preparation flavoured with coffee

moelle – bone marrow

moelleux – soft, creamy, similar to *fondant*

mollet(te) – soft or soft-boiled eggs

mont blanc – rich puréed chestnut dessert with crème *chantilly*

morille – morel mushroom

morue – salt cod. See *brandade de morue*

mouclade – mussels in a creamy white wine sauce

mouette – gull

moules – mussels

mousseline – preparations to which whipped cream has been added. The sauce comprises hollandaise mixed with an equal amount of stiffly whipped cream and warmed gently

mousseron – St George's agaric, a small field mushroom

mousseux – sparkling (as in wine) or a light and frothy sauce of butter cream and egg yolks accompanying fish

moutarde – mustard

mouton – sheep

mulet – grey mullet

muscade – nutmeg

museau – muzzle

mure – blackberry

myrtille – bilberry

nage – a herby *court bouillon* with vegetables used for cooking fish or shellfish

nantaise – chicken sautéed with root vegetables and white wine served with onions, carrots, mushrooms, artichoke hearts and hollandaise sauce

nantua – a cream sauce made with crayfish butter and tomato purée. Prawns sometimes substitute for crayfish

nappé – masked or covered

navarin – a mutton stew with onions and potatoes. With other root vegetables it is a *ragout à la printanière*. Also a soup of puréed peas with crayfish tails and parsley

navet – turnip

neige – snow, as in oeufs à la neige – poached egg whites with vanilla custard

nem – small spring roll

nesselrode – name given to several preparations including fillets of fish stuffed with a pike and lobster forcemeat in puff pastry, served with a lobster sauce and oysters. Also a soup of puréed woodcock and chestnuts, garnished with woodcock quenelles and croutons. An iced pudding of maraschino-flavoured custard mixed with chestnut purée, candied peel, crystallised fruit soaked in Malaga wine frozen in a charlotte mould and served with *marrons glacés*

newburg – sliced cooked lobster or other seafood sautéed in butter with brandy or Madeira with paprika, cream and egg yolks added. Also a sauce for boiled, baked or grilled shellfish of butter, brandy and Marsala, cream and paprika with egg yolks added and a dice of lobster coral if served with lobster

niçoise – name for dishes which contain tomato and garlic, anchovies, capers and olives, soups being garnished with tomato, chervil and green beans

nid – nest

noisette – hazelnut or round slice of meat from the fillet or rib of lamb or other meat e.g. venison. Also applies to small rounded shapes. **pommes noisette** – small potato balls fried in butter till golden brown

noix – nut or walnut

noix de coco – coconut

normande – meat or fish cooked with apple cider or calvados. Also a method of cooking partridge in a casserole on a bed of stewed apples

norvégienne – omelette à la norvégienne is a baked alaska. Also the name for several savoury preparations including a thick cream soup of puréed swedes garnished with *julienne* of beetroot. Poached salmon presented with a decoration of prawns, cucumber *timbales* filled with

smoked salmon purée, eggs stuffed with shrimp *mousseline* and a Russian sauce
nouilles – noodles

oeufs brouillés – scrambled eggs
oeuf dur – hard-boiled egg
oeuf mollets – soft-boiled egg
oie – goose
omble chevalier – char, also known as **ombre chevalier**
onglet – cut of beef – the skirt, used primarily in *carbonnades*
oreille – ear
orge perlé – pearl barley
ortolan – European bunting
os – bone
oseille – sorrel
oursin – sea urchin

paillard – a flat, thin slice, usually applied to veal
paille – straw, as in **pommes paille** – deep-fried straw potatoes
paillettes – long, fine sticks of vegetables especially potatoes (as in **pommes frites paille**) or flavoured pastry sticks
pain complet – wholemeal bread
pain d'épice – gingerbread
pain perdu – *brioche* or crustless slices of bread soaked in egg and milk and fried in butter
paleron – chuck (of beef)
palmier – sweet icing sugar-coated puff pastry often heart-shaped
palombe – wild pigeon
paloise – *béarnaise* sauce flavoured with mint instead of tarragon, or a mint-flavoured hollandaise
palourde – clam
pamplemousse – grapefruit
panaché – mixed or mixture
panais – parsnip
pan bagna – bread soaked in olive oil and filled with a *niçoise* mixture of anchovies, olives, peppers and onion
pané – breaded
panier – basket
pannequet – pancake
papillote – **en papillote** – to cook in a paper bag or aluminium foil
Paques – Easter
parfait – used to describe a creamy savoury mousse. Also an iced sweet akin to ice cream and usually suffixed by **glacé**. They are of a single flavour only
Paris-Brest – ring-shaped choux pastry sprinkled with almonds and filled with praline cream
parisienne – small balls of potato tossed in dissolved meat jelly and sprinkled with parsley
parmentier – preparations with potato. **Pommes parmentier** are cubed potatoes cooked in butter. Also puréed potatoes, as in *hachis* parmentier. The name given to potatoes cooked with the meat with which they are served
pate – general term for pastry including pasta, as in pates fraiches, (fresh pasta)
pate brisée – short-crust pastry

pate d'amandes – marzipan
pate feuilletée – flaky pastry
pate frolle – short crust pastry with almonds and egg used for flans and sweet pies
patelle – limpet
pate moulée – raised pie pastry
pate sucrée – sweet rich short crust pastry, made with sugar, eggs and vanilla
paupiette – thin slice of meat or fish (usually sole) rolled around a forcemeat or mousse and braised
pavé – flat cut of meat or fish. Also a cold pie or mousse set in a square or rectangular mould
paysanne – as *fermière*
peche – peach
perdreau – young partridge, **perdrix** – partridge
périgourdine – name given to dishes garnished with truffle and *foie gras*
périgueux – classic sauce with chopped truffles and Madeira
persil – parsley
persillade – a mixture of parsley and other chopped herbs
petit salé – salt pork usually served with lentils or cabbage
petits fours – general name given to the selection of tartlets and small pastries served at the end of a meal
petits gris – variety of snail
petit salé – salt pork
pétoncle – small scallop
pholiottes – thick orange fungus found in the South of France
pichet – jug or pitcher
pied – trotter
pignon – pine kernel
piment – pimento, hot pepper, chili
pimenté(e) – hot, spicy
piment doux – sweet pepper, also **poivron**
pintade – guinea fowl, **pintadeau** – a young bird
pipérade – Basque speciality of green peppers, onions, garlic and basil stewed in oil and thickened with beaten eggs
piquant(e) – spicy
piqué(e) – spiked
pissaladière – Provençal dish similar to pizza but with no cheese
pissenlit – dandelion
pistou – French version of Italian pesto usually served with **soupe au pistou**
pithiviers – rich puff pastry cake usually filled with almond paste but also can be of chocolate. Savoury versions also
plat du jour – dish of the day, **sur le plat** – cooked and served in a shallow dish
plateau – a large platter as in **plateau de** *fruits de mer*
plie – plaice
poché(e) – poached
poelé – pan-fried
à point – medium-rare (steak)
pointe – tip (as in asparagus tip)
poire – pear
poireau – leek
pois – peas, also **petit pois** (garden peas) **pois gourmands** (snow peas)
pois-chiches – chick peas

poisson – fish
poitrine – breast (in lamb) or belly (in pork)
poivre – pepper
poivré – peppered
poivron – sweet pepper
pomme – apple; (but occasionally, especially on menus) potato, as in
pomme de terre
pommes frites – french fried potatoes
pont-neuf – as in pommes Pont-Neuf – extra thick
french fried potatoes
porcelet – suckling pig
pot-au-feu – dish of boiled meat and vegetables. When chicken is used
it is known as **poule-au-pot**
potage – thickened cream soup
potée – rich meat and vegetable stew usually made with pork and
cabbage
potiron – pumpkin
poularde, poule, poulet – fattened hen or chicken, boiling fowl and
spring chicken respectively
poulpe – octopus
pourpier – purslane (a salad herb)
poussin – very small chicken or spring chicken
poutargue – a paste of salt mullet or tuna roe, also *boutargue*
praire – clam, see *palourde*
praline – crumbed or ground mixture of caramel and almonds
praliné(e) – praline or toasted almond-flavoured
pré-salé – a name given to lamb reared on Atlantic salt meadows
pression – as in **bière pression** – draught beer
princesse – asparagus tip garnish
printanière – usually a garnish of mixed young vegetables
printemps – spring
provençale – name given to certain dishes which include garlic and often
tomatoes and olive oil
prune – plum
pruneau – prune

quasi – chump end of loin
quetsch – a plum used as the base for the *eau de vie* **de quetsch** as well
as in sweet tarts
quenelle – a very light, poached mousse
queue – tail (**queue de boeuf** is oxtail)

rable – saddle, as in **rable de lièvre** – saddle of hare
radis – radish
radis noir – black radish
rafraichi(e) – chilled, cool
ragout – a stew
raie – skate (**raie au beure noir** is a dish of poached skate served
in browned butter with capers)
raifort – horseradish
raisin – grape, also sultana
rapé(e) – grated
rascasse – scorpion or hog fish – a constituent of *bouillabaisse*
ravigote – highly seasoned white sauce served hot or cold
rechauffé(e) – reheated, or a dish made with ready cooked ingredients

régence – sauce *normande* for fish prepared with white wine, mushrooms and truffles. For chicken a *supreme* sauce is used

réglisse – liquorice

reine-claude – greengage

reinette – variety of apple

reinette giroflée – clove (spice)

religieuse – a cake with choux pastry

rémoulade – mayonnaise with chopped chervil, tarragon, spring onions, gherkins, capers, parsley and sometimes anchovy essence if served with cold fish

rhum – rum

rillettes – potted meat or fish, served cold

rillons – well-browned pieces of pork breast

ripopée – slow simmered dish of various beef cuts

ris – as in **ris de veau** – sweetbreads

rissolé(e) – fried or browned

riz – rice

robert – classic brown sauce

rognon – kidney

rognon blanc – testicles

rognons de coq – red kidney bean, also gonads of male fowl

romanoff – usually applied to strawberries with *chantilly* cream and curaçao liqueur

romarin – rosemary

rosette – cured sausage from the Lyons region

rossini – garnish for *tournedos* and *noisettes* of *foie gras*, truffles and *demi-glace* with truffle extract and Madeira

roti(e) – roast

rouget – red mullet, also called **rouget-barbet**

rouelle – round slice

rouille – fiery sauce served with Mediterranean fish soup. It is an *aïoli* made with pounded chilis and lobster coral (though tomato is sometimes used to make it pink)

roulade – 'swiss roll' with sweet or savoury filling

roulé(e) – rolled, or a savoury or sweet roll as in swiss roll

rubané(e) – ribboned, striped

rumsteak – rump steak

sabayon – thin custard made with white wine instead of milk, sweet and savoury uses

sablé – usually a thin, circular rich shortbread-like biscuit often layered with fresh fruit and *chantilly* cream. Savoury **sablés** are made with cheese

sabodet – pig's head sausage

safran – saffron

saignant – very rare, bloody (usually applies to steaks)

Saint Germain – a thick soup made with fresh peas. Also the name of a garnish whose principal ingredient is fresh peas

Saint-Honoré – a gateau with choux pastry and *crème patissière*

Saint-Jacques – scallop – short for **coquille Saint Jacques**

Saint Pierre – John Dory

saison – season, **saisonier (saisonière)** seasonal

salé – salted

salmigondis – a ragout of several reheated meats

salmis – a stew of poultry or game birds

salpicon – diced meat, fish, fruit or vegetables bound in a sauce

sandre – zander
sanglier – wild boar. See also *marcassin*
sarladaise – potatoes cooked in goose fat with garlic. Also a garnish for lamb of truffles and diced potatoes cooked with thick gravy
sarriette – summer savory, a herb
saucisse – sausage
saucisson sec – salami
sauge – sage
saumon – salmon
sauté – lightly browned or fried
sauvage – wild
savarin – yeasted cake usually in the form of a ring, soaked in rum or kirsch-flavoured syrup. A larger version of a *baba*
savoyarde – as *dauphinoise* but with stock instead of milk or cream and no garlic
seiche – squid or cuttlefish
selle – saddle (of lamb)
semoule – semolina
soissons – large white haricot beans
soubise – name given to dishes including onions in their preparation. The sauce is an onion purée mixed with *béchamel*
souris – simmered very gently
spätzli – German noodles also **spätzel**
suppions – tiny squid
supreme – usually a breast (of poultry). Also a *velouté* sauce with cream and mushroom extract
sur l'os, à l'os – on the bone

tablier de sapeur – Lyonnais dish of tripe cooked in bouillon, then fried in egg and breadcrumbs
tagine – North African stew made in an earthenware dish of the same name
tapénade – a Provençal purée of capers, black olives, anchovies and olive oil
tarbais – Tarbes haricot beans
tarte tartin – caramelised upside-down apple tart
tartine – slice of bread with various toppings
tete de veau/porc – calf/pig's head, as in brawn
thé – tea
thermidor – method of serving lobster, with a *bercy* sauce mixed with English mustard and parmesan
thon – tuna
tian – typical *Niçois* dish: any mixture cooked in layers in a gratin dish
tiède – warm
tilleuil – lime tree, leaf and/or blossom
timbale – a thimble-shaped mould usually of pasta, rice or vegetable purées
tisane – herbal tea
topinambour – Jerusalem artichoke
tournedos – small round fillet steak
tourteau – large crab
tout-épicé – all spice
tranche – slice
trevise – red chicory (radicchio)

tripes à la mode de Caen – beef tripe cooked with vegetables, cider and Calvados
tronçon – chunk, also a *darne*
tuile – very thin almond biscuit
turban – combination of ingredients cooked in a ring mould

unilatéral – method of sautéeing fish slices skin-side down only

vacherin – a meringue ring filled with *chantilly* cream and fruit and/or ice cream
vallée d'Auge – a garnish of cooked apples with cream and Calvados
vapeur – steam
VDQS – vin délimité de qualité supérieure
veau – veal
velouté – a white sauce made with veal or chicken stock
vénus – large clam
verjus – juice from unripe grapes. Also the name for certain thickened soups
vermit – large clam
véronique – garnish of white grapes
verte – green, also a mayonnaise blended with pounded spinach, watercress and parsley
vert-pré – watercress garnish
verveine – verbena
vessie – **en vessie** is to cook in a bladder
viande – meat
vichy – garnish of glazed carrots
vierge – frothy blend of butter whipped with lemon juice, salt and pepper; virgin (olive oil)
vieux – old
vignot – winkle, periwinkle
villeroy – *velouté* sauce with truffle essence often used as a coating before deep frying in egg and breadcrumbs
vinaigre – vinegar
vin jaune – yellow wine from the Jura, used in sauce-making and for cooking poultry and other light meats
volaille – poultry or fowl

walewska – garnish for poached fish of mornay sauce, lobster and truffles
waterzooi – Belgian speciality of chicken or fish simmered with vegetables and white wine
witloof – white Belgian chicory

xérès – sherry

yaourt – yoghurt

zéphir – any light or frothy dish, sometimes applied to light mousses or mousselines
zingara – garnish of ham, tongue, mushrooms and truffles in *demi-glace* flavoured with tomato and tarragon

Glossary compiled by Mario Wyn-Jones

Index

READERS' COMMENTS

Please use this sheet, and the continuation overleaf, to recommend hotels or restaurants of **really outstanding quality and to comment on existing entries.**

Complaints about any of the Guide's entries will be treated seriously and passed on to our inspectorate, but we would like to remind you always to take up your complaint with the management at the time.

We regret that owing to the volume of readers' communications received each year, we will be unable to acknowledge all these forms, but they will certainly be seriously considered.

Please post to: Egon Ronay's Guides, 35 Tadema Road, London SW10 0PZ

Please use an up-to-date Guide. We publish annually. (Paris 1995)

Name and address of establishment	Your recommendation or complaint

Readers' Comments continued

Name and address of establishment	**Your recommendation or complaint**

Your Name (BLOCK LETTERS PLEASE)

Address

Date